PLANTS
FOR DRY CLIMATES
HOW TO SELECT, GROW AND ENJOY

REVISED EDITION

PLANTS
FOR DRY CLIMATES

HOW TO SELECT, GROW AND ENJOY

REVISED EDITION

MARY ROSE DUFFIELD
Landscape Architect
and
WARREN D. JONES, FASLA
Landscape Architect

PERSEUS
PUBLISHING

Many of the designations used by manufacturers and sellers to distinguish their products are claimed as trademarks. Where those designations appear in this book and Perseus Publishing was aware of a trademark claim, the designations have been printed in initial capital letters.

Major photography: Mary Rose Duffield and Warren D. Jones

Main cover photo: Mary Rose Duffield

Landscape design in cover photo: Mary Rose Duffield and Guy Greene

Additional Photography:

Steve Carter, Boyce Thompson Arboretum: *Eucalyptus torquata*, page 96; *Hardenbergia violacea*, page 188; *Parkinsidium* Desert Museum hybrid (two photos), page 76

Greg Corman, Tucson Botanical Garden: *Acacia greggii*, page 52

Debra Hodson and John Babiarz, Greenfield Citrus Nursery: Minneola tangelo, page 81 and 84; Valencia orange, page 81; Washington navel orange, page 84, all compliments of www.greenfieldcitrus.com

Carl Olson, University of Arizona: Flat-headed borers, page 42; tent caterpillar nest, page 44; grapeleaf skeletonizers, page 44; aphids, page 42 (top)

Amy Smith: Snow on desert plants, page 4

Illustrations: David Fischer and Mary Rose Duffield

Cataloging-in-Publication data for this book is available from the Library of Congress.

Perseus Publishing is a member of the Perseus Books Group. Find us on the world wide web at www.perseuspublishing.com

Perseus Publishing books are available at special discounts for bulk purchases in the United States by corporations, institutions, and other organizations. For more information, please contact the Special Markets Department at the Perseus Books Group, 11 Cambridge Center, Cambridge, MA 02142, or call (617) 252-5298.

NOTICE: The information contained in this book is true and complete to the best of our knowledge. All recommendations are made without any guarantees on the part of the authors or Perseus Publishing. The authors and publisher disclaim all liability in connection with the use of this information.

First printing, October 2001

Acknowledgements

We would like to thank the following individuals for their help in preparing this revision: Bill, Helen and Howard Fisher, publishers; Scott Millard, our first editor and a contributor to this revised edition; Judith Ratliff, MSLA, special assistant; Sarah Trotta, our present managing editor; Melanie Mallon, our present editor; Steve Martino, landscape architect, for his talents; John Begeman, Pima County extension service; Margaret Livingston, Ph.D., professor of landscape architecture, University of Arizona; Terry H. Mikel, area horticultural agent, University of Arizona cooperative extension; Patricia H. Waterfall, extension agent, Landscape Water Conservation; Elizabeth Davison, lecturer, plant sciences, University of Arizona; Ed Mulrean, Ph.D., Arid Zone Trees; Cecily Gill, Tucson Botanical Garden; Carl Olson, Ph.D., entomologist; Ron Gas and Janet Rademacher, Mountain States Nursery, Glendale, Arizona; Greg Starr, Starr Nursery, Tucson, Arizona; Tony Balda; Michael A Reuwsaats, Kelley Green Trees; Matthew Johnson, Ph.D., Desert Legume Project, University of Arizona; Nancy Laney, Arizona Sonora Desert Museum; Doug Larson, Arizona Sonora Desert Museum; Brian and Garrett Ham, landscape contractors; Dave and Paul Deppe, landscape contractors; Jan Ferguson, contract administrator, Western Sod; Leroy Bradey, landscape architect, Arizona Roadside Development, Arizona Department of Transportation; Georgiann Carroll, enthusiastic gardener; Pat Ewing, enthusiastic gardener; Johanna Stein, garden lover. And to our many clients from whom we have learned so much.

We would like to thank the following individuals, whose work on the previous editions led the way for this revision: Rick Bailey, publisher; Randy Summerlin, executive editor; Scott Millard, editor; Cindy Coatsworth, managing editor; Tony L. Burgess, Ph.D, botanist; Christopher Duffield, Ph.D, for the climate map; Carol Crosswhite, Ph.D., and Frank Crosswhite, Ph.D., Boyce Thompson Southwestern Arboretum; Steve Fazio, retired professor of plant sciences, University of Arizona; William Feldman, Ph.D, Director, Boyce Thompson Southwestern Arboretum; John M. Harlow Jr.; Christie Ten Eyck, landscape architect, Phoenix, Arizona; Genevieve Jasper, Harlow's Nursery, Tucson, Arizona; the late Eric A. Johnson, landscape consultant, Palm Desert, California; Matthew Johnson, Desert Legume Project, University of Arizona; James G. Jerry Lewis, landscape architect, El Paso, Texas; Michael MacCaskey, horticulturalist, Palo Alto, California; Laila and Ralph McPheeters, Catalina Heights Nursery, Tucson, Arizona; Charles T. Mason Jr, Ph.D., retired curator, Herbarium, University of Arizona; Charles Sacamano, Ph.D, retired Arizona cooperative extension horticulturalist, University of Arizona; Carol Shuler, landscape architect, Phoenix, Arizona; Darrell T. Sullivan, professor of horticulture, New Mexico State University; the late Harvey Tate, extension horticulturist, University of Arizona; the late James Tipton, Ph.D., extension horticulturist, University of Arizona; Lance Walheim, horticulturist, St. Helena, California; Jim Wheat, landscape architect, Phoenix, Arizona; the late J.D. DiMeglio, landscape contractor; George Brookbank, Arizona cooperative extension horticulturalist.

Contents

Many think of a desert as barren, but the natural Sonoran desert (top), really a semidesert, has a mood all its own and is quite unlike the arid plains of Jordan (left) and other parts of the Middle East and North Africa.

Growing plants in a hot, dry, sunny environment is pioneering in a real sense. Interior valleys and desert areas present special challenges: Extremes of heat, aridity and problem soils make gardening different, even difficult, at times.

Experienced gardeners in these regions have learned many lessons. Out of necessity, they have learned which plants accept the rigors of the climate or they have devised ways to grow and protect plants unadapted to these extreme conditions.

It has become apparent that the huge population shift to the arid West and Southwest will continue. The most critical element necessary to support the various needs of the growing population is water. To meet the demands of climate and population growth and to stretch the water supply as far as possible, people in the landscape field have been pioneering in new ways:

• Specialists have developed drip irrigation, a dependable and inexpensive technology.
• Plant explorers have introduced plants adapted to dry climates from all the arid regions of the world.
• Scientists have experimented with new ways of planting.
• Designers have created unique and attractive landscapes attuned to the environment.
• Landscape contractors have developed

better ways of dealing with difficult soil conditions and installing water-efficient irrigation systems.
• County cooperative extension services and master gardeners have produced up-to-date information for people needing help.

This book is about growing plants in warm interior valleys, the desert and similar climates. It too is a pioneering effort, dedicated to helping you create your own low-maintenance, energy-saving, drought-resistant landscape, using both desert and lush garden plants.

Defining an Arid Climate

What makes a locale arid is not how much rain falls, but how much accumulates in the soil. Evaporation of water exceeds the amount of rainfall deposited on the ground, preventing any accumulation of moisture. This imbalance between rainfall and soil moisture and evaporation is what all arid lands have in common, whether it is along a southern coast or hot interior valleys of California, the high cool plateau of northern Mexico or the hot sands of the Sahara.

Low rainfall
Five inches (127mm) or less rainfall per year also makes a region arid. However, some places that get much more precipitation are

(continued on page 4)

Arid Climates

Warm, arid climates can be grouped into three general zones, plus the arid grasslands that surround these zones. The zones are based on how often the temperature drops below freezing, how far it goes below freezing and how long it stays there. No matter what you do to modify climate, cold is the deciding factor. All plants have a cold-tolerance point below which they are severely damaged or killed.

Low-zone climates are the closest to tropical climates. Elevation ranges from sea level (some areas are even below sea level) to 2,000 feet (610m). In the lowest arid latitudes, this climate will extend to a slightly higher elevation. The growing season—days between killing frosts—ranges from year-round along the coast to 302 days in Phoenix, Arizona. Average winter minimum temperature is 36 to 37F (2 to 3C). Freezing temperatures can occur, even in coastal deserts, and drop to 20F (-7C) in some locations. Average summer maximum temperature ranges are near 102F (39C) and are much higher in drier interior locations, away from marine influence. Highs of 120F (49C) are not unusual. Summer nights also remain warm, often staying above 80F (27C). Annual rainfall is 10 inches (254mm) or less; some areas receive less than 5 inches (127mm). Wide temperature variations exclude some tropical plants inland that thrive in milder coastal climates. Fall months signal the beginning of the planting year in this zone. Early fall planting of annual flowers permits a full life cycle before the high temperatures of late April and May.

Middle-zone climates generally have mild winters. Their median 2,500-foot (762m) elevation causes the growing season to be shorter than in low-zone climates, ranging from 220 to 242 frost-free days. Occasionally, these zones can reach a short-term minimum temperature of 15 to 18F (-10 to -8C). Summer maximum temperatures may also be lower by 5 degrees or more than in low-zone climates. Summer nights are more comfortable, often dropping to a cool 70F (21C) or lower. These moderate summer nights, along with an earlier cooling trend in the fall, allow many cool-weather plants to succeed. Precipitation is generally higher than in the low zone, especially in regions subject to summer rains, such as Tucson, Arizona. Some areas have summer and winter rains, receiving as much as 10 to 15 inches (254 to 381mm) annually. This relatively high rainfall does not take these areas out of the arid classification. Evaporation during the long dry periods between rains prevents any real accumulation or penetration of moisture into the soil. Subtropicals and tender plants must be protected from the hard frosts that can occur here. September, October and November are ideal months for planting annuals, perennials and basic landscape plants.

High-zone climates lie generally between 3,300 and 5,000 feet (1,006 to 1,524m) in southern latitudes but exist at lower elevations farther north. Saltillo, Mexico, and El Paso, Texas, are examples of high-zone cities. This zone is transitional and many temperate plants grow here. Growing season lasts 200 to 220 days. Areas that are located at higher elevations in lower latitudes will have about the same expected annual low temperatures as other high elevation zones, but the growing season will be longer, with frost ending earlier in the spring. Temperatures approaching 0F (-18C) have been experienced in most high arid or desert regions, but 15 to 18F (-9 to -8C) is the usual low for the season. Minimum winter temperatures average around freezing, providing the necessary chilling for such landscape plants as lilac and stone fruits. Winters are mild enough and summers are hot enough in most of this zone to grow oleander (*Nerium oleander*), loquat (*Eriobotrya japonica*), southern magnolia (*Magnolia grandiflora*), glossy privet (*Ligustrum lucidum*) and pomegranate (*Punica granatum*). Rainfall is often higher because many of these regions are close to mountain ranges.

Arid grasslands, or savannahs, have growing conditions similar to the three climate types above. In fact, they often border these regions. The only difference is that rain falls at a time when it can accumulate in the soil. This enables the soil to support a complete cover of grass, usually an annual grass, but only briefly. Bakersfield, in California's interior valley, as well as warm, dry valleys of southern California and regions of the southern Mediterranean are examples of this climate. The low rainfall coastal strip along the southern California coast is an arid grassland, except summers are cool. Plants that require high heat, such as mesquite (*Prosopis* species) and palo verde (*Cercidium* and *Parkinsonia* species), may not bloom and may grow very slowly. But the majority of plants in this book perform well in this region. These areas have the same variations in temperature and modifying conditions as desert climates. Rainfall is generally as low as the bordering desert or slightly higher (7 to 15 inches, 178 to 381mm). Most home landscapes need to be irrigated nine to ten months of the year—sometimes all year.

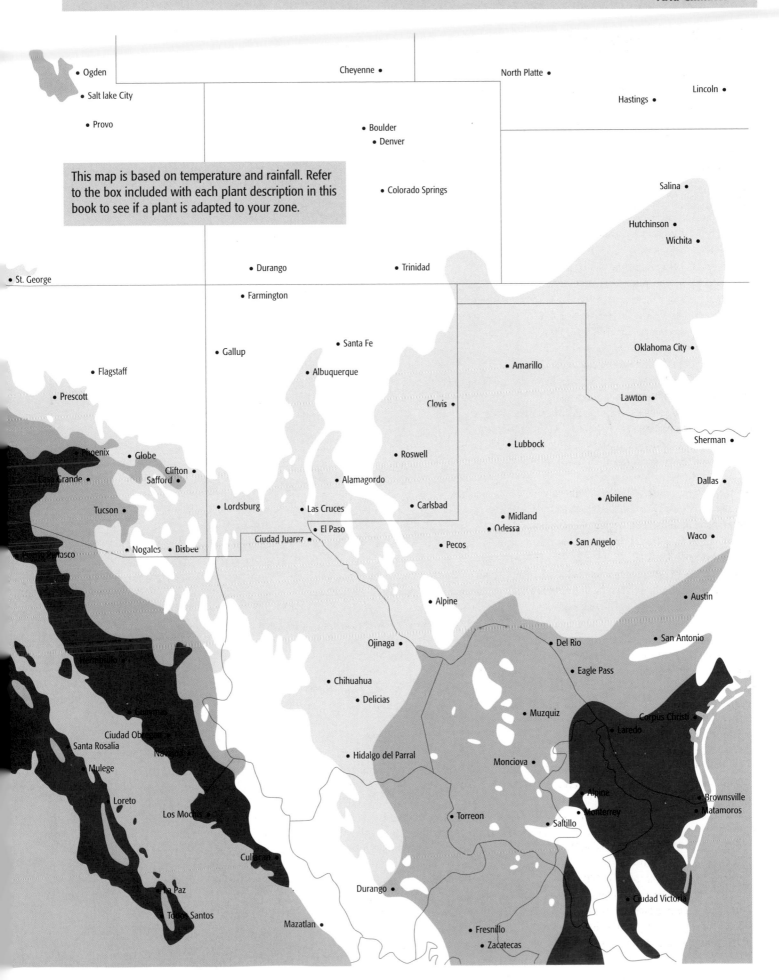

This map is based on temperature and rainfall. Refer to the box included with each plant description in this book to see if a plant is adapted to your zone.

Ogden

Salt lake City

Provo

Cheyenne

North Platte

Lincoln

Hastings

Boulder

Denver

Salina

Colorado Springs

Hutchinson

Wichita

St. George

Durango

Trinidad

Farmington

Santa Fe

Oklahoma City

Gallup

Flagstaff

Albuquerque

Prescott

Amarillo

Lawton

Clovis

Phoenix

Globe

Clifton

Roswell

Lubbock

Sherman

Safford

Casa Grande

Alamagordo

Abilene

Dallas

Tucson

Lordsburg

Las Cruces

Carlsbad

Midland

Nogales

Disbee

El Paso

Odessa

Waco

Ciudad Juarez

Pecos

San Angelo

Puerto Penasco

Alpine

Austin

Ojinaga

Del Rio

San Antonio

Hermosillo

Eagle Pass

Chihuahua

Delicias

Muzquiz

Corpus Christi

Guaymas

Laredo

Ciudad Obregon

Santa Rosalia

Navajoa

Monciova

Mulege

Hidalgo del Parral

Alpine

Brownsville

Loreto

Torreon

Monterrey

Matamoros

Los Mochis

Saltillo

La Paz

Culiacan

Durango

Ciudad Victoria

Todos Santos

Mazatlan

Fresnillo

Zacatecas

classified as arid. When and how a region gets its rainfall are important factors. An area can have as much as 15 inches (381mm) of rain annually and still be arid if rainfall is spread evenly over the year, with periods of windy, very dry weather between rains, which causes evaporation (moisture is unable to accumulate in the soil). If rain falls in a concentrated time span, especially if the air is cool and moist at that time, moisture will accumulate. Such an area is then able to support a solid cover of grass and, occasionally, shrubs and trees.

Heat

Contrary to popular belief, heat is not a standard ingredient of arid climates. For instance, Saltillo, the capital city of the Mexican state of Coahuila, is considered a prototype for the dry, cool subtropic Chihuahuan Desert. Summers there are pleasant and it has become something of a resort—a place to escape the summer heat of the northeast Mexican lowlands.

Low Humidity

Low humidity is not a universal indicator of a desert, either. Some of the most desolate are fog deserts: the bleak northern Chilean coast and the western coast of Baja California, for example. Cold ocean currents along the shore produce a cool climate with little rain (fog is the only moisture) and no summer heat.

There are many kinds of arid climates, including deserts in cold high latitudes that merge into the Arctic Circle. This book, however, concentrates on subtropical to somewhat cool arid and desert lands and the adjoining regions, the arid grasslands. Arid grasslands are regions that are dry the balance of the year, with a short wet season. They briefly support a cover of annual grass. As hot and windy as true deserts, they sustain many of the same landscape plants. Southern California near the coast is an example of an arid grassland that, because of the climate, can support many plants, including tropical plants if irrigation water is available.

Your Climate Ingredients

Several major factors limit and influence plant growth in hot, arid regions. All these factors combine to make gardening different. Elements described in the following discussion, combined with your microclimates and the composition of your

At first glance, snow on desert plants may seem unusual, but snowfall is not uncommon in arid lands. Normally the amount that falls is slight and melts in a few hours.

soil (see pages 7 and 29), make up your plant's environment. Knowing these "ingredients" will take you a long way in learning how to select and care for landscape plants.

Cold and Frost

Temperature is the key ingredient in selecting and using plants. As we mention on page 2, cold is the limiting factor in determining whether a plant will grow in a given area. In addition to the low point, the length of time the temperature remains below freezing determines the extent of damage tender plants will sustain.

Freeze damage generally occurs when air temperature reaches 28F (-2C), but only if it remains there for several hours. For

example, how often the 28F (-2C) temperature occurs and its duration establish the upper cold limit of the citrus belt. This is because 28F (-2C) is the temperature at which citrus and most other sensitive plants sustain damage.

Heavy freezes. Day-to-night temperature changes in winter for many arid areas are not nearly as much of a threat to plants in the desert as occasional arctic cold fronts. These fronts, or polar waves, sweep down from the north, bringing unusually cold temperatures. Unexpected heavy freezes periodically kill many plants, such as *Bougainvillea*, that might otherwise do well in these climate zones. The cold is all-pervading. Radiated heat from the sun collected on south walls or

Anatomy of a Frost

At sundown the earth begins to radiate skyward the heat it has accumulated during the day. Just before dawn, the earth reaches its coolest temperature. If the dew point is reached—the point when the ground and plants are cooler than the air—moisture will be deposited. However, the lower the humidity of the air, the closer to freezing the dew point will be. If the temperature drops below freezing, the moisture passes directly to the ground and plants as frost. This is most likely to happen on a still, clear winter night when the earth is unprotected by cloud cover.

A cold night with enough moisture to produce heavy frost may not be as destructive to tender plants as one (with the same minimum temperature) having humidity so low that no frost forms. This condition is sometimes referred to as a *black frost*. White frost on the foliage actually prevents the leaf from losing moisture. Low humidity on a very dry night causes foliage to lose moisture by evaporation. This lowers the leaf temperature below that of the air. Therefore, a wet surface can actually form ice or frost, even though the air temperature stays 4 to 5 degrees above freezing.

pavement during the day is not enough to compensate for the cold. Warm microclimates are also overcome and get almost as cold as surrounding areas.

Covering your plants (see page 40) may give adequate protection during normal winter cold, but not during a polar wave. Use heating devices such as electric lights to increase the temperature close to sensitive plants, even those in normally warm and protected spots. Flood irrigation can also help warm the plant environment a degree or two.

Polar waves are particularly destructive if they follow a period of springlike weather. Plants at that time have put out succulent new growth that has not had time to "harden off," meaning to become woody. This can be a serious problem even with a normal freeze. New succulent growth is naturally more susceptible to freezing than the rest of the plant. Even plants tolerant to cold, natives included, can suffer damage.

Prickly pear cacti (Opuntia) *can function as barrier and windscreen.*

Temperature Fluctuations

Plants must also be able to tolerate the alternating heat and cold between day and night, as well as winter lows. Inland deserts and interior valleys have greater temperature fluctuations than areas adjacent to large bodies of water, which tend to moderate temperatures. Annual variations may be 100F (38C) or more between a summer high and a winter low. Fluctuation between day and night temperatures is also pronounced, especially in spring and fall.

High Heat and Sunshine

Except in arid regions by the sea, the most stressful period for plants is late May through September, when temperatures are

Dry brown spots on leaves are signs of sunburn.

high and solar radiation is intense. During this period there may be forty-five to ninety or more consecutive days of sunshine with temperatures reaching at least 100F (38C). In regions where there are summer thunderstorms, the heat is moderated somewhat by afternoon cloud cover and humidity during stormy spells.

During this period of intense heat, the zone of greatest temperature variation is where radiant heat from the sun is absorbed— the ground surface. Bare rocks, concrete and other dense objects can reach temperatures as high as 180F (82C) on a summer afternoon. These temperature extremes are especially tough on plants— dehydrating, bleaching, and actually cooking young seedlings. This is why many plants appreciate shade on hot summer afternoons, especially in the low zone. With intense heat, broadleaf plants not adapted to the arid environment cannot transpire water to cool themselves rapidly enough to keep up with the intensity of the sun. They wilt or suffer leafburn, a killing of all or part of the leaves. This happens most often if the soil is allowed to dry out and there is not enough water available. A moist soil surface is cooler, of course, and raises the humidity. Mulches play an important role in modifying soil temperatures. They are discussed in detail on page 38.

Some plants stop blooming, shifting down metabolically, when the daytime temperatures begin to hit the 100 to 105F (38 to 41C) mark. Plants may stop growing,

trying just to hang on. Any damage is slow to repair due to this shutdown. If they do bloom, their petals or fruiting parts are often damaged and they will not set fruit. Rose and gardenia blooms tend to dry out rapidly in the heat. With some plants, the continued warmth of night temperatures affects flower fertilization and fruit set. For instance, corn and tomatoes cease bearing when the minimum temperature stays above the mid-70s F (23 to 25C). Conversely, some plants, such as Bermudagrass, do not begin to grow well until the weather warms and night temperatures are in the 60s F (15 to 21C).

Rainfall

Some arid regions have a winter and a summer rain season. The summer storms can be quite dramatic, coming on an area very quickly. They are often accompanied by strong winds that create a wall of dust and sand immediately preceding the storm. The rains last only a short time and are usually localized, seldom spreading more than three miles in diameter.

In areas that receive little rain, watering is especially important in early summer when plants are still trying to grow fast. They need lots of water to grow and to cope with the heat. As the hot season intensifies, plants may become semidormant and look poor until the cooler temperatures of fall, when they may again put out new growth. Plants from Mediterranean climates (where summers are dry) may be hard to grow where summers are hot and dry. These plants need some irrigation but can die from a soil fungus if the soil is too wet or drainage is poor. (See page 36 for discussion of irrigation practices.)

Winds

Hot summer winds are often laden with dust and can be seen preceding a thundershower, covering all in their path with clouds of soil. The winds not only take their toll by drying your skin but also suck moisture from tender succulent tissues of many plants.

Another desert occurrence during warm weather, especially when the ground is warmer than the air, is the dust devil or whirlwind. It is much like a small tornado and may be started by something as small as the movement of a rabbit or by a car driving on a dirt road. Superheated air near the ground is set in motion, turning rapidly and spiraling upward, burdened with dirt and debris. It leaves a path of destruction or annoyance across the open spaces until it dissipates in a grove of trees or other barrier.

Dust devils are a common sight to travelers crossing the desert during the summer months. Sometimes the only protection a desert dweller has against these great natural forces is a windbreak or windscreen of plants. Cities benefit from the foliage of tall trees, breaking the force of the wind. Trees lessen the force of windflow through the "canyons" created by city buildings. Rows of trees planted at the edges of fields, along roads or close to houses or settlements in the open country filter the wind and make life in the desert environment more desirable. (See page 21 for how to shelter your home with windbreaks.)

Humidity

Atmospheric humidity has a direct bearing on how much water plants must have to thrive, because much less ground moisture is needed where the air remains moist. The presence of humidity, either hot or cool, greatly reduces a plant's water demands. The amount of water required for transpiration—keeping the plant cool—far surpasses the amount required for plant growth. If the summer is cool and humid, a surprising amount of vegetation can exist even if annual rainfall is low.

Humidity also plays a part in

Home Microclimates

Your own backyard has areas with different climatic conditions, called *microclimates*. Variables in sunlight, temperature, humidity and wind make each home landscape different, even from the site next door. Understanding your microclimates will help ensure success with your landscape plants. For example, cold-tender, sun-loving plants will perish if located in a cool, shaded part of your lot. Plants not adapted to high temperatures will die when exposed to the intense reflected heat from a south or west wall.

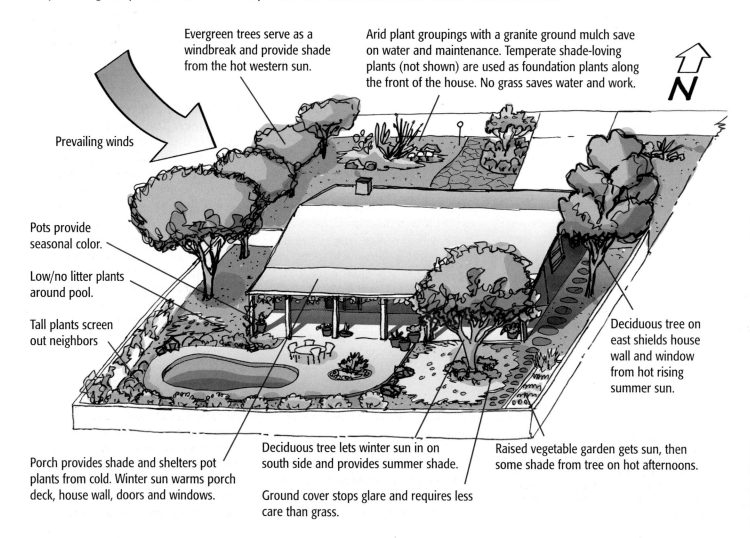

Evergreen trees serve as a windbreak and provide shade from the hot western sun.

Arid plant groupings with a granite ground mulch save on water and maintenance. Temperate shade-loving plants (not shown) are used as foundation plants along the front of the house. No grass saves water and work.

N

Prevailing winds

Pots provide seasonal color.

Low/no litter plants around pool.

Tall plants screen out neighbors

Deciduous tree on east shields house wall and window from hot rising summer sun.

Porch provides shade and shelters pot plants from cold. Winter sun warms porch deck, house wall, doors and windows.

Deciduous tree lets winter sun in on south side and provides summer shade.

Ground cover stops glare and requires less care than grass.

Raised vegetable garden gets sun, then some shade from tree on hot afternoons.

determining which plant species will succeed in an area. It is the climatic ingredient that is most difficult to adjust. Sprinkling the ground near plants raises humidity slightly, and the subsequent evaporation cools the area. Plants create a more humid environment as they transpire through their leaves. During summer rain periods or in irrigated farm areas, the humidity will often increase to an uncomfortable level. This is especially true in the hotter low deserts, coastal deserts and in wide low inland valleys that get little in the way of breezes.

Most regions with high humidity will support many of the plants traditionally associated with the tropics. As long as their irrigation needs are supplied, they perform as if in a truly tropical habitat. Landscape plantings in arid coastal desert cities such as San Diego, California; Guaymas, Mexico; and Jidda, Saudi Arabia, support many of the traditional tropicals.

Microclimates

No absolute lines can be drawn to define climates. You cannot cross a given boundary and find yourself in the next zone. Instead, there is a gradual change as each merges with the next. Within each climate region you will also find many small climates, called *microclimates*. These places can be as large as a canyon or as small as a corner of your backyard. The slope of the ground, its surface composition, the direction and intensity of wind and sun, topography, structures, nearby bodies of water and other factors combine to create these variations.

Large microclimates that are generally warmer than the surrounding climate are called *thermal belts*. They are usually areas of higher ground facing south or southwest.

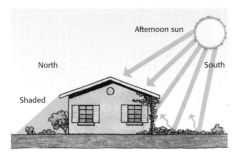

A vine-covered wall and grass or a ground cover will absorb the sun's rays and prevent glare. They also cool the air through evapotranspiration, giving off humidity. Plant shade-loving plants on the north sides of buildings and heat-loving plants, tender to cold, in the sunny shelter of a hot south wall with an overhang.

Because thermal belts receive maximum exposure to the sun's rays, their surfaces store up heat during the day and release it at night, while the cold air drains to lower levels. This keeps the minimum temperature higher, so a larger range of plants can grow there.

Microclimates generally cooler than the surrounding climate are called *cold air drainage basins*. These are caused by cold air flowing down hillsides along natural drainage ways. Cold air is heavy and follows the same contours of a hillside as a river would. In the early morning hours, it settles as "puddles" in low areas such as canyon or wash bottoms or the pockets of a valley. In a smaller sense, cold air can be contained by a solid wall or fence around your house. If there is an abrupt change in topography, the early morning temperature variations can be startling, even within short distances. You can check your own microclimates by walking around your property in early morning. In some instances a difference of 15 degrees can be recorded between a low bottomland location and a nearby higher slope with good air drainage.

Modifying Elements

Large bodies of water also have an effect on the local climate. By absorbing heat, they keep temperatures warmer when it is cold. Through evaporation, they keep places cooler when it is warm. By the same token, a region adjacent to irrigated agriculture or a heavily watered landscape area such as a golf course or park has a lower nighttime minimum temperature because of evaporation at night.

Cities modify the minimum and maximum temperature ranges. Buildings and pavement act as heat sponges during the day, much like rocks or gravel, and radiate heat at night. Heated buildings, factories and automobiles contribute additional heat and pollutants. The pollutants not only foul the air but put an atmospheric umbrella over the whole region, holding in the warmth at night like a giant greenhouse. This additional warmth is a benefit to the gardener. It is well known that the range of dependable plants increases to include more tender plants as the size and density of the city increases. Conversely, tall buildings can create cold wind tunnels, or canyons, that may affect plants.

The surface of a given area also affects the minimum and maximum temperatures. Rock outcrops, gravel and open sandy areas or bare earth will be warmer than areas covered with vegetation.

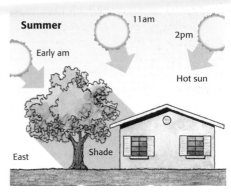

A deciduous tree on the east side of a home can intercept the rising summer sun and keep a house cooler by up to 10 degrees until the sun beats on the unprotected roof later in the day. The tree also prevents glare off hard surfaces from reflecting into windows.

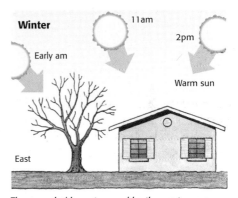

The same deciduous tree enables the sun to warm the house on a winter morning.

Indicator Plants

Certain plants growing in nature can be indicators of microclimates. In the Southwest, for example, you might notice Arizona rosewood (*Vauquelinia californica*) and Mexican blue oak (*Quercus douglasii*) growing at a lower elevation on a north slope. This would indicate a cool location. A short distance away on a south slope, the presence of native plants such as jojoba (*Simmondsia chinensis*), brittlebush (*Encelia farinosa*) and ironwood (*Olneya tesota*) would indicate a warm spot. If you see ironwood growing naturally in an area, for instance, this would be a desirable location for citrus.

Backyard Microclimates

Microclimates in your own backyard follow the same principles as the larger areas just described. The direction of winds and air circulation cause temperature modifications. Paving, buildings, walls, trees, turf and other plantings affect the penetration and absorption of the sun's heat. Pavement and walls that face south store heat during the

This Bougainvillea *is taking advantage of the microclimate created by a warm south wall and overhang. Heat accumulated by the wall during the day is released at night, which helps protect the plant from cold.*

day and radiate it at night, moderating temperatures. Even after the sun has been down for some time, you can feel the warmth coming from a south wall. Because this warmth is released gradually during the night, cold-sensitive plants such as *Bougainvillea* may be grown here with success, yet fail just a few feet away in an open garden.

Likewise, the north sides of buildings are shaded and cooler than those of the hot south. This is the place for temperate plants such as *Viburnum*, which would burn up if grown in the open western sun.

All of these factors operate within your general climate zone. Microclimates have a great deal to do with the success or failure of your plants.

Adaptations of Arid-Land Plants

The uniqueness of desert and arid-land plants and their successful adaptations to their environment are important to consider. By understanding some of their adaptive functions you can better understand how your landscape plants, desert and otherwise, cope with the arid environment. Even though you will probably select plants to create an integrated landscape, you should locate plants in zones according to their water needs.

For successful results, most nondesert plants require moderate to ample irrigation, while established desert natives and other

plants from arid regions may require only occasional supplemental water. Some stay a lush green on modest amounts of water and continue to bloom over a long period.

Arid and desert plants are especially adapted to arid landscaping and have learned to live with dry conditions in a variety of ways, a few which sound like science fiction.

Evaders and Endurers

Plants with adaptations to periods of drought beat heat and water deprivation in two ways: They evade it or they endure it, the latter by using water more efficiently.

Drought-evading plants simply disappear into a sort of time capsule until the temperature and moisture are right for them to grow again. The heart of the plant rests in seeds, bulbs or fleshy roots until moisture, temperature and the length of daylight signal them to germinate or reappear.

For the most part, arid-land plants have found ways to endure periods of drought and high heat. The Mexican palo verde tree *(Parkinsonia aculeata)* is a prime example of an endurer. It has evolved many functions that combine to allow it to live in the desert. As a drought persists, this tree gradually sheds leaflets, then midribs, even twigs. By reducing tissues, a tree can maintain life in its core as long as possible until water returns. The tiny leaves of the palo verde and other arid-adapted trees and shrubs absorb little heat and transpire less. Their open-branch forms allows rain or dew to collect and flow down the tree to the roots. The green bark of palo verde trees is filled with chlorophyll and continues photo-synthesis (food production) even when leaves are absent. A shallow, fibrous root system extends outward near the soil surface to the drip line and beyond, to absorb traces of rainfall. While most trees in arid landscapes have wide shallow root systems, they may also have one or more tap roots that seek moisture at a deeper level and help to anchor the tree as well.

Arid-land plants have evolved a number of other fascinating adaptations. Many have white or silvery leaf surfaces that reflect the sun. Some plants have the ability to turn away from the sun or fold up to protect themselves. Others, such as Texas ranger *(Leucophyllum frutescens)*, have leaves that store water. Plant leaves become spongy and greenish during a rainy period, then turn small and reflective during a dry season.

Cacti and other succulents also store water in their tissues. Their surfaces, green from chlorophyll, produce food, and their tough, waxy skin prevents moisture loss. They often do not have leaves, or they may have leaves that are temporary or undeveloped. Thorns growing at the bases of the undeveloped or temporary leaves protect them from animals.

Most plants continuously transpire water into the atmosphere and exchange carbon dioxide and oxygen through their

One of the ways the palo verde (Cercidium *species) endures drought is by gradually dropping leaves, twigs and branches to conserve moisture. Green bark allows photosynthesis to continue even after leaves have fallen.*

The leaves of Texas ranger (Leucophyllum frutescens) *are green and plump when water is plentiful. In dry periods, the leaves shrink and turn a reflective silvery color.*

leaves for their metabolic processes. A few desert plants have actually learned to "hold their breath." They close their stomata, tiny leaf pores, during hot days and open them only at night for necessary exchanges with the atmosphere. Others can store carbon dioxide and metabolize indefinitely within their bodies. Keeping their pores completely closed allows them to exist for indefinite periods during hostile climatic conditions, until moisture becomes available. Such plants are usually slow growing and long-lived. The giant saguaro cactus is an example.

Water Gatherers

Many plant forms have developed specialized water-gathering functions. They take any available moisture and guide it down the plant toward the root zone. The corrugated ribs of cacti and *Euphorbias* accomplish this, as do the radiating leaf forms of the *Aloes* and *Agaves*. The open-branching form of desert trees, such as the palo verde, does the same. Thorns on some plants, such as ocotillo *(Fouquieria splendens)*, are believed to collect dew, somehow absorbed by the plant. Foggy coastal deserts, such as the Atacama in Chile, receive so little rain that plants have evolved that can survive solely on the humidity in the air.

The fleshy root parts developed by some plants, such as cat-claw vine *(Macfadyena unfuis-cati)*, asparagus fern *(Asparagus densiflorus)* and queen's wreath

Aloe ferox, like other cacti and succulents, stores moisture in tissues when water is abundant. This moisture sustains the plant through dry periods.

(Antigonon leptopus), enable them to contend with extended dry periods through adaptations. They store moisture in the roots and use it when water becomes short.

Creosote bush *(Larrea tridentata)* has such efficient water-gathering roots that it prevents other plants from growing in its vicinity. This eliminates competition for water. Only when the soil has been soaked by rains will annual grasses or flowering plants grow for brief periods beneath creosote. After flowering and new leaf growth in spring, the waxy leaves of the creosote go dormant in early summer until the summer rains come, when the plant appears more verdant and may even produce a few more flowers. Salty leaves that drop from tamarisk tree *(Tamarix aphylla)* are thought to prevent new plants from competing.

Arid land plants often have two kinds of roots:

1. Wide-ranging surface roots take up the slightest traces of moisture and nutrients. They function as soil holders and therefore make good erosion-control plants.
2. Taproots go deep into the earth to seek out moisture stored below. They also anchor the plant against strong winds and the scouring action of fast-flowing water that accompanies desert storms. The taproot of the desert hackberry *(Celtis pallida)* will penetrate to 50 feet (15.2m); mesquite *(Prosopis* species) roots can penetrate to 150 feet (45.7m) or more. Taproots make it hard to transplant or pull out tiny seedlings of mesquites, palo verdes and other desert plants. A 2- or 3-inch (5.1- or 7.6-cm) seedling may be anchored in the ground by a 10-inch (25.4 cm) root.

Some plants from arid regions, such as Bermudagrass, have developed the ability to penetrate the hard cement like layers of caliche soil. The roots of the evergreen pistache are known to penetrate rock by secreting a dissolving acid.

Riparian Plants

Not all plants you see in the desert and other arid lands are drought-resistant. Plants that grow along washes, river flood plains, and other places where water collects are part of a riparian, or water-related, community. Trees such as desert hackberry *(Celtis reticulata)*, Arizona walnut *(Juglans major)*, Arizona ash *(Fraxinus velutina)*, the sycamores *(Platanus* species), and the cottonwoods *(Populus*

Creosote bush (Larrea tridentata) *goes dormant until rains come.*

*Cottonwoods (*Populus *species) are riparian plants. They require regular moisture throughout the year.*

species) are riparian plants, although the latter two require a slightly wetter situation than the first three. They will grow only in locations where moisture is available all or most of the year.

The growth habit of mesquite also depends on how much water is available. It may never grow larger than a shrub on the dry mesa, but it becomes a large tree along flood plains or water courses, indicating ample moisture below. If the water table drops slowly, the mesquite adjusts by sending its roots deeper, to as much as 150 feet (45.7m), following the moisture. If you should see a grove of dead mesquite trees, it could be that the water table dropped too fast or too deep for the roots to follow and the trees died of drought. The main problem with mesquites in the landscape is that ample water enlarges the crown without balancing the growth of a wide root system. In outgrowing their root spread, trees may blow over in the wind, unless crowns are thinned to allow wind to move through.

Outdoor room off a study takes advantage of the distant view yet has a close-up view of waterfalls and plants. It is a pleasant place to look into or be in, to listen to the sounds of nature and to watch birds come and go and plants change through the seasons.

Most people have an idea of what they want their landscape to be, but many don't feel they are getting the most from their outdoor space. An undesirable landscape is often the result of poor planning, caused by seasonal urges, nursery promotions, or a natural desire to plant anything that will add color or greenery to a bare lot. The immediate effect is an improvement, but plants that are hastily selected and poorly located will develop into a hodgepodge. Established plants are difficult and expensive to move or replace if you change your mind. The final result is a landscape you spend most of your time caring for, rather than enjoying.

The Outdoor Room

Rather than go through this frustrating exercise, plan before you plant. One way to approach a landscape plan is to treat your outdoor area as an outdoor room—an extension of your home. Your room will have a "floor," "walls," and a "roof." The floor can be anything: lawn, brick, wooden deck, ground cover or any combination of these. Walls can be rows of trees, a hedge, a wood or vine-covered fence, or an actual masonry wall. The roof can be made of wood, aluminum, shade cloth or canvas, a canopy-shaped tree, or the sky. Other plants and pots and the like are the "furniture" with a color theme and a specific effect.

Above all, keep two things in mind as you make your plan: First in importance is that your outdoor room will serve the interests of you and your family. Second, it should be a beautiful place, something you enjoy looking at or being in. When these two features are skillfully blended together, the landscape is a success.

Hardscape

When designing your outdoor room, think of built items such as paved patios, decks, walks, walls and so on (frequently called the *hardscape*) as you would think of walls, hallways, and rooms of different uses when planning a house. The hardscape forms the spaces and is usually the landscape backbone. Major trees, hedges and grass areas are also part of the structure of your landscape. You should finish your hardscape before you begin planting.

Ask Yourself Some Questions

Planning begins with knowing what you want from your outdoor space. Before you rush out to the nursery, think about what you and your family like to do outdoors. The size and makeup of your family will be major factors. Small children, for example, have completely different needs from adults. Try to plan for multiple uses later on as interests change. For example, a sandbox can be easily transformed into a raised bed for vegetable gardening when your child's interest in sandcastles wanes.

Following is a list of questions to help you narrow down what you want and need out of your landscape plan.

The entry drive is walled with an inviting door at the entrance.

- **Do you understand your CC & Rs and zoning restrictions?** Many subdivisions have covenants, conditions and restrictions (CC&Rs) that state what homeowners may or may not do. City or county zoning restrictions may also affect you. For example, the distance of a structure from a property line may be spelled out in the CC&Rs or in a city or county code. In subdivisions with CC&Rs, there is usually a homeowners' association with an architectural committee that must approve your plans.

- **Do you need space for recreation?** Backyards and family games are nearly synonymous. Lawns and paved areas support a number of activities for all ages. Perhaps you will want a special play yard for children, visible from indoors.

- **Do you want fruit, vegetable or flower gardens?** Gardening for food is increasing in popularity. Raised planter beds are neat self-contained areas for growing vegetables or flowers. Improving the soil is also easier and more economical in a raised bed, especially if you use a soil mix. The low walls of the raised beds enable you to sit as you tend your plants.

Consider fruit trees, including citrus. Dwarf varieties take up less space than their full-size counterparts and they grow well in large containers. Espaliered plants (plants attached to and trained on walls or fences), including some fruit trees, work well in small spaces. Such treatment is decorative and does not interfere with fruit production. Fruit trees trained on a wall or fence produce fruit in a very small space.

A small lawn and a vine-covered pergola that shades the living room and protects sensitive plants from the extremes of weather.

- **Do you need privacy, such as a private garden?** A private place in your own backyard has a special appeal, offering retreat, relaxation and possibly even a spa. You may want to preserve scenic views, while screening the neighbor's view of you.

- **Will you do much entertaining?** Patio areas adjacent to the house are desirable for large outdoor parties or small family gatherings. The size of your get-togethers naturally determines how large your patio should be. A paved area or plot of lawn nearby can serve as an overflow area for extra-large gatherings. A low seatwall at the edge of a terrace can provide extra seating for a crowd as well as help to define the space.

- **Does your climate require modification?** Unchecked, the arid climate creates harsh living conditions indoors and out. Most sites have to be modified. Proper placement of shade structures, trees, shrubs and ground covers will help make your home more livable than any other single factor. (See page 19 for details on using plants to temper difficult climates.)

- **What kind of gardener are you?** This is an important question, because it deals with how much time you have or want to spend caring for your landscape. For example, don't plan to have a large lawn if you really hate to water, mow and fertilize. Do you plan to have help maintaining your landscape? Consider too the total water requirements of your plants. The minioasis landscape (a small intensively planted green area by the house, transitioning to arid plants farther out) may be perfect for you. Are you more interested in plants that can grow in hot climates but require more water? The low-water-use, easy-care landscape is not for everyone.

- **Do you have any special needs?** For instance, elderly or physically challenged people may not be able to negotiate steps. Also consider areas for pets, storage, compost, work, or hobbies. Open multiple-use areas allow for changes as the family grows or interests change. Do you wish to preserve and enhance a special view? As they do in Japan, you can "borrow" the view of your neighbor's lovely tree. Are there eyesores you would like to screen?

- **Do you wish to fit your landscape into the flavor of the neighborhood?** If your neighbors have a plant theme, such as desert or natural, do you want to follow suit? Will the theme fit in with your home? Or do you prefer contrast?

- **How much money do you have to spend?** As a general rule, plan generously. Then, after you have roughed out costs, you may discover that you will have to start with smaller plants, reduce the size of the patio or deck area slightly, or use less expensive building materials. Perhaps your landscape will have to be built a little at a time. Plant trees and shrubs first if they won't interfere with your future hardscape: They take the longest to develop. Watch for sales and nursery promotions, but don't compromise the basic quality of your plan. Add to it gradually as your budget allows. If you can't

do the planting yourself, talk to some contractors to find out what they would charge. Or ask your neighbors for referrals—perhaps they use a yard-maintenance company or know someone who can help you out. (See page 15 for more information on costs.)

The Landscape Plan

The preceding questions have probably created a jigsaw puzzle of ideas in your mind. You can better organize your ideas if you create major headings and lists. Then rate the items on the lists according to their importance from first to last. After you have formulated your thoughts, sit down and put the pieces of your landscape together. One of the best methods, used by professionals and amateurs alike, begins with a large sheet of graph paper. Excellent tools besides pencil and eraser include an architect's scale, a triangle or other straight edge, French curves and circle templates. Use the graph squares to equal a unit of measurement (each square equals one foot, for example) so it will be simple to plot distances.

To create a landscape plan, you will first need a base plan of your house and lot, from property line to property line, drawn as accurately as possible.

- **Show the outline of your house on the lot.** To correctly place your house on your plan, measure the distance from two points on the front of the house to the two front corners of your lot. Then measure side yards and the distance to the back lot line.

- **Show windows, doors, the electric box, gas meter, hosebibs, and other features.**

- **Draw drains from the roof and where the water goes from there.** Note runoff from paved areas, or drainage from a higher part of the property, and where the water goes.

- **Show property lines, power poles, underground utilities, walls, fences, views, existing trees and shrubs— anything that will affect the beauty and livability of the design.** This will also include notes on prevailing winds and how the sun shines on your lot in summer and in winter and where the greatest extent of the shadow is in winter. Knowing these details will be important if you want to have a windscreen, trees for shade, plants to handle runoff from rain or shade-tolerant plants.

When you are satisfied that the major features of your site are represented on the graph paper, cover it with a sheet of tracing paper and sketch your ideas. Experiment. Modify. Erase. Analyze. Be bold. Changing a plan is simple; moving a landscape around is not. Start with the hardscape, including dominant existing plants. When that is completed you are ready to do your plant design. It might be helpful to follow these guidelines:

- **Begin with a simple, unified plan.** Think of plants as groups and masses. Limit their forms, colors and textures. (We discuss specifics on selecting plants on page 17.) Likewise, limit the types of construction materials and repeat design elements of the house if possible.

- **Work toward a basic concept.** Don't concern yourself with minor details—they can be added later. It always helps to have a landscape theme to follow. (Several are described on page 15.)

- **Consider water needs.** Try to place plants with similar water and sun exposure needs together. Plants in shade will require less water than those in the sun. Small plants will need more frequent but shorter irrigations. Trees and large desert shrubs will require much longer irrigations given at less frequent intervals. Cacti can use a little help with occasional irrigations while they are becoming established and can be left pretty much to survive on their own later, depending on their native origin.

Landscape Tip: Sleeving

Before digging, be sure you know what is underground. It is a good idea in putting down anything of a permanent nature to know where any underground utilities are located and to put in enough sleeving (pipe tunnels to run wire or irrigation tubing through) under paving and decks to be sure you can reach all planting areas with irrigation piping and wires for outdoor lighting. Sleeving (sometimes called a *chase*) doesn't cost much and, with a little planning, can save you a lot of grief. Use 2-inch schedule 40 PVC or 2-inch ABS pipe. Double sleeving (two pipes side by side) is a good idea because it can give you plenty of space to weave your lines through. One pipe can be for irrigation and one for electrical wires.

A Bubble Diagram Helps You Plan

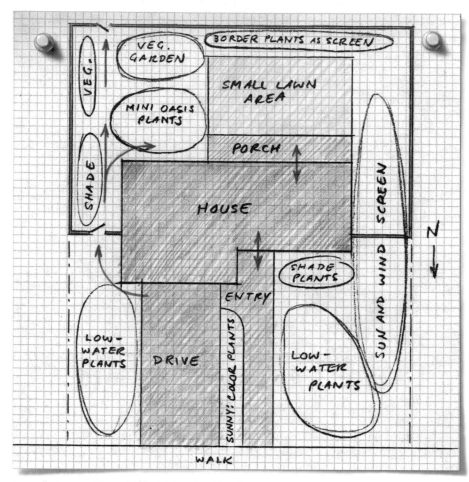

Map your house and lot to scale and make a list of your needs and desires. Then make a bubble diagram, as shown above, indicating the placement and approximate size of the plants you want. Show your traffic patterns with arrows.

• **Keep plant size in proportion to your home.** Those innocent-looking plants in the one-gallon containers can grow up to become giants. If large-growing plants are located near an entryway or sidewalk, you will have to battle their natural growth habits, pruning and cutting them back continuously. In addition, the appearance of those plants will suffer. It is important to know the mature size of your plants and allow space for their growth. Some plants come in large, medium and small selections. There are often smaller or more compact forms of plants of the same variety that won't outgrow the allotted space.

• **Picture yourself in your completed garden.** Having a good imagination is a real advantage in deciding if your proposed landscape is right for you. Spend some time outside during the day and night. Walk along pathways you are considering and envision how your proposed trees and shrubs will look after they have matured. Sit on the "deck" you have penciled on your plan and admire your view. Projecting yourself into your future landscape will give you a real feel of how you will like living in your outdoor room.

To check on dimensions, use a tape measure and outline your landscape elements by making lines on the ground with flour or spray paint. Another method is to use a rope or a garden hose to lay out a curved line or a straight border. This will help you to estimate size, visualize your finished plan, and make changes before it is too late. Measure the altered distance each change makes and mark it on your plan.

Professional Help

If you don't feel confident about your plan, or you wish to have the benefit of a professional opinion, you might want to consult with a licensed landscape architect. The least expensive way is to have a landscape architect visit your homesite for a consultation. Prices change, but to give you some idea, some landscape architects charge anywhere from $50 to $100 per hour, possibly more depending on where you live. A complete professional plan with the design of hardscape (including a pool, spa, or other water feature; plant plan and lighting plan with schedules; irrigation notes or design; and complete specifications) can start at $1250 (or less) to $2500 and up depending on the size and complexity of the job. This isn't a lot for a well-designed, integrated plan if you are considering investing your energy and hundreds or thousands of dollars in plants and building materials. And for a small area, it could be a lot less.

Consider having a licensed landscape architect work with you to design a plan from scratch. Be sure to ask the following questions of any firm you consider:

• **What are their qualifications?**

• **What services do they provide?**

• **How much do they charge for what kinds of services?**

• **Besides consulting and designing, what help can they offer you in installing your landscape?**

• **Is this a design/build firm? Or can this person help you identify suitable contractors for competitive bids? Can he or she work with a contractor for a seamless installation?** Some charge by the

Landscape Tip: A Lower Water Bill

Whether you design your own landscape or have someone else do it, pay attention to capturing rainwater to help irrigate your garden. Capture roof runoff in containers that can be tapped for irrigation. Contour the landscape so that trees are placed in a low area to which water runs as it comes off your roof, your patio or your drive. There are numerous ingenious ways to capture and use the water nature gives you and therefore save on your water bill, especially in areas with rainy summers.

hour, others charge a percentage of the construction cost or charge a set fee. Fees will vary according to region.

If you have a small site or section of a landscape you want to have developed, some landscape architects will make a single trip to your home and draw a plan on-site. This reduces their time, thus your cost. You will get a simple plan with a professional touch. Such a plan is fine for a small area. For larger spaces or many requirements, it may be better to work with the designer over time to make sure you get what you want.

Landscape Themes

A space can be designed in many different ways. Consider not only the items above, but also the style of the home, the effects desired, plant water requirements, and how best to divide space and to fit in any amenities such as pools, spas, fountains, cooking centers and play yards. A single landscape plan can produce several different effects, depending on which plants and building materials you use and how you combine and maintain them.

A theme gives your home and landscape a personality. It can be merely suggested by a few select plants or carried out to the last detail. If you unconsciously tend to be a "one-of-this, one-of-that" kind of gardener, a theme can still serve as an organizing and unifying device.

You'll find that masses of plants of a similar nature are more pleasing to the eye than a collection of many different kinds of plants. And it is important to group together plants with similar water requirements. Don't force a style on your home; it will only appear contrived and unnatural. Get a feel for what will work best with your architecture, the layout of your site, what neighbors have done and your family's way of life.

Mexican or Mediterranean type patios are suitable with homes of a similar style. Usually at least partially walled, they acquire a picturesque look with large paved areas, a wall or central fountain, numerous container plants and vines. Palms and citrus look at home here. Paving materials can be rustic—such as pebbled concrete, brick or adobe-looking material—or sleek, in a formal symmetrical layout, depending on the surrounding architecture.

Rustic landscapes can be produced by using rough, weathered materials, such as railroad ties, used bricks, flag- or fieldstone,

Landscape Costs

If you are budget conscious, try to figure the cost of landscaping and get an idea of materials and plants available. Visit large stores that deal in home improvements; stone and materials yards; irrigation supply stores; outdoor lighting stores and nurseries. If you take your plan along and it has accurate dimensions, trained personnel there can help you figure out how much of a material you might need and how much it will cost. Many deliver. Some may have the names of people who can help you do all or part of the work. Having a contractor install your landscape costs more, but it can save a lot of effort.

Cost will increase with increased size or additional features. For instance, if you wish to have a spa, you will find a large cost range depending on whether you plan for a custom-designed in-ground spa or a portable or drop-in model. To save money, you may decide to use brick edges to define plant beds and the edges of terraces and walkways. Then use decomposed granite or gravel to fill in the walk or terrace instead of bricking the whole thing. Stepping stones are available at a range of prices from preformed concrete pavers to more expensive flagstone set in mortar. The more complex your plan, the more it will cost to install.

Constructed elements, such as swimming pools, need to be accessible to trucks and should be put in before plants or other items that would be disturbed if you decide to do this construction later. Complex plans and installations with many constructed elements (pools, fountains, terraces, walls) will be costly, sort of like building a house outdoors. Plants cost less than the hardscape.

If you plan to sell your home, maybe in five years, how much can you spend on landscaping and still get the amount back when you sell? You can safely spend 10 percent of the value of an average home on landscaping. The more valuable the home, the higher the budget should be to create a suitable setting. Real estate experts will tell you that good landscaping is a good investment. A house needs what they call "curb appeal"—an attractive and inviting appearance from the street. A grim-looking landscape discourages buyers from looking further.

The patio is another selling point. Many people will plan to change the carpet or remodel the kitchen to match the magazine clippings they have saved. But they may buy the house because they fall in love with how the patio looks from the living room or how it makes them feel as they walk out on it. You will find it easier to sell your house and get your asking price if you have a pleasing landscape.

If you plan to stay in your home for a longer period, or it is your dream house, you are landscaping it for yourself and it should match your dreams. Even if you spend more, it will be worth it to you for the enjoyment of living there. You can bet that if you do decide to sell your home and you like your landscaping, others will, too.

One travel agent found after creating her dream patio that she had made her home a resort. She preferred to stay home instead of gallivanting around the world. Bad for the travel business. But it is true that you can recreate that special feeling of a vacation place you loved so you have your own resort at home.

boulders and exposed-aggregate concrete. Construction is done in a loose, free manner. Plant forms should be natural and free in shape. Trim or thin to maintain a subtle control of the plants, but don't shear or shape. Maintenance is casual, and a certain amount of litter is acceptable.

Formal or tailored landscapes are created with a feeling of control, geometry, precision and containment. Bricks or paving with sharply defined edges are appropriate elements. Plants that grow naturally into contained shapes or accept clipping and

training well are at home here. Hedges, sheared screens and topiaries define the formal look. An English garden may have formally shaped beds, but, contrary to popular belief, plants in an English border can grow to their natural size and mingle, giving a feeling of well-being and exuberance without losing the formal quality of the landscape.

Natural, wild and desert have similar themes. All such gardens are informal in character with flowing lines, open spaces and rough textures. Stones, broom-swept earth,

The Mediterranean/Mexican patio has paved spaces and lots of pots. It is usually a private space, either partially or wholly surrounded by the walls of the house.

This desert garden shows a collection of bold succulents.

A rustic feeling was created here with berms, rock banks, a rustic fence and casual plantings.

Topiary is sometimes used in formal gardens. It is created by forming a plant into a special shape, such as this leaping dolphin, or a three-tiered tree. Animal shapes are usually formed by letting a plant grow into a wire frame and clipping the leaves as they grow out from the wires.

earthy mulches and gently contoured mounds of earth fit well here. Plant placement is subtle, natural and random. One way to achieve an informal look and break the tradition of row planting is to set plants in triangles or lazy "M" patterns.

A natural landscape in its true form includes plants native to an area, whether desert, chaparral or subtropical. It may or may not be enhanced by the addition of similar non-native plants.

A wild landscape may or may not include native plants but gives the same feeling as a natural garden. A bird or butterfly garden with a small pond or water dish for drinking, and plants attractive to these creatures would be at home here. Plants are allowed to have a natural appearance and may grow into a dense tangle, giving birds places for hiding, nesting and nurturing young. Such gardens would include plants that feed the larval stages of butterflies, so you will need to accommodate caterpillars.

Desert landscapes may or may not include cacti, but most people consider cacti integral to the desert. In real deserts, however, there are a variety of other types of plants. Desert plants generally have wide soil and irrigation tolerances. The desert garden can be neatly planted, like a collection, or arranged more randomly for a natural appearance.

Transitional landscapes may take place between the green minioasis and the truly low- or no-water landscape. They include plants that look at home with the cultivated, tended garden as well as the low-water landscape. The main function is to blend the two garden types together to create a unified whole.

Subtropical landscapes are somewhere between the rather sparse desert landscape and the verdant tropical landscape. There is a festive feel to the plants in this type of garden—many have bold, striking leaves; others have feathery leaves. Palms and citrus fit well here, as do flowering annuals and perennials of bright and contrasting colors. Subtropical landscapes will have some bloom or color all year and be especially exuberant with color in the warmer months. Bold succulent forms such as *Aloes*, *Agaves*, or spiky *Yuccas* used as accents play against the frilly foliage of the color plants and draw attention when the color providers are dormant in the winter.

Tropical landscapes generally work best in small, preferably enclosed and protected areas in hot and dry climates, such as in an entryway, small bathroom, patio or atrium area. Plants used here require

This naturalistic garden is a functional wash, bermed on the sides and planted sparingly with native arid-land plants.

protection from extreme cold, heat and wind. They are characterized by dense greenery, rich vibrant color and bold leaf forms. Create a relaxing oasis and cooling effect by adding a water feature or a suggestion of water, such as near a dry wash or pebbled stream bed.

Oriental gardens are landscapes of suggestion and illusion. They are seldom symmetrical. To Western eyes, Oriental landscapes may appear sparse and serene. Plants and materials are objects of art and sculptural beauty. Careful attention is given to natural effects. Small, informal water elements, or even suggested streams in the form of dry streambeds, work well here. Combining rocks, wood, gravel and other natural materials with picturesque plants makes the Western version of the Oriental garden particularly attractive in arid regions. The style is well adapted to a small space,

This entry transitions from olive trees and rosemary near the house to arid-land plants and mesquite trees at the parking area.

This planter has something in color most of the year, giving a subtropical feeling. Many of the plants are attractive to hummingbirds.

such as an entryway, atrium or townhouse patio. The Oriental effect is quite striking, yet requires little care. You don't have to use pines, bamboo and the like: Desert plants with character can carry out the Oriental garden philosophy when properly chosen, but avoid cacti, *Yuccas* and similar plants.

Woodsy landscapes are informal and rustic, with curving lines and natural materials. Vines and low ground covers in contrasting shades of green along with tender little ground plants such as violets, shaded by trees, can give this effect. Woody or pine-needle mulches, stony outcrops and overstory tall trees are important features. The woodsy garden might include coniferous plants, such as pines or junipers, but also requires deciduous trees that offer fall color. Colorful flowers, add the finishing touches.

Container gardens, from one pot to a whole garden of nothing but pots, are loved by almost everyone. Those who fall in love with the Mexican patio (a patio full of pots) think container gardens are especially attractive and practical. From contained herb gardens by the kitchen door to color spots by the entry, containers have many uses. Not all pots need to contain plants. Some can be thought of as sculpture or character pieces.

Specialized landscapes, from play yards to bird or butterfly gardens, can be achieved by furnishing any of the above themes with decorative paths, lawns or groundcover, or plants that attract birds and butterflies (see page 201 for examples).

Selecting Plants

For many people, choosing plants at a nursery can be a bewildering experience. Row upon row of plants, most of them unfamiliar, await your selection. So, before you buy plants, take some time to familiarize yourself with plants that can grow in your area. A nursery or display garden with labeled plants is an excellent place to educate yourself. There you can study them and sort out your feelings about foliage texture, color and structure. You can also examine plants at various stages of growth. For example, you can look at a tree species in a one-gallon can, five-gallon can and a fifteen-gallon can, noting changes that occur with age and size.

Ask questions of the nursery people or other plant professionals who are knowledgeable about the plants you like. Beware of impulse purchases of nursery plants or you may end up with a collection of unsuitable plants and a disappointing result.

A protected entry patio, perfect for tropical plants.

The stone path, like a dry stream, leads to the gazebo, which might be an American version of a Japanese tea house.

A botanical garden is another source of information. Botanical gardens have labeled plants, may have demonstration gardens, give classes suitable to your location, and usually have helpful books in their shops.

Getting to know plants and their needs will help you with your selection. Don't actually purchase your plants until you are ready to plant them and have the holes dug and any necessary soil preparation done (see chapter 3 for information on planting preparation). Plant selection will depend on your needs and the effect you are trying to create. Make a list of the plants you want and the uses you will want them to fill. Try to choose the right plant for a particular use. Vary forms, sizes, foliage texture and color, but limit your plant palette so you end up with a design, not a collection. Keep in mind which plants are evergreen and which deciduous. It helps to have evergreens mixed in with deciduous plants so everything won't look bare at once. Plan to have something

Container gardens offer a world of possibilities from riots of color to prim succulents, from hanging pots to rustic containers that make interesting planters. Not all pots need to be planted. Some are art objects on their own.

Garden pathways don't have to be straight. These flagstone stepping stones to the play yard make getting there an adventure.

blooming at all times of the year. Observers tend to see only the colorful or attractive plants, which overshadow the dull-looking plants out of season.

Do not purchase plants that are too small or too large for the container. Avoid plants with weeds or bugs, or those that just look sickly. Select plants that will not outgrow the space allowed, or you will always be cutting. Many plants have cultivars of different sizes. Be sure you know what you are getting. Stay with your design list even if the plant is out of season and doesn't look like it did when you first saw it. Avoid impulse buying. Trust your design judgment.

Water Needs

An even more important part of plant selection is the amount of water each plant requires. There are few arid-land regions where water use isn't a concern. This dramatically modifies the approach to landscape planning and critically affects plant selection. Plants naturally have varied water needs, from little to ample. Before you finalize your design and purchase plants, examine their total water needs. Are you willing to spend what it will take to keep them growing? Does your region have that much water to spend?

One or more tall sheltering trees and leafy under-plants create a woodsy effect.

The Minioasis Concept

For many, the ideal landscape is lush, green and inviting, filled with beautiful, healthy plants. At first this kind of landscape may seem difficult, expensive or even impossible in hot, arid regions. However, even with limited water, you can have your own lush green place. The minioasis concept works like this: As you begin to select plants for your design, group them by their water needs. Concentrate those with high water requirements in one small area close to your house, entry, patio or pool—this is your minioasis. These plants should be your favorites—the ones you like to look at and touch. They should be attractive at close range and look nice all year. A minioasis is the perfect place for a small, lush carpet of grass if you feel you must have a lawn. Treat it like an area rug. Or you can have a paved terrace with plants and pots all around and no grass, or some of both.

Areas beyond this well-watered zone can include plants having lower and lower water needs, blending from a transitional plant zone to an arid one. The zoning of plants by their water requirements can be as extensive as you want to make it.

A newer term for the low-water landscape is *Xeriscape*™. "Xeric" means "dry" in Greek. The "scape" part comes from landscape. This concept may or may not allow for a minioasis. It is primarily concerned with the water budget.

The essence of the minioasis concept is also water budgeting—spending water where you will enjoy it the most. If you use more sensitive plants from other regions that require improved soil, you also confine these to a single area. Areas beyond the minioasis need not suffer in appearance. Attractive drought-resistant plants are available to shade, screen or cover the ground just as efficiently and sometimes more colorfully than their water-demanding counterparts.

Modifying Your Climate

One of the most important services plants can provide is increased human comfort. Plants are beautiful to look at, but in hot arid regions they also play an important part in tempering severe climatic conditions. To modify your climate effectively requires careful placement of plants. You want to place the right plant where it will do the best possible job of modifying sun, wind and temperatures. Some homeowners merely guess at which plants they should grow and where they should be placed. But considering the amount of time it takes a tree to reach maturity and provide shade or act as a screen, it makes sense to choose and locate it carefully.

The first step in controlling your climate is knowing what needs to be modified. Study your site: Is your patio unprotected, facing the hot western sun? Do cold winter winds rip across the backyard, nearly always coming from the west? Are there windows in the house directly exposed to the summer sun? As you watch the weather on your site, you'll begin to notice particular patterns. Using this knowledge, and being aware of your microclimates (see page 6), you can make the best plant selections and place them where

This walled minioasis with trees has concrete aggregate instead of a lawn and is edged with easy-care plants and annual flowers.

Typical of the Mediterranean region, this deciduous grape vine shades the porch in summer but lets the warming sun come in when in its leafless winter state.

they will do the most good for your indoor and outdoor environment.

The Sun

In hot arid regions, the most powerful climatic force is the sun. For example, the average maximum temperature in Palm Springs, California, for July is 110F (43C). In Phoenix, Arizona, it's 105F (41C). Modifying these kinds of temperature extremes should be one of your first landscaping priorities.

Due to the earth's rotation, the angle of the sun and its relationship to your home changes. During summer, the sun is high in the sky and the rays shine at a more direct angle and for a longer period. This increases temperatures. Conversely, the winter sun is lower in the sky. The less direct angle and shorter days produce lower temperatures. The point is, you need to know these

Plants and Pollen Allergies

Many people are allergic to certain plants. Some allergies are caused by direct contact with the skin or by breathing in an allergen that's released from a blossom within a limited range. It is a good idea to check on your family's allergic reactions before selecting your plants. Beyond close range, certain plants with wind-blown pollen can affect people over a wide distance. Generally, plants with small colorless flowers are the most troublesome. They rely on the wind for pollination and produce tremendous amounts of pollen. Some of the worst offenders are the male mulberry (*Morus alba*), African sumac (*Rhus lancea*), olive (*Olea europaea*), ash (*Fraxinus* species), tamarisk (*Tamarix* species) and common Bermudagrass (*Cynodon dactylon*). Plants with fragrant, colorful flowers also produce pollen, but it is heavy and sticky and transferred by insects, not wind, as they go from flower to flower. Some of these plants, such as the *Acacia* species, produce a cloud of pollen near the plant, which may bother certain nearby individuals, but it is not spread widely by the wind. Some communities forbid the planting of some or all wind-pollinating plants. Note that there is now a grafted selection of fruitless olive called 'Swan Hill' that does not give off free-blowing pollen.

seasonal changes to choose the best location for your shade-producing or shade-loving plants. Keep mental notes or, better yet, sketch on paper the sun's path as it passes over your home. If you are new to your home and don't know how the sun will pass over in the respective seasons, ask your neighbor for help.

Because the sun is such a powerful force, it pays to use it to your best advantage. One of the best ways is with shade trees, properly placed to shade home or outdoor areas. Deciduous shade trees are those that lose their leaves each fall and produce new leaves in the spring. This works perfectly for climate control. When the summer sun is at its hottest, trees are in full leaf and block the hot rays. A house with a shaded roof remains 10 to 20 degrees cooler inside. The same tree during chilly winter weather allows the sun to shine through its bare branches, warming the house. (See illustrations on page 7.) Thus deciduous trees save energy both seasons, reducing cooling bills in summer, heating

bills in winter. Try to select trees with high arching branches that will create a canopy over your roof. Solar-energy installations require special consideration—they cannot be shaded from the sun. If you are considering placing a solar unit on your roof, plan the placement of your trees accordingly.

Evergreen trees can also be used for shade, but because they are in leaf the entire year, getting the benefit of summer shade and winter sun is not as simple as with deciduous trees. One way is to grow evergreens that will be tall enough to shade the high summer sun, yet have a high enough canopy to allow the low winter sun to shine beneath, unimpeded. To do this, the tree has to be carefully trained and placed at just the right distance from your house.

Evergreens, as well as deciduous trees, can be used to block the low hot rays of the summer setting sun. Because the sun sets in the northwest in midsummer compared to southwest in winter, there is no risk of

blocking the desirable winter setting sun.

There are other ways of modifying the sun's heat and glare. Vines can be trained to grow on hot south and west walls, or trained on trellises to provide fast shade. Cat-claw vine (*Macfadyena unguis-cati*) climbs by itself and is one of the best plants for a hot wall. For summer shade and winter sun, deciduous grape vines (see *Vitis vinifera*) are outstanding and fast-growing, with the added benefit of fruit. Annual vines are fast temporary covers. Try using temporary vines or other covers until shade trees have grown.

Don't forget about manmade structures that provide shade. Overhangs above windows deflect the high summer sun but allow the lower winter sun to enter. Wooden trellises, lattice work, retractable awnings, shadecloth and other materials overhead will also reduce the sun's intensity and create shade.

Reducing Glare

When the sun hits light-colored pavement or buildings, bare earth or shiny objects, it reflects at an angle—partly as heat and partly as intense light. This reflection often heats the surroundings, enters buildings through windows, and is hard on the eyes. Tall trees that shade the building and the ground intercept the sunlight above building level and eliminate reflected light from the ground's surface. Ground covers, such as lawns, *Myoporum* species, trailing indigo bush (*Dalea greggii*), junipers (*Juniperus* species) and rosemary (*Rosmarinus officinalis*), absorb the sun's rays, eliminating glare. These and other ground covers, when placed on the south sides of buildings, prevent the angled sun's rays from bouncing up into windows. Through transpiration, a living ground cover cools the air above it by about 10 degrees. Vines and espaliers on walls also cut down on heat reflected from light-colored surfaces. Paving, gravel and rock increase temperatures by storing heat during the day and releasing it at night.

Controlling Wind and Airflow

Wind is a special problem in arid regions. It exaggerates the harsher elements. Wind-whipped sand and dust can be picked up and carried for miles, unimpeded by natural barriers. Hot dry winds that occur in summer are more drying than still air, and cold winter winds are more penetrating.

Plants used as windscreens or windbreaks can play an important part in controlling and guiding air movement.

Seasonal Sun Patterns

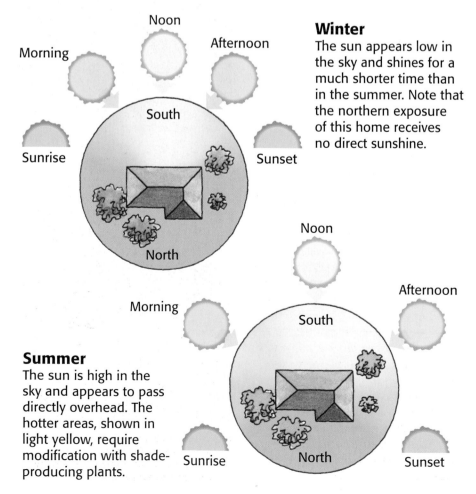

Winter
The sun appears low in the sky and shines for a much shorter time than in the summer. Note that the northern exposure of this home receives no direct sunshine.

Summer
The sun is high in the sky and appears to pass directly overhead. The hotter areas, shown in light yellow, require modification with shade-producing plants.

A hedge placed 10 feet (3.1m) from a house will deflect the wind over the building.

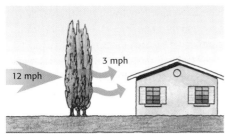

12 mph   3 mph

A screen that allows some wind flow is more effective for a greater distance because the wind slows as it filters through.

Windscreens give shelter to homes and outdoor areas. They help alleviate dust problems along highways and keep topsoil from blowing away.

In urban areas, windbreaks shield playing fields, parks and school playgrounds. They help break up the wind-tunnel effect on city streets. Placement of trees around a structure can affect its ventilation and alter the climate by blocking or guiding the wind. You can create a pocket of relatively still air by placing a hedge 20 feet (6.1m) upwind of a building. A hedge placed 10 feet (3.1m) from a house will deflect the wind over the building and open windows will only get a low breeze backwash from the opposite side.

Windscreens set in the open are most effective when set perpendicular to the prevailing wind. A vertical, somewhat penetrable planting that covers to the ground, with a 50 to 60 percent density, generally affords more protection than a wide dense one. A screen that allows some wind flow is more effective for a greater distance because the wind slows as it filters through. A solid screen blocks the wind completely for a short distance, deflecting it upward. But after the wind passes over the screen, it comes back to earth with greater force. For this reason, a mix of plant sizes building from low to high will do the best job at reducing wind flow.

Broadleaf evergreens, such as certain *Eucalyptus* and *Acacia* species, or conifers, such as pines, junipers, and cypress with foliage that reaches to the ground are best as year-round windscreens. Tall grasses, such as giant reed (*Arundo donax*), pampas grass (*Cortaderia selloana*), and bamboo (*Bambusa* species) are good low plants as the first line of defense at outer edges. Deciduous trees lose their leaves in winter, so their effectiveness is reduced.

Even more important to the effectiveness of your windscreen is placement of plants. To figure out the prevailing wind patterns of your site, use a variation of the airport wind sock. Strips of cloth placed on stakes will show you at a glance which way the wind tends to blow. Chart the direction and intensity of the wind for a period of time, preferably both summer and winter. You'll notice patterns and will then be able to place plants to filter any strong annoying winds. As a general rule, optimum protection from the wind is obtained at a distance of three to seven times the height of the windbreak on the sheltered side. Ideally then, a row of 20-foot (6.1-m) trees should be placed 60 to 100 feet (18.3 to 30.5m) away from the area you want to protect. Most home lots are not large enough to accommodate this kind of spacing, so placement will depend upon what space you have.

Not all winds are undesirable. Summer breezes have a cooling effect, so you may want to direct them toward your site by creating a breezeway. Again, this takes careful thought and research to be done effectively, but the end result is well worth the effort.

Herb Gardens

Many herbs are easy to grow in arid zones. While the weather is generally harsher than in the Mediterranean region, it is possible to grow Mediterranean plants and herbs here. Some, such as rosemary, sage, bay trees and olive trees, are grown as landscape plants. Other herbs grown as landscape plants are lavender, catmint and catnip, *Santolina*, *Verbena*, lamb's ears and *Aloe vera*. Useful for refreshing air in residences are the decorative branches cut from *Eucalyptus pulverulenta* and *E. cinerea*.

Locate your herb garden where it will get about six hours of sunshine and have afternoon shade. Plant in large pots, raised beds or create a traditional rectangular garden with a path entering from each direction and leading to a fountain, birdbath or other ornament in the center, making it more of a garden spot. Herbs can also be combined with seasonal vegetables or flowers.

Herbs do best in porous soil with good drainage and will need to be lightly fertilized every few weeks. Chives, mint and parsley like moist enriched soil. Once the herbs are up and growing, you will need to harvest from many of them to keep them producing and to keep plants from bolting to seed.

Besides the perennial bay trees and bush or dwarf rosemary, there are annual herbs, such as the many flavors of basil, to be planted in spring. Chives are mainly summer plants that go dormant in cold winters. Fennel is a summer annual, which also feeds the friendly bugs you want to keep around to

Herb gardens can be as simple as a few pots on a cart or by the kitchen door, to an edging by the garage, to a large formal space cut in quarters by walks with a fountain in the center.

This raised vegetable garden gets full sun most of the day and is used for growing both warm and cool weather vegetables. A raised bed is easier to service and allows you to fill it with prepared soil.

eat plant pests. Plant winter annuals, such as chamomile, cilantro, dill and parsley, in fall. Thyme of many kinds is generally a root-hardy winter-dormant perennial. It looks attractive grown between stepping stones or in rock gardens.

Vegetable Gardens

Many gardeners are surprised to discover that arid climates are among the best anywhere for growing vegetables. Irrigated desert valleys produce a huge percentage of the world's vegetable crops, especially in winter. The word "winter" emphasizes a very important aspect of vegetable gardening in the warm arid regions: It's a two-season affair, and winter is often the most productive season. Planting at the right time is the key to success in these regions. The dates to plant your favorite crops are not as clearly defined as in temperate zones. In fact, you will be better off in most cases ignoring any "spring fever" planting urges.

An important part of knowing when to plant your garden requires a little understanding about vegetables as plants. Not all vegetables have the same cultural requirements. Some are better adapted to cool weather and can tolerate light freezes. Others require warm soil and temperatures to germinate and grow properly. Vegetables are generally divided into two climate

categories: cool season and warm season. Because cool-season crops are hardy, frost tolerant and germinate in cool soil, they are usually planted from late summer to early spring, depending on your climate. Warm-season plants will not tolerate frost and need warm temperatures to set and mature fruit. Extreme heat prevents fruit set and reduces plant and fruit quality.

When to Plant

The following are some planting guidelines for your climate zone (according to the map on pages 2 and 3). Keep in mind that climate varies greatly within a zone and from year to year. Your own experiences or those learned from your neighbor, cooperative extension service, botanical garden or a knowledgeable nursery are invaluable when making planting decisions.

There are two main planting periods in the low and middle zones: late summer to winter for cool-season crops, early spring for warm-season crops. In the high zone there is one main planting period: spring to early summer.

Cool-season garden. The best time to garden in the low and middle zones is late summer to fall. Cooler temperatures, lower water needs and fewer pests make it easier to grow plants. This is the prime time to grow a cool-season garden: leaf crops, such as lettuce, cabbage and chard, and beets, carrots and turnips from seed. In the milder areas in these zones, you can sometimes grow early-maturing summer crops like corn and tomato at this time. Many summer vegetables have trouble setting fruit when night temperatures stay up in the 70s and 80s F (21 to 32C). The cool but not cold night temperatures of early fall allow plants to come into bloom and set fruit. In the high zone, early frosts prevent fall planting in most areas. A late-summer cool-season crop planting with early-maturing varieties can sometimes produce before winter cold takes over.

Warm-season garden. Late winter

through early spring is the time to plant warm-season vegetables in the low and middle zones. Generally, the lower the elevation, the sooner you can set out plants. The idea is to get plants such as tomatoes, beans and corn established as soon as possible so they will bloom and set fruit before the high heat of summer. The fruit will then mature during summer, even though blossoming or fruit set may cease. If blooms start setting again when nights cool in fall, these same plants may bear a bonus crop before frost cuts them short.

Tender young plants require protection from frost. Cover them at night with protective devices. If you don't set out your plants early, the midsummer bounty of vine-ripe vegetables is difficult to achieve. Some crops blossom and set fruit during midsummer heat: the melon and squash group and a few other heat lovers such as peppers, eggplant, okra and sweet potatoes. They are usually planted in midspring.

In the high zone, because of late frosts, a late spring planting date is necessary. Again, put plants out as soon as possible and give them frost protection to stretch the growing season.

Cultural Requirements & Care

The basics for a successful vegetable garden in hot arid regions are the same as for any other area. Soil preparation, a site with plenty of sunlight, and regular care and irrigation are necessary. The following chapter on planting and plant care (chapter 3) can help you with some of the fundamentals. You can plant vegetables in large pots, barrels, a stack of old tires or raised beds. Raised beds are perhaps the easiest way to have a vegetable garden. Masonry walls, boards or railroad ties fastened together and filled with a good soil mix can get you started quickly. Before adding the planter mix, put heavy black plastic around the inside edges of a board or railroad tie planter to keep water from leaking out. Sides to 2 feet (0.6m) high can give you an edge to sit on while you do your gardening. Beds no wider than 4 feet (1.2m) allow you to reach in comfortably from each side. While you are at it, why not add a few herbs to your garden? For more information, read George Brookbank's *Desert Gardening: Fruits & Vegetables* (Fisher Books).

Container Gardens

One way to extend your garden, especially for annuals and other color plants, is by using

When Containers Dry Out

Beware: If a container has been allowed to dry out and you water it, the water may go down the sides, between the edge of the soil (where it has pulled away from the container) and the container itself, draining out the bottom. Don't think the plant is saturated. It is not. Water it several times and test the soil with a sensor or your finger to be sure it is thoroughly wet. This may occur more frequently in small ceramic containers, which are more likely to dry out quickly.

pots and other containers. Containers come in many sizes and materials. Plastic pots have become popular because they are lighter to pick up and move around. There are thick-walled and thin-walled containers. Avoid thin-walled plastic containers, especially if they will be in the sun. Plastic containers with thin walls placed in the sun create a very hot and damaging root environment and will eventually break.

Pots made of fired clay are old standbys. Italian and other high-fired pots are harder and less porous, so they last longer than low-fired containers. Low-fired pots, like many of the containers from Mexico, last only a few years and may start peeling and flaking even in the first year of use.

There are glazed and decorated containers, many of a high-fired nature, that will last a long time. But don't be fooled. Some glazed pots have cracks in the glaze that will allow the underlying clay to absorb water and start to pop off the glaze and eventually crumble.

To deal with pots that will crumble, always waterproof at least the inside with a clear sealer or plastic roofing cement. Then you can put a plastic bag into the pot and put the planting mix into that. Be sure to make a hole for drainage in the bottom and cut the extra plastic off just above soil level, leaving enough to prevent water from seeping over

A small Bermudagrass lawn

the sides and into the pot. Another possibility is to not plant in low-fired containers at all, but use them either as pot sculpture or as holders for plants within other containers.

Concrete, concrete/fiberglass and some thick-walled plastic commercial containers come in large sizes and should last a long time. The larger containers have other advantages. They become an architectural statement, keep roots cooler because of their size, and can have mixed bouquets blooming in them or surrounding a taller, permanent anchor plant. Saucers compatible with container size can help keep water drainage from staining decks. Fill the saucer with gravel or Styrofoam peanuts or set the pot on three bricks set in the saucer. This gives the plant some humidity and allows air to dry any waste water quickly.

Some self-watering containers come with a built-in well and wicking system that draws water into the soil from the well in the base. These are less likely to stain decks from

draining water, but plants may become waterlogged or salt-burned in time.

All sorts of plants make interesting pot plants, from cacti to ground covers that spill. Cacti prefer porous well-draining soil mix. Some plants, such as geraniums, prefer a heavier clay soil that doesn't dry out as fast. You can mix dirt and compost or dirt with the potting soil to get the mix you want. When planting the new plant, make the rootball the same height as the potting soil—no higher. Then, as the potting mix settles around the rootball, you can add more potting mix or mulch to bring the level up to rootball level.

If you want a deck garden or a grouping in a special area, place the containers in groupings you find attractive. Then buy the plants. Try to match a plant's cultural needs to the site in which you want it to grow. Remember that a few plants mixed with objects of interest can make an attractive arrangement.

Brick, gravel or styrofoam peanuts in saucer

— Cart

Containers on a wheel dolly allow you to move plants from place to place as the weather and seasons change. Or, as plants become more or less attractive, you can show them off or move them to a less prominent spot. The dolly also allows air to circulate under the container, drying out waste water.

Invasive Grasses

One area of concern in planting a new grass not native to your area will be whether it will escape and become a pest in other yards or in areas of native plants. This has happened with fountain grass (*Pennisetum setaceum*) to the detriment of both gardens and ecologically sensitive areas. Such invaders will eventually change the local ecology because as non-native plants introduced without their native pests and diseases to keep them in check, they can gradually take over in an area where they are adapted. Ask your county cooperative extension service or an experienced nursery person.

Caring for Container Plants

In caring for your plants, be sure you don't let containers dry out completely. Use an inexpensive moisture probe to test the soil moisture or stick your finger in the soil about an inch. If the soil feels just a little damp and the surface is dry, it is time to irrigate. Sometimes in summer heat you will need to do this twice a day. You can do the watering, or use an emitter system on a dedicated valve. Adjustable spray emitters, sometimes called *shrubblers*, can be used for pots. They can be set in place with little plastic stakes. Set the clock to how many times a day you wish to water and for how long. As the seasons change, change the clock.

While small adjustable sprays on an irrigation system are helpful, there is nothing like your personal attention and hand watering, which can also include feeding the plant liquid fertilizer. Personal attention to container plants will catch anything amiss quickly, including pests, diseases or nutrient deficiencies.

Lawns

There is nothing quite as green or inviting in hot, dry climates as an expanse of lawn, however small. At first thought, it may seem that having a lawn in such an environment is difficult. But it isn't a question of whether a lawn will succeed; it's how much money, time, water and effort you are willing to spend. Lawns are actually very successful in arid regions, if you plant the right kind of grass. All things considered, lawn is still the best ground cover for holding down large areas of dirt. It is also excellent for reducing or preventing glare from reflecting off pavement into windows. A lawn will soften the landscape. In addition, grass is nice for

children and dogs to play on. Grass actually does not use as much water as an overwatered Xeriscape. Depending on which grass you plant and how you care for it, you can use comparatively little water.

Selecting the Right Grass

There are two kinds of grasses: warm season and cool season. Summer heat is the limiting factor in growing a lawn in hot dry regions. Many well-known temperate-zone or cool-season grasses, such as ryegrass, bluegrass and bentgrass, will thrive in arid regions in winter but are unable to survive a long hot summer in the sun. Warm-season grasses such as Bermudagrass, St. Augustinegrass and occasionally Zoysiagrass are the best choices.

In arid climates, the hybrid Bermudas put in as ready-made lawns (called sod) are the most popular. The softer, finer-textured hybrid Bermudas—the 'Tif' series ('Tif-dwarf,' 'Tifgreen,' 'Tifway,' 'Tiflawn'), 'Santa Ana,' 'Easyturf' and 'Midiron'—can produce a lawn equal to the best bentgrass lawns. They require more water and fertilizer and more frequent mowing compared to common Bermuda, but they have advantages. They seldom go to seed, and their fine texture is more pleasing to the eye and the touch than common Bermudagrass. Before selecting which hybrid to grow, talk to the grower to see which might be the best one for you.

Bermudagrass (*Cynodon dactylon*) is by far the most common lawn grass for these areas. Seeded Bermudagrass was the original warm-season grass grown before the hybrid Bermudas were developed. It is very tolerant of alkalinity, hard water, and hard rocky or caliche soils. It is relatively free of diseases and insect pests except pearl scale and Bermuda mite. If you give it regular water, fertilizer, proper care and mowing, you can achieve a first-class turf, comparable to lawns anywhere. Bermudagrass can be very invasive, however, so consider the planting site accordingly. Once established, it is difficult to get rid of. Bermudagrass does not grow in deep shade. If not mowed it develops seed heads that can cause allergies. Seedheads spread it around the yard and around the neighborhood. Because of its invasiveness and its allergens, some housing developments and even communities ban its use. That is not a problem with the hybrids. However, for durability, heavy use and survival in neglected situations, Bermudagrass is hard to beat.

St. Augustine grass (*Stenotaphrum secundatum*) makes a very thick, bright green lawn in hot, wet climates, such as along the Gulf Coast of the United States. It does reasonably well if irrigated in hot and dry areas.

Vigorous and rather coarse-bladed, it spreads rapidly and is adapted to areas where there is both sun and shade. A newer selection called 'Palmeto' is more tolerant of sun and can be used most successfully in areas spotted with sun and shade. St. Augustine needs more water than Bermudagrass to keep it looking nice. Problems sometimes occur with caliche subsoil that may cause it to become yellowish and chlorotic, requiring an application of iron chelates. Cold weather brings on dormancy. The turf turns brown when temperatures go below freezing. Overseeding with winter grass, a common practice with Bermudagrass, is not recommended for St. Augustine lawns.

Zoysiagrass (*Zoysia tenuifolia*) is fine-textured like hybrid Bermudagrass, slow to develop, and can form a series of small mounds that can be attractive in a small lawn meant for viewing. Although it tolerates traffic once established, the mounds make walking difficult. While tolerant of shade, like St. Augustine, it is subject to chlorosis due to caliche and calcareous soils. It also has more insect and disease problems than Bermuda types or St. Augustine. Zoysia goes dormant early in cold weather and seems to stay brown for a longer period than either Bermuda or St. Augustine. Overseeding is not recommended. If you want a green lawn in winter, applying a lawn dye over the surface is the best solution (see page 26).

Buffalograss (*Buchloe dactyloides*) **and Blue grama** (*Bouteloua gracilis*) have recently come into use and are often planted together in higher and cooler areas. Buffalograss grows to 4 to 6 inches (10.2 to 15.2cm) high and spreads along the surface of the soil by rooting runners. It can stabilize and bind soil and makes a durable drought- and cold-tolerant lawn that withstands traffic and has few if any pests. A warm-season grass, it is dormant during the cool season and may go dormant during extremely hot, dry summers. It bounces back with water or rain. When unmowed, it looks like a shag rug. Mow a few times over summer for a more groomed appearance.

Blue grama is a bunch grass native to the high plains. A warm-season grass, it can be the most drought-tolerant lawn

Dichondra grows amid the stepping stones in this sheltered, "secret" garden.

mentioned here. It grows 12 to 18 inches (30.5 to 45.7cm) high with thin blades, making a fine-textured sod. Blue grama is easy to grow from seed and is cold hardy, disease free, pest free, tolerant of poor soils and adaptable. It can be left unmowed for a meadow effect or cut once a month or so to make a lawn. It makes a good companion for Buffalograss because it can be established quickly and because as a bunch grass, it does not compete with Buffalograss.

Wild grasses. Fescue grasses can be kept green throughout the year with special care. Sheep fescue (*Festuca ovina*) grows to 12 inches (30.5cm) high and can be mowed. Red fescue (*Festuca rubra*) can take shade, grows to 12 inches (30.5cm) high, needs fertilizer and can be mowed. It needs moderate to ample irrigation to succeed.

Other previously wild grasses more recently tried as lawns are streambank wheatgrass (*Agropyron riparium*) and western wheatgrass (*Agropyron smithii*). All of these grasses can give a meadow appearance and are attractive with a few wildflowers thrown in the mix. They are currently available only as seed. These

grasses are important to mention because of efficient water use, minimum care and a minimum need for fertilizer, which is often a polluting source in runoff water. Seek information in your area.

Planting a New Lawn

For good results, prepare the seedbed before installing a lawn. Rototill the soil to a depth of 6 inches (15.2cm) minimum. Remove rocks over 1/2 inch (1.3cm) in diameter. Add

3 inches (7.6cm) of mulch and rototill it in. A mulch mixed with the soil can be sand, nitrogen-reinforced forest mulch, well-composted manure, vermiculite, perlite, or a diatomaceous material. Use alone or in combination to break up and aerate the soil and help with drainage. Rake and level the seedbed. If you plan to start your lawn from seed, put on an organic top dressing and moisten the seedbed well. Well-rotted manure has served well in this capacity over

Establishing a Winter Lawn: Step by Step

1. Scalp warm-season grass to 1/2 inch (1.3cm). Dethatch if necessary.
2. Sow seed.
3. Top-dress with sand, manure or forest mulch to 1/4 inch (0.6cm).
4. Keep damp for seven days, sprinkling three times a day, then once a day until after second mowing. Then water as needed depending on the weather, from every two days to once a week.
5. Fertilize with 16-20-0 about two weeks after planting, then regularly with 1 pound of nitrogen to every 1,000 square feet (305 square meters) at four- to six-week intervals. Use a blend of 21-7-14.
6. Mow at 1-1/2 inches (3.8cm) after two weeks, then down to 1 inch (2.5cm).

the years. It significantly increases the moisture-holding ability of the seedbed. Once germination begins, constant moisture is necessary, or the seedlings will quickly die. This may mean watering lightly four or five times a day until the grass is up. To plant, mix the seed with sand and scatter it with an inexpensive seed spreader. Birds consider the seed and seedlings a feast, so you may have to reseed more than once before you get a good stand of grass.

Other ways of starting a lawn besides seeding include sodding, plugging, sprigging or stolonizing. These are considered *vegetative* means of propagating a lawn. Vegetative methods are best done in the early warm part of the year: May, June and July.

Sodding produces an instant lawn and is the easiest and least time-consuming way to go. You lay down rolls of mature turf in strips like a carpet. Although more costly than a lawn from seed, the effect is immediate.

Plugging is done by cutting small chunks or plugs of sod and planting them in a prepared seedbed. Spacing depends on how close you can afford to plug and how soon you want a complete cover. For example, 'Tifgreen' hybrid Bermuda placed at 8-inch (20.3-cm) intervals should cover in three to five months. Daily watering is necessary until new growth becomes established.

Stolonizing is the most often recommended method of vegetative propagation. You spread shredded turf segments over a moist, prepared lawn bed and cover lightly with soil or organic mulch. This covering must be kept constantly moist until the individual segments have put down roots and have established themselves. Short of sodding, stolonizing is the fastest and smoothest way of establishing a hybrid Bermuda turf.

Keep in mind that no matter what method you use, it is very important that you thoroughly prepare and moisten the soil before you plant and keep it moist until the grass has well sprouted. Even moisture is one of the most important things you can do to ensure your lawn's success. (Soils and soil amendments are discussed in detail in chapter 3.)

Individual Planting Requirements

Bermudagrass. The usual way to start a seeded Bermudagrass lawn in the low and middle zones is to sow in the warmest part of the year—April through August. This allows the new grass to grow fast and establish itself before winter stops growth. If you live at a higher elevation, plant in late spring. Hybrid Bermudagrass varieties produce no viable seed, so they can only be started by one of the vegetative methods described above.

St. Augustine is sometimes sodded (if sod is available) but is more often plugged or stolonized.

Zoysia can be established by planting stolons or plugs, but not by seed. Perhaps one of its biggest drawbacks is that it is so terribly slow to cover and takes a season or more before creating a lawn.

Buffalograss is not competitive with bermudagrass or weeds and is slow to cover because the seed germinates in stages over time. Sow in summer, 4 to 8 pounds of pure live seed per acre. It can also be planted in plugs or as a sod, in some areas.

Blue grama. Sow seeds in summer, 2 to 3 pounds of pure live seed per acre.

Wild grasses (such as fescue and wheatgrass): Wheatgrass is best sown about 2 pounds per 1,000 square feet. Fescue can be sown or planted from small divisions of overgrown clumps.

The Dormant Lawn

Warm-season grasses such as Bermudagrass hybrids go dormant and turn a straw color in winter. Some people prefer an all-year green lawn so they overseed with cool-season winter grasses. Overseeding means essentially planting another quick-growing grass over existing dormant turf. The overseeded grass, adapted to cooler winter temperatures, will stay green and thrive through the dormant period of the warm-season grass. It then dies or is crowded out as hot weather comes on in spring and the warm-season lawn really begins to grow. Overseeding is generally done in the fall (usually around October 15) when there is still enough mild growing weather ahead, allowing the winter lawn to establish. A hybrid Bermuda planted as sod in the cool of the year will come from the grower green with overplanted ryegrass.

Winter Grasses

Perennial ryegrass (*Lolium parvifolium*) has become the most common grass for overseeding to make a winter lawn. Rather fine textured and a deep rich green, it grows very fast. However, because most winter grasses grow in clumps, the rate of seeding has to be fairly heavy to get an immediate effect. As with other grasses, you may need to reseed because birds eat the seed. Perennial ryegrass has just about replaced annual ryegrass because it needs less mowing and less water. It may also remain in partly shady areas where Bermudagrass languishes. Occasional light applications of nitrogen fertilizer will keep your lawn looking attractive. Follow the directions on the package. Damping off fungus is sometimes a problem. Stop watering in April, before Bermuda starts. 'Manhattan,' 'Pennfine' and 'Denny' are some recommended selections of *L. parvifolium*.

Low-Water Lawns

In arid regions where water is at a premium, a dormant Bermudagrass lawn can be a blessing in disguise. It covers and protects the ground with a vegetative carpet, without requiring nearly as much water as would a year-round green lawn. In areas where dust and erosion control are problems, a Bermudagrass lawn can be established, then gradually allowed to dry out until it goes into a drought-induced dormancy. Afterward, supply just enough moisture periodically to stimulate new growth and keep the turf intact. Bermuda retreats into clumps if kept dry too long.

This kind of lawn serves as a good walk-on ground cover. With irrigation, it becomes a vigorous green lawn in a short time. Alternating watering and drying Bermuda turf works very well for playgrounds, parks and other large areas where water is costly or in short supply. In regions where summer rains occur, there is the welcome bonus of having these lawns suddenly turn green for a period after a good storm. In higher elevations, Buffalograss does well.

Another way to have a low-water lawn is to have lawn in winter only, allowing the area to lie fallow in the summer. This can be done each fall by seeding cool-season annual or perennial grasses—those used to overseed dormant warm-season grasses. A winter lawn makes a lot of sense in many situations: It takes much less water to achieve a green effect in cool periods than it would to keep a lawn green all summer. And, even though the turf is dead during summer, dust and erosion are reduced.

Lawn Tints or Dyes

While not seen as often these days, a dormant lawn can be painted green for the winter. Dying or spraying dormant lawns with a special green paint may sound like a strange activity, but it was common in the past. It is one of the alternatives if you can't stand the tan dormant color of your warm-season lawn. Over the years, firms doing the spraying have developed some fairly natural-looking colors, but most everyone who lives in Bermuda country has seen dubious "dye jobs" on occasion. Quality dyes applied correctly by a reputable company will not wash or rub off. There is also an advantage compared to overseeding: Overseeded winter grass often delays the spring recovery of the Bermuda.

Lawn Substitutes

Besides the newly introduced wild grasses mentioned under "Planting a New Lawn," it is possible to use some wide-spreading ground covers, such as *Myoporum* species, *Dalea greggii*, or colorful *Lantana montevidensis*. A one-gallon plant can spread up to 5 feet (1.5m) or more over hot sunny surfaces, giving a cooling effect. (See also the list of ground covers on page 200.)

Dichondra *(Dichondra micrantha)*, also known as "pony foot," is perhaps the most attractive if the most finicky of the nongrass, walk-on ground covers occasionally used in arid landscapes. This creeping plant has small, round, bright green leaves, giving it a fresh, cool appearance. It will not withstand excessive foot traffic or scorching sun if allowed to dry out, so use it in small areas or between stepping stones in partly shaded areas, or in places where mowing is difficult. Dichondra grows well in both sun and partial shade. It needs a rich well-prepared soil and ample moisture. Sow seed in the spring and fall, or plant from plugs or sod, if available.

Dichondra is sometimes attacked by flea beetles. This pest can completely wipe out an entire lawn. Cutworms may also appear in spring. Their voracious appetites can wipe out a lawn if it is not sprayed. Rabbits love the tender leaves and can be a problem all year. Contact your county cooperative extension service for controls.

Lippia *(Phyla nodiflora)* is excellent on banks, where it holds soil with its deep-rooted runners. Lippia will withstand more foot traffic than Dichondra but it has one drawback: It produces an abundance of cloverlike blossoms that attract bees. Avoid it if you like to run barefoot across the lawn. Lippia's small leaves are bluish green or almost grayish, especially if grown in full sun. It is quite drought tolerant after it is established, but if you want a first-class cover, supply with regular irrigation. Lippia is

Ryegrass is planted over dormant Bermudagrass as a winter lawn.

available in flats at nurseries. Establish by setting out small plugs 12 to 18 inches (30.5 to 45.7cm) on center in a prepared bed. Nematodes are sometimes a problem.

White Dutch clover *(Trifolium repens)* is often planted to fill in a turf during the dormant season, or as a temporary cover until a permanent lawn can mature. Clover is a fairly vigorous, spreading plant that rarely gets over 4 or 5 inches (10.2 to 12.7cm) tall in arid regions. It can achieve a solid cover when planted as a lawn or bank cover. Clover also produces white blossoms that attract bees. It is tough and especially vigorous during the winter months, when some of the other walk-on ground covers are dormant. Clover is often combined with dichondra. Although the textures are different, a mix of the two does make a fairly dependable year-round green cover. Mowing helps improve growth and creates a tighter lawn. Sow seed in fall and water regularly to keep healthy.

There are also seed mixes containing several of the above species. The effect is not the smooth look of a uniform lawn. However, it is practical in that each plant type grows well in the environment of its choice.

Lawn Care

A regular fertilization program is necessary to keep lawns growing well. Because desert lawns require so much water, nutrients are quickly leached from the soil. Rates for different grasses vary. Applications of a nitrogen fertilizer every six weeks during the growing season are recommended for hybrid Bermudagrass varieties.

If your lawn shows signs of chlorosis (yellow color), it probably has a caliche (calcium carbonate) underbase or the soil is too alkaline. Add iron in the form of iron

chelates. In fact, one way to cut down on mowing yet keep a very green lawn is to feed it frequently with the iron chelates and cut down on the ammonium sulfate.

When it comes to lawn irrigation, keep one thing in mind: Never allow the soil to dry out completely if you want a healthy-looking turf. Although Bermudagrass will withstand a certain amount of drought, it will look unattractive if kept too dry. If you have deep well-prepared soil that retains water, you can space irrigations during hot weather three to four days apart to maintain an attractive appearance. Fast-draining sandy soils require more frequent lawn irrigation. Winds and high temperatures greatly increase water needs. The best advice is to get to know your lawn and water when it needs it. Sign of water stress are a bluish cast or footprints that remain indented after you walk across the lawn.

Watering during cool weather requires a different set of guidelines. An actively growing winter lawn requires deep watering once or twice a week, depending on the weather and rainfall. Again, your own experiences and observations will determine the proper irrigation schedule.

Dormant lawns also need some irrigation. It is a common belief that they do not need water, but roots continue to develop even though surface growth has stopped. Many fine Bermuda lawns have been damaged when allowed to get bone dry. Soak dormant lawns at least once a month during the winter if no significant rainfall occurs.

These healthy plants show the importance of basic plant care. Take care of your plants and they will take care of you.

No matter what kind of climate you live in, hot, arid or otherwise, the key to success with plants depends on understanding their needs for growth. Plants have extremely varied cultural requirements, but the basics remain the same: They need a suitable soil that drains well, appropriate amounts of sunshine, a uniform supply of moisture and nutrients, and protection from the elements. It is important to give plants what they need to maintain health and growth. Knowing the basics of planting and plant care will take you a long way toward a successful landscape.

After deciding on your landscape design and layout, it is time to select your plants and draw them on the plan. First you need to know a few things about the planting environment your plants will be in. This will help you narrow down your choices and pick the right plants for the job.

Soil: Alkaline versus Acidic

The key to successful planting is understanding the alkaline soils of arid lands and how they differ from the more acidic soils of temperate regions. Most arid-adapted plants are used to alkaline (high pH) soils with little or no humus in them. Plants not adapted to arid soils are used to acidic soils (low pH) that contain humus. To determine the nature of your soil, use a pH test: A pH of 7 is neutral. A pH of 7.5 and above is alkaline. A pH of 6.5 and below is acidic. Kits are available to test soil pH. Or take a sample to a soil lab to find out what you need to do.

Plants Adapted to Alkaline Soils

There are three basic types of alkalinity in arid soils: saline, sodic and calcareous. These conditions can exist separately or in combination. All types can cause nutrient deficiencies in plants because they prevent such minerals as iron, zinc and manganese from dissolving so that plants can absorb them. This results in unhealthy plants with reduced growth and vigor. The visible symptom of iron deficiency is new leaves that look yellow with green veins. The visible symptom of nitrogen deficiency is the yellowing of old leaves.

Saline soils contain soluble salts such as sodium chloride—common table salt. Soluble salts may be present naturally in the soil, but they can also come from irrigation

This band of caliche (or hardpan) is impervious to water. It is necessary to break through this layer when digging a plant pit so that the pit can drain.

water or sea spray. You can often see salts as a white crust on the soil surface, left by evaporated water. Similar crusts may also form in the bottom of a plant pit, which can crowd or burn roots. Most salts are easily leached below root depth by occasional deep soakings.

Sodic soils are sometimes referred to as **alkali, black alkali** or **slick-spot** soils. They are caused by having too much sodium in the soil in relation to the amounts of calcium and magnesium. Sodic soils usually have a pH higher than 8.5. When dampened, they are often dark and become slick and slimy on the surface. Their structure as a soil

has broken down. They are impervious to water, have no air spaces and do not allow roots to grow. Sometimes sodic soils occur in combination with soluble salts, called sodic-saline soils. Few plants can grow under either condition. Adding large quantities of gypsum to the soil can help, but if you think you have one of these soils, consult an expert for treatment.

Calcareous soils usually contain calcium carbonate, which is only slightly soluble in water. This material is most troublesome when it forms an impervious layer known as *caliche* or *hardpan*. This layer can be 6 feet (1.8m) thick or even thicker. It is formed when rain or surface water continually deposits calcium at a certain soil depth, usually 6 to 20 inches (15.2 to 50.8cm) over long periods of time. The water either evaporates or is absorbed by plants, leaving the calcium to accumulate in a cementlike layer.

Plow pan is similar in effect to caliche. It is found in old orchards or areas farmed for commercial crops, where soil has been tilled for a period of time to a certain depth. A layer of salts may accumulate at the surface of the unbroken subsoil, or the subsoil may become packed. Plant roots sometimes find it difficult to break through. In both cases, water will not soak into the subsoil and instead forms standing pools. Before planting, break up and soak the subsoil to wash away salts.

If you have questions about soil quality, check with your local cooperative extension agent, a qualified nursery professional or, better yet, have your soil tested by a private soil lab. A soil-analysis test is relatively inexpensive.

Planting Arid-Adapted Plants

The latest recommendation for planting arid-adapted plants is to dig a hole that is three to five times the width of the root ball and the same depth as the root ball. (If you are planting a hedge with a number of plants in a row, you can make a long ditch, but the width should follow the rule of three times the width of the root ball.) Then use the soil you took out as backfill, after you remove large rocks and other pieces of debris over 1/2 inch (1.3cm) in diameter.

Do not add amendments to backfill for arid-adapted plants. This idea is new and uncomfortable for many who have added soil amendments for years, but landscape professionals agree with research scientists that arid-adapted plants seem to do better and grow faster if they are planted without amendments. This is, in fact, a practice widely used for native plants in many other regions.

One reason for the change is that plant roots find it difficult to grow from the amended soil into the surrounding soil. This "wall" is referred to as the *soil interface* between the surrounding soil and the loosened improved soil in the pit. The goal is to get the roots into the native soil as early as possible. Arid-adapted plants may otherwise inhabit what is essentially a container underground and may never spread their roots into the surrounding soil.

Testing Soil Drainage

Most dense arid soils, whether they are gravelly, claylike, sandy or rocky, don't have much, if any, organic matter. Unless the soil is sandy or gravelly, it may not drain well. So when you dig the hole, test it by filling it with 3 or 4 inches (76.2 to 102mm) of water. If all water has not drained in three or four hours, you will need to provide a "chimney" in the bottom, to one side of where the root ball will be. Test again and go deeper to a more porous layer. If the drainage is still poor, consider planting elsewhere or putting in plants such as mesquite, palo verde, or other plants adapted to such conditions.

Creating a Water Basin

If you are not going to provide an irrigation system, you will need to provide a basin for deep irrigations. This can be done by building a dam or a planting basin around the plant or tree at a distance that will allow water to penetrate the soil to beyond the

---

Landscape Tip: Planting Distances

If you plan to make a grove of similar trees or a mass planting of a particular shrub or ground cover, take the estimated mature width of the plant and space the second plant that far from the first plant to have the plants touch each other at maturity. This is referred to as *on center* (oc), meaning from plant center to plant center. Space informally so that many mature plants will touch if you want a natural grove. Space plants wider apart if you don't want them to touch. This is referred to as *edge to edge*.

If you feel impatient because a shrub will be slow to cover, you can do one of two things.

1. You can intersperse a temporary color plant or ground cover that will die out, be shaded out or removed later on.

2. You can put plants closer together and plan to remove every other one by cutting them out when things become crowded. Do not dig out the plants to be removed as their roots will be intertwined with those of the plants to stay. If you dig out the plants, you will injure the ones you want to save.

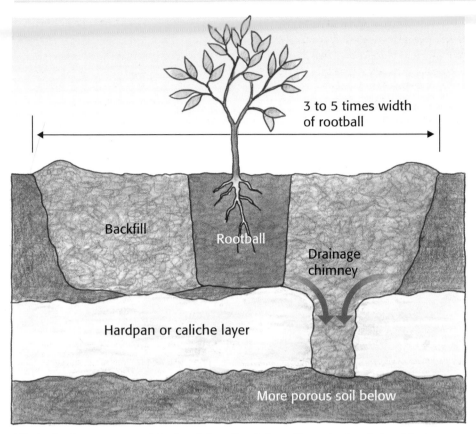

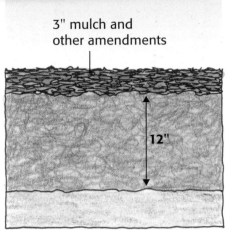

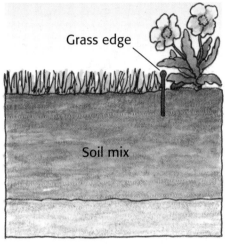

This drawing demonstrates a carefully planted plant with a drainage chimney dug through the caliche (or hardpan) layer.

For grass, flowers and ground covers, dig a bed 8 to 12 inches (20.3 to 30.5cm) deep and mix soil well with 3 inches (7.6cm) of mulch and other amendments.

edges of the plant canopy (the drip line). The perimeter of this catchment will need to be expanded as the plant grows to bring water out beyond the spread of the plant leaves. (See page 36 for more information on irrigation options.)

If you are grouping one-gallon or smaller plants together and are installing bubblers or no irrigation system at all, create a basin large enough for all of the plants. If the planting is to be wider than 5 or 6 feet (1.5 to 1.8m), create more than one basin to be sure the soil can be level enough to wet all the plants. Check the lay of the bed several times a year to be sure the soil is level and water is spreading out. Dirt has a way of moving around, and water may not get to the high spots.

Plants Adapted to Acidic Soils

Most plants from temperate regions are used to acidic soils with humus. To grow them, you must modify the alkaline soil conditions of arid lands to suit their needs. This includes mixing humus and soil acidifiers, such as soil sulfur, into existing soil, a technique called *soil improvement, amendment* or *modification.*

Soil Amendments

A *soil amendment* is any material added to the soil to improve soil texture or chemistry.

In nearly every instance, what people think is a "good soil" is high in organic matter. When you amend the soil with organic matter, you improve drainage, and the resulting spongy soil is able to retain moisture and nutrients longer in the root zone. Organic amendments include nitrogen-stabilized forest products, Canadian peat moss, grass clippings, well-rotted manure and homemade compost. Inorganic amendments include perlite, sand and possibly gypsum (no redwood with its damaging oils). The coarseness of these amendments is an advantage. They take longer to decompose and they "fluff up," or aerate, the soil.

Unless the organic products you choose are nitrogen stabilized, you will need to add nitrogen to your soil mix because it aids soil organisms in breaking down the organic matter. Use ammonium phosphate or other slow-release nitrogen fertilizer that will not burn roots. Follow the manufacturer's directions. Manures, depended on heavily in the past, are not used as often today as amendments in arid areas because of their

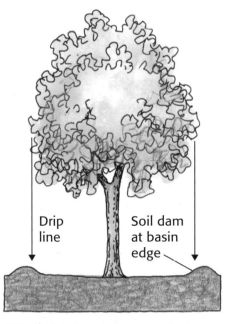

Without an irrigation system, you can water effectively by ringing a tree or shrub with a soil dam under the drip line of the canopy or beyond. Then fill the basin to 2 to 3 inches (5.1 to 7.6cm) with water periodically, depending on the tree's watering needs.

Planting from Containers: Step by Step

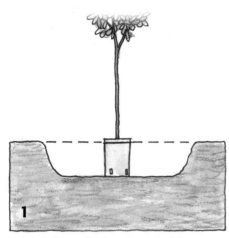

1

Dig hole three to five times the width of the root ball and only as deep as the root ball. When the plant sits in the pit, the dirt line of the plant should be a little higher than the top edge of the hole. Remove rocks larger than 1/2 inch (1.3cm) and test for drainage (see page 30).

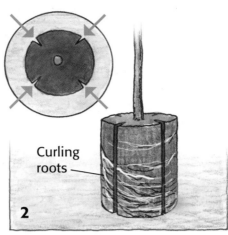

Curling roots

2

Carefully remove the plant from the container. If the roots crowd around the outside of the root ball, make four vertical cuts about ½ inch (1.3cm) deep through the outside roots and into the root ball from top to bottom.

3

Place the plant in the center of the plant pit and fill the hole with the same soil you removed from the hole (with rocks removed). Never allow the soil to cover the plant deeper than it was in the container. Also be careful to keep the graft union above the soil if you have a grafted plant.

4

Carefully press the soil around the roots to remove air pockets. Wetting the soil as you add backfill helps to pack it down.

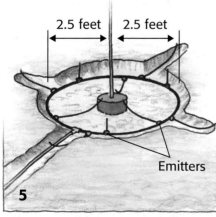

2.5 feet | 2.5 feet

Emitters

5

Set the irrigation around the plant. Shown here: a drip irrigation system with single port emitters (see page 36 for more information on irrigation systems).

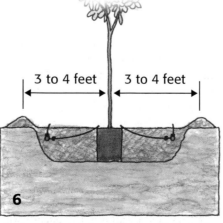

3 to 4 feet | 3 to 4 feet

6

Continue to fill the hole until the ground is level with the edge of the hole. Make a temporary well by mounding earth around the tree at 3 to 4 feet (0.9 to 1.2m) from the trunk. Soak the entire root zone area.

---

high salt content: Arid-land soils are often too salty to begin with. Composted manures are sometimes used as a top dressing on a new lawn. If you do use manure, be certain it is well composted. Leach away salts with several soakings before incorporating manure into the soil.

Planting Non-Arid-Adapted Plants

To make a friendly environment for acid-loving, tender shrubs, vines and other shallow-rooted plants of one- to five-gallon size, follow the planting instructions for alkaline soils (page 30), digging a hole three to five times the size of the root ball, but amend the existing soil. Mix well before backfilling 1/3 of the existing soil, 1/3 sandy loam, and 1/3 of the following combined: compost (or nitrogen-stabilized forest mulch), soil sulfur and ammonium phosphate (follow package instructions). Some use manure as part or all of the compost mix. If the manure was not well composted, you can leach out manure salts by heavily watering the plant bed for ten to fourteen days before planting.

Dig the mix into the bottom and sides of the hole, making rough edges (no straight slick ones) to allow water and roots, to penetrate from the prepared soil into the existing soil as the plant grows. Otherwise the soil interface between improved soil and existing soil may prove impenetrable for growing roots. Always settle the soil with water as you fill the plant pit. This prevents large air pockets, which are bad for roots and will also allow more settling than you want as the air pockets deflate. Compacting the soil at the base of the hole will keep a plant from sinking after it is planted. Because organic material in arid climates breaks down more rapidly and disappears over time, you can keep adding it by applying compost, forest products or composted manure as a top dressing or mulch.

If you want to plant one-gallon plants, ground covers or other small shallow-rooted plants in a common area, consider digging up and enriching the top 8 to 12 inches (20.3 to 30.5cm) in the entire area they are to cover. It will be easier for the plants to spread if their whole bed is dug up and enriched.

Bare-Root Planting

Deciduous plants, such as shade trees, roses, fruit trees and shrubs, can be planted bare root during their dormant season in the cool of the year. While the practice has waned somewhat in recent years, bare-root plants are less expensive than plants in containers.

Buy fresh stock at the beginning of the bare-root season in your area. Be sure roots are not dried out, and check to see there are no whitish spring roots showing. Then check the buds at the tops of the branches to be sure they have not been broken. Cut off cleanly any torn or deformed roots.

To plant, make a damp mound of soil mix in the center of the hole. Set the plant on the mound, spreading the roots. Make sure the bud union (or graft), the place on grafted plants where the top joins the roots, is above ground level. Allow at least 2 to 4 inches (5.1 to 10.2cm) for settling. Fill hole to this level, settling the soil by pressing down around roots and watering as you go. Adjust the soil as needed. For starters, add an earth berm for a watering basin, even if you are putting in an irrigation system, and soak frequently until you see new growth appearing, which indicates the plant is taking hold. Then follow a regular watering schedule for the plant as given in the plant descriptions.

After planting, many gardeners selectively cut the tops of the plants by as much a 1/3 to reduce the water needs of the tops as they leaf out to balance the now smaller root system. This is done because the grower trimmed the roots, so there are fewer of them to support the top.

Staking Trees

Some young trees need to be staked for support, especially if strong winds occur in your area. Place stakes at right angles to the strongest wind. For example, if the wind comes from the west, put one stake on the north side of the tree and one stake on the south side. You can also use stakes to encourage a shrubby plant or a plant with a weaving trunk to become more erect in form. Often you will want to use more than one stake. Lodge poles available at nurseries make good stakes for trees.

Tie loosely with a pliable material or flexible nonbinding tie such as cloth or a soft plastic. Cloth ties can eventually rot away, freeing the tree if you forget to do so. Tie the tree so it can move in the wind between the stakes and gain strength on its own. Loosen

Planting Bare Root: Step by Step

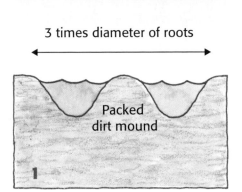

Dig a hole at least three times the diameter of the roots and test for drainage (see page 30). The hole should have a wet, packed-down mound in the center over which the roots will spread equally on all sides.

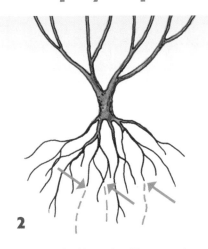

Purchase fresh, healthy stock and keep roots damp until planting. Cut off cleanly any torn or discolored roots.

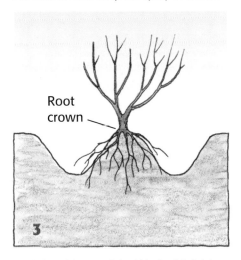

The hole and the mound should be the right height so that the root crown of the plant will be level with the sides of the hole.

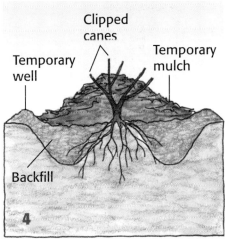

Cover the roots with the original dirt from the hole (with large rocks removed) or prepared soil if the plant requires it. Remove top growth by 1/3 to balance it with the reduced number of roots. Make a temporary earth mound around the edge of the hole, creating a well, and soak the root zone. Mound a temporary mulch around the plant cane to 1/3 their height to keep them from drying out.

ties as the tree grows to keep from girdling (choking) it. Remove supports as soon as the tree will remain erect on its own, often in less than six months. Always remove the stake it came with from the nursery.

If a tree has branches to the ground, leave all the lower branches on for the first year or two to help the tree make food for growth and to provide enzymes to help it develop a strong trunk. If lower branches are in the way, shorten them partway to encourage vertical growth. This practice will keep the tree from using energy to extend the side branches and will encourage vertical growth. Once the tree attains stature of 6 to

8 feet (1.8 to 2.4m) or more, you can trim off these temporary lower branches and select the *scaffold branches*, the major framework branches. These first branches at the base of the crown should be above head-height and form the foundation of the crown.

Pruning Trees

Do not severely prune trees. The old idea of cutting branches back to nubbins is over. Tree pruning must be done carefully. Less is better. After selecting and pruning to form the scaffold branches (basic framework branches) to give the tree its mature form,

Staking a Tree

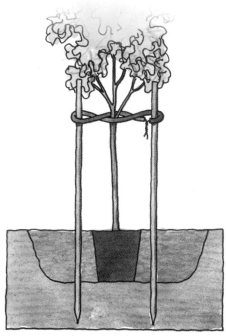

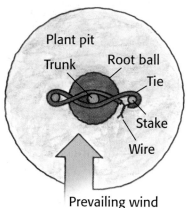

Plant pit

Trunk

Root ball

Tie

Stake

Wire

Prevailing wind

Drive two sturdy stakes on either side of the tree, outside the root ball, perpendicular to the prevailing wind. Stakes should be at least 12 inches (30.5cm) into the undisturbed earth beneath the plant pit. Thread a rubber hose or soft cloth with wire and wrap around the trunk and stakes in the form of a figure 8. Twist wire ends together to secure. Remove tie and stakes in six to twelve months.

prune only to thin out water sprouts, crossing branches, branches hanging too low for pedestrians or vehicles, dead branches, branches with mistletoe attached, or to carefully sculpt or thin the tree for some particular function. Major pruning, to thin the crown and remove large branches, should be done just before a tree breaks out of dormancy. Otherwise sunburn or dripping sap can occur. Light trimming and shaping can be done any time to shape or thin if needed.

Prune fruiting and flowering plants after spring bloom is over. Prune evergreens after the coldest weather is over and just before they break dormancy. Quicker recovery and wound healing seems to occur in desert trees and *Eucalyptus* trees if they are pruned in early May. To remove freeze-damaged wood, prune after new growth begins so that you can distinguish the surviving healthy branches from the damaged wood. Prune for safety any time branches grow toward windows, electric lines, stop signs, below head-height or over walks on an as-needed basis. Prune to repair wind damage and disease any time as well.

Use sharp tools that make clean smooth cuts, which will heal faster from the outside to the center. Sterilize instruments with a 10 percent bleach solution before you start and between cuts on a diseased tree and be sure to disinfect tools as you move from one plant to another.

Remember not to do heavy pruning during warm weather, especially summer when the tree can suffer sunburn on the bark after shade is removed. When pruning to form the scaffold (foundation) branches of a tree, select branches at a desired height that are in different positions around the trunk and that are pointing upward and outward at the 10 o'clock or 2 o'clock position. Always cut back to a crotch. (See diagram on page 35.)

Why Trees Fail

It is widely held that the number-one reason for the shortened life and decline of a tree is improper pruning. Every time a branch is removed from a plant the following occurs:

- Leaves that make food and energy are reduced.
- The tree must draw energy from other reserves to heal wounds.
- Growth-regulator chemicals that signal roots to grow shut off or slow growth.

Other reasons trees fail:

- Poor location
- Mechanical damage
- Soil compaction
- Improper irrigation

Trees weaken from any or all of the above and, as they weaken, they can become diseased or attract pests. It is a downward spiral.

Pruning and Thinning Shrubs

Carefully thin shrubs with handclippers to hold their natural form. Cut a long twig back to a crotch with a shorter outward-pointing twig inside the plant. This is called *selective pruning* and will encourage new growth and a fresher, fuller look to the shrub. The new growth will shield the bark from sunburn. Clipping and light trimming can be done any time to maintain a desired size or shape.

The dotted lines indicate what to clip to reduce the size of a shrub. Reach into the shrub and clip back to a fork with a shorter, preferably outward pointing twig. Be careful not to leave nubs—clip twig completely off.

Landscape Tip! Arborists

Trees need to be looked at every year or two by an arborist (tree expert). Trees that develop heavy crowns, especially if their roots are not developing as fast or as well as the crown, can be blown over in wind storms, common with mesquites and, to a lesser extent, palo verdes. Arborists will also note cross branches, weak branches, horizontal branches likely to break, suckers, and infestations of mistletoe as well as spot borers, other pests, and nutrient deficiencies that cause chlorosis (yellowing of the foliage) or poor leaf development.

Pruning a Tree: Step by Step

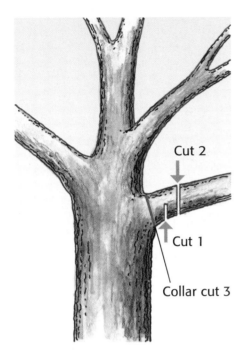

A scaffold of angled branches makes a good tree structure. Horizontal branches or sharp V-shaped crotches weaken the structure. When cutting a branch off next to the trunk, follow these steps:

1. Look for the collar (sort of a wrinkled place) next to the trunk at the base of the branch.
2. Make a cut upward an inch (2.5cm) or so up from the bottom of the branch, about 2 inches (5.1cm) from the trunk. This will keep bark from stripping off as the branch falls.
3. Then saw through the branch about 4 inches (10.2cm) from the trunk.
4. Make a third, finishing cut by sawing just outside this collar. This place will heal better and faster if you don't leave a long stub or cut too far into the trunk.

Major trimming on evergreens needs to be done just before spring growth begins. On deciduous shrubs, major pruning is best done in midwinter, during the dormant season.

Shearing plants gives an unnatural box or lollipop look, cuts leaves, reduces flowers and may expose plants to sunburn or expose unattractive leafless twigs. If for speed's sake you need to use hedge trimmers to cut a plant back, you can make some slant cuts into the foliage, giving an uneven appearance. The plant will grow out with a more natural look. Avoid shearing unless you want a formal hedge or topiary.

Watering Basics

"When" and "how much" irrigation to give depends on many variables: the needs of the particular kind of plant, its size and age, the soil composition, time of year, climate zone, sun exposure, and what water it may get from other sources. While we can't tell you exactly what to do in your individual situation, these watering guidelines will get you started.

1. Keep new plantings damp for ten to fourteen days (longer in warm weather) until they begin to grow, indicating that they are becoming established. Then gradually reduce the watering schedule to match the plant's particular needs.

2. Think of root depths. Tree roots spread widely, even beyond the outer edges of the foliage (drip line) and with roots to 3 feet (0.9m) deep. Think of shrubs as having roots at least as wide as the foliage spread and 2 feet (0.6m) deep. Lawns, ground covers and flowers are shallowly rooted, to 1 foot (0.3m) deep. The point of thorough irrigation is to soak the root zone.

3. Try to water plants just before they begin to show signs of stress. Look for slightly wilted foliage, a loss in luster, or color change that is darker, grayer or bluer than normal. Other signs are curling or falling leaves. If leaf edges turn dry or brown, or leaves yellow, this indicates a more advanced state of drought. Greenish yellow leaves can also indicate overwatered plants, but bright yellow leaves scattered throughout a rapidly growing plant in spring or summer are usually just old leaves about to drop.

4. Deep periodic irrigations for established trees and shrubs are usually best for plants in any region, but they are especially useful in arid lands because of the high percentage of soil salts. Long, slow soakings of the root zone, up to four hours or more, will wash salts from the root zone. Letting the soil get somewhat dry between irrigations allows air, necessary for plant life, to get to the roots.

5. Never allow soil to become bone-dry, except for well-established desert plants. Never leave plants in standing water that creates a swampy situation, denying oxygen to the roots.

How to Create a Natural Look Using Hedge Trimmers

1. Shear the shrub back as far as desired into a rounded shape.

2. Make angled cuts at intervals into the shrub.

3. Allow the shrub to grow out so it has a natural look.

6. You can test the soil with your finger or with an inexpensive moisture sensor from a hardware store or garden shop. Usually when the surface is dry to the touch, but some dampness is indicated below the soil surface, is a good time to irrigate. For larger plants, such as trees, you can drive a

Drip Irrigation System

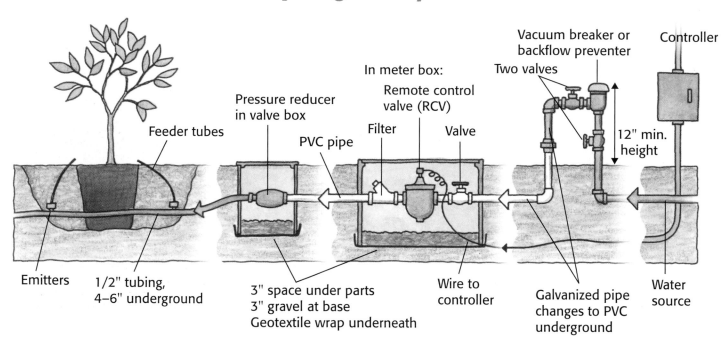

Vacuum breaker or backflow preventer

Controller

Two valves

In meter box:

Remote control valve (RCV)

Pressure reducer in valve box

Filter

Valve

Feeder tubes

PVC pipe

12" min. height

Emitters

1/2" tubing, 4–6" underground

3" space under parts
3" gravel at base
Geotextile wrap underneath

Wire to controller

Galvanized pipe changes to PVC underground

Water source

The construction of a drip system, going backward from the plant (left side of illustration), goes in this order: The feeder tubing that delivers water to the plant is attached to an emitter, which is plugged into a tube approximately 1/2 inch (1.3cm) in diameter. The tube is attached to a pressure reducer that takes the usual house water pressure of about 60 psi (pounds per square inch) and reduces it to between 20 and 30 psi. The pressure reducer used will depend

on the length of the line and the number of gph (gallons of water per hour) to be delivered by the emitters. Upstream from the pressure reducer is a filter, usually a simple device with a fine screen to filter out pieces of debris that might plug the system. Beyond the pressure reducer and the filter is the valve that turns the water on and off. Unless the system is operated by hand, the valve will be an RCV (remote control valve) with a wired electrical

connection to the timer that turns the valve on and off. You can set and reset the timer to run the system according to the season and the water needs of the plants. Between the water source and the valve will be the code-mandated vacuum breaker, or backflow preventer, to keep irrigation water from being sucked back into the potable water supply if the source system should go off.

metal stake (such as rebar) into the soil until it stops. This will show you how far down the damp pliable soil goes before the stake hits the dry hard stuff and stops.

Seasonal Watering Guidelines

Heavily soak the root zone of most plants in early spring, slightly later in higher and colder zones. It can be done just prior to the first feeding of the year. The deep irrigation leaches salts from root zones that may have collected in the soil during the previous year or over winter. Maintain steady soil dampness during spring to encourage growth, flowering and fruiting. Plants that are stressed do not perform as well.

In summer, especially if the weather is hot, sunny and dry, maintain a diligent watering schedule. This is the period of greatest stress on plants, because they are trying to put on spring and summer growth and to transpire enough water from their leaf surfaces to keep themselves cool. Stressed plants become weak, and weak plants are more subject to pests and disease and general failure. Stressed plants do not bloom well and will drop fruit. In areas of summer rain, do not depend on the rain entirely. It may not have penetrated deeply enough into the soil to replace irrigation.

Taper off water as autumn nears to harden growth so that it becomes less succulent, and woody enough to tolerate a

freeze. Ample water encourages succulent growth that can be damaged by cold, even in cold-hardy plants. Don't forget to water plants periodically in winter. Roots continue to grow, but at a slower rate. Unless you live in an area that gets winter rains, which may suffice, the lack of winter irrigation can damage plants and ultimately cause decline and death.

Irrigation Choices: Which System Is Right for You?

Hose watering: Hand watering with a hose that has various spray or sprinkler attachments is not very efficient. It is also time consuming and arbitrary. You have to remember to turn the water on and off, both easy to forget.

Bubblers, sprays, and lawn sprinklers engineered to fit the yard work well on timers. These systems put out a lot of water and are often wasteful, with water wetting a larger area than is needed or overshooting the area as runoff. One consideration is to

Native Plants Need Water, Too!

Natives and other drought-resistant plants are often neglected when they are first planted because of their reputation for toughness, but the plant location you choose does not necessarily give all the advantages plants in the wild receive. Treat native plants with the care you would give any nursery plant, and give them regular irrigation for at least the first year.

Three Ways to Install an Emitter

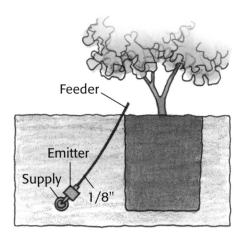

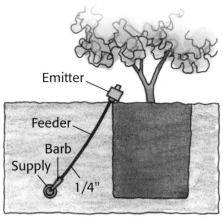

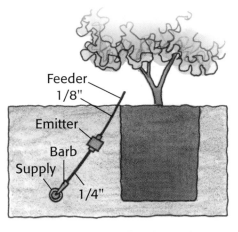

1. Emitters can be directly plugged into the supply (1/2-inch tubing) with feeder tubes (1/4 or 1/8 inch) running from each emitter to the surface, delivering water to each plant. This method prevents water loss if the tube is separated from the emitter.

2. Sometimes, where animals will not cut the small tubes, a barb is put into the supply tube with a feeder tube attached to it. The feeder tube runs to the surface where an emitter is attached.

3. A good, though more complicated, system is to put a barb into the supply line, attach 1/4-inch feeder tubing to it and attach an emitter at 3 to 4 inches (7.6 to 10.2cm) below the surface. Put a 1/8-inch feeder tubing at the other end of the emitter and take it up to the plant.

have lawn sprinkler heads on a triple-swing joint or a flexible tube to facilitate height adjustment.

Drip irrigation has become the preferred method of watering trees, shrubs and many other plants. These systems deliver water directly to the root zones of plants, where it is needed. Systems are easy to install and inexpensive. A well-designed system on a timer can be not only efficient and economical with water, but with proper maintenance can last for years. Systems do need periodic tuning, like your car, to continue to serve you faithfully. Such maintenance includes backwashing the filter, fixing leaks, replacing any stopped-up emitters, clearing root-strangled lines, checking for rodent damage and so forth.

A combined system of lawn sprinklers and drip irrigation works well with the sprinklers on one or more valves and the drip system on one or more valves.

Drip Irrigation Systems

Drip irrigation is a low-pressure system that gives a slow application of water to only the root zones of plants where it is needed. Emitters are designed to deliver a specific amount of water over an hour of time. This is expressed as gph (gallons of water per hour): 1 gph, 2 gph, 1/2 gph and so on. Flexible 1/2 inch tubing set 8 to 10 inches (20.3 to 25.4cm) under the soil surface is used to deliver water to the emitters.

Emitters. Emitters to look for are those with silicon diaphragms, which are self

flushing and pressure compensating. Such emitters will flush themselves of most sand or debris, which may have entered the system. They will also "compensate" by delivering only the amount of water they are designed to emit even if the system goes up or down hill or the line is very long. These emitters are also less likely to stop up or become encrusted with mineral deposits from hard water. While these emitters are more costly, they will help you avoid many headaches and will last for years.

Flag emitters are sometimes used where it is desirable to have the emitter at the surface and there is no danger of animals cutting the line to them. They are less expensive and they can be easily cleaned if they stop up from mineral formation. They are not pressure compensating, so you cannot count on having even water distribution, and plants at the line end may get little or no water.

The spot vortex emitters are probably the least expensive. These are tiny emitters that you can plug directly into tubing or put at the ends of microtubing. In water with a high pH, they usually work for only a year or two before calcium crusts stop them up.

How many emitters? Space emitters equally around the plant and on the uphill side if the plant is on a slope. As plants grow, they will need more emitters. Arid-land plants should be on a separate valve that is used only while the plants are establishing and then only during hot dry weather or during rainless winters. No irrigation for

cacti but a little hand-soaking now and then during hot dry weather.

Trees are a larger question. They need to expand their roots far beyond the original root ball as the crown spreads out. Because people seldom go back to add more emitters as a tree grows, put in the number of emitters the tree will eventually need at the time it is planted. Emitters should be placed 2-1/2 feet (0.8m) apart from the root ball edge to about 10 feet (3.1m) from the trunk, making a cross with the tree in the center. At a distance of 5 feet (1.5m) from the trunk, add a second line so that the most distant emitters make eight rays instead of four.

One way to take advantage of the water from the extra emitters not yet used by the tree is to put in a temporary water-wise ground cover that you hope can hang on until the tree grows and spreads out. Another idea is to put goof plugs into the ends of feeder tubes to stop water flow. (Remove them when tree spreads out.)

Other tips for using drip irrigation. Water basins are not required around plants with a drip system. There are fewer weeds with drip irrigation because there is not as much surface water. If a 2- or 3-inch (5.1- to 7.6-cm) layer of mulch, such as decomposed granite or forest mulch, is placed over the soil around the plants, it will not only help to prevent weeds, it will help to prevent the irrigation water from evaporating and will keep the soil surface cooler, avoiding plant roots cooking in the sizzling summer heat.

Some Thoughts on Irrigating Arid-Adapted Plants

Some arid-adapted plants imported from many regions of the world are opportunists where water is concerned. In their native habitats they may have temporarily come into leaf and bloom during a short rainy period before going dormant for the rest of the year. Or they may have had another adaptation, which kept them living from rain period to rain period. While these plants can survive and grow with a tight water budget, they become lush, verdant and often overgrown when given large amounts of water. Such treatment is tempting because of the lush look and generous bloom, but if you are trying to live on a water budget, you are defeating your purpose in having arid-adapted plants. A verdant garden of arid-adapted plants is greedy and can use as much or more water than a lawn. So be mindful of your garden and find the balance between the plants looking good and using a minimum quantity of water. An exception will be a long hot, dry spell when all plants need at least some water to maintain life and more water to look good.

If you have digging dogs or other animals likely to harm your system, consider using metal or rigid plastic piping and install either bubblers with glass jars or a commercial cover over them to prevent animals gnawing on the heads. Another possibility is to put plastic tubing with emitters attached in perforated pipe under the surface of the ground. Placing rocks and stakes around emitters and plants can discourage dogs as will placing fencing around a new sod lawn you may lay.

When purchasing equipment, consider going to an irrigation supply store where the professionals go. They will have all the parts you need and many will help you put your system together as well as offer advice. Commercial-grade drip equipment is sold in standard sizes and will always be available for replacement. The items at a hardware store may be sized differently from those at an irrigation supply store and may not always be available. Purchase everything from one source.

In designing a minimal drip irrigation system, you can balance water needs of plants on a single valve by varying the sizes and numbers of emitters. This is the usual system put into housing developments by the developers who are also likely to install a manual valve or put the system on a single-station clock. Better yet is to have more than one valve and a timer that can handle at least four valves: one for trees, one for shrubs and ground covers, one for containers and one for a small plot of grass or other use. More complicated plant palettes incorporating areas with sun and shade, high- and low-water-use plants will ideally have more valves with a clock to accommodate them—plus at least one extra valve station in case you want to add to your landscaping later.

Mulches

A mulch is any material used to cover the soil. Mulches can be organic or inorganic: Bark products, shredded bark, wood chips, hay, shredded newspaper, leaf mold, grass clippings, compost and composted manure are organic mulches. Inorganic mulches are gravel, decomposed granite, rock and fiberglass landscape fabric.

Mulches have many uses in the landscape. On a small scale, they can be used around plants to modify temperatures, reduce loss of moisture and reduce weeds. Weeds that blow in and sprout in the mulch are usually easy to pull out. The cooling effect mulches have on a plant's root zone is of great value in hot climates. For example, soil is approximately 10 degrees cooler when covered with a 3-inch (7.6-cm) layer of mulch.

Organic mulches can hold water, shade roots and improve soil structure as they decompose. This is especially important for acid-loving plants. Although some organic mulches fade in color and may sometimes float away in a downpour or carry seeds that may sprout, they are still highly beneficial to plants. Replenish the mulch periodically.

Inorganic mulches are inexpensive, low-maintenance ways to cover large areas. They can be a permanent, attractive part of a landscape design and are frequently used in landscapes featuring arid-adapted plants.

Weed Control

Unless you are willing to pull a few weeds, a pre-emergent spray or granule is often the preferred method of weed control. A pre-emergent is a mild poison that is applied to the soil, usually in early spring, and often again in fall to kill weed seeds before they germinate. This is by far the easiest way to control weeds. There are several kinds: some applied as liquids, some as granules or powders. To save water, wash the pre-emergents into the soil before a good rain.

If you see weeds growing after you have applied the pre-emergence, then the weed seeds had already germinated before the pre-emergence was applied or it did not yet penetrate the soil. Hand pull or spray these unwanted volunteers with Roundup or another systemic weed killer.

Many products that commercial companies are not allowed to use because of the environmental damage they do are strangely still available to homeowners. Be sure you do not mistake a soil sterilant, such as Triox or Hybor-D, for a pre-emergence product. Read the label before you buy. Soil sterilants not only kill the weeds, they sterilize the soil so that nothing can grow there. They also spread by leaching and will kill any neighboring plants that absorb them.

Chlorosis

Chlorosis means a yellowing of plant leaves, which indicates a lack of chlorophyll. Besides iron chlorosis in garden plants, the hot temperatures of summer, extremes of wet or dry soils, inadequate depth of watering, salty soils or caliche (high-calcium) soils cause it. In early spring, plants may look chlorotic if the air is warm, making plants want to grow, but the soil is cold and roots are still dormant. Feedings and adding organic matter will help. If you have continued problems with chlorosis, consider planting a more adapted plant.

There are other, less common deficiencies not covered here. If a plant response or characteristic seems strange, harvest some leaves and some living roots, put them in a plastic bag and take them to a qualified nursery or your local county cooperative extension office to see what can be done about it.

Plant Nutrition

Like people, plants need proper nutrition to be healthy. They take nutrients and make their own food from sunshine, carbon dioxide and water. Sometimes nutrients are missing or are unavailable. Nutrients most often needed in arid climates are nitrogen and chelated iron. Slow growth, small leaves and a pale to yellowish look, especially on old foliage, can indicate a need for nitrogen. New leaves that are yellow with green veins show a need for iron. Ammonium sulfate in small quantities can give a quick shot of nitrogen. A short-term iron fix is to spray chelated iron on plant foliage. Add iron chelates to the soil for a more permanent solution. When planting, many landscape professionals put fertilizer pellets in the soil under each emitter. Pellets last up to two years and are easy to replace. A slow-release fertilizer is better than a quick fix because it will provide nutrients over time.

Look at package labels to see what is in the fertilizer as well as how much to apply. Labels on fertilizer packages identify contents of nutrients with three numbers, such as 29-9-9. The first number is the percentage of nitrogen, the second is the percentage of phosphorus and the third is potassium or potash. Plants in soils with high pH and a high lime content do not usually need potash. But container plants in acidic potting mixes, grasses (including turf) and palms may need it. Look for fertilizer mixes that are high in nitrogen and be careful how you apply them, because too much applied the wrong way will burn plant roots and may kill the plant.

There are fertilizers formulated for certain plants, such as gardenias, citrus or plants in containers. Many nurseries put out their own fertilizer, especially balanced for local soils and conditions. Some gardeners swear by adding an organic mulch of compost or composted steer manure over plant beds once or twice a year. This treatment serves as soil enrichment as well as mulch.

Trees mainly need nitrogen. Try a complete fertilizer that contains nitrogen and chelated iron along with other micro-ingredients. Some gardeners swear by feeding trees with a composted steer manure under the whole canopy. Citrus trees have their own needs, which can be found on page 80.

Three Ways to Protect Plants from Cold or Sun

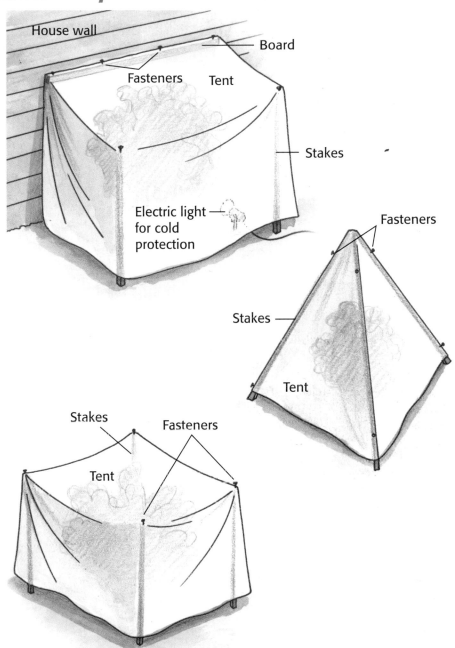

To protect a plant from cold, use canvas, sheeting or burlap, lifting it during the day to let the sun in. An electric light beneath the tent will also help warm the plant.

To adapt a plant to sun, use shade cloth over the plant the first summer. Take the cloth off in fall (or the next spring if as a young plant it might be tender to cold) and let the plant adjust to the intense summer sun as the weather warms up.

Landscape Tip: No Nitrogen for Legumes

Mesquite, palo verde, and ironwood are examples of legumes (members of the family Fabaceae, formerly Leguminosae), which make their own nitrogen, adding it to the soil. This benefits not only the legumes, but also provides nitrogen to surrounding plants within their range. Do not feed legumes nitrogen. They will stop making it and will lose the ability to do so!

Protecting Plants from Environmental Damage

Cold protection is sometimes necessary for borderline plants or if an unusual cold spell occurs. A floodlight or light bulb placed in or near plants or under constructed tents can produce quite a bit of heat. Christmas tree lights can add a little heat, or burning petroleum blocks or candles can make the difference of a few degrees, especially if there is a covering over the plant. If possible, move container plants under shelter or indoors temporarily. Giving a heavy irrigation just before a freeze arrives can raise the temperature of the soil just enough to keep a plant from freezing. Sometimes a covering is all a plant needs to see it through a light frost. Burlap or an old sheet or bedspread will work well. Avoid using plastic.

Sunburn can damage many plants, especially newly planted trees or any plant from a shaded nursery that is suddenly placed in the hot sun without an adjustment period. Young citrus, fruit trees, ash, magnolia and many others can suffer severe bark burn unless the trunk is protected. Cover trunk with a latex paint or commercial wrap to prevent damage. Drought-stressed

Ten Reasons Why Plants Fail

1. Selecting the wrong plant: a plant not adapted to the situation
2. Selecting a plant with problems: too small or poorly rooted in the nursery container
3. Wrong exposure: too much or too little sun.
4. Faulty planting techniques: set too deep in soil, plant pit too small, wrong backfill
5. Irrigation requirements not met
6. Lack of nutrients
7. Mechanical injury: injuring the roots by digging, weed devices, and so forth
8. Neglect, such as leaving stakes and ties on plants, especially trees, for so long that they girdle the plant or tree
9. Pests: animals and insects attacking the weakened plant
10. Diseases attacking the weakened plant

Six Ways to Control Pests

1. **Beneficial insects**
2. **Biorational controls:** soaps and oils applied by spray
3. **Organic pesticides:** Neem, pyrethrum, rotenone, nicotine sulfate
4. **Mechanical:** water spray, hand removal, and preventatives such as yellow sticky traps and shiny metal hoops at plant bases
5. **Exclusionary control:** using row covers or geotextile fabrics to cover plants
6. **Other materials:** diatomaceous earth, which rasps insect coats, and synthetic pesticides.

If you want to use an insecticide, use one that targets a specific pest. Broad spectrum insecticides kill everything, good bugs as well as bad. Some insecticides still in use in the home garden, such as Diazinon and Sevin, are contact pesticides for many sucking and chewing insects. Malathion is a contact insecticide for both soft-bodied insects and bugs with harder shells. Acephate is a systemic insecticide absorbed by nonedible plants for sucking and chewing insects, but it also kills beneficial pollinating and nectar insects, bees, and butterflies, and should not be used on edible plants.

plants can develop dry spots on leaves, which indicate sunburn. Small delicate plants suddenly put out in the sun in hot weather may wilt and die as the surface of the soil heats up on a hot sunny day.

To help new plants adapt, you can create a tent frame with sticks and put shade cloth over them. Or leave plants in their nursery containers for a few days, putting them out in the sun for increasing periods until they adapt. Be sure they are not drought stressed during the adjustment process or after.

Why Plants Fail

A plant's decline and eventual death is usually caused by one of three things: improper growing conditions, insect pests, or diseases. Pests and diseases are sometimes unavoidable, but landscape plants are dependent on you to supply a proper environment for growth. Some of the more basic causes of plant decline are too high or too low temperatures, too much or too little water, and soil that is inadequate for proper root growth. When plants are weakened by their circumstances, they become more susceptible to pests and diseases

Developing good gardening habits as described in the preceding section will help prevent plant problems before they start. Following soil preparation guidelines and maintaining a regular program of watering, fertilizing, weeding and pruning will keep plants growing vigorously. Healthy plants are resistant to attacks from pests and diseases. And, by caring for your plants regularly, you become more familiar with them. If a problem occurs, in most cases you will be

able to spot it and treat it promptly.

Problems are caused by weed killers, soil sterilants, mechanical injuries from weed trimmers or digging in the root zone, toxins poured on the soil, such as crank case oil or paint thinner, or building debris left in place and covered over with dirt by building contractors. Planting in a place known to have a toxic pest or disease like Texas root rot can also cause problems. If you have continued plant failure in an area, you can test your soil by planting radish seeds. If they fail to germinate in a few days, you may have toxic soil. You can also send a soil sample to a soil lab for testing.

Common-Sense Pest Control

Every insect you see is not out to destroy your landscape plants; many are beneficial. In addition to the well-known ladybug and praying mantis, there are many parasitic wasps, spiders and other insects, including lacewing and the common black ground beetle, that prey on plant-damaging pests. Keep them working in your yard by having plants they feed on, such as sweet alyssum or fennel. Using these "good guys" is an important part of the developing science known as *Integrated Pest Management (IPM)*. The basic principle of IPM is to use the simplest, least disruptive means of control first, reserving the most poisonous remedy as the last resort.

Many pests can be controlled without chemical sprays if they are discovered early, but there are times when sprays are necessary to save valuable plants. Some chemical controls are suggested below, but

How to Protect Plants from Small Animals

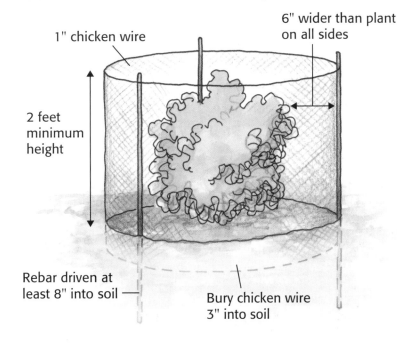

1" chicken wire

6" wider than plant on all sides

2 feet minimum height

Rebar driven at least 8" into soil

Bury chicken wire 3" into soil

When plants are located in exposed areas, subject to being eaten by small animals, they need protection until they develop their oils or enough size and woodiness to survive some damage.

because many chemicals become banned and treatments change so rapidly, it is best to consult a reputable landscape professional or your county cooperative extension agent. If you do use chemicals to control pests, do it thoughtfully. Read the label and follow directions.

Common Plant Pests

Knowing a little about the habits of insects and other pests will help you control them. Weather has a great influence on their behavior. Winds aid their spread. Erratic

A packrat nest

climatic variations often cause unpredictable insect infestations.

Another significant factor in arid areas is the lack of vegetation during most of the year. Winter and spring rains cause annual and perennial wild plant growth, resulting in a corresponding increase in insect populations. With the onset of hot, dry weather, natural vegetation quickly dies and dries up. The insects then migrate to your irrigated landscape to survive.

The following descriptions cover many common pests found in arid climates. We have followed the recommendations of the United States Department of Agriculture regarding use of chemical insecticides.

Animals. Rabbits, packrats and other rodents, javelinas, deer, and raccoons can be serious plant pests. They especially love tender, young, newly planted plants. Repellent sprays are not that effective and have to be applied after each rain or irrigation. The best protection besides a good fence or wall is a barrier such as 1-inch (2.5-cm) chicken wire hoops, wider than the plant and held in place by sturdy stakes driven well into the ground. When the plant is large enough and woody enough to withstand attacks without being destroyed, remove the barrier.

Agave weevils. Large century plants such as *Agave americana* and some other

large *Agaves* are especially susceptible to damage caused by this stout 3/4-inch (1.9-cm) long black weevil—a snout-nosed beetle—and its grubs. They usually attack Agaves near maturity, boring into the soft tissue of the heart and laying eggs. The larvae damage the plant and enable bacterial or fungal diseases to inoculate and finish off the plant. Avoid planting susceptible *Agaves* if *Agaves* in the neighborhood have been affected or the pests will spread.

Ants. Mix boric acid and apple jelly and put in a covered perforated box (or some other container accessible to ants but safe to pets and children) and set it near targeted plants or near the anthill. Ants carry it back to the colony to eat.

To gas an anthill, blend orange peel and a little water in a blender to make a syrup and pour into an anthill and around it during the hottest part of a summer day.

For harvester ants, the ants that strip leaves from plants, place Tanglefoot around the hole or shiny metal several inches wide around a plant likely to be attacked.

Amdro is a commercial poison. Use it carefully.

Aphids. These small, innocent-looking sucking insects on new growth secrete honeydew on the stems of plants they infest. They can reproduce very fast, since each aphid is female and born pregnant. Their thin-skinned bodies leave them vulnerable to dehydration, but they can be very damaging during mild weather.

Agave americana dead from agave snout-nosed weevil but still blooming.

Aphids

Detergent Spray

To use a dish detergent spray, mix 2 tablespoons detergent in one gallon of water; spray; then wash it off after thirty minutes. It will have done its work and should not remain on the plant. Remember that just because a household product is harmless to us doesn't mean it is harmless to a plant. Also remember that even if an insecticide is biologically based, that doesn't mean it isn't a poison to other forms of life, including us. Pyrethrums from chrysanthemums and the nicotine in tobacco tea are a case in point. Using anything at all changes the natural balance in ways we may never dream of. So always be thoughtful about what you are doing.

If the problem seems overwhelming, instead of going to the store and in frustration purchasing the deadliest thing you can find, call your county cooperative extension service to see what they would recommend.

twigs and bark of trees and shrubs, and are nearly invisible to the eye. These eggs are highly susceptible to a dormant oil spray, usually applied before a plant buds out in spring. Summer oils may be applied to some evergreen and growing plants. Read the product label.

• Insecticides such as malathion and Diazinon will stop aphids from feeding and will protect the plant from reinfestation for a few days. Depending on your plants and the degree of aphid damage you will tolerate, weekly applications may be necessary. This is especially true if the weather is suitable to their reproduction. Spray intervals will be noted on the product label.

Eucalyptus long-nosed borer. Introduced from Australia in 1984, the larvae eat trails under the bark and can girdle the tree, causing branches to die back and maybe even killing the tree. This is most serious in drought-stressed trees. Little is known about remedies. Eucalyptus borers may be sapped over by healthy trees like bugs in amber.

Eucalyptus redgum lerp psyllid. This pest is called *redgum lerp psyllid* (also known as the *tortoise beetle*) because the psyllid forms a lerp, a secretionary structure of crystallized honeydew excreted by nymphs. It forms a protective cover resembling those of scale insects. These pests cause severe leaf drop, killing saplings and weakening older trees. The lerps litter the ground under infested trees. This is a new pest that seems to attack *E. camaldulensis* and *E. sideroxylon*, both covered in this book, as well as *E. rudis*.

• There may be a newly introduced wasp predator from Australia that may help the situation.

• Diversify the *Eucalyptus* trees you plant.
• Don't fertilize or overwater trees and don't remove old branches, which will encourage new growth attractive to the lerps.
• Give deep irrigations at wide intervals at some distance from the trunk.

Flathead apple borers. Of the various kinds of borers, flathead apple borers are frequently a problem. They attack roses, *Pyracantha*, elms, olives, Mexican palo verdes, fruit trees and others of the rose family, but are usually considered a secondary pest. They follow other problems, such as sunburn of the trunk, pruning wounds and the like. They seldom invade undamaged bark. Borers mainly attack fruit trees or other plants already weakened by lack of water, or some other stress. They also attack mesquite trees.

Flathead borers on mesquite

• The honeydew secreted by aphids protects them somewhat from drying. A mild detergent solution—one tablespoon per gallon of water—will dissolve the honeydew so the aphids are more likely to dry out. Wash off the detergent soon after you have sprayed the aphids to avoid injuring the plant.
• Strong blasts of water from the hose, done frequently, will sometimes control aphid infestations.
• Aphids fly in on winds. Eggs are laid on

• Aside from injections given by a professional, you can use a lindane spray to wet trunks thoroughly two or three times a month. The trouble is that the pesticide creates havoc with the natural balance.

• Consider removing some branches a few inches below the infestation and get rid of the infested branches.

Giant palm borer. This borer attacks stressed palms of the *Washingtonia* and *Phoenix* groups. It is often found in large old palms transplanted from old groves into residential and commercial landscapes. Palms are stressed if fronds are removed from above the horizon line and are carelessly transplanted and poorly maintained thereafter.

• Prevent borer attacks by maintaining transplanted palms with plenty of water until they are well rerooted.

• Transplant only during the warm season.

Grubs. These pests are often found in the soil. They look like a thick, curved white worm. They are the larval stage of June bugs, May beetles and other beetles. Grubs are root feeders, the unseen enemy.

• Try solarization: wetting the earth and putting black plastic over the soil, keeping the temperature at 105 to 110F (41 to 43C) for ten days or longer in summer.

• When you plant, remove by hand any grubs that you find in the soil.

• There are other drenches, but seek advice from the your county cooperative extension service or a qualified landscape professional before you purchase one. Then always read and follow the directions on the label.

• A good nematode attacks grubs. Ask the cooperative extension service about availability in your area.

Mites. The eriophyid mite causes witches' broom in Mexican palo verdes and growth deformities in *Aloe saponarias*. The only control seems to be removing the plant.

Palo verde borers. The adult palo verde borer is up to 3 to 4 inches (7.6 to 10.2cm) long and 3/4 inch (1.9cm) wide. It is reddish brown to black, with long antennae. Larvae are 4 to 5 inches (10.2 to 12.7cm) long and an inch (2.5cm) or more in diameter. They feed on roots of the palo verde and deciduous fruit and shade trees, causing extensive damage. They may feed for

four or five years before reaching maturity. Symptoms are a decline in tree vigor with some branches dying back completely. Since there are few if any really effective controls, try to enhance tree growth with supplemental water and nutrients, which may help it outgrow the damage.

You may also notice 1/2- to 3/4-inch (1.3 to 1.9cm) holes in the soil near trees after rains. These are holes through which adults have emerged to mate. Adults may re-enter these same holes to lay more eggs or make new holes. Consider a mechanical prevention by laying down window screen or hardware cloth so the borers cannot exit the holes. Do this in late spring before the mating season. Grubs of the palo verde borer are well insulated by several inches of soil, so control is difficult. Insecticides may be pressure-injected at about the time adult beetles emerge—late spring to early summer. If you suspect this pest is damaging your trees, check with your county cooperative extension service for the latest control methods.

Scale. These usually small, hard-shelled, immobile pests cluster on plants. Some appear as tiny dots. Others look like little oysters. Cochineal scale looks like cotton stuck to prickly pear pads. If you touch it, a red liquid will appear. This scale is the source for the dye used by Native Americans known as Mexican pink.

• For some scale insects, particularly in small infestations, hair spray seems to work.

• Forceful sprays from the hose, plus a dish detergent spray (see box on page 42) are helpful.

• Some kinds of scale are susceptible to summer and winter oil sprays, but oil sprays will damage certain cactus plants and should not be used in the summer.

• The recommended insecticide is Sevin. Orthene, a systemic, is also effective.

• If the scale is particularly thick, scrape off as many as possible with a stiff brush before applying any controls. Take care not to cut into soft inner growth.

Skeletonizers. Grapeleaf skeletonizers are tiny yellow-and-black-striped worms that literally "skeletonize" the leaves of grapevines and other plants. Several generations may appear in one summer. You will find them on the underside munching away. They stay together in a colony when newly hatched, then separate as they get older. Watch for the symptoms and pick off the infested leaves if

Aloe *sick from aloe mite*

Mexican palo verde diseased with palo verde borer

Cochineal scale on prickly pear

you can. Texas mountain laurel gets a different skeletonizer. The destruction of a few leaves is of little concern. When they devastate a plant, it represents an overpopulation.

• Small initial infestations may be picked off by hand if you get to them early.

• Paper wasps are natural enemies.

• *Bacillus thurenginesis* (Dipel, Thuricide) is a safe biological control but works slowly.

• Sevin or malathion will also control but use only as a last resort.

Scale on silverberry

Grapeleaf skeletonizers

Damage from grapeleaf skeletonizer

Tent caterpillar nest in an aspen

Spider mites. These pests attack all needled evergreens, Italian cypress, junipers and other plants, such as *Pyracantha* and loquats. They are sucking pests that work from the ground up. Unlike aphids, these tiny spiderlike pests thrive in hot, dry, dusty weather. Expect them any time of year, but they are more active during warm periods. Early detection of spider mites requires an experienced, observant eye. Leaves will begin to appear a little dusty and there may be a speckling of tiny yellow spots or red dots. Shake foliage over white paper to see if little dark specks fall on it. Turn the leaves over and look for tiny silvery webbing. Rub your fingers over the leaf to feel for a gritty residue. Finally, look for the tiny mites with a small magnifying glass.

- Just as drying destroys aphids, spider mites are discouraged by moisture. Washing plants weekly during summer with a forceful blast from the hose will help prevent population build-ups. But this is only a preventive measure.
- Spraying with detergent water (see box on page 42) once a week can break their reproduction cycle and control small infestations. If the webbing is very thick, it may actually repel water. The addition of a commercial wetting agent, called a *surfactant*, such as Exhalt 800 or Spray Mate, will enable the spray to penetrate the webbing and work more effectively.
- By the time much webbing is evident, some chemical control will be necessary. For the latest chemical control, call your county cooperative extension service.

Tent caterpillars. They're easy to spot: They make tentlike structures of webbing, usually at branch tips high in trees. Cottonwood and willow trees are favorite hosts. The caterpillars are protected within the tent and feed there until time to pupate.

- Remove the tents of these pests from branches by using a long pole that has either a cone-shaped brush or several nails on one end. Wind the webs on the pole and then remove them from the tree and burn them. If you have a pole pruner, it may be simpler to prune away the branch tips supporting the tents.
- A strong spray of detergent water (see box on page 42) may help break up the tents, making the caterpillars more susceptible to other predatory insects, weather and insecticide sprays. *Bacillus thurenginesis*

is effective if the spray can penetrate the webbing. Malathion or methoxychlor will control.

Whiteflies. These annoying, pure white, flying insects suck vital juices from plants. They reproduce fast, so the key to their management is early control while numbers are small. Once a large population is established, it is virtually impossible to eliminate them until inclement weather reduces their numbers.

- Sprays of dish detergent water help control. (See box on page 42.) Be careful that the detergent doesn't injure plants.
- A commercial spreader-sticker, such as Exhalt 800, is another control method. Materials of this type essentially glue the tiny whiteflies to leaves.
- Whiteflies are attracted to the color yellow. Sticky yellow boards can be used as flypaper near infested plants.
- The botanical insecticide pyrethrum is relatively effective if used frequently. The synthetic imitation of pyrethrum, resmethrin, provides control that is more effective.
- Whatever method you use, be persistent. Spray every four to seven days, or as the product label directs. It is all-important to cover the plant thoroughly with the spray, especially the undersides of leaves.

Diseases

Arid climates are unfavorable for many common plant diseases. Most require considerable humidity to develop. The following diseases are those most likely to be a problem in arid landscapes. Remember that the best prevention is to choose a disease-resistant plant. As a rule of thumb, you can use Bordeaux, a copper product, to prevent or treat fungal diseases. Bacterial diseases can sometimes be effectively treated with sprays of Bordeaux or antibiotics such as Streptomycin sulfate sprays or shots. Be sure you know the disease your plant has and how to treat it. To help plants recover, improve their soil environment by adding mulches and nutrients.

Aleppo pine blight. You'll recognize this disease when clumps of foliage suddenly dehydrate on sun-exposed sides of actively growing trees. Affected needles first appear whitish green then turn brown. In more severe cases, sap may exude from affected twigs. Some die-back usually occurs, but many blighted branches survive. The "blight" seems to be a weather-induced shock to tender, actively growing foliage. It occurs during early winter and is apparently caused by shifts between day and night temperature extremes. It seems to be worsened by drying winds, because it is typically found on the sun-exposed windward sides of trees. Also, blighting seems to be more common to trees receiving frequent, shallow irrigation, especially in lawn areas. To prevent the blight from occurring, avoid light, frequent watering. Water deeply when you do water.

Armillaria root rot or oak root fungus. This disease is encouraged by excessive soil moisture at the plant's crown. Tree declines in vigor, foliage yellows and leaves drop. Fan-shaped plaque appears between bark and wood at trunk. This is mainly a problem in the higher deserts and grasslands and seldom affects oaks in the hotter low zone, but it does occur at sea level on the Pacific coast. Oaks may die but more frequently experience stunted growth and lack of vigor. Surrounding plants may be killed. Prevent by not overwatering near the trunk. If your plant contracts this disease, contact your county cooperative extension agent.

Crown gall. A very common plant disease caused by a bacteria, crown gall can destroy large fruit trees, such as peach and almond, and also plagues roses and grapes. Round, woody, lumpy growth appears near the soil line, although in some cases the galls form below ground or well above the soil line. Growth is poor, foliage is thin and plants eventually succumb.

Check plants for any suspicious bumps before taking them home from the nursery. Remove growth and add organic matter and perhaps sulfur to the soil to lower the pH. Crown gall does not thrive in acidic soil.

Fire blight. Fire blight is a bacterial disease that primarily affects members of the rose family, like *Pyracantha*, pears, loquats, *Cotoneaster*, hawthorn and sometimes even roses. Plants are infected through their blossoms. Blight is first apparent on bloom spurs shortly after bloom, when blossoms and leaves of the fruit-spurs dry and turn a blackish brown. The disease progresses to limbs and bark if not treated. Prevent it by not overfertilizing and by planting resistant plants if possible. Treat by cutting out infected wood. Be sure to wash your tools in a bleach solution between cuts so as not to spread the infection. Plants can be sprayed at blossom time with an antibiotic, such as streptomycin sulfate, a weak Bordeaux mixture or with Agrimycin 100. Seek more information from your county cooperative extension service.

Powdery mildew. This well-known disease is all too common in arid regions. It is more prevalent in spring and fall than in summer. Plants commonly attacked are roses, crepe myrtles, *Euonymous*, grapes, zinnias and dahlias. A form of sulfur, lime-sulfur, wetable sulfur or sulfur dust is a good preventive measure, but it will not eradicate the disease once it is established. Useful fungicides include Acti-dione PM and triforine. Bayleton (triadimefon), a systemic, lasts several months, killing any powdery mildew on plant leaves.

Root-knot nematodes. These microscopic wormlike animals parasitize plant roots, reducing plant growth and health. Use nematode-resistant plants when possible. If you suspect nematodes are damaging your plants, consult an expert. Diagnosis and control require professional help.

Texas root rot or cotton root rot. This fungus requires special attention. Left untreated, it can gradually spread through your garden, killing most of the plants in its path. The only plants that are immune are the grasses or grasslike plants—plants with fibrous roots such as palms, bananas and bamboos. Resistant plants are the pines, *Eucalyptus*, citrus from sour orange rootstock, cypress, oleander, pomegranate, jasmine, myrtle, *Pyracantha*, elderberry, rosemary, olive and juniper.

This is mainly a problem at altitudes below 3,500 feet (1,067m).

Plants afflicted with Texas root rot often wilt and die rapidly, leaving the wilted drying leaves on the plant. Sometimes plants decline the first summer and die the second. Take action immediately. Remove the plant at once or plant resistant types, as listed above.

Verticillum wilt. This disease, often seen in olives but sometimes in carobs and other trees, is most active in cool, wet soils, especially in spring, but sometimes shows up in fall. It is introduced to the soil by infected plants. Symptoms are branches that die back progressively on one side of the tree from base to tip. When cut, the wood beneath the bark shows a dark, discolored layer.

Purchase healthy plants. Treat by promoting plant vigor. Work 3 inches (7.6cm) of organic matter into topsoil around the drip line. Feed with light applications of ammonium sulfate every six weeks during

Crown gall plant problems

growing season. Trees that have lost whole branches can sprout new ones and recover, but they may be attacked again when and if conditions are right.

New pests and diseases occasionally arrive, making it still more complicated to keep your plants healthy and uninfested. For instance, the prickly pear decimator *Cactoblastus cactorum*, now in Florida, may spread west. For information on any new problem, consult your local county cooperative extension agent or a knowledgeable nursery person.

Choosing the right combination of plants is the key to a thriving landscape you will enjoy for years to come.

This chapter describes more than 400 plant species and cultivars adapted to warm, arid environments. Plants are listed in alphabetical order, according to botanical name. You may find the botanical names cumbersome at first, but there are sound reasons for their use: A given plant may have many common names, or different plants may be known by the same common name. Common names also change from region to region within the country, or the world, while the botanical name will be the same whether in Japan, France or the United States, regardless of the language. (See page 49 for a closer look at botanical names.)

From a practical viewpoint, the most important aspect of using botanical names is that you know exactly what you are getting. This is not always the case with common names. If you select a juniper for low ground cover, there's a difference between *Juniperus horizontalis*, with a maximum height of 18 inches (45.7cm), or *Juniperus chinensis* 'Pfitzerana,' which will reach up to 15 or 20 feet (4.6 or 6.1m) in height. If you know plants only by their common names, see the index for reference. (See also chapter 5 for more plant descriptions.)

How to Use This Chapter

This chapter covers widely used plants such as dominant trees and woody plants, plus some standby shrubs and color plants. It includes descriptions of individual species as well as genuses, such as *Acacia* and *Yucca*. Chapter 5 lists more excellent plants charted according to the niches they fill in your landscape. If you can't find a particular plant in this encyclopedic section, look in chapter 5 or check the index.

Each plant entry that follows includes scientific (genus, species, family) and common names, a general plant description, cultivars and other notables species (as alternatives), special design features, uses, disadvantages, planting and care guidelines, and cultural requirements.

Cultural Requirements

Growing plants is not an exact science but a learned art. It depends on myriad changing conditions, but mostly, it depends on you, the grower and caretaker.

The boxed cultural guide with each plant description gives you the plant's basic requirements as to soil, sun, water, temperature and maintenance. It also indicates the zone or zones where that plant is best adapted (see the climate map on pages 2 and 3 to determine which zone you live in). The zone adaptations are only guides, not hard and fast rules. Temper the information with your own experiences, and with the guidance of your nursery and a cooperative extension agent.

The following are explanations of the cultural terms used in the plant descriptions.

Soil

Tolerant: Plant will grow in a wide range of soil conditions.

Well-prepared or improved garden soil: Ample planting pit with 1/3 humus (organic amendment) and possibly 1/3 sand mixed with existing soil. Water drains freely.

Average garden soil: Soil of established gardens.

Well-drained soil: Sandy loam; sandy or gravelly soil with fast drainage. It may or may not have organic matter in it.

Heavy soil: Soil with high clay or silt content that drains poorly because it is dense.

Sun

Full shade: No direct sun. Interiors or areas under overhangs or roofs. North sides.

Part or filtered shade: Dappled sun. Under trees with open shade or under lath cover.

Open shade: Shaded but open to the sky, such as on the north side of a building.

Part sun or afternoon shadow: East sides of buildings or near trees where shade is cast during afternoon hours.

Full sun: Full exposure to the sun at all times, away from reflected heat.

Reflected sun, reflected heat: Near or against south or west walls or next to pavement that collects and reflects the sun.

Glossary of Terms

Alkaline: Soils with high pH—above 7.0.

Berm: A mound.

Bare root: Not potted in soil. Some dormant plants are sold and planted bare root at certain times of the year, usually late winter or early spring.

Bracts: Colorful specialized leaves surrounding the true flowers of some plants, such as bougainvillea and poinsettias.

Buttress roots: Roots extending out on the surface of the ground at the base of trees.

Caliche (hardpan): Impervious, rocklike cemented layer of lime in soil.

Catkins: Long, slender, fuzzy, usually greenish flowers.

Chlorosis: Abnormal yellowing of plants, often caused by iron or nitrogen deficiency.

Crown: Top of a tree from where it branches out or area of roots from where they meet the trunk (the root crown).

Deciduous: Plants that shed all of their leaves all at once each year (usually in autumn).

Drip line: The outer edge of a tree's crown.

Drought deciduous: Plants that shed all or part of their leaves when stressed by drought.

Espalier: Plants pruned and trained to grow flat against a wall or fence.

Evergreen: Plant foliage remains green through the year. Conifers with needles or scaly leaves can shed at any season. Some, such as pines, shed seasonally. Some, such as junipers, do not. Broadleaf evergreen plants, such as *Xylosma* or magnolia, may shed leaves in spring or summer as new leaves come out and growth begins.

Foliage: The mass of leaves on a plant.

Foundation plant: Plants used at the bases of buildings to integrate plants and structures with the site.

Glochid: Tiny stickers around the areola of a prickly pear pad. The pad may or may not have longer thorns.

Harden off: Give less irrigation to prevent new growth that will be tender to cold.

Herbaceous: A plant with no woody parts.

Humus: Organic matter that is in, or added to, the soil, usually composted or treated in some way.

Leach: To wash salts out of the soil with long, slow irrigation.

Leader: Dominant shoot of a plant. Usually grows vertically in the center of the plant.

Leggy: Tall and spindly. A plant is leggy usually because of lack of light or overcrowding. Certain species, however, are naturally leggy.

Microclimate: Small area within a climate zone where temperatures are modified by terrain, sun exposure, wind flow and other factors. Microclimates may be warmer or cooler than the prevailing climate. Even north or south sides of buildings can be considered microclimates.

Mulch: Layer of material laid on the soil to retain moisture, modify soil temperature, and prevent weeds. Mulches can be organic, such as hay or wood chips, or inorganic, such as decomposed granite or gravel.

Naturalized: A plant so well adapted to a nonnative area that it has reseeded naturally and become a part of the landscape.

Overstory: Tall tree or plant above smaller plants.

Pinching: Manually removing burgeoning bud tips to keep twigs from growing out.

Phyllodes: Broadened leaf stalk (petiole) that ordinarily connects the leaf to the stem. Forms the center rib of the leaves except there is no "leaf" extending from this rib. This may briefly support a true leaf at the tip, which soon drops off. The broadened phyllodes carry on the function of the leaves and, unless closely examined, appear to be typical leaves. Many Australian *Acacias* have phyllodes for foliage. In this work, to avoid confusion, we refer to phyllodes as "foliage" or "leaves."

Refurbish: To replant an area, especially one that has been neglected or abused.

Rejuvenate: To renew and create a more youthful growing pattern, usually by pruning.

Rhizomes: Thick horizontal stems that spread laterally through or on the soil.

Scarify: To scratch a seed along one side to allow water to penetrate so that germination can take place. Also to rake the hard-packed soil or lawn surface to facilitate water penetration.

Soil amendment: Any material mixed in with existing soil to create a friendly environment for the roots of certain plants.

Specimen: Single plant used alone in the landscape as an eye-catcher. Also specially selected plants that must meet certain standards.

Standard: Tree or shrub trained into a small treelike form with an erect single trunk and often a clipped, rounded crown.

Stolons: Runners or vegetative parts that are used in plant propagation. Stolons also describe runners that certain spreading plants, such as Bermudagrass, use to expand over the soil surface.

Systemic: Pesticide that is absorbed by the plant, making the plant poisonous to pests.

Suckers: Vigorous shoots that sprout from the base, trunks or major branches of plants.

Swale: A shallow depression that covers a horizontal distance. Swales are often used to channel substances to or from a location, such as water from the downspout of a house to a tree basin. Rock-covered swales prevent erosion.

Topiary: Method of pruning that shapes plants into hedges or other artificial forms.

Transitional area: Area between a heavily irrigated landscape and a drier landscape treatment.

Underplant: Smaller plant beneath a taller plant.

Irrigation

Ample: Irrigate to keep soil damp to the touch.
Moderate: Irrigate when the top 2 inches (5.1cm) of soil are dry.
Occasional: Irrigate deeply, soaking the root zone, but at wide intervals.
None: No water in addition to rainfall. In very dry climates or during long hot dry periods, some water may be required. **Note:** Even drought-tolerant plants require water when first planted. Be sure plants are established before gradually stopping irrigation.

Temperature

Tolerant: Accepts a wide range of temperature. Plants generally tolerate heat and average cold of their adapted zones.
Heat-tolerant: Plants will grow in hot locations, even in the low zone. A plant may be heat tolerant but not hardy to cold.
Tender: Sensitive to cold and may be damaged or killed by freezing temperatures.
Hardy: Adapted to cold of the climate zones covered in this book. A plant may be hardy but not heat tolerant.
Temperature ranges: Whenever possible, we give a low-temperature range. There are so many variables—whether a plant has hardened off (succulent plant parts have become woody), unseasonable frosts, microclimates—that these ranges are not absolute.

Maintenance

Constant: Continual care of some sort. Plants to be fussed over.
Periodic: Tolerant. Requires some regular care.
Seasonal: Needs attention at certain times of the year: feeding, pruning, and grooming.
Little: Rarely needs any attention.
None: Can largely be ignored once established, although occasional pruning, grooming, and irrigation will usually improve any plant's health and appearance.

Gazania and *Verbena*

A Close Look at a Botanical Name

Genus: Plants consisting of one or more species sharing many characteristics, usually similar flowers and fruit. Species within a genus have more in common with each other compared to other species. The plural is genera.

Species: Plants with certain discernible differences from other plants within the same genus. Their characteristics normally continue from generation to generation.

Cultivar: After the species name you may have a cultivar name. The word "cultivar" comes from the combination of the words "cultivated" and "variety," meaning they are cultivated (bred) for their desirable characteristics.

Acacia redolens 'Desert Carpet™'

Family: *Fabaceae*
(Leguminosae)

Former family name

Family: The broadest botanical classification used in this book. Plants within a family share some general characteristics but differ enough that they can be further categorized into genera and further still into species.

Trademarked plants: There are also many varieties of trademarked plants, which have a "™" after their names. They are plants that nurseries have developed for a particular characteristic. The name of the variety of the plant appears in quotes or italics after the genus and species names. While other nurseries may take cuttings and grow the same plant, they are not allowed to call it by the same name unless they pay a royalty to the trademark owner.

Varieties: Variations in species that occur in nature are varieties. A variety is usually quite different from the typical plant of the species. For example, the honey locust *Gleditsia triacanthos* has thorny branches. The variety *Gleditsia triacanthos inermis* has no thorns.

Acacia species

Family: Fabaceae (Leguminoceae)

The first *Acacia* species brought from Australia to the hot interior valleys and deserts of the Southwest performed poorly or failed entirely. Most were species previously introduced into the western part of California. They were successful in the coastal regions because they were native to similar mild climates in Australia, but they could not tolerate the desert heat and soils. Many new introductions from the Australian deserts have since been tested successfully in the Southwest and are now available and widely used. Australian *Acacia* species, or wattles as they are called Down Under, are thornless and often spectacular bloomers.

Most are large shrubs that with staking and pruning can be trained into patio-size trees. A few are distinct trees and grow larger than the other species. Most plants produce a heavy spring bloom followed by a large crop of seed that can litter and look unattractive. Some species blow over because their tops outgrow their roots. The Australian *Acacias* have phyllodes instead of leaves. They are resistant to drought because of their leathery,

waxy exterior. True leaves sometimes grow out of the tip of the phyllodes after germination.

There are also *Acacia* species native to the Americas, Europe, North Africa and the Middle East. These have feathery leaves, are often thorny and produce showy blooms. A number of species are well adapted to arid conditions and are currently in use as attractive landscape plants.

Most *Acacias* can be planted from containers any season, except for frost-tender species that are best planted in spring and early summer. Fall and winter are usually the best planting time for fast root development. Many *Acacias* can also be grown from seed sown directly in soil, which avoids root distortion—a common problem with container-grown plants, especially if contained so long they become rootbound.

Special design features: Desert to subtropical effect. Some species have an interesting silhouette. See individual species descriptions.

Uses: Patio or street trees. Desert, natural or transitional gardens. Light shade. Grouped for grove or barrier.

Disadvantages: Some litter from leaves and seeds. Caterpillars may defoliate in spring, but leaves quickly come out again. Occasional infestations of desert mistletoe. Thorns can be a nuisance if planted near walkways.

Planting and care: Plant any time from containers. If starting from seed, scratch seeds to allow water penetration. Space 12 to 15 feet (3.7 to 4.6m) for a row or grove, 5 to 6 feet (1.5 to 1.8m) apart for a barrier. Prune side branches and stake one or more main leaders to train as a tree.

Acacia species

Zones: See individual species descriptions.
Evergreen to partly deciduous: See individual species descriptions.
Soil: Most soils, but provide good drainage.
Sun: Full sun. Tolerates reflected sun and heat.
Water: Highly drought resistant, but ample moisture will stimulate growth until desired size is achieved. Then irrigate occasionally to maintain satisfactory landscape appearance.
Temperature: See individual species descriptions.
Maintenance: Little maintenance required if you use it appropriately and give it space to grow.

Acacia aneura

Acacia berlandieri

Acacia aneura
Mulga

This large erect evergreen shrub to small-size patio tree grows up to 20 feet (6.1m) high and spreads 12 to 20 feet (3.7 to 6.1m) or so wide, with rounded contours. Plants are densely covered with small, undivided, silvery gray leaves and showy yellow rod-shaped flowers in March, June and September. An Australian desert native, it is well-adapted to desert conditions.

A special design feature is its fairly compact, dense growth—unusual in desert plants. Mass for screening, as a space definer or as a background planting. Also a nice tree for small patio or row planting at property edges or along streets. Prune in October. Can be slow to develop. Overwatering causes chlorosis. Hardy to about 15 to 18F (-9.4 to -7.8C) in low and middle zones.

Acacia berlandieri
Guajillo

A small, dense, deep green ferny shrub of moderate growth rate to 15 feet (4.6m) high and wide. To a degree, it can be used to

replace the more tender *Lysiloma watsonii thornberi* (feather bush) where temperatures go below 28F (-2.2C) but stay above the midteens. Can survive 15 to 20F (-9 to -7C) in low zone and warmer areas of middle zone. It can be kept as a large shrub for screening or trained as a small tree for patios or entries where a lush look is desired. Evergreen in warm areas but naturally deciduous. Creamy puffballs from February to May produce large woody pods in summer. The soil and water requirements are the same as with other arid-land *Acacias*, but it needs good drainage and regular watering in summer to look its best. Prune in June. Protect from rabbits in open areas until trunks become woody and reach 1 to 2 inches (2.5 to 5.1cm) in diameter.

Acacia constricta
Mescat Acacia
Whitethorn Acacia

The tough and durable whitethorn acacia is native to the deserts of the Southwest where it may receive 10 inches (254mm) or less of annual rainfall. This deciduous plant tolerates a wide range of unfavorable conditions, including heat and cold; drought; poor, stony or alkaline soils; and hot winds. It naturally forms a thicket of dark thorny branches 6 to 8 feet (1.8 to 2.4m) high, spreading 6 to 8 feet (1.8 to 2.4m) wide, which makes it a good barrier or erosion-control plant. It can also be used in desert repair, as a bank cover or in a wild garden or natural area. Pruned and trained, it becomes an attractive single or multiple-trunk tree that grows to 18 feet (5.5m) and spreads as wide, with some irrigation. Twigs and branches of first new growth have white thorns about 1/2 inch (1.3cm) long, but slower growth on more mature plants do not. Occasionally, plants will have no thorns at all.

Feathery, finely cut foliage appears in midspring and provides filtered shade. Small, fragrant puffball blooms, attractive to birds, appear mid- to late spring for several weeks and sometimes again after summer rains, followed by small papery beans. Potential problems include profuse seeding, defoliation by caterpillars, and mistletoe. Hardy in all three zones.

Acacia craspedocarpa
Waxleaf Acacia

A solid, shrubby evergreen with a slow to moderate growth rate from 10 to 15 feet (3.1 to 4.6m) high and as wide. This Acacia is a large shrub or small tree with a dense mass of small, rounded gray-green leaves. Rod-shaped yellow flowers brighten the landscape for a long period in late winter through spring, sometimes into early summer, followed by seedpods. Works well as background shrub, privacy screen, windbreak shrub, space definer or small tree. May be slow to develop. Hardy in low zone and warm areas of middle zone.

Acacia cultriformis
Knife Acacia

This is a large evergreen shrub to small tree, 10 to 15 feet (3.1 to 4.6m) high. Knife-shaped silvery gray leaves to 1 inch (2.5cm) long form an interesting pattern along stems. Abundant soft-yellow flowers clothe the plant in early spring, followed by 3-inch (7.6-cm) bean pods. Grows naturally into a multistem thicket, but can be trained into a gnarled yet interesting specimen tree.

As a mounding large shrub with interesting foliage pattern, it contrasts nicely with other plants and works well as a specimen plant. Use for banks, roadsides,

screens, barrier planting and for dust and wind control in tough situations. Hardy in low zone and warm areas of middle zone.

Acacia farnesiana
Popinac • Sweet Acacia

Native to the tropics and the subtropics of the Americas and grown in warm climates throughout the world, this multibranched umbrella-shaped shrub with ferny foliage grows 8 to 10 feet (2.4 to 3.1m) tall. Trained as a single or multiple-trunk tree, it grows 15 to 20 feet (4.6 to 6.1m) high with an umbrella-shaped crown spreading 15 to 20 feet (4.6 to 6.1m). A profusion of fragrant yellow puffball flowers appears in late fall and lasts over a long period. Small beans follow the flowers.

In addition to creating a tropical or subtropical effect, this Acacia works well as a patio or street tree, a transitional plant, or in tropical or desert groupings. Its disadvantages include beans that may litter pavement and slow recovery from cold damage, which necessitates complete retraining. Occasionally caterpillars may defoliate and leave webs in spring, but tree leafs out again. Hardy in the low and middle zones.

Note: There is a great difference in hardiness among A. farnesiana, depending on where the seed came from. It ranges from the tropics into the Sonoran and Chihuahuan Deserts. For a time, the hardier types from the northern populations were classified first as A. smallii. Later, botanists changed it to A. minuta and eventually lumped it back into A. farnesiana, saying it was not different enough to qualify as a separate species. Some nurseries still carry the hardier strain under the name of A. smallii or A. minuta. If you plant the tree in the middle zone, it is worth your while to get plants from the northern populations. The plants grown from the seed of more tropical populations will sustain frost damage in colder areas of the low zone.

Acacia greggii
Cat-Claw Acacia • Devil's Claw
Texas Mimosa

This native of the southwestern United States and northern Mexico naturally forms a rugged tangle of thorny branches 6 to 8 feet (1.8 to 2.4m) high. With training, it can become a 10-foot (3.1-m) tree with a spread of 12 feet (3.6m) or more. Feathery gray-green foliage appears in midspring. Branches

Acacia constricta

Acacia craspedocarpa

Acacia cultriformis

Acacia farnesiana

Acacia greggii

Acacia notabilis

Acacia salicina

followed by flat rust-colored beans up to 3 inches (7.6cm) long. A second but less spectacular bloom may appear after summer rains. Rough, dark bark and picturesque form of plants trained into multiple-trunk trees make this an attractive landscape subject, with or without foliage, for a subtropical effect, when in leaf, or in desert, naturalistic, or transitional gardens. It is useful in refurbishing the desert in disturbed areas, for harboring wildlife, or for banks, property edges, or as a shrub forming an impenetrable barrier. A trained plant makes a handsome silhouette against plain walls or the sky and provides filtered shade for a patio or courtyard. It is also a nectar plant for butterflies. Its disadvantages are that it needs training to look good, has snagging thorns, is prone to desert mistletoe and may be attacked by caterpillars in spring. Hardy in all zones.

Acacia notabilis
Notable Acacia

A large graceful evergreen shrub that grows quickly to 6 to 8 feet (1.8 to 2.4m) high, occasionally to 15 feet (4.6m), and as wide. Large, narrow, dark to bluish green or gray-green leaves to 6 inches (15.2cm) long cover the plant densely to the ground. Rounded form at maturity. A show of bright yellow puffballs in spring appear on its sprawling form. Looks like *Acacia redolens*, but leaves are longer and form is more upright. Established plants survive without irrigation in areas with 12 inches (305mm) or more of rainfall.

Provides a bright green accent for the arid landscape when given space to grow. Unusually dense for a desert plant. Sharp clean form is excellent for screening, background planting, roadsides and large residential areas where it can grow at the outskirts of the garden or serve as transition between high- and low-water areas. Hardy in low zone and middle zone and probably warmer areas in the high zone (it is likely damaged in the high teens Fahrenheit).

Acacia pendula
Weeping Acacia • Weeping Myall

Weeping, cascading branches clothed with abundant gray willow-like leaves to 4 inches (10.2cm) long are notable features of this evergreen tree. Plants are highly variable in shape and may grow to 25 feet (7.6m) high

and 15 feet (4.6m) wide. Small, yellow puffball flowers appear sporadically from February to April but are not showy.

Unique pendulous form makes this a dramatic accent or specimen tree. Silvery gray foliage is striking in contrast with other greener plants. Occasionally, individual plants become distorted or take on an unattractive sprawling form that is difficult to train. Prune in April at end of bloom. Can be slow to develop. Hardy to below 20F (-7C) in the low and middle zones and protected areas of high zone.

Acacia redolens
(*A. ongerup*)
Prostrate Acacia

This spreading, evergreen shrub may cover an area as broad as 12 to 15 feet (3.7 to 4.6m) in diameter if given space. Species may mound to 5 feet (1.5m) or more if crowded or untrimmed. A trademarked selection, 'Desert Carpet,' is said to get no higher than 2 feet (0.6m) and spread 8 feet (2.4m) or more wide. It is one of the best sprawling ground covers for hot arid climates and can compete root-wise with *Eucalyptus*. Numerous leathery gray-green leaves are narrow pointed ovals spaced interestingly along the stems. Small, yellow rod-shaped flowers bloom along stems briefly from February to April.

Use as ground cover for medians, banks and large open areas. Be aware that plants might overwhelm smaller restricted spaces, and can get woody with time. Prune in April, at end of bloom. Plants die out in some situations, which is sometimes attributed to overwatering. Hardy to low and middle zones and warmer areas of high zone, to 18 to 20F (-8 to -7C).

Acacia salicina
Willow Acacia

A semiweeping, fast-growing evergreen tree to 20 to 40 feet (6.1 to 12.2m) high and up to 15 feet (4.6m) wide, with long, slender willow-like leaves. Small creamy puffball blooms appear from October to December. Tolerates high heat, poor soil, brackish water and drought. Weeping form with abundant foliage evokes a cool oasis feeling in the landscape. Also use as shade tree for homes, public spaces, roadsides, reforestation and as a tall screen. May naturalize. Wood is sometimes brittle in wind. Blows over easily, especially if overwatered or if drip emitters

and twigs covered with small thorns resemble the sharp, curved claws of a cat, which take hold with tenacity if you brush them. Profusion of fuzzy light yellow catkins appear in late spring or early summer,

are not placed at or beyond drip line so roots do not spread out to stabilize the tree. Plant any time from containers, but best in cool months. Space 20 to 40 feet (6.1 to 12.2m) apart. Hardy in low zone, to 22F (-6C). May be damaged during coldest winters in middle zone, where planting time is early spring after danger of unusual cold is past.

Acacia saligna
Blue Leaf Wattle

Fast-growing, large evergreen shrub or a small umbrella-shaped tree (with training) with long, narrow, blue-green leaves. Gorgeous display of yellow-orange puffballs appear in early to midspring. Dense leaves and branches cover plants nearly to the ground unless trimmed. The dark, dense, lush foliage makes an attractive mounding mass. Prune up for interesting multistem structure or stake and train as a single-trunk patio-size tree. Use for screening, mass planting on slopes and banks, and revegetation. Plant singly or in a group to form mass or a grove for rich green foliage and early to midspring color. Best in informal settings. Plants are subject to being blown over in early development stages because of rapid growth unless staked securely. Irrigate widely to spread and strengthen root system. Spread irrigation emitters around trunk and set so they fan out from it to a desired future drip line to develop a strong root system. Hardy in low zone and warm areas of middle zone, to 22F (-6C). Older uncared-for plants can become unattractive.

Acacia schaffneri
Twisted Acacia

A small tree from Mexico with unique thorny, twisting branch structure clothed tightly with small, feathery, deep green leaves. Reaches 18 feet (5.5m) high with a spreading crown. Evergreen to deciduous depending on moisture supply and temperature. Small, fragrant, yellow puffball flowers appear among foliage in March and April. Thorns on branches are not conspicuous while in leaf. Generally a see-through tree, it makes a unique silhouette with tentacle-like twigs—interesting in contrast with neighboring plants or against plain walls or the sky. Use as small tree, character plant, desert or tropical effects plant, or barrier plant. Somewhat slow-growing. Thorns may be a problem in the

development stage for maintenance personnel or passersby. Prune in May. Hardy in low and middle zone, to 20F (-7C).

Acacia smallii
(A. minuta)
Hardy Sweet Acacia
Western Sweet Acacia

Once thought to be a separate species and now considered to be a regional variation of *A. farnesiana*, which it is similar to with two distinctions—it is hardier to cold and begins blooming in early spring, or as early as December. Raised as a multiple-trunked or low-branching tree, it keeps its small frilly canopy for a long time. It can be planted any time of year. While sweet acacias lose leaves and can be damaged at 20F (-7C) and even killed at 15F (-9C), this hardier form can tolerate temperatures of 15F (-9C) or below, so it grows well in the high zone as well as the middle and low zones. Benefits from some pruning and training to develop a desirable tree form. Prune in April.

Acacia stenophylla
Shoestring Acacia • Dalby Myall • Eumong

Erect to bending in form, with an open crown, this unusual Australian tree has a sparse showing in youth of dark gray-green threadlike leaves, 1 foot (30.5cm) in length, that produce a weeping effect. Leaf threads are not true leaves but function as such. As the tree grows at a moderate rate to 20 feet (6.1m) tall and spreads to 15 feet (4.6m) wide, the foliage becomes denser, filling in the crown. A sparse showing of creamy-white puffball blooms may appear from October to November. Tree is remarkably tough and tolerant of drought, heat and poor soil conditions. Trees severely topped because of power lines overhead go on to develop a thick crown that hides the lopped off branches.

This *Acacia* has many uses: a tree narrow enough for townhouse side yards; interesting grouping in a small grove; silhouette plant against structures or sky; transitional plant; specimen plant; visual screen or break—distinct and effective but not dense; and dusty situations. Light shade beneath allows other plants to grow, although it also looks good with bare earth or rock mulch. It grows in the low and middle zone and is marginal in the high zone. It is hardy to 18F (-8C) but may be damaged below that. Other than some pruning and training,

Acacia saligna

Acacia schaffneri

Acacia stenophylla

this tree requires little maintenance. Prune in January.

Acacia visco
Visco Acacia

Previously named *A. abyssinica* in error (the seeds were erroneously thought to be from Ethiopia), this tropical-looking tree has been reclassified and correctly identified as *A. visco* from South America. It resembles the *Jacaranda* but leaves are smaller and tree is hardier. Evergreen in mild climates, deciduous with hard frosts, it has an erect and open-branched structure with feathery lush-green foliage. It grows at a moderate rate to 20 to 25 feet (6.1 to 7.6m) high,

Acacia willardiana

sometimes higher. Spreads to 30 feet (9.2m) if given room. To train as a single trunk tree, the first branches should be 8 feet (2.4m) or more above ground. Mildly fragrant, creamy-yellow puffball blooms appear midspring. Brown pods follow. Heavily furled bark on old trees is an attraction.

Meager irrigation slows development. Accepts ample water in flower beds or lawns. Tolerates periods of drought but will show stress and become unattractive if kept too dry. This *Acacia* can make a patio look like a vacation spot. Use for tropical or subtropical effects, on patios, in lawns or gardens, or as a large planter subject. Can grow up through a hole in the roof or toward the sky in an atrium patio. Disadvantages include possible splitting in wind and unattractive foliage when frozen. Foliage turns brown and stays on the tree until new growth resumes in spring. Leaf midribs are difficult to sweep up after they fall, so use a blower. Best in the middle and low zones. Loses leaves when

temperature suddenly drops to upper or mid 20s F (-1.7 to -5C). The twigs and branches tolerate temperatures lower than 20F (-7C).

Acacia willardiana
Palo Blanco • White-Barked Acacia

Decorative, small, open-branched, to 20 feet (6.1m) high by 15 feet (4.6m) wide in warm areas, this somewhat wispy, weeping tree with white peeling bark looks good in small spaces protected from hard freezes. It likes hot spaces with reflected heat, such as in planters along the south side of buildings, and is for the low zone or protected microclimates in the middle zone. It is particularly appealing as a multi-trunked silhouette plant. Blooms in March and April. Prune in April, after bloom. Protect young trees from cold in mid 20s F (-3 to -5C) or below until trunks reach at least 1 to 2 inches (2.5 to 5.1cm) in diameter. In open areas, protect saplings from rabbits.

Agave species

Family: Agavaceae

Because of their striking form and general tolerance of most species to cold, heat, sun, drought and poor or alkaline soils, *Agaves* are some of the most useful plants in the hot arid regions. Size varies from 1 to 6 feet (0.3 to 1.8m) tall, with many interesting leaf and color variations. The fleshy pointed leaves are usually armed with thorns at the tips, which often extend down along the edges. The leaves sometimes grow in rosettes around the center. This formation allows them to capture minute amounts of rain, guiding the moisture down the leaf to the roots. New growth and eventually the flower stalk rises from the center of the plant. Many *Agaves*, such as *A. americana*, can survive in areas receiving a mere 3 inches (762mm) of rain per year. While they are useful under such conditions, they are stunted and not necessarily attractive.

Agaves form a group of bold succulents that are recognizable by their form of thick, pointed radiating leaves. Most have spines and should be planted away from traffic areas. The majority bloom once after many years of growth, producing flowers on tall stalks anytime from May to August, dying after bloom.

Special design features: Bold form and foliage contrast.

Uses: Outstanding plant for harsh environments or difficult situations in which other plants fail, such as in shallow soils. Specimen or accent plant, or mass for a bold effect against structures. Rows for a barrier. Sculptural space definer or windscreen. Desert, subtropical or natural gardens. Banks for erosion control. Many are excellent container plants.

Disadvantages: Lower leaves may become dry or untidy looking and need to be removed. Snout weevils can kill some *Agaves*, usually the large ones with soft leaves rather than the smaller ones, which have a harder and thicker skin. They mostly attack in the mature stage as the plant gets ready to bloom, unless prevented by chemical treatment (see page 41). Some *Agave* species produce numerous offsets at their base, which can become invasive and a nuisance in some locations. In the wild, young *Agaves* can be rabbit food, even cow food. Plants can also become too large for allotted space. Be sure species in the ground are where you want them and have enough space to grow to maturity. Sharp tips of agaves near walkways or other high-use areas need to be cut off to avoid accidents. Better yet, plant away from frequented areas. Once an *Agave* blooms, it dies and the drying remains should be

removed. This can be difficult and costly if the plant is large. The removal of a bloomed-out agave, especially a large one, is a big job, but you receive many years of enjoyment before the bloom. The dry bloom stalks produce great silhouettes and many people just remove the dry leaves, allowing the dry bloom stalks to remain for many years.

Planting and care: Plant any time from containers, seeds or offsets. In dry climates, supply young plants with water occasionally until established or when plants show stress by wilting or withering. Prune in September.

Agave species

Zones: See individual species descriptions.
Evergreen
Soil: Tolerates most types except waterlogged.
Sun: Accepts part shade. Some species prefer shade in low or middle zones. Most are suitable for planting in full or reflected sun.
Water: Occasional to none in areas with more than 3 inches (762mm) annual rainfall or where plants receive extra runoff. When summers are dry, supply some water to keep leaves plump.
Temperature: Hardy from 0 to 20F (-18 to -7C), depending on species. Many species are damaged when temperature remains below 20F (-7C) for a long period, and some tropical species will tolerate only a light frost. Slow to recover.
Maintenance: Little to none unless you wish to groom.

Agave americana
Century Plant • Magay

Most important of the desert *Agaves*, this bold sculptural plant has stiff grayish blue-green leaf blades that reach 3 to 5 feet (0.9 to 1.5m) in length. It grows up to 6 feet (1.8m) in height and as wide or wider before the 20-foot (6.1-m) bloom stalk makes its appearance. Stalks grow fast—6 to 14 inches (15.2 to 35.6cm) a day—and look like a giant asparagus sprout until the horizontal arms open outward and the greenish yellow blooms appear. The woody stalk has an interesting silhouette and is often left standing even after it dies. This *Agave* is often a prolific producer of offsets. Leaf blades are well armed with saw-toothed edges and sharp points at the tips and should be placed at least 6 feet (1.8m) away from frequented areas. Leaves and entire plant may be injured in cold winter areas. This *Agave* looks good in large containers and urns, where it becomes stunted and remains small.

Agave americana 'Marginata'
Variegated Century Plant

'Marginata' is similar in form to *A. Americana* but slightly more refined and smaller in scale. Its narrower leaf blades are gray-green with a yellow stripe down each margin. It is more susceptible to grubs and should be treated annually to prevent infestations. This *Agave* looks nice in the garden as a contrast in color and form to other plants. It blends well in desert or tropical groupings and is an attractive container plant. Moderate water is acceptable, with occasional deep soakings. It survives without any irrigation in areas with 10 inches (254mm) or more annual rainfall. Like *A. americana*, it is well armed and should not be placed near paths or walkways. Space plants 3 to 6 feet (0.9 to 1.8m) apart for a mass effect. Also attractive as a container plant.

Agave americana 'Media Picta'
Picta Agave

Another *Agave* thought to be a variety of *A. americana* is this small decorative plant that grows no more than 3 feet (0.9m) high and forms numerous offsets. Each well-armed gray-green leaf has a wide white stripe along its center. Leaves tend to curl back in an appealing and decorative way.

This is a good pot plant for areas away from pedestrian traffic (because of the thorns). Picta tolerates garden conditions if it has good drainage and makes a dramatic contrast with other succulents, in a perennial garden, or against green background shrubs. If small *Agaves* are set out in an area unprotected from animals, they may be eaten. This *Agave* can grow in full shade to full sun, but not reflected sun and heat. Otherwise its needs are about the same as *A. americana*.

Agave attenuata
Nova • Century Plant

Soft succulent with luminescent smooth-edged leaves of pale green-gray in a rosette to 5 feet (1.5m) across. Trunks reach up to 5 feet (1.5m) high on mature plants. Offsets form clumps several feet in diameter that may be divided. Unlike most *Agaves*, mature plants continue to grow after blooming. Provide garden soil and moderate water. Protect from frosts or hot sun. In extreme climates, use as container plant in location protected from sun and cold. A handsome container plant in any zone.

Agave bovicornuta
Cow's Horn Agave

Very green and highly decorative with interesting marginal teeth, this *Agave* is good for close-up viewing in atriums and entryways, especially in afternoon shade or in filtered light under trees. Grows fast to mature size, 3 feet (0.9m) high by 4 feet (1.2m) wide, and is hardy to the mid 20s F (-3 to -5C). Can withstand lower temperature where it is protected by a tree or overhang. While not fatal, freeze-damaged leaf-tip burn is slow to disappear the next spring due to the slow growth rate. Although the plant survives, it is not a good choice in areas where this happens on a regular basis.

Agave colorata
Mescal Ceniza

Moderate growth rate to 3 to 4 feet (0.9 to 1.2m) high and as wide, with strong, broad leaf blades appealingly scalloped along the margins between sharp spines. Gray-green leaves show markings of other leaves and are sometimes cross-banded and red-tinted, ending in long, sharp terminal leaf spines. May be damaged in high to mid teens F (-7 to -11C). Very drought tolerant and

Agave americana

Agave americana 'Media Picta'

Agave attenuata

Agave bovicornuta

Agave colorata

Agave murpheyi

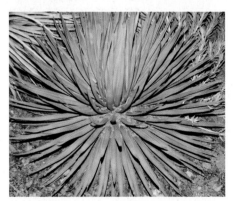

Agave ocahui

Agave salmiana

suitable for transitional zone planting or in a true desert application. It has a fairly long life, taking about fifteen years to bloom and die. The smaller selection with wider leaf pads is of great decorative interest.

Agave franzosinii
Franzosini's Agave

This *Agave* is similar to, and perhaps a form of, *A. americana* or a relative but has leaves that are lighter in color, less rigid and sometimes curved. At maturity, in as long as forty years, one has been measured at 9 feet (2.7m) wide from tip to tip and 7 feet (2.1m) high from ground to highest tip. Like *A. americana*, it is well armed along the edges and has a sharp tip. Plant it where it will have room to grow without impinging on walks or other places with foot traffic. These large *Agaves* have soft leaf surfaces and mature plants are more subject to attack from snout weevils than many of the smaller *Agaves*. Dramatic landscape form.

Agave geminiflora
Twin-Flowered Agave

Dense and symmetrical with numerous thornless, soft, flexible dark green leaves ending in sharp points, sometimes with thready edges, this plant grows moderately fast to 2 to 3 feet (0.6 to 0.9m) high by 2 to 4 feet (0.6 to 1.2m) wide. Prefers filtered sun or afternoon shade. It looks like a smaller, greener version of *Dasylirion wheeleri* with narrower leaves. Damaged by cold in mid 20s F (-3 to -5C). Excellent in containers or in the lusher landscape. Protect from hungry animals in open areas.

Agave lophantha
(A. univittata)
Holly Agave

A small, very green *Agave* with vertical stripes on its rosette of sharply pointed leaves, this plant forms colonies, which makes it useful as a barrier with its razor sharp marginal thorns and wickedly sharp tips. It prefers part shade, at least on hot afternoons, but will adapt to a sunny exposure. Decorative small *Agave* that looks good under palo verde trees or combined with larger, bolder succulents. Also makes an excellent barrier plant. Being clump-forming, there are always other plants to cover the hole left by the exit of a mature plant after blooming.

Agave murpheyi
Murphey's Agave

An *Agave* for cooler areas, tolerating temperatures below 10F (-12.2C) as well as those of the low desert where it grows naturally. This light gray-green *Agave* with stiff, fairly narrow barbed leaves gets to 3, even 4, feet (0.9 to 1.2m) high and as wide. Native Americans have used the center as food, particularly as their main source of sweets. The heart, as it buds out to bloom, is high in sugar. The flower nectar is attractive to birds (and bats).

Agave ocahui
Ocahui Agave

A small to medium dark green plant with a strong symmetrical growth pattern that looks like a spiked ball, *A. ocahui* grows in full sun with little water at a slow to moderate rate to 2 to 3 feet (0.6 to 0.9m) high and wide. If heavily watered or grown in the shade, it loses its distinctive appearance. Not particular about soil—can grow in a small pocket of soil on a rock cliff. Grow in containers away from traffic patterns, in dry areas accented by boulders, in Xeriscapes or in desert-effects landscapes. Hardy to mid teens F (-7 to -11C), probably even lower.

Agave parryi huachucensis
Huachuca Agave

Striking in form with strongly patterned leaves set in wide rosettes, this *Agave* is pale gray-green with black leaf margins edged with sharp thorns that end in a wickedly barbed tip. Highly decorative as a specimen or a group planting in a Xeriscape or desert garden. It can form offsets that can be transplanted or left to form a cluster.

   A. p. truncata (gentry agave) is similar to *A. p. huachucensis* but forms more of a globe shape. It is especially decorative and much sought after by *Agave* collectors.

Agave salmiana
Pulque Agave • Salms Agave
Maguey de Pulque

Formerly listed in error as *A. weberi*, this bulky *Agave* is known to grow 5 to 6 feet (1.5 to 1.8m) high and 10 to 13 (3.1 to 4m) feet wide. Bold guttered leaves 10 to 13 inches (25.4 to 33cm) wide have wavy edges and a long sharp spine at the tip. Individual plants vary in color from dark green to gray green.

The bloom stalk may rise to 25 feet (7.6m) high. There are a number of varieties with varying tolerances of cold. This is the *Agave* from which people of Mexico make pulque, an alcoholic beverage. It is grown on upland plantations in north-central Mexico. Just as the stalk starts to bloom, they cut off the developing bud and then cut into the center of the plant, making a bowl. The bowl collects great amounts of juice that can be gathered day after day. The juice is then fermented into pulque. Subtropical to desert effect.

Agave vilmoriniana
Octopus Agave • Midas Agave

Blue-gray with a sprawling, twisted form and leaf blades more slender than *A. americana*, the octopus agave is a striking specimen plant in the ground or in containers. It is one of the few *Agaves* without sharp points on leaf ends or saw-toothed thorns on the leaf margins. It seldom reaches more than 3 or 4 feet (0.9 to 1.2m) high but may spread to 6 feet (1.8m) wide.

Blends with tropical or desert settings or with rocks and other structural materials.

Give moderate water in summer and protect from cold and reflected sun. Accepts shade and does nicely in garden situations. Space 3 to 6 feet (0.9 to 1.8m) apart for massing. Use only in the middle and low zones because it is sensitive to cold. May bloom in three to five years. Treat to prevent grubs.

Agave weberi
Weber Agave • Smooth-Edged Agave

Similar to *A. americana* but slightly smaller and more refined, this *Agave* grows to as much as 6 feet (1.8m) high and 13 feet (4m) wide. Smooth-edged, almost luminous leaves can be gray-green or a a deeper blue-green. Leaves are 4 to 6 feet (1.2 to 1.8m) long and about 8 inches (20.3cm) wide and are armed only at the tip, without the saw-toothed edges of most desert *Agaves*. The bloom stalk can rise to 23 feet (7m) or higher. Plant is noticeably sensitive to light and closes up when conditions are too hot or too bright, even showing some light patches similar to sunburn on the outer leaves. This usually goes away if the weather moderates and it receives rain or irrigation. It is more tolerant of cold than even *A. americana*.

Agave vilmoriniana

It needs some supplemental irrigation, especially in hot summer areas. Plants may bloom within four or five years or so. *A. weberi* spawns offsets, but not as vigorously as *A. americana*. Several offsets are produced over the life cycle and can be transplanted or left in place to fill in after the parent has bloomed and died. It is a worthy plant for a tropical effect when combined with other bold foliage or colorful plants.

Ailanthus altissima

Family: Simaroubaceae
Ailanthus • Tree of Heaven
Copal Tree • Varnish Tree

This is the tree from the book *A Tree Grows in Brooklyn*, one that grows and thrives in pollution and other poor conditions. Versatile, with a handsome form and medium green foliage, it grows rapidly to 20 feet (6.1m), spreading 15 feet (4.6m). Later it grows more slowly to an eventual 50 feet (15.2m) by 40 feet (12.2m), if the soil is deep. These trees will accommodate the space they are given, and are often seen in a row against buildings or as a grove of saplings. Often the grove multiplies because of its tendency to produce suckers. Decorative seeds appear in summer on female trees after a spring bloom (April or May). While not as refined as some trees, this Chinese native should not be overlooked as a fast-growing shade tree.

Special design features: Vertical trunk with interesting twig structure. Heavy shade. Winter deciduous—gives winter sun and summer shade. Golden fall color. Tropical

effect, especially in rows, when it forms thickets sprouting from roots. Strong, strange scent.

Uses: Ailanthus is often condemned as a "weed tree," but, although it does have its faults, there are few trees that thrive under such harsh conditions. It grows almost anywhere—city, sanitary landfill, street or yard. Plant several together to make a sapling grove for a narrow space. Try it where conditions are poor but shade is needed. Naturalizes in alleys, along walls or railroad tracks where it gets extra water.

Disadvantages: Root suckers come up in lawns. Large trees can develop buttress roots and heave structures if set too close. May reseed profusely. Very invasive in poorly maintained areas in both town and countryside. Odd scent.

Planting and care: Plant any time of year from containers or bare root in winter. It can also be grown from viable seed. Trees have stout trunks and usually do not need pruning and training. If pruning is necessary, trim in late winter during dormant season. Remove suckers near base unless you desire a sapling grove. Suckers in lawns can be mowed out.

Ailanthus altissima

Ailanthus altissima

All Zones
Deciduous
Soil: Tolerant. Widely adaptable.
Sun: Part shade to full or reflected sun.
Water: Moderate to ample. Drought tolerant for periods when established. Grows with runoff in areas receiving 10 inches (254mm) or more of annual rainfall.
Temperature: Hardy to 0F (-18C). Tolerates heat.
Maintenance: Periodic to seasonal. None in areas where spread of plants isn't a problem.

Aloe species

Family: Liliaceae

Native to Africa and the Middle East, *Aloes* are generally smaller in scale and less tolerant of cold than their American counterparts, the *Agaves*. They make dramatic accent plants in containers or in landscapes of the low zone where there are no hard freezes. Some survive well outside in the middle zone and will recover quickly from a freeze. The blooms appear on stalks above the plants, some in candelabra forms and some on single stalks. All flowers are tubular and range from yellow to orange to red depending on the species. In drought, the leaves dry up from the tip and the *Aloe* turns a brownish red. Irrigation makes them look succulent and green, with rusty tints. They usually form colonies and bloom annually (some semiannually) without dying. There is a mite that deforms the flowers and leaves of some aloes.

Special design features: Spiky succulent leaves. Some species may have two or more bloom periods. Hummingbirds love flowers. Tropical or desert effect. Periodic bloom lends color and a vertical effect.

Uses: Desert or rock gardens and transitional areas. Attractive as scattered clumps with bare earth and rocks. Attractive in containers. Underplant for palms or *Yuccas*.

Disadvantages: No pests or diseases except an occasional infestation of a mite that deforms plants. Old clumps may look unkempt after blooming and need to be groomed. Plants located in direct or reflected or summer sun will have a dry and unkempt look unless given enough water.

Planting and care: Plant or transplant from containers or divisions in spring. Set single plants about 18 to 24 inches (to 45.7 cm) apart to establish a dense clump in two or three years, after which time the clumps may be separated. Immediately discard plants damaged by thrips.

Aloe hybrid 'Blue Elf'

Aloe species

Low zone and warmer areas of middle zone
Evergreen
Soil: Tolerant. Good drainage.
Sun: Open or part shade. Full or reflected sun.
Water: None to moderate.
Temperature: 28F (-2.2C) to 25F (-4C). Root hardy and tolerant of high heat.
Maintenance: Periodic. Thin overcrowded colonies and remove dead bloom stalks.

Aloe ferox

Aloe saponaria

Aloe arborescens
Tree Aloe

A treelike *Aloe* that thrives in milder coastal regions but isn't hardy enough to tolerate the extremes of heat and cold of the middle zone. Can reach 18 feet (5.5m) high and has many arms and thick gray-green spiny leaves. Spiky clusters of red to yellow flowers bloom in winter. Tolerant of salt spray but damaged at 29F (-1.7C).

Aloe barbadensis (see *Aloe vera*)

Aloe ferox
Tree Aloe • Cape Aloe

Thick, succulent terminal leaf rosettes grow as wide as 3 feet (0.9m). Top trunks may reach 6 to 8 feet (1.8 to 2.4m) or higher over time and are clothed in dried leaves unless stripped. Leaves will persist if not removed. Large-branched stalks up to 4 feet (1.2m) above the plant produce a brief show of scarlet tubular flowers that are damaged at 28F (-2C). Use as bold statement or accent plant with a striking silhouette in areas protected from heavy frosts. This *Aloe*, as many plants do, grows much larger in the frost-free marine influence and humidity of California.

Aloe hybrid 'Blue Elf'
Blue Elf Aloe

This clumping *Aloe* grows to 18 inches (45.7cm) tall by 2 feet (0.6m) wide with narrow silver-blue leaves, which contrast with the orange-red flowers that bloom January through April. Tolerates full sun in the low zone with no signs of sunburn, but will freeze if the temperature goes below 20F (-7C).

Aloe saponaria
(A. latifolia)
African Aloe

This *Aloe* from South Africa is a low clumping plant that reaches 1 foot (30.5cm) high, with pointed succulent leaves growing in a rosette form. Leaves are pale to medium green, tinged red, with dull white spots. Thorny brown teeth edge the leaf blades, which are sometimes dry and twisted at the tips, especially in dry or cold weather. Plants show more red in cold weather if exposed to strong sunlight or if irrigation is meager. Plants grown in the shade are more green and succulent. Scarlet to yellowish flowers appear two or three times a year. Purplish stalks add a vertical dimension, rising 18 to 30 inches (45.7 to 76.2cm) above the 9- to 12-inch (22.9- to 30.5-cm) plant. One plant produces a dense clump in three or four years by sending out numerous offsets. Sometimes, old clumps become so dense that they die out in the center, resulting in a ring. It's best to replant before it reaches this point or you essentially throw away two-thirds of the plants.

Use for tropical or desert effect; in desert, wild or rock gardens; in transitional areas; as ground or bank cover; or as an underplant for palms or *Yuccas*. Spiky foliage adds interest and periodic bloom lends color and a vertical effect. Good container plant. Very susceptible to the deforming Aloe mite.

Aloe vera

(*A. barbadensis, A. perfoliata vera*)
Medicinal Aloe • Barbados Aloe

Aloe vera, originally from North Africa, was brought by Spanish padres to the New World and planted in mission herb gardens. It has been used for centuries as a treatment for burns and skin afflictions. Leaves of spiky succulent rosettes grow upward to 12 or 18 inches (30.5 to 45.7cm). They have sharp tips and whitish to reddish teeth along the margins. In March and April, bloom stalks rise to 3 feet (0.9m) above the plant, bearing dense arrow-shaped clusters of yellowish flowers (or orange, if a hybrid), which hummingbirds love. May have two or more bloom periods. One plant quickly spawns many offsets, forming a dense clump in a few years. Clumps of old plantings may reach widths up to 10 feet (3.1m) if not divided. Prune and thin in May. Plants are very drought- and heat-resistant. Hardy in the middle and low zones, to 25F (-4C).

Aloe vera

Araucaria bidwillii

Family: Auricariaceae
Bunya-Bunya

This genus once grew widely throughout the world but is now found in nature only in the Southern Hemisphere. It is the genus of the pre-Ice Age trees of the petrified forest in Arizona. Bunya-bunya, an Australian native, is an erect conifer with horizontal branches that droop downward at the tips. Juvenile leaves are a shiny dark green with sharply pointed tips, prickly to the touch. Mature leaves are small woody ovals up to 1/2 inch (1.3cm) long that grow in overlapping spirals. These leaves do not appear for a number of years, until the tree has attained height and maturity. It is not known how tall a bunya-bunya will get in the desert, but specimens in the coastal valleys of California reach 80 feet (24.4m) with vertical broadly spreading crowns that are rounded at the top. Mature trees produce heavy cones that drop with a crash: not a tree to picnic under. Mature plants are skyline trees.

Special design features: Bold vertical dome-like form with spreading, somewhat pendulous branches. Interesting structure and foliage.

Uses: Excellent container plant for several years before it outgrows the space. Specimen or emphasis plant for large public spaces (away from high-use areas) or for impressive entrances to residential or institutional projects. Silhouette plant against tall structures. Mature trees are thought to be too large for the average residence but do not get that large for many, many years.

Disadvantages: Slow grower. Prickly juvenile foliage can be annoying near frequented areas. If walks are established near trees later, remove lower branches. Foliage may brown out in extreme or prolonged cold or if soil becomes too dry. Iron chlorosis in alkaline soils. Heavy cones on old trees fall and could injure people under the tree.

Planting and care: Plant from containers in spring when danger of frost has passed. Be sure tree has an ample planting hole with good drainage. This ensures room for maximum root growth. Stake trunks on young trees until they are self-supporting.

Araucaria bidwillii

Araucaria bidwillii

Low and middle zones; protected locations in high zone
Evergreen
Soil: Tolerant, but needs good drainage and adequate soil moisture. Prefers improved garden soil.
Sun: Part shade to full sun.
Water: Moderate to ample, especially when young.
Temperature: Foliage on young trees or container plants browns in intense or prolonged cold below 25F (-4C). Older trees in the ground tolerate much colder temperatures without damage.
Maintenance: Periodic.

Asparagus densiflorus 'Sprengeri'

(A. sprengeri)
Family: Liliaceae
Sprenger Asparagus
Asparagus Fern

This festive plant of the Victorian Age is back in style. It is a multiple-branched trailing plant with small, bright yellow-green prickly needlelike leaves. It grows fast in spring and moderately the rest of the year. On the ground it mounds 1 foot to 2 feet (30.5 to 61cm) high or cascades over walls, banks or containers with branches trailing to 4 feet (1.2m) or more. A sparse late-spring bloom of tiny white flowers may produce a few bright red fall berries. Roots develop fleshy nodules that store water, allowing the plant to withstand periods of drought or neglect.

Cultivars and other notable species: 'Sprengeri Compacta' is like the regular 'Sprengeri' with a more compact mounding form and tighter growth habit. 'Myers,' Myers asparagus, is different in form from the trailing asparagus fern. The bright green foliage in spiky bundles like fox tails is decorative. Good container plant, for close-up viewing or as an accent. Less tolerant of cold than 'Sprengeri,' but recovers quickly.

Special design features: Ferny effect. Color and texture contrast to dark evergreens.

Uses: Containers, especially hanging pots. Attractive trailing and spilling over planter walls or banks. For low borders or edgings, especially framing colorful flower beds. A billowing underplant, ground cover or foundation plant.

Disadvantages: Iron chlorosis. Sometimes develops dry stems and foliage if neglected or if growing conditions are too hot or too dry.

Planting and care: Plant from containers in spring after danger of frost has passed, or in protected areas any time. Space 30 inches (76.2cm) apart for a ground or bank cover. Groom by cutting back the longest trailers or removing dried ones. Plants may be cut back severely to rejuvenate. Prune and thin in July. Give extra iron for deeper green foliage.

Asparagus densiflorus 'Sprengeri'

Asparagus densiflorus 'Sprengeri'

Low and middle zones
Evergreen
Soil: Tolerant. Best in enriched soil with good drainage.
Sun: Any exposure, but becomes stringy in deep shade.
Water: Moderate to ample. Established plants with well developed roots tolerate some drought.
Temperature: Freezes back at about 28F (-2C). Recovers quickly in warm weather. Because plants are usually grown in more protected places or they are brought indoors in winter, freezing is seldom a problem.
Maintenance: Periodic.

Asparagus falcatus

Family: Liliaceae
Sicklethorn Asparagus

A bold, rapidly growing, twining vine native to tropical areas from Ceylon to Africa. Leaves are slender, elongated, shiny and light green. They grow in clusters of three to five at branch ends. The sickle-shaped thorns on the branches help it climb and twine over structures to 10 or as much as 40 feet (3.1 to 12.2m) in frost-free zones. It will also climb over trees and neighbors' shrubs and could be invasive in adjoining areas. If allowed, new growth will twine around support wire or a lattice. Plant will eventually develop fleshy roots that store water, enabling it to survive dry periods. Tiny, fragrant, white flowers bloom May to June, followed by brown berries. Flowers aren't showy but plant has an excellent foliage mass.

Special design features: Dense cover; refined foliage.

Uses: In frost-free areas, a fast-growing ground cover or vine in large-scale plantings or over structures. A surprisingly good container plant, tolerating heat and occasional drying out. It becomes more compact with the roots restricted in the container.

Disadvantages: Thorns make it difficult to prune. Possible reseeding and naturalizing in adjacent areas. May die all or partway back in freezes, but recovers fast in spring.

Planting and care: Plant from container in spring or early summer and guide its growth. Prune in March. This plant needs plenty of room to grow. Avoid confined areas.

Asparagus falcatus

Asparagus falcatus

Low zone; marginal in middle zone
Evergreen unless frozen back
Soil: Garden soil with good drainage.
Sun: Full to reflected sun. Gets leggy in shade.
Water: Ample water until established. Weekly deep irrigation to maintain a good appearance. Fleshy roots enable it to withstand brief periods of drying out.
Temperature: Tolerant to the mid 20s F (-3 to -5C); foliage freezes at 28F (-2C).
Maintenance: Little in large-scale informal plantings. Train and selectively prune if using in a container or over fences and other structures.

Atriplex species

Family: Chenopodiaceae

Saltbushes are an important group of somewhat drab and weedy plants, which grow naturally in most arid regions of the world. They are amazingly well adapted to arid conditions, withstanding saline-alkaline soils, wind, heat, cold and drought, surviving on as little as 3 inches (762mm) of annual rainfall and accepting seawater irrigation. Their often spongy leaves are used for water storage. As the water is used over an extended period, the leaves contract, turning from gray to white or silver. This color change occurs when the plant absorbs and deposits salts from the soil through the leaf pores. The lighter color helps reflect the sun's intense rays. These adaptations make the saltbush plant group extremely important for vegetating the driest land, and also as a browse for animals. With a little extra water from runoff or irrigation, saltbushes do well. Blooms from March to May.

Special design features: Informal, rustic. Many tolerate regular clipping into formal hedges.

Uses: Valuable for replanting open areas, or in desert or wild gardens where little or no care is given. Ground or bank cover. Boundary, transitional, or desert edge plant in Xeriscapes.

Disadvantages: Some species are difficult to obtain. Sometimes rangy or unkempt.

Planting and care: Plant from containers or cuttings or sow from seed in spring. Space randomly for a natural look. Protect young plants from cold and irrigate until they are well established. Prune or trim in July.

Atriplex canescens

Atriplex species

All zones except as noted
Evergreen to deciduous
Soil: Tolerant of most soils. Many species require good drainage, but some even tolerate (or are native to) tight clay soils that drain poorly.
Sun: Full to reflected sun.
Water: None to moderate. Looks best with deep occasional irrigation.
Temperature: Variable according to plant origin—hardy to somewhat tender, usually to about 0F (-18C). Tolerant of heat.
Maintenance: Little.

Atriplex canescens
Four-Wing Saltbush • Chamiso
Cenzo • Saltsage

This multiple-branched, gray-green shrub is found throughout the western part of the United States and Mexico at elevations from 150 to 7,000 feet (45.7 to 2134m). Plants are fairly slow growers, reaching 3 to 6 feet (0.9 to 1.8m) high spreading 4 to 8 feet (1.2 to 2.4m) wide. They may be sparse or densely foliated with narrow leaves 1/2 to 2 inches (1.3 to 5.1cm) long. Fruits cluster at the ends of young branches, forming golden cascades, are somewhat decorative. Set out seedlings or start from cuttings in spring (young plants are tender to cold). Space 1-1/2 to 4 feet (0.45 to 1.2m) apart for a hedge or screen, which may be clipped or shaped any time. Water until established. Grows fastest and looks best with regular irrigation.

Atriplex lentiformis
Quail Bush • Lens-Scale
White Thistle • Big Saltbush

A showy shrub native to the low and middle deserts of the Southwest. Given ample water, it grows at a moderate to fast rate to 12 feet (3.7m) high, spreading 8 to 15 feet (2.4 to 4.6m) wide. It grows slowly to about 5 feet (1.5m) in dry areas without supplemental irrigation. Bare in winter but handsome in summer: Hollylike blue-gray leaves are 1-1/2 inches (3.8cm) long on slender, sometimes spiny branches that are pale gray to whitish in color. Clusters of decorative fruit show at the branch tips late spring to early summer. Tolerant of high heat and cold. Can survive on 3-1/2 inches (889mm) of rainfall a year in deep soils where its deep root system can penetrate to draw on subsurface moisture.

Atriplex lentiformis breweri
Brewer Saltbush

The best saltbush for garden use. There is almost a lush quality to this gray-foliaged shrub with its soft, triangular, 2-inch (5.1-cm) leaves, which cover the plant densely. A slow to moderate grower, this mounding plant reaches 3 to 8 feet (0.9 to 2.4m) high and 6 to 8 feet (1.8 to 2.4m) wide, depending on growing conditions. Heavy decorative clusters of golden fruit appear at the top of the foliage in late spring. Neglected plants growing under difficult circumstances have a rangy appearance. Attractive with some shaping; it makes an excellent clipped hedge.

Atriplex semibaccata
Australian Saltbush

A drought-tolerant and widely adaptable plant, the Australian saltbush was introduced in California in the 1880s, where it has naturalized. It was later brought to Arizona and New Mexico, probably carried in the wool of sheep from California or Australia. Of the varieties found in the United States, 'Corto' possesses the most desirable combination of characteristics: uniform growth habit, drought tolerance and cold hardiness. This semiherbaceous, semi-prostrate plant grows rapidly from seed to 8 to 10 inches (20.3 to 25.4cm) high with a spread of 6 feet (1.8m). Leaves are gray-green and numerous. Inconspicuous flowers produce fleshy fruit that turn red at maturity and are attractive in the fall. Plants reseed themselves and spread under favorable cond-itions. An evergreen perennial in warm areas. Older plants are killed back to the crown at 20F (-7C) or below. Young plants should recover in spring from winter temp-eratures of 17F (-9C); probably killed at 10F (-12C).

Atriplex lentiformis breweri

Baccharis centennial hybrid

(*B. pilularis* x *B. sarothroides*)
Family: Asteraceae (Compositae)
Centennial Coyote Brush

A billowing ground cover for larger areas. This hybrid may grow 2 to 3 feet (0.6 to 0.9m) high and 3 to 5 feet (0.9 to 1.5m) wide. Blooms from September to November. A female plant that produces tufted cottony seeds in fall, but not in the great abundance of its relative *Baccharis sarothroides*. Tolerant of heat, cold, root fungi and other diseases. When plant is established, cut irrigation by one-third, which will help keep the plants more compact in form. Long lived in low zone and not particularly susceptible to damping off like *B. pilularis*.

Cultivars and other notable species: *Baccharis centennial* hybrid 'Starn Thompson™' is an outstanding spreading evergreen male plant that produces no seedheads and thus no mess. Difficult to tell apart from *B. centennial* unless in bloom or are bearing trademark or patent tag. Both are a bright green even when water is restricted.

Can grow to 3 to 4 feet (0.9 to 1.2m) tall by 4 to 5 feet (1.2 to 1.5m) wide.

Special design features: A refreshing bright green mound in the arid landscape.

Uses: One of the better bank or ground covers for large- or small-scale plantings in arid regions. Best in large spaces such as golf courses, commercial projects, parks, highway medians and naturalistic areas. Can withstand temporary flooding of retention basins.

Disadvantages: Female produces a few airborne seedheads in fall that may sprout and appear more like one of its parents, creating a messy look unless pulled out. May become woody with age.

Planting and care: Plant from containers from fall to spring in hot low and middle zones; any season in high zone. Plants installed in summer are slower to develop. Cut back in spring before new growth starts. Feed with nitrogen.

Baccharis centennial hybrid

Baccharis centennial hybrid

All zones but best in the high zone
Evergreen
Soil: Tolerates most soils.
Sun: Sun to part shade.
Water: Weekly the first hot season to aid developing plants. Irrigate at wider intervals after cover has been established, reducing water by 30 percent to maintain compact size.
Temperature: Hardy to at least 5F (-15C) and tolerant of hot summers once established.
Maintenance: Little care except to prevent weed invasion with a pre-emergent. Prune out old branches in fall or winter to rejuvenate by encouraging new growth and prevent woody appearance. Avoid pruning in summer to avoid sunburning interior growth.

Baccharis pilularis

Family: Asteraceae (Compositae)
Dwarf Coyote Brush • Chaparral Broom

A dense planting of this low-mounding California native looks like a patch of giant moss from a distance. Small, closely set, bright green toothed leaves densely cover this trailing, ground-hugging plant. Plants grow at a moderate rate 6 to 24 inches (15.2 to 61cm) high, trailing 3 to 6 feet (0.9 to 1.8m) wide or wider. Fastest growth is in the cool of the year. Plants look best in spring and may merely hold their own in summer. To avoid the cottony blossom fluffs the females produce, seek plants grown from male cuttings. The species is somewhat rangy and is not planted as often as the cultivar below.

Cultivars and other notable species: 'Twin Peaks' is a male selection, cutting grown and very dense and low.

Special design features: Dense mounding or billowing plant. Oriental effect. Attractive poolside appearance with water and rocks and adapted waterside plants.

Uses: Ground cover and rock gardens. Low edging or filler plant. Erosion control. Fire retardant.

Disadvantages: Subject to infestations of red spider mite in June and July. Branches become woody and need to be cut back. Plants seem to be weak in hot summer areas and may die out or brown suddenly.

Planting and care: Plant from flats or containers any time except in the heat of summer. Space 30 inches (76.2cm) apart for cover. In fall remove old woody branches and thin to rejuvenate. Fill in bare spots. Spray for red spider mite.

Baccharis pilularis

Baccharis pilularis

All zones, but marginal in low and middle
Evergreen
Soil: Tolerant. Accepts damp situation in cool weather, but needs good drainage in summer.
Sun: Does best with full sun. Accepts part shade or reflected sun.
Water: Occasional to moderate. Looks best with winter irrigation and infrequent waterings in summer; allow to dry out in between.
Temperature: Mostly hardy to cold. Some frost damage in the coldest areas. Tolerant of some heat. Tends to damp off and fail in hot summers of low and middle zones, especially during periods of summer rain.
Maintenance: Periodic.

Bambusa species

Family: Poaceae (Graminae)

Bamboos are perennial grasses of great ornamental value. They range in size from low, ground-hugging plants to the giant timber bamboo, with woody canes 35 feet (10.7m) or more in height and up to 6 inches (15.2cm) in diameter. Bamboo canes may be hollow or solid, and are divided into sections called *internodes* by joints called *nodes*.

Nodes on the upper part of the plant produce buds that develop into leaf-bearing branches. In larger bamboos these divide into secondary branches that bear the flat leaf blades.

Bamboos are of two kinds—running and clumping. Running bamboos, represented in this book under *Phyllostachys*, have underground rhizomes that rapidly grow horizontally to varying distances from the original plant before rising from the ground to start new stands. Large groves can shoot up in a number of years unless the rhizomes are controlled. Running bamboos are generally hardier to cold than clumping bamboos and are also more self-contained in a garden, not spreading out of control.

Clumping bamboos (*Bambusa*), more tropical in nature and more tender to cold, expand outwardly cane by cane as new shoots spring up at the clump edges. They do not send out horizontal stems or rhizomes. In a new planting, canes are small at first, no wider in diameter than the original shoot. Old plantings develop into tight clumps with the canes growing to maximum size. Many bamboos flower only once after many years of growth. They usually die after flowering but in rare instances have recovered after several years of intensive care. Whole stands and even the divisions taken from them over the years will flower at the same time, no matter where they are located.

While it is often said that bamboo (especially the running types) is difficult to eradicate, this is not necessarily so. To eliminate bamboo, cut out all canes and trim off all shoots as they start to grow. The plants will exhaust their vigor and die. In arid regions, the easiest way is to eliminate watering.

Special design features: As a landscape plant bamboos give a special mood and character to a place, evoking mystery, intimacy, the tropics, or the Orient, depending on the setting. The rustling sound of bamboo leaves in the wind is an added dimension to the ambiance.

Note: Most bamboos are from the tropics and subtropics. Some are temperate-zone plants hardy enough to grow in even the northern states. Because conditions of generally lower humidity and greater seasonal temperature fluctuations are hard on bamboo in arid lands, only a few of the more successful are listed here. In the gardens of Japan, bamboo stands are thinned out to show just a few canes as a restrained design feature.

Uses: Planters and containers. Specimens, screens, style or mood setters. Many tropical species make great feature plants in protected intimate gardens sheltered from cold. While not hardy in all three zones, they can be used in any protected situation, with water availability the only limitation.

Disadvantages: Looks scraggly in cold winters or after periods of drought stress. Greedy roots. Leaves litter in swimming pools but attractive as a ground mulch.

Planting and care: Plant tender species from containers in spring, when danger of frost has passed, or divide old clumps in spring and replant. Plant hardy types any time. When dividing, cut away a segment with at least three shoots and cut those shoots back to 2 or 3 feet (0.6 to 0.9m). Be sure segment contains numerous roots. Replant where desired, setting 2 to 3 feet (0.6 to 0.9m) apart if you want the planting to fill in. Keep constantly damp until new growth begins. For fastest growth, feed with nitrogen and potassium and water regularly as you would a lawn. Do not cultivate or walk near clumps, as new shoots may be damaged.

Bambusa species

Zones: See individual species descriptions.
Evergreen
Soil: Tolerant. Prefers improved garden soil. Dislikes alkaline situations.
Sun: Part shade to full or reflected sun.
Water: Moderate to ample.
Temperature: See individual species descriptions.
Maintenance: Periodic care to thin out old canes.

Bambusa glaucescens 'Alphonse Karr'
(B. verticillaga)
'Alphonse Karr' Bamboo

This lush medium-size bamboo is an outstanding clumping variety, exceptionally graceful and attractive. Somewhat slow to develop, cane shafts eventually reach 10 to 15 feet (3.1 to 4.6m) in height, up to 30 feet (9.2m) with optimum conditions. Cane diameters are usually about 1/2 to 3/4 inch (1.3 to 1.9cm). 'Alphonse Karr' is recognizable by the pink and green stripes on the bases of the young stems. Great for oriental, tropical or jungle effect. Handsome silhouette. Verdant plant for the summer garden. Unthinned it makes a good screen visually and for sun and wind. Hardy in low and middle zones to 15F (-9C).

Bambusa multiplex riviereorum
(B. argentea nana)
Chinese Goddess Bamboo

A dwarf bamboo with solid stems and fernlike foliage, the Chinese goddess bamboo grows only 4 to 6 feet (1.2 to 1.8m) high, with occasional plants reaching 10 feet (3.1m) under favorable conditions. This plant is unusually refined and graceful in the summer garden, especially for close-up viewing in a small space. Use as a background for garden sculpture or lanterns, or as a specimen. Combines well with masonry or natural materials. Leaves often

Bambusa multiplex riviereorum

Bambusa oldhamii

have dry edges and may be completely straw-colored in winter. Plants sometimes look unkempt, especially in cold areas. Hardy in low and middle zones. Low temperature range is 15F (-9C). Requires part shade in hot, arid locations, with shelter from hot dry winds.

Bambusa oldhamii
(*Sinocalamus oldhamii*, *Dendrocalamus latiflorus*)
Oldham Bamboo
Clump Giant Timber Bamboo

Native to China and Taiwan, this tall, rustling, clumping grasslike plant gives a cool feeling of retreat and contemplation. Once established, it is a fast grower, with canes reaching 15 to 25 feet (4.6 to 7.6m), occasionally 40 feet (12.2m), with a diameter of 3 inches (7.6cm). New canes suddenly pop up and grow at an amazing rate but are never larger in diameter than the original sprout. Deep green canes sometimes turn a golden hue when older. The medium green and dry leaves give a variegated effect. It produces no runners. The plant spreads laterally and sends up even taller canes as the clump matures. Cultivation should be kept at a

minimum around bamboo clumps during the growth period to avoid injuring the new sprouts. A fast hedge or screen. Great for high protected courtyards away from winter chill, or against tall buildings on southeast, south or west sides. Anywhere in mild winter areas. Foliage damaged at 20F (-7C). New or developing canes may be injured around 28F (-2C).

Bambusa glaucescens 'Alphonse Karr'

Bauhinia species

Family: Fabaceae (Leguminosae)

Flowering trees and shrubs from the edge of the tropics, orchid trees present a spectacular display of delicate 2-inch (5cm) orchid-like flowers for a long period. Large bright green leaves shaped like round-winged butterflies cover plants most of the year, dropping for a short period after the bloom. An exception is summer-blooming *B. forficata*, which may be evergreen in warm areas. Because of their spectacular flowers and handsome foliage, orchid trees are very desirable in the right location. They are not attractive when frozen back regularly because they bloom on last year's wood and must go through a recovery period. This is especially true of *B. variegata*. Plants will survive, but may not have many seasons of bloom. If you have a warm sunny spot you may want to grow this tree. Give it added protection during the first few years when it is most sensitive to cold.

Special design features: Tropical effect with a spectacular bloom.

Uses: Patio or courtyard. Street trees in mild winter areas.

Disadvantages: Frosted plants go through a long unattractive recovery period. Sometimes older foliage looks mangy in between blossom periods. Susceptible to iron chlorosis.

Planting and care: Plant from containers in spring when weather warms up. Stake and prune young trees carefully. With cold-damaged trees, wait until foliage reappears before pruning, so that you don't trim living wood. Pale trees may need extra feeding in alkaline soils. When leaves are burned from soil salts, give long slow soakings to leach soil.

Bauhinia forficate

Bauhinia species

Low zone and protected locations in middle zone
Briefly deciduous
Soil: Tolerant. Leaves may burn in alkaline conditions.
Sun: Part shade to full or reflected sun.
Water: Moderate to ample.
Temperature: Hardy from 20 to 25F (-7 to -4C), depending on species.
Maintenance: Seasonal.

Bauhinia blakeana
Hong Kong Orchid Tree

With stunning tropical effects at the peak of its bloom, this *Bauhinia* is one of the showiest flowering specimens or accent trees for the oasis zone in a mild-winter landscape. In near frost-free areas, the tree grows to 15 to 30 feet high (4.6 to 9.2m) with equal spread and an umbrella-shaped crown. Gray-green double-lobed leaves to 6 or 8 inches (15.2 to 20.3cm) across are partly deciduous from fall into winter flowering period. With no leaves, the flowers are more showy. Flowers to 6 inches across (15.2cm) range in color from pink to purple to maroon. No seeds. Trees like full sun to part shade but no hot drying winds that tatter foliage and dry it out. When established, mature trees need irrigation every week or two depending on the weather. Selectively trim young trees for a good form and appearance. Frosty temperatures may eliminate the flower crop, and intense cold will disfigure it. In highly alkaline, salty, or poorly drained soils it can become chlorotic.

Bauhinia forficate
(B. corniculata, B. candicans)
White Butterfly Orchid Tree

A small tree with medium green foliage, the white butterfly orchid tree is a moderate grower to 20 feet (6.1m) with a wide flat crown. Plant silhouettes are often picturesque, with a leaning trunk and angled branches, thorny at the joints, becoming twisted with age. Delicate white flowers resembling butterfly orchids may appear in late spring, continuing as a pleasant sprinkling through summer. Flowers in clusters open at night, lasting into the following day. Hardy to below 20F (-7C) but becomes deciduous. This South American native is the best orchid tree for the middle zone because blooms appear in spring after frosts. It is also a hardier plant.

Bauhinia lunarioides
(B. congesta)
Chihuahuan Orchid Shrub
Anacacho Orchid Tree

This deciduous, delicate large shrub or small tree grows at a slow to moderate rate to 6 to 8 feet (1.8 to 2.4m) or higher, spreading to 8 feet (2.4m) wider, depending on water availability. The thornless branches support small leaflets that grow in pairs, resembling

butterflies. Tiny orchid flowers ranging in color from white to shades of pink cover plant from spring into summer. May bloom again in fall in response to rain. It is propagated from seed. A white one is available commercially. Tolerates most soils. May need a little pruning and shaping after bloom to guide its form and prevent wind damage. It can tolerate complete drought in areas with 12 inches (305mm) of annual rainfall when established, but looks better if given a monthly soak. Can be grown as a delicate small patio tree, specimen, or overplant to smaller plants that want a little summer shade. Good as a background shrub. A fine-textured spring and summer color plant. Grows in low, middle, and high zones and is hardy to at least 5F (-15C). Protect from rabbits until it forms a trunk or trunks to 1-1/2 or 2 inches (3.6 to 5.1cm) in diameter.

Bauhinia punctata
(B. galpinii)
Red Bauhinia • Red Orchid Shrub

This is a typical *Bauhinia* with red orchid-like flowers. It can be a sprawling shrub or trained as a small tree. Its almost vining character lends itself well to espalier; the abundance and vibrant color of the blossoms allows it to be used like a *Bougainvillea*. Thrives in hot locations and is as hardy as *B. variegata*.

Bauhinia variegata
Purple Orchid Tree

This native to India and China grows at a moderate rate to 30 feet (9.2m) with a broad bushy crown of medium green foliage. Most attractive when grown with multiple trunks, but will grow as a standard as well. Bloom begins in midwinter and lasts into spring. Bloom is massive, covering tree with 3-inch (7.5cm) or wider orchid-like flowers. Each broad, overlapping petal ranges in color from lavender to magenta and purple, sometimes white. Central petal is marked dark purple. Bloom often continues while leaves are falling, which is sometimes unattractive. The most spectacular blooms occur when leaves have fallen early from cold or prolonged drought and masses of flowers grace the crown. New leaves appear as bloom ends. Trees may have heavy crop of beans. Hardy to 22F (-6C). Best in low zone, but performs satisfactorily in warm protected locations in middle zone.

Bauhinia lunarioides

Bauhinia variegata

Bauhinia punctata

Bauhinia variegata 'Candida'

Bougainvillea species

Family: Nyctaginaceae
Bougainvillea

One of the most delightful and rewarding of the color plants is *Bougainvillea*, a native of Brazil. In bloom it creates beauty and flamboyant color in any environment and is now grown and appreciated in warm climates throughout the world. *Bougainvillea* color is not from blossoms, but from bracts, specialized leaves, which enclose the two or three small blossoms. Brachts appear in masses of purple, magenta, red, orange, yellow or white. Most *Bougainvilleas* are woody vines that naturally climb by hooking their sharp thorns into support. Some are newly developed shrubs. In cultivation vining types can be trained as large, sprawling, shrubby masses over banks or trellises or formed into standard trees. Vines grow as high as 30 feet (9.2m) and spread to 20 feet (6.1m).

The two original species of *Bougainvillea* are *B. spectabilis* (sometimes refered to as *B. brasiliensis*), purple, and *B. glabra*, red. *B. spectabilis* is more hardy to cold and a more vigorous grower and bloomer in cool summer areas than *B. glabra*. Throughout the years these plants have been so manipulated by horticulturists that it is difficult to tell which species each plant came from. Below, unless we are listing the unaltered species, we ignore the species name and list the cultivar name only.

Special design features: Riot of tropical color. Promotes a festive mood.

Uses: Color or emphasis plants for warm locations, such as south or west walls. Against hot walls with overhangs in areas where some frost is expected. Striking on trellises. Hot banks in the warmer zones where they will not be frozen back. Specimens. Containers. Train as trees in warm areas.

Disadvantages: Root balls tend to fall apart when plants are taken from container or transplanted. Aggressive grower—it can take over in frost-free areas. Frost-damaged plants are slow to recover in spring. Trim off damaged wood in mid-April or so, after plant has a chance to recover. Plant begins recovery from base, so unless you give it a chance to sprout new growth, you may be removing live wood. Too thorny for areas near walks or doorways.

Planting and care: Place where plant will have plenty of room to spread out. Set out new plants in spring after danger of frost has passed. Remove from containers carefully to keep root ball intact. To avoid problem of a crumbling root ball, slice or perforate containers and remove bottoms before planting, then set in ground. This will allow roots to spread. Metal containers will rust away with time. Supply spring and summer feedings, but keep in mind that overfertilized or overwatered plants bloom little, if at all. Bloom comes on new wood at branch tips. Train vines by tying to supports. Cut off unwanted branches. To train vines as bank covers, tie to hairpin-type stakes in the ground. To train as a vine or as a tree in a frost-free climate, tie to a pole and prune back occasionally to a basic framework to form a strong structure.

Vines:

'Barbara Karst': red in sun to magenta in shade. Hardiest of the reds, it recovers quickly from frost, grows vigorously and blooms early in the season. Loves the desert summer.

'San Diego Red' ('Scarlet O'Hara,' 'American Red'): similar in color to 'Barbara Karst,' but with larger leaves and fewer but larger blooms in clusters. One of the hardier strains, this cultivar recovers quickly from cold, but blooms later than 'Barbara Karst.'

'Texas Dawn': one of the closest to pink *Bougainvilleas* yet developed. Vigorous grower, it blooms profusely over a long period in summer after 'Barbara Karst' has

Bougainvillea cultivars

Bougainvillea species

Low zone, protected locations in middle zone
Evergreen in mild areas

Soil: Tolerant. Needs good drainage.

Sun: *B. spectabilis* prefers cool summers. All others appreciate heat of full or reflected sun. Plants tolerate partial shade but do not bloom well.

Water: Moderate to ample. Requires little water once established.

Temperature: Damaged between 30 and 25F (-1 to -4C) depending on situation and hardiness of variety. Most plants stop blooming as nights cool, but reflected heat from a wall can extend bloom period. Established plants damaged by cold usually recover quickly in warm weather.

Maintenance: Very little except when training is required. Some removal of frost-damaged wood in spring. Some cleanup of fallen bracts, which hold their color for a while and can be attractive floating on the breeze or even in the pool.

finished. Appreciates high heat and some humidity.

'Rainbow Gold': burnt orange; blooms vigorously.

'Orange King': tender to frost, but loves long hot summers. More open in growth, with bracts that turn from orange to copper to pink.

'California Gold': bears golden bracts profusely for a long period. More sensitive to cold than red *Bougainvilleas*.

'Jamaica White': white bracts, tinged pink in cooler weather. A fairly new cultivar, it is not known how it performs in winters of the middle zone.

Shrubs:

'La Jolla': red bracts. Performs well and recovers from freezes in the middle zone even in containers.

'Crimson Jewel': red bracts densely cover plant over a long period.

'Convent' (also called 'Panama Queen'): shrubby with large clusters of magenta purple bracts that appear over a long season. There are many more cultivars available for landscape use, some with double bracts.

'Torch Glow': a fairly recent introduction that has pinkish red bracts and leaves spaced closely together on upward pointing branches that need no support. It serves well as an accent or a decorative row. Can grow to 6 feet (1.8m) high. Can be trained by staking into a small tree where climate permits.

Cool summer plants:

'Torch Glow': shrub (see above).

'Texas Dawn': vine (see above).

'Temple Fire': shrub with red-bronze bracts. Grows to 4 feet (1.2m) high and may spread to 6 feet (1.8m) wide.

'Tahitian Dawn': vine with gold bracts that turn a pinkish purple.

Bougainvillea 'Rainbow Gold'

Brachychiton populneus

(B. diversifolia, Sterculia diversifolia)
Family: Sterculiaceae
Bottle Tree • Kurrajong Tree

The bottle tree from Australia has a vertical form with a pyramidal crown. A moderate to fast grower, it can reach a height of 20 feet (6.1m) in five or six years, eventually reaching 30 or even 50 feet (9.2 to 15.2m) in warm areas. Crown of young trees is narrow and dense and becomes wider on older trees. Foliage is shiny and lobed, rustling like a poplar in the wind. The trunk, covered with patterned greenish bark, is thick at the base but suddenly tapers inward several feet above the ground, resembling a bottle. Clusters of small bell-shaped flowers are dusted pink, appear in May or June and are followed by decorative woody seedpods shaped like boats. Tree revels in heat. Sometimes will almost completely shed leaves just before blooming, only to quickly refoliate afterward.

Special design features: Refined and pleasing at close range. Bright green vertical form.

Uses: Specimen tree or sapling grove. Row plantings make an attractive and effective screen or background. Does well where space is limited, but can heave sidewalks or paving. Roadside tree or windbreak.

Disadvantages: Susceptible to Texas root rot and iron chlorosis. Fuzz inside seedpods is prickly and can be irritating to skin.

Planting and care: Plant from containers in spring. Root systems are fragile, so handle with care. Young trees may need staking until trunks thicken. Give extra iron to avoid chlorosis. Prune in February.

Brachychiton populneus

Brachychiton populneus

Low zone and most of middle zone
Evergreen
Soil: Tolerant. Needs good drainage. May yellow in alkaline soils.
Sun: Full to reflected sun.
Water: Occasional deep soakings of root zone, although it also seems to do well in lawns with moderate or ample water.
Temperature: Young trees killed and foliage damaged on older trees at about 18F (-8C). Fast recovery in spring.
Maintenance: Little to none.

Brachychiton populneus

Brahea armata

(Erythea armata)
Family: Arecaceae (Palmae)
Mexican Blue Palm
Big Blue Hesper Palm • Rock Palm

This fan palm from Baja, California, is very much at home in the desert garden. It tolerates greater extremes of heat, cold, wind and other adverse conditions than most palms. Grows slowly to 25 or 30 feet (7.6 to 9.2m), sometimes higher, with a crown spread of 8 to 10 feet (2.4 to 3.1m). Crown is wider than high, formed of stiff waxy fronds that retain their blue-gray color until they bend down to the trunk. Fragrant, whitish flower garlands to 18 feet (5.5m) long in summer mature to reddish brown and produce hard berry-like fruit. Not as graceful as other palms as it matures because of heavy trunk, small head and stiff leaves. However, younger plants are lush and attractive and remain so for many years.

Cultivars and other notable species: *Brahea edulis*, Guadalupe palm, is another fan palm that is often used in these areas. In appearance, it is much like *B. armata*, with light green leaves and not as heavy a trunk. It is a moderate grower that stays in scale with the average home landscape, with a maximum height of approximately 30 feet (9.2m). It is an excellent plant for a tropical effect.

Special design features: Interesting blue-gray foliage. Informal. Vertical with age.

Uses: Specimen, grove or row. Residential, street or public area. Informal areas, subtropical, desert or wild gardens. Complements other desert plants.

Disadvantages: Does not seem to have any special problems.

Planting and care: Plant any time from containers, but best in spring. Transplant spring or early summer. Larger plants are difficult to transplant successfully.

Brahea armata

Brahea armata

Middle and low zone, protected microclimates in high zone
Evergreen
Soil: Tolerant. Grows naturally in limestone soils. Prefers improved garden soil.
Sun: Tolerates part shade to full or reflected sun.
Water: Drought tolerant. For best results, irrigate deeply at wide intervals.
Temperature: *B. armata* is hardy to 15F (-9C); *B. edulis* to 20F (-7C).
Maintenance: Little. Some cleanup of old fronds and fruit.

Butia capitata

(Cocos australis, C. campestris)
Family: Arecaceae (Palmae)
Pindo Palm • Jelly Palm

This is a graceful small-scale feather palm, originally from Brazil and Argentina. One of the hardiest exotic palms. It can be used in a small area for many years without outgrowing the space, growing slowly to 10, sometimes 20 feet (3.1 to 6.1m) with a spread of 10 to 12 feet (3.1 to 3.7m). Vertical trunk and gray-green fronds deeply recurve as they bend downward. Palms are most attractive in youth before they develop the rather heavy trunk with vertical leaf bases, which sometimes become marred by fungus. Try to keep leaf cuts the same length to create an even pattern, or skim them off to create a smooth, fibrous trunk. Female trees produce edible pineapple-flavored fruit, used to make tasty jelly or preserves.

Special design features: Light festive appearance. Refined eyecatcher in youth. Tropical effect with tropical plants.

Uses: Emphasis or accent plant for containers, tubs, planters or gardens. Because of its gray color, combines with arid or desert plants or contrasts with tropical plants, Resistant to Texas root rot.

Disadvantages: Plants may be hard to locate. Trunks on older specimens sometimes awkward and unattractive in appearance. Subject to infestations of root knot nematodes and bud rot. Leaf stumps and trunks sometimes get a fungus, which eats and deforms them. Poor drainage and alkaline soils sometimes cause iron chlorosis.

Planting and care: Plant from containers any time of year, but transplant in warm weather. Remove old, drooping or dry fronds and spent blossoms. Do not wet crown to avoid infecting palm with bud or trunk rot. Plants need careful grooming as they age to keep a tidy appearance. Give extra iron if foliage pales.

Butia capitata

Butia capitata

Middle and low zones, warmer microclimates of high zone
Evergreen
Soil: Tolerant, but needs good drainage. Best in improved garden soil.
Sun: Full to reflected sun.
Water: Moderate.
Temperature: Hardy to 15F (-9C).
Maintenance: Periodic trimming.

Buxus microphylla japonica

Family: Buxaceae
Japanese Boxwood

This shrub from Japan has been used for centuries as an outstanding hedge plant for formal or contained gardens—it accepts clipping very well. Slow growing to an eventual 4 to 6 feet (1.2 to 1.8m) high and as wide unless contained, it makes a dense, rounded form if allowed to grow naturally. When trimmed, Japanese boxwood will remain a low, compact hedge for a long time. Shiny bright green leaves are small and rounded and cover plant to ground.

Special design features: Dependable and durable formal plant.

Uses: Specimen or hedge plant for low or medium hedges or edgings. Excellent in formal or contained gardens as a box hedge, space divider or topiary plant.

Disadvantages: May sunburn if clipped too closely late in the season. Subject to browning in spots from reflected heat or yellowing from iron chlorosis.

Planting and care: Plant any time from flats or containers. For continuous planting, space plants from flats 6 to 9 inches (15.2 to 22.9cm) apart, gallon plants 9 to 12 inches (22.9 to 30.5cm) apart. Begin clipping and shaping plants when they are young. Give regular feedings and extra iron to encourage green foliage during growing season, especially in alkaline situations. Any heavy clipping should be done in fall or late winter before heat arrives. Shear as needed to keep neat.

Buxus microphylla japonica

Buxus microphylla japonica

All zones
Evergreen
Soil: Tolerant. Prefers improved garden soil. Accepts some degree of alkalinity.
Sun: Open shade, part shade, full sun. Burns in reflected sun.
Water: Moderate.
Temperature: Hardy. Accepts heat with adequate water.
Maintenance: Periodic clipping and feeding.

Buxus microphylla japonica

Caesalpinia gilliesii

(Poinciana gilliesii)
Family: Fabaceae (Leguminosae)
Yellow Bird of Paradise

Also known as Mexican bird of paradise before the introduction of *C. mexicana*, this exotic, angular and picturesque plant bears numerous pyramidal clusters of yellow flowers with long red stamens that look like tropical birds. Generally open in form with a slender trunk, branches bear finely cut medium green leaflets. Branches, leaves and fruit may be flecked with brown specks. Flat pods 4 to 5 inches (10.2 to 12.7cm) long follow March to September bloom. Mature pods literally explode with a pop or bang, showering seed in all directions. Bird of paradise is generally deciduous, except in the warmest places, but is never its best in winter. With water it grows rapidly to 6 feet (1.8m) high or higher. Usually a lower- and slower-growing plant, especially where it has to struggle. A native of South America and Mexico, it is widely adapted to the Southwest, where it has naturalized.

Special design features: Warm weather color. Arid, desert, tropical or subtropical effects.

Uses: Specimen or mass. Accent or silhouette plant, alone or in combination.

Disadvantages: Brown fuzz on stems. Twigs and seedpods produce unpleasant odor, and seedpods are poisonous. Plants may become pests in some places because they reseed profusely.

Planting and care: May be grown from seed. Plant from containers any time. Irrigate until established, especially during first summer. Prune in June and January to keep groomed and to remove pods. May be cut back severely in winter, its most unattractive season. It will grow and bloom as a thick, low shrub in spring, or you can train it to become a tall and open plant. Survives drought and neglect, but may go dormant. Needs supplemental water during bloom season to look best and to have a good show of flowers. Plants grown in an arid environment survive with no summer moisture but stay small and seldom bloom.

Caesalpinia gilliesii

Caesalpinia gilliesii

All zones
Deciduous
Soil: Tolerant of a wide variety of soils.
Sun: Full and reflected sun, also part shade.
Water: Accepts any amount. Needs some supplemental water in the arid climates to look good.
Temperature: Hardy to about 10F (-12C) where it may die back to the ground. Recovers quickly in warm weather.
Maintenance: Periodic to none.

Caesalpinia mexicana

Family: Fabaceae (Leguminosae)
Mexican Bird of Paradise

This tough shrub to small tree is a native of Mexico. Small round to oblong leaflets are coarse and remain green during mild winters. Branches are spineless. Open crown. It grows fairly rapidly to 8 to 10, even 15 feet (2.4 to 3.1, even 4.6m) high and can spread 8 to 12 feet (2.4 to 3.7m) wide. Prune to keep it a shrub. This plant bears 6-inch (15.2-cm) lemon yellow flower clusters along branches from March to October, all year in mild winter areas. Seed pods, a few inches long, follow.

Special design features: Color, open form. Arid, desert, tropical or subtropical effects.

Uses: Boundary plant, small patio tree, wild garden. Open form gives shade to underplants. Large shrub form makes a great background.

Disadvantages: As with all *Caesalpinias*, the seeds are poisonous. Will reseed in irrigated areas. Seed litter can be a problem.

Planting and care: Plant in warm weather and train as needed. Prune in June to contain size or allow to grow into a small open tree. For a shrub, prune long, lanky branches to shorten and create more foliage and flower clusters. Remove lower branches to create a small tree. May need to clean up seed litter in a groomed landscape.

Caesalpinia mexicana

Caesalpinia mexicana

Low zone and all but the coldest areas of the middle zone
Evergreen
Soil: Tolerant.
Sun: Full sun to part shade.
Water: Drought tolerant, but looks and blooms better with occasional water in warm weather.
Temperature: Hardy to about 20F (-7C)
Maintenance: Seasonal. Remove seedpods to improve appearance and encourage bloom. Otherwise, maintenance depends on use.

Caesalpinia pulcherrima

(*Poinciana pulcherrima*)
Family: Fabaceae (Leguminosae)
Red Bird of Paradise • Dwarf Poinciana

The brilliant orange-red and yellow flower clusters and lush, medium green ferny foliage of this summer bloomer add a vibrant tropical effect to the landscape. A native from Mexico and the West Indies, it thrives in the hottest places where little else will grow, blooming continuously during the warm season (March to October). A vase-shaped shrub with large, finely cut, feathery leaves and sometimes prickly branches, dwarf poinciana is slow to get started but becomes a vigorous grower and profuse bloomer after a year or two. Once roots are established, a plant cut back in late winter to a mere 10 inches (25.4cm) can attain a height of 3 feet (0.9m) or more early in the season and bloom by early summer. Established untrimmed plants in areas seldom nipped by frost may reach 6 feet (1.8m) or higher and become almost treelike. Spectacular flowers in flat pyramidal clusters at branch tips produce flat 3- to 6-inch (7.6- to 15.2-cm) seedpods that, when ripe, pop open and scatter the seeds. Give extra water in warm season for plant to look lush and bloom well.

Cultivars and other notable species: 'Phoenix' has bright yellow flower clusters.

Special design features: Warm seasonal color. Tropical effect.

Uses: Specimen as accent or massed for effect. Rows for screening. Natural, arid, tropical, rock and desert gardens. Spruces up bare areas.

Disadvantages: Fruit is poisonous. Plants slow to start and may not grow or bloom much during the first year or two. This is especially true in dry summer areas lacking sufficient water. Unattractive in winter. Sometimes gets Texas root rot.

Planting and care: Start from seed or plant from containers in spring when frost is past. Space 3 to 5 feet (0.9 to 1.5m) apart for rows or massing. If plant is twiggy in appearance in winter, cut back 4 to 6 inches (10.2 to 15.2cm) above the ground. This also encourages branching. Prune in November.

Caesalpinia pulcherrima

Caesalpinia pulcherrima

Low and middle zones; protected locations in high zone
Evergreen in warm climates
Soil: Tolerant of wide range of soils.
Sun: Full to reflected sun.
Water: Moderate to ample during flowering. Occasional during dormant season. Tolerates small amounts during warm season but with little bloom.
Temperature: Foliage becomes purplish in cool of winter. Freezes to ground around 28 to 30F (-2 to -1C). Mulch roots and lower stems in cooler areas to help plants recover from much lower temperatures.

Carissa macrocarpa

(C. grandiflora macrocarpa)
Family: Apocynaceae
Natal Plum • Amatungula

Natal plum has almost succulent leathery leaves, a scattering of fragrant white flowers and decorative red edible fruit. This South African native revels in heat, including warm soils, and tolerates salt wind in seaside plantings. A fast to slow grower, depending on soil and available moisture, to 5 to 7 feet (1.5 to 2.1m), sometimes more, and as wide. Short green thorny stems support closely set, shiny, rounded 3-inch (7.6-cm) dark green leaves. Fragrant, waxy, starlike flowers are scattered over plant from May to June, followed by 1-inch (2.5cm) beet-shaped fruit, delicious in fresh salads or in preserves.

Cultivars and other notable species: 'Fancy,' to 6 feet (1.8m) high, is an ample flower and fruit producer. 'Ruby Point' is the same size, with red new leaves through the growing season. Low forms include 'Boxwood Beauty,' 'Prostrata,' 'Green Carpet' and 'Tuttle' ('Nana Compacta Tuttle').

Special design features: Rich, dense, dark green. Tropical, formal or informal designs. Oriental effect.

Uses: Handsome, refined but thorny barrier plants. Taller forms make clipped or unclipped hedges and screens in warm areas, foundation or wall plants against south or west walls under overhangs in the middle zone, or against any wall in the low zone. Low plants can be clipped and shaped into low hedges or forms, trained on walls or used in containers or as ground covers in warm areas (or where protected from cold).

Disadvantages: Winter browning in areas of frost. When frozen branches are removed, it may not be attractive until new foliage and branches fill out.

Planting and care: Plant in spring when danger from frost is past. Space larger plants 4 feet (1.2m) apart for continuous planting, low plants 1-1/2 to 3 feet (0.5 to 0.9m) apart, depending on spread of cultivar. Cut back vertical shoots on ground covers to encourage spreading. Do any heavy pruning in May.

Carissa macrocarpa 'Prostrata'

Carissa macrocarpa

Low zone; protected areas in middle zone
Evergreen
Soil: Average garden soil with good drainage.
Sun: Widely tolerant. Prefers full or reflected sun. Growth is more open in shade, with fewer flowers and fruit.
Water: Moderate to ample. Tolerates some drought when established. A deep irrigation every week or two in the warm season, every month or so for old plants, and it will survive but may look poor.
Temperature: Damaged at 28F (-2C). Recovers quickly in spring.
Maintenance: If you choose a cultivar appropriate to the specific place or use, it looks great with almost no care except periodic trimming.

Carnegiea gigantea

(Cereus giganteus)
Family: Cactaceae
Saguaro • Sahuaro
Arizona Giant • Giant Cactus

A spectacular plant of great character, this well-known tall columnar cactus is native to southern Arizona and northern Mexico. Saguaros grow very slowly to 60 feet (18.3m) or higher and are long-lived, up to 250 years. It takes many years for plants to reach just inches in height. When sixty to seventy-five years old and about 20 feet (6.1m) tall, they may sprout budding branches, or arms. A saguaro may develop a single arm or several and each arm may develop an arm. In late spring or early summer, wreaths of white flowers appear at the top and branch tips, opening at night and lasting into the next afternoon. Summer fruits are green, then red. They split open, revealing the sweet red pulp and the black seeds inside. Saguaros and other cacti are expensive and heavily protected by law. They require tags from the United States Commission of Agriculture for legal purchase or to be transplanted from one place to another. Purchase plants from a supplier.

Special design features: Strong dramatic vertical. Spectacular skyline silhouette. The ultimate plant of the desert landscape.

Uses: Desert or natural gardens as an emphasis or accent plant.

Disadvantages: Plants over 8 feet (2.4m) high don't transplant well. They may hang on a few years and gradually succumb. Bacterial necrosis, mainly a problem affecting older specimens or weakened plants, is fatal if not treated in the early stages.

Planting and care: All specimens over 4 feet (1.2m) high are heavy and should be transplanted by professionals with special equipment. To transplant small saguaro, mark the north side and dig carefully to maintain as many roots as possible. Cut roots cleanly and apply sulfur. Lay plant in shade to allow wounds to dry. Plant in a wide shallow hole with the same side of the saguaro facing north as before. Irrigate occasionally to help it establish.

Carnegiea gigantea

Carnegiea gigantea

Low and middle zones; warm pockets of high zone
Evergreen
Soil: Prefers rocky or loose soil with good drainage.
Sun: Full or reflected sun. Tolerates part shade.
Water: Moderate when getting established, then none to occasional. Supply some water during extended hot dry weather. Plants receiving a little extra water will establish better and grow faster.
Temperature: Sometimes damaged by long, hard freezes around 20F (-7C).
Maintenance: None.

Carya illinoensis

(C. oliviformis, Hicoria pecan)
Family: Juglandaceae
Pecan

This native of the southcentral United States to northeastern Mexico grows surprisingly well in arid areas if supplied with deep, nonsaline soil and irrigation. A handsome, well-structured tree, it grows at a moderate rate up to 70 feet (21.3m), with an equal spread in favorable situations. Most commonly seen as a garden tree, 25 to 40 feet (7.6 to 12.2m) high, but can be kept smaller by pruning. Compound medium to deep green leaves are long and have eleven to seventeen pointed leaflets to 7 inches (17.8cm) long. Trees are usually erect with single trunks and billowing crowns. Inconspicuous flowers in spring produce a nut borne in a husk in late summer or fall. Pecans are a cash crop in the Southwest. Plant at least two different species for a better crop of nuts.

Cultivars and other notable species: Numerous are available. Select the ones that best suit your climate. Seek recommendations from a qualified landscape professional.

Special design features: Dominant green statement in the summer landscape.

Carya illinoensis

Woodsy look. Shade tree that produces edible nuts. Handsome silhouette in any season. Yellow fall color.

Uses: Quality shade tree that does well in lawns. Slower growing than some trees, but worth waiting for. Groves or specimens in lawns or gardens. Especially attractive when given room to spread. South sides of buildings where it gives shade in summer and allows sun in winter.

Disadvantages: Brittle branches. Subject to attack by aphids and a number of other pests and diseases, including Texas root rot. Nuts sometimes attacked by pests. Pecan rosette, abnormal clumping twigs, is caused by a lack of zinc. To treat, use zinc sulfate spray or add compound to soil.

Planting and care: Plant from containers any time or bare root in winter. Deep wide holes are best, especially in difficult soil. Be sure bud union on grafted trees is above ground. Train tree to have well-spaced branches the first two to three years by pruning in winter. In February, after deep watering, feed with 1 pound (0.5kg) each zinc sulfate and nitrogen per inch (2.5cm) of trunk diameter. Broadcast nitrogen over three feedings, six weeks apart. Contact your county cooperative extension agent if interested in raising nut crops.

Carya illinoensis

All zones
Deciduous
Soil: Don't plant in rocky or caliche soils. Deep soil is best so tree may send down taproot for fullest development.
Sun: Full to reflected sun.
Water: Moderate to ample.
Temperature: Hardy. Takes dry heat with ample water.
Maintenance: Periodic. Prune dead branches and control weeds underneath tree.

Cassia species

Many of the plants formerly listed here under the genus *Cassia* have been reclassified as *Sennas*. Some of the familiar species names have changed as well. Familiar names are noted with the new ones.

***Cassia artemisioides*, feathery cassia,** see *Senna artemisioides*

***Cassia nemophila*, hardy cassia,** see *Senna artemisioides filifolia*

***Cassia wislizenii*, shrubby senna,** see *Senna wislizenii*

Cassia artemisiodes has been renamed as *Senna artemisiodes*.

Cedrus atlantica

(C. libani atlantica)
Family: Pinaceae
Atlas Cedar

One of the three or four true cedars, the atlas cedar comes from North Africa. The blue Atlas cedar, *C. atlantica* 'Glauca™', is probably best known. A slow to moderate grower to 100 feet (30.5m) in its native Atlas Mountains, it is not yet known whether this tree will attain such heights under cultivation in lower arid climates and soils. Tree is irregular in youth, but grows into a flat-topped, pyramidal vertical giant with stiff horizontal branches. Branches are clothed in tuftlike clusters of tiny blue-green needles. Train for a symmetrical form or leave untrained for a rustic and irregular shape.

Cultivars and other notable species: 'Glauca' is a grafted selection with silvery blue foliage and pyramidal form. It gives a rustic effect but is most often used as an accent or specimen in large containers. 'Glauca Pendula' is a weeping kind with sprawling, cascading branches.

Special design features: Rustic, oriental or woodsy effect. Blue color of some varieties.

Uses: This tree is seldom seen, but deserves wider use. Strong vertical and skyline tree for large spaces such as parks or large lawns. Mass as a tall screen near bodies of water to filter the air. The rustic blue Atlas cedar is more commonly used as an accent or specimen in a planter or container. It will look nice for a few years, until it becomes rootbound and begins to decline. In the ground it develops into a rustic small gnarled tree.

Disadvantages: Trees lacking sufficient irrigation die back from the top.

Planting and care: Plant from containers any time. Set species 16 to 30 feet (4.9 to 9.2m) apart for a grove. No special care, pests or problems have been noted so far with this uncommon tree. Pinch tips to shorten long, heavy branches on young trees.

Cedrus atlantica

Cedrus atlantica

Middle and high zones
Evergreen
Soil: Well-prepared garden soil. Avoid light gravelly soils.
Sun: Part shade to full or reflected sun.
Water: Moderate. Established trees can accept short periods of drought but need deep irrigation at least every month during long hot dry periods or they will begin to die back.
Temperature: Tolerant of heat and cold.
Maintenance: Periodic grooming and trimming.

Cedrus deodara

Family: Pinaceae
Deodar Cedar

The most widely planted of the true cedars, the deodar makes a dramatic statement in the landscape. Graceful and pyramidal, with a youthful form reminiscent of a Christmas tree, this Himalayan native grows at a moderate to fast rate to 80 feet (24.4m) high with a 40-foot (12.2-m) spread at the base. Silhouette is partly open so you can see the sky through the horizontal branches, which bend downward near the ends. Older trees have a bobbing leader or main branch, which leans to one side. Silvery gray to gray-green foliage darkens with age. Needles 2 inches (5.1cm) long grow in tufts along branches. Cones are up to 5 inches (12.7cm) long and sit erect on branches. Individual cultivars vary in form and color.

Cultivars and other notable species: 'Prostrata' will grow flat on the ground, such as on banks, or will hang over planters. 'Compacta' is slow growing, rounded and dense. 'Pendula' has a weeping form. Another true cedar that should be used more is *C. libani*, cedar of Lebanon. It is a fine tree for arid climates. Erect and conical in youth, it develops into a broad-headed form with several main trunks at maturity. A mature tree will reach the same size as *C. deodara*. Foliage is bright green in youth, becoming dark green with age. Requires ordinary garden care, with the same cultural requirements as *C. deodara*.

Special design features: Tall accent or silhouette. Skyline tree. Foliage contrast with broadleaf evergreens or lighter green or gray plants.

Uses: Accent or specimen tree, or mass for effect and screening in a park or large open area. Plants set close together can be trimmed as a hedge.

Disadvantages: Trees that don't receive deep root-zone irrigation at least every month during long dry and especially hot periods will begin to die back from the top.

Planting and care: Plant from containers any time. Prune in May to shape or to encourage dense bushy growth. Plant area under tree with a needle-absorbing ground cover, such as a low juniper or English or Algerian ivy, or leave unraked to create a mulch of needles. Give extra iron if tree seems pale or yellows from chlorosis.

Cedrus deodara

Cedrus deodara

Middle and high zones; marginal in low zone
Evergreen
Soil: Best in heavy soils, especially well-prepared garden soil. Avoid light or gravelly soils.
Sun: Full to reflected sun.
Water: Prefers moderate. Accepts occasional deep irrigation, which is essential during dry and especially long hot periods.
Temperature: Hardy to 5F (-15C).
Maintenance: None to periodic.

Celtis reticulata

(C. douglasii)
Family: Ulmaceae
Western Hackberry
Netleaf Hackberry
Sugar Berry

Growing naturally as a riparian tree, netleaf hackberry is seen along streams and washes at elevations from 2,500 to 6,000 feet (762 to 1,829m) throughout much of the Southwest and northern Mexico. A craggy tree with pendulous branches and interesting nubby light gray bark, it grows at a moderate rate to 25 to 30 feet (7.6 to 9.2m) and spreads as wide. Leaf form may vary in size and shape and in density depending on individual tree and conditions. Insignificant spring flowers bloom June to August and produce orange to purple 1/4-inch (0.6-cm) berries in clusters late summer into winter, loved by birds.

Special design features: Picturesque character plant, almost oriental in form, especially when bare. Informal.

Uses: Specimen tree in arid, desert or wild gardens where it receives some irrigation. Bird gardens, parks, playgrounds or lawns. A larval food plant for baby butterflies (caterpillars). Birds love berries.

Disadvantages: Reseeds profusely where there is some concentration of moisture. In periods of drought, tree dies back, becomes sparse and unkempt.

Planting and care: Plant from containers any time or bare root in winter. Space 20 to 30 feet (6.1 to 9.2m) apart for a row. Prune only to remove dead branches or to shape. Prune in January.

Celtis reticulata

Middle and high zones; low zone with extra water
Deciduous
Soil: Tolerant, but prefers loose sandy soil with some depth.
Sun: Full to reflected sun.
Water: Needs moderate irrigation or ample deep soakings in spring and summer, especially in low zone or areas with less than 10 inches (254mm) of annual rainfall.
Temperature: Tolerant of heat and cold. Hardy to about 10F (-12C).
Maintenance: Periodic in garden situations.

Celtis reticulata in summer

Celtis reticulata in winter

Ceratonia siliqua

Family: Fabaceae (Leguminosae)
Carob • St. John's Bread
Algarroba • Locust Bean

The carob is native to the eastern part of the Mediterranean. Variable form but usually seen as a very dark green, dense, wide-spreading tree, sometimes pyramidal in form. The carob has crinkled leathery compound leaflets and a heavy trunk. Individuals grow at a slow to moderate rate 30 to 40 feet (9.1 to 12.2m) tall and spread their crowns 25 to 30 feet (7.6 to 9.2m) or wider. Males have attractive pinkish blossoms in spring. Females have small red blossoms that produce dark flat pods about 12 inches (30.5cm) long. Beans are used for the production of carob powder, a substitute for chocolate. It is believed that this is the locust tree whose pods fed St. John the Baptist in the wilderness in Biblical times.

Special design features: Dense shade with interesting foliage. Mediterranean oasis.

Uses: Street or park tree or in large patios or courtyards. In large areas it can be grown in closely set rows as a hedge or screen, allowing low branches to remain clear to the ground. Not for narrow planting areas.

Disadvantages: Buttress roots may heave paving or walls if planted too close or if there is an irrigated area on the opposite side. Subject to wind breakage. Leaf, flower and, from females, large bean pods create litter. Flowers on male trees produce a strong scent objectionable to some. Young trees are frost sensitive until they develop woodiness. Subject to Texas root rot, verticilium wilt, sooty canker, crown rot and nematodes.

Planting and care: Grow from seed or plant young trees of the desired sex from containers in spring after frost danger has passed. Space 35 to 40 feet (10.7 to 12.2m) apart for row planting, 10 to 15 feet (3.1 to 4.6m) apart for a hedge. Trees naturally branch low, so they accept severe pruning and staking when young to make a high crown. Protect cold-sensitive young trees for the first few years in winter. Trees frosted when young often develop into multiple-trunk trees, which is quite attractive.

Ceratonia siliqua

Ceratonia siliqua

Best in low zone; marginal in middle zone, except in hot spots
Evergreen
Soil: Best in deep fertile soil. Accepts sandy soil with good drainage and some alkalinity. Intolerant of heavy, wet soils.
Sun: Part shade to full or reflected sun.
Water: Drought tolerant, but grows fastest and looks best with occasional deep irrigation, such as a monthly soak, once established.
Temperature: Young trees are tender to cold below 22F (-6C). Mature trees may suffer only superficial foliage damage at that temperature and are known to survive freezes to 18F (-8C) and below.
Maintenance: Periodic. New plantings need staking and pruning to develop a tree form. Thin the crown in windy locations to prevent damage.

Cercidium floridum

(C. torreyanum, Parkinsonia torreyana)
Family: Fabaceae (Leguminosae)
Blue Palo Verde • Wash Palo Verde

This tree is the first palo verde to bloom in spring, becoming a striking mass of golden flowers. Native to the southwestern United States and northern Mexico, it grows along washes and on sandy alluvial fans. A wide-spreading tree with a rounded crown and a naturally low, sweeping branching habit, the blue palo verde grows fast up to 25 feet (7.6m) high and as wide. Bark and foliage are blue-green, but lower trunks of older trees become rough and gray. Tiny compound leaves with rounded leaflets shed in cold or drought. Midspring bloom is followed by numerous seedpods. **Note:** Botanists are regrouping *Cercidium* as *Parkinsonia*.

Special design features: Spring color, desert or subtropical effect. Picturesque.

Uses: Street, patio or garden tree. Specimen, grouping, row or silhouette plant. Naturalistic gardens.

Disadvantages: Litter of flowers, beans and leaves. Roots are sometimes attacked by larvae of the palo verde beetle, which seldom kills the tree but may kill a few branches. Desert mistletoe may infest the crowns. Older trees are not as attractive as younger ones. Trees tend to be short-lived, from twenty to forty years. Roots produce nitrogen.

Planting and care: Plant seed that has been scarified (scratched) so water can enter the seed. Sow in place or in deep containers, because plants are difficult to transplant successfully from the open ground. Plant from containers any time. Space 20 feet (6.1m) or more apart for street tree or row planting, 15 feet (4.6m) for a grove. Some young trees need careful staking and tying. Prune branches high on young trees if they are near walks, and to reveal their interesting structure, especially on multiple-trunk specimens. Cut out infestations of mistletoe immediately, preferably by cutting off the branch at a crotch some distance below infestation. Remove dead branches and interior twigs to groom. Beans may be cut off before they fall.

Cercidium floridum

Cercidium floridum

All zones (to 4,000 feet; 1220m)
Deciduous
Soil: Tolerant of most soils, but needs good drainage. Prefers sandy soil. Accepts some alkalinity.
Sun: Full to reflected sun.
Water: Volunteers can grow without irrigation, surviving on rainfall alone in areas of 11 to 12 inches (279 to 305mm) of rain a year. Nursery-grown trees grow best with some irrigation for a while. Older trees will look their best with some water, especially in dry summer areas. Accepts occasional irrigation or lawn watering. Established trees tolerate periods of drought but may lose leaves.
Temperature: Hardy to about 10F (-12C). Accepts heat when adequate water is supplied.
Maintenance: Periodic, once trained.

Cercidium microphyllum

(Parkinsonia microphyllum)
Family: Fabaceae (Leguminosae)
Little-Leaf Palo Verde • Foothill Palo Verde • Mesa Palo Verde

Usually smaller and tougher than the blue palo verde, the little-leaf palo verde has yellow-green bark and leaves, and blooms a little later in the season (April or May). Native to the rocky foothills and mesas to 4,000 feet (1,220m) in the Southwest and northwestern Mexico. Young trees are irregular and craggy in form, with upward pointing branches that make them more vase shaped; older trees are rounded and somewhat weeping, like the blue palo verde. The fleshy-looking trunks divide near the ground, possibly from being eaten down by rabbits over the years of its youth. Numerous twigs support tiny rounded leaflets that drop in periods of cold or drought. During a long drought, the tree will self-prune and small branches die and drop off. It is slow growing to 10 to 12 feet (3.1 to 3.7m), much faster and larger with irrigation. Creamy yellow flowers cover the tree in midspring for a long period, followed by beans. These trees reach venerable ages in nature where they can be seen as saguaro nurse plants. A saguaro will start under a tree, achieve maturity over many years and then die—often the palo verde remains. Sometimes you will see a saguaro that has accepted the shelter of a palo verde and outlived its mentor.

Special design features: Spring color. Subtropical, desert or rustic effect.

Uses: Patio tree. Wild, naturalistic gardens, patios, dry sites, but not in lawns.

Disadvantages: Heavy litter of beans, leaves and flowers. Larvae of palo verde beetle grubs (prionid beetle) may eat the roots and cause branches to die, sometimes killing the whole tree. Mistletoe infestations. Because of its slower growth, not widely available in the nursery trade.

Planting and care: Purchase nursery plants or plant seeds in containers any time. Scratch or sandpaper seed so that it will absorb water. Space 10 feet (3.1m) or more apart for massing. Prune as desired to shape. Remove mistletoe by cutting off the branch at a crotch well below the point of infestation if possible.

Cercidium microphyllum

Cercidium microphyllum

All zones
Deciduous
Soil: Tolerant. Prefers loose gravelly soil with good drainage. Will grow in caliche.
Sun: Full to reflected sun.
Water: Tolerates little to none in areas of 12 inches (305mm) or more annual rainfall, but grows slowly and does not reach its maximum size. New plantings require moderate irrigation for a year or two. It grows faster and looks better with some supplemental irrigation; requires irrigation in low rainfall areas or over long hot dry spells.
Temperature: Hardy to cold, tolerant of heat.
Maintenance: Periodic grooming or sculpting to reveal sculptural form.

Cercidium praecox praecox

Family: Fabaceae (Leguminosae)
Palo Brea • Sonoran Palo Verde

From Sonora, Mexico, comes this small yellow-flowering tree that grows 12 to 20 feet (3.7 to 6.1m) high and as wide, occasionally larger in optimum situations. Smooth apple-green bark clothes the picturesque trunk and branch structure. Tree usually has deciduous periods from drought or possibly cold, but it can hold its small, luxuriant, feathery leaves all year. Bright yellow blooms appear midspring, covering the canopy and showering the ground with tiny blossoms. A heavy crop of small green pods follows the bloom and eventually drops. Where winters aren't frosty, it is by far the most attractive of the palo verdes listed here.

Cultivars and other notable species: *C. p. glaucum*, Argentine palo brea, grows slowly to moderately fast, forming an open-structured patio-size tree about the same size as *C. p. praecox*. It is hardier than *C. p. praecox* but is winter deciduous. It requires no supplemental irrigation in areas of 5 inches (12.7cm) or more rainfall, but grows faster and looks better with monthly summer soakings.

Cercidium sonorae, hybrid Sonoran palo verde, is a natural hybrid of *C. microphyllum* and *C. praecox*. It differs from both by having tighter, less luxuriant foliage and darker green bark and twigs, although the spring flower display is just as spectacular as *C. praecox*. It is also hardier, suitable for the middle zone. It is not usually grown by nurseries but is easy to propagate from seed. Although it is a hybrid, it grows from the seed of wild plants. Good as a small median tree, a flowering accent, screen, buffer or patio tree, it grows at a slow to moderate rate to about the same size as *C. praecox*. It is cold and drought deciduous.

Special design features: Umbrella-shaped patio tree with unique apple green bark, a handsome structure and a spectacular spring bloom.

Uses: Small tree for street or residence, roadsides, medians, subtropical garden effects.

Disadvantages: Borderline cold tenderness and hardiness can vary, even within a batch of seed. Does not recover quickly from cold damage. Heavy crop of beans after bloom.

Planting and care: Plant from containers in spring in cooler areas, any time in frost-free regions.

Cercidium praecox praecox

Cercidium praecox praecox lime green bark

An Exceptional Palo Verde Hybrid

Cercidium hybrid *(Parkinsonia aculeata* x *C. floridum* x *C. microphyllum)*, sometimes called *Parkinsidium* hybrid or Desert Museum hybrid, is exceptionally handsome, hardy and fast-growing to 15 to 25 feet (4.6 to 7.6m) high. Grows a single trunk with well-developed branches and a symmetrical crown. Abundant bloom with large flowers in long clusters from March to May; occasional flowers throughout the season. Must be grown from cuttings to be the true hybrid. Otherwise, cultural requirements are the same as for other *Cercidiums*.

Cercidium hybrids

Cercidium praecox praecox

Low and middle zones
Deciduous
Soil: Accepts all arid soils, but needs good drainage.
Sun: Reflected sun and full sun.
Water: Highly drought resistant. Can survive on as little as 7 inches (17.8cm) of rainfall a year, but will remain small. Best with moderate water in the warm season to develop and grow. Accepts anything from occasional irrigation to lawn watering.
Temperature: In most cases, *C. p. praecox* tolerates temperatures as low as 19F (-7C). In a large planting, one or two trees may show cold damage while the rest will not, possibly a genetic difference.
Maintenance: Requires little attention other than cleanup of pod litter and some staking and pruning to shape into tree form.

Chamaerops humilis

Family: Arecarceae (Palmae)
Mediterranean Fan Palm
European Fan Palm

The Mediterranean fan palm is a well-behaved palm native to southern Europe and North Africa. It is always attractive and lends itself to a wide range of uses. A small-scale palm, it has a rounded head of fanlike leaves 4 to 5 feet (1.2 to 1.5m) or more across. It suckers and forms a clump of several heads at the tips of several trunks, which lean outward from the center. If numerous heads are undesirable, remove them to develop a single-trunk palm, which is excellent for a narrow planting space. Development is usually slow, about 6 inches (15.2cm) a year. Fronds vary in color from deep green to grayish or yellowish green. Leaf petioles (stems) are thorny and have lots of fiber at the base. Trunks 6 to 8 inches (15.2 to 20.3cm) in diameter emerge as old fans are removed. In time, trunks grow to a height of 10 or 20 feet (3.1 or 6.1m) and side trunks lean outward so a single plant may sprawl to 20 feet (6.1m) or so. July bloom is unobtrusive. Fruit clusters on female trees are below leaves, around the trunk. Fruit look like small, shiny black beads.

Special design features: Bold accent, tropical effect. Mature multitrunk palms make attractive accents.

Uses: Small garden palm for containers and small to large planting areas (if used in a small area, you may need to remove the side trunks as they appear). Linear barrier or screen. Transitional plant. Specimen or mass as an underplanting for taller palms. Good tough plant for poolsides where it accepts the intense heat of the beating sun and heat-reflecting deck.

Disadvantages: Young plants somewhat tender to cold in high zone. Occasionally attacked by heart rot fungus during humid periods in late summer. Hard to trim and groom the thorny petioles.

Planting and care: May be planted from containers any time, or transplanted during warm season. Accepts neglect without complaint, but grows faster and larger with ample feedings and water. Prune in August.

Chamaerops humilis

Chamaerops humilis

All zones
Evergreen
Soil: Tolerant. Accepts alkaline conditions. Prefers rich, moist soils.
Sun: Full, open or filtered shade. Part or full sun.
Water: Accepts periods of drought when established, but stays stunted. Prefers moderate water. Does nicely with occasional deep irrigation. Tolerates ample water, such as in a lawn area, if the drainage is good.
Temperature: Tolerant of heat and temperatures as low as 12 to 15F (-11 to -9C). Has survived brief spells at 6F (-14C).
Maintenance: Little. Rarely needs attention unless you trim it into one or a limited number of trunks and want to leave clear trunks by removing old leaves.

Chilopsis linearis and C. linearis linearis

Family: Bignoniaceae
Desert Willow • Flowering Willow
Willowleaf Catalpa

This plant is no relation to the true willow but it does have long weeping leaves. It can be found as a sprawling shrub, 6 by 6 feet (1.8 by 1.8m) in dry locations, or as a tree reaching 30 feet (9.2m). Native trees are usually open, with a twiggy structure, smooth gray bark and slender leaves, either straight or curved. Constant production of fragrant, trumpet-shaped flowers begins in April and continues until late summer. Flowers are shades of white, lavender and pink, followed by long slender pods, which may hang on branches all winter.

Cultivars and other notable species: The plants from the east side of the Continental Divide are usually cultivars of the subspecies *C. l. linearis*. They are more upright and have thicker, greener foliage. Some are partial hybrids of this subspecies crossed with the more willowy Western form. 'Barranco™' has curved leaves and ample pink to lavender flowers. 'Lois Adams™' is pink and has few if any pods.

'AZT Bi-Color™' produces abundant blooms over the growing season against a canopy of narrow, weeping, deep green leaves. 'AZT Desert Amethyst™' has dark purple flowers and more upright leaves.

Special design features: Weeping form. Summer bloom. Evokes waterside effect.

Uses: Specimen or grove in patio, lawn or garden. Subtropical, desert or wild gardens, or transitional areas. Windbreaks, visual screens. Hummingbird and butterfly gardens. Erosion control. Streets, roadsides, median strips. Plant with cold-hardy evergreens to mask its winter dormancy.

Disadvantages: Suckers from roots. Some seedpod litter. Not attractive in winter, especially if it retains a lot of seedpods.

Planting and care: Seeds planted shallowly in moist soil in May will emerge in a week if soil is kept moist. Plant from containers any time. May also be planted bare root in winter. Trees with ample water will grow 3 feet (0.9m) a year for the first few years before slowing. To form a tree, remove basal suckers and train a strong central leader. Slender leaders may need staking until they become strong. Prune to shape as

Chilopsis linearis

Chilopsis linearis and C. linearis linearis

All zones
Deciduous
Soil: Adaptable. Prefers deep loose soils with good drainage.
Sun: Part shade to full or reflected sun.
Water: Moderate to ample in summer. Occasional soakings are satisfactory.
Temperature: Hardy to cold and tolerant of heat.
Maintenance: None in natural areas. Periodic in patios and gardens, especially if you want to develop a significant tree.

Chitalpa tashkentensis hybrid (Chilopsis linearis x Catalpa bignonioides)

Family: Bignonia
Chitalpa

This fast-growing tree, a fortunate cross between species, with training becomes a delicate small to medium, usually multitrunk, tree with upward pointing branches that may then cascade down. Grows to 20 or 30 feet (6.1 or 9m). Slender bright green leaves are 4 to 5 inches long and 1 inch wide (2.5cm). Large frilly pink, white or purple trumpet flowers in clusters bloom from April through September. All are cutting-grown.

Cultivars and other notable species: 'Morning Cloud' has white flowers with purple throats. 'Pink Dawn' has pale lavender flowers with yellow throats and can bloom summer through fall.

Special design features: Attractive for close-up viewing. Color display over long period.

Uses: Oasis tree, patio tree, specimen, cluster or screen.

Disadvantages: None observed.

Planting and care: Give garden care. Prune in November.

Chitalpa tashkentensis hybrid

Chitalpa tashkentensis hybrid (Chilopsis linearis x Catalpa bignonioides)

All zones
Deciduous
Soil: Tolerant, but responds best if given some soil improvement and good drainage.
Sun: Full sun.
Water: Once established it can accept short periods of neglect, but it looks and performs its best with weekly soaks of the root zone in summer, especially where summers are hot, and bimonthly in winter.
Temperature: Hardy to 10F (-12C) and summer tolerant with irrigation. Briefly deciduous after a frost.
Maintenance: Little other than training and cleanup of some leaf litter in fall.

Chorisia insignis

Family: Bombacaceae
White Floss Silk Tree
Palo Boracho
Bottle-Trunked Tree

A moderately fast grower to as high as 50 feet with a crown spread of 30 to 40 feet (9 to 12m). Briefly winter deciduous, this tree has a striking form with a bulbous trunk, smooth green bark and conical thorns on the trunk and lower branches of younger trees. The trunk turns gray with age and may lose the thorns. Compound waxy leaves like spreading fingers on a hand cover the irregular canopy. Lilylike flowers, 2 to 3 inches (5.1 to 7.6cm) long and creamy yellow (may fade to white) appear any time from fall into winter. They produce a 5-inch (12.5-cm) long capsule filled with silky auburn seeds—thus its name.

Special design features: Unusual form and showy flowers.

Uses: Horticultural curiosity. Tree for large spaces or the south side of public buildings away from walks. Sheltered places where frosts are common.

Disadvantages: Sharp, woody, slender to broad-based conical thorns on trunk. Frosts damage young trees and may stop the

bloom on more mature trees.

Planting and care: Propagate from cuttings or plant from container. Prune and train to encourage small tree form. Remove lower branches as tree grows to reveal interesting trunk. Some cleanup.

Chorisia insignis

Low zone and protected microclimates of middle zone
Briefly deciduous in winter and anytime the temperature goes below 27F (-3C).
Soil: Tolerant of most soils if drainage is good.
Sun: Full sun.
Water: Once established, soak root zone thoroughly every month in spring and early summer. In late summer, reduce irrigation to bring on a heavy bloom and increase woodiness, which will prevent the freezing of succulent new growth.
Temperature: Best in frost-free or sheltered areas. Leaves fall and young trees are frost damaged at 27F (-3C).
Maintenance: Little to periodic, depending on use.

Chorisia insignis

Chorisia speciosa

Family: Bombaceae
Pink Floss Silk Tree
Kapok Tree • Palo Boracho

A great tree of the Gran Chaco in South America, this is the plant from whose large seedpods kapok (used to stuff pillows) is harvested. Erect in form, the floss silk tree grows rapidly at first, then slowly to 30 feet (9.2m), sometimes to 60 feet in frost-free areas (18m), with a crown spreading 30 feet (9.2m) or more. Young trees in more open areas can spread their branches out at a lower level if trained. The bright green slender trunk sometimes thickens, turns gray with age, and may develop a pattern of gray thorny projections that disappear on some older individuals. Large bright green leaflets radiate from the center of the palmate leaves like a fan. Abundant large lilylike flowers in September and November, and again in June, may be rose to orchid to wine in color with brown-flecked white centers. Seed capsules to 8 inches (20.3cm) long hold the kapok. Plants grown from seed will vary, but excellent grafted selections are available in the nursery trade, which will produce plants of predictable size, form and flower color. This striking tree originates in Brazil and Argentina and is now widely cultivated in the warmer regions of the world.

Cultivars and other notable species: 'Monsa Majestic Beauty™,' a graft, has a smooth thornless green trunk and makes a good yard tree in warmer areas, providing summer shade and fall flower color.

Special design features: Tropical forest feeling. Fall flowers. Shade.

Uses: Featured tree for courtyards or south sides of buildings where protected from cold. Not considered a lawn tree but seems to accept lawn conditions in arid climates if it has good drainage.

Disadvantages: Susceptible to cold—it may recover rapidly but form could be permanently distorted. Spines on trunk.

Planting and care: Plant from containers after danger of frost has passed and weather has warmed up. Give ample room and fast drainage for roots. The tree naturally prunes itself by dropping branches as it grows, so prune lower branches beforehand to prevent them from falling on someone. Protect trunks on young trees from sunburn. Set away from walks because of spines on trunk. Prune in February.

Chorisia speciosa

Low zone and protected areas of middle zone
Evergreen to briefly deciduous
Soil: Prefers prepared garden soil. Fast drainage is important.
Sun: Part shade to full sun.
Water: Ample in early summer. Reduce water in late August to September to encourage bloom and harden tree for winter. Supply occasional deep irrigation during the cool of the year. With too little water, it becomes drought deciduous.
Temperature: Foliage may drop at 27F (-3C). Wood badly damaged at about 20F (-7C) on mature trees.
Maintenance: Periodic garden care.

Chorisia speciosa

Chorisia speciosa

Citrus species and selections

Family: Rutaceae

One of the delights of living in a warm and sunny climate is growing citrus. Citrus plants are mostly evergreen spiny shrubs or small to medium-size trees, useful for fruit and flower production and for landscape use. Most originated in south or southeast Asia and the Malay Peninsula and have been planted and widely developed for centuries in relatively frost-free areas of the world. Few planted today are of original stock, being hybrids, seedlings or bud sports. Most are grafted on sturdy roots adapted to different soil conditions and resistant to disease.

Limitations of Cold, Heat and Soil

Citrus may be planted in almost any climate as outdoor/indoor container plants as long as they are taken inside during severe winters, in the manner of the European orangeries. Cold is the prime controlling factor when planting citrus outdoors for landscape use or for fruit production. Heat also causes problems. When summer heat begins, plants are under great stress and "June drop" may occur, a situation that startles many gardeners when they find dozens of small green immature fruits on the ground. Leaf burn occurs during hot arid summers with little cloud cover. Other limiting factors are excessively alkaline or rocky soil, poor drainage and salty water.

Meyer lemon *(Citrus lemon 'Meyer')*

Hardiest citrus are the ornamentals: calamondin, sour orange and bouquet orange, in that order. They may be planted where the temperature does not fall below 20F (-7C). They have, however, survived several days of below freezing temperatures that at times dipped to 18F (-8C). While mature trees of fruiting varieties have survived temperatures 20F (-7C) and lower, fruit may be injured below 29F (-2C). The hardiest fruit-bearing citrus is kumquat, then grapefruit, then tangerines (mandarins and tangeloes) and improved Meyer lemon followed by sweet oranges. Lemons are sensitive to 29 to 30F (-2 to -1C), and limes are most sensitive, being primarily tropical plants that enjoy not only higher temperatures, but also higher humidity.

It is important to realize that the low-temperature tolerance is not the absolute factor in determining hardiness to cold. Also consider how long the temperature stays down and how often low temperatures occur.

Common Citrus Problems

Cold damage: Leaves may freeze and fall off, but tree will recover. If the sap freezes, branches may rupture, which usually kills them. If the trunk ruptures, the tree may die. Do not trim cold-damaged trees until new spring growth pinpoints the dead wood.

Fruit drop: Trees have many more blossoms and set much more fruit than they can actually produce, so a certain amount of fruit must drop off. Unless excessive, fruit drop should not be alarming, because only 5 percent of the initial flowering on a healthy tree can develop into a normal crop. In late spring or early summer, fruits are about the size of a pea and are lightly attached to branches so that they readily fall off in times of stress. When a mild spring turns to summer heat, the tree is put under stress. If hot dry winds coincide with insufficient watering, the tree is placed under a great strain. Stress at this time can be caused not only by heat and insufficient water, but also by lack of fertilizer at proper times in spring. Application of fertilizer after flowering and before the fruit is golfball size sometimes causes more stress and more fruit to drop. It is during critical fruit development that you should be sure watering is uniform and sufficient.

Salt burn: Appearance of brown leaf edges or spots 1/8 to 1/4 inch (0.3 to 0.6cm)

Sour orange *(Citrus aurantium)*

across on the leaves indicates need for soil leaching.

Sunburn: Trees with insufficient moisture may develop rolled up or dry leaves as well as drop fruit in times of high summer heat. Also, leaves and fruit on south side of trees are most likely to get burned.

Gummosis: A fungus disease caused by exposing trunks of citrus trees to too much moisture. It is also called brown rot gummosis and foot rot. It is a brown, gummy discoloration of the inner layer of the tree, the cambium. If it goes completely around the trunk, it may kill the plant. Prevent by never letting trunk stand in water. Build a dike around but away from the trunk to keep irrigation water from wetting it. If the tree is infected, remove discolored bark and wood to a point just beyond the infection, and treat with a Bordeaux paste mixture.

Pests: Aphids may appear at growing tips in early spring months. Tiny citrus thrips cause crinkled leathery leaves and scarred fruit. They can be damaging to young trees. Orange dog is a curious but not dangerous pest that looks like a bird dropping on a leaf. It is the larval stage of the swallowtail butterfly. Watch for and treat red or brown scale. Citrus red mite is recognizable by the red eggs it lays along the top midrib of a leaf. Eggs look as if they are strapped to the leaf by tiny cables. Shake branches over a white sheet of paper. Mites are nearly microscopic, but will appear as tiny specks.

If you recognize any of these problems or experience any others, immediately consult a reputable nursery, your county cooperative extension for the latest method of treatment. See the section on Plant Problems, page 40.

Planting Citrus

Time to plant: March or April when frost danger is over.

Place: If you are in a borderline area, locate plants in a warm microclimate (see page 7 for more information on microclimates).

How to plant: Prepare the hole before you buy the tree (but after you've decided which tree you want). Holes should be at least three to five times the size of the root ball and should have good drainage. Check drainage by filling hole with 4 inches (102mm) of water. If water is gone in four hours, the drainage is acceptable. If drainage is poor, dig a "chimney" through impervious soil layers to gravel. Fill hole partway with sandy loam and organic material combined with soil from the hole. Leave enough depth so you can put the tree in the center and fill around it, creating a water basin.

Selecting a tree: Trees one or two years old are best for easy handling. They should be about 3 to 4 feet (0.9 to 1.2m) tall with a trunk 5/8 inch (1.6cm) in diameter. Be sure the crown does not appear too large for the root ball, which should be no less than 18 inches (45.7cm) across and about 24 inches (61cm) deep. The root ball may be covered with burlap or tar paper or planted in a plastic or metal container. Trees in plastic containers are reported to recover from transplant shock more quickly than others. Larger trees may be transplanted, but require special handling not covered here.

Putting the plant in the hole: The method depends on how roots are contained. Be sure the hole has been soaked so the soil has settled and will not sink once tree is planted. Plant should be set in the center of the hole, making sure the bud union is no deeper than when it was in the container. Plants in plastic containers should be removed from the container before being set in the hole. Wet roots thoroughly and remove carefully so as not to shatter root ball. Plants with roots in burlap may be set in the hole and burlap loosened from the trunk and spread out. It will rot in the hole and does not have to be removed.

Plants with roots wrapped in tar paper may also be set in the hole and the tar paper can then be cut off. Fill soil in around roots, pressing it down to be sure there are no air pockets. Form a basin with a 3- or 4-inch (7.6- or 10.2-cm) berm at the outer edge to hold irrigation water. The basin should be as wide as the hole and should be enlarged as tree grows. Water newly planted trees immediately.

Care of Young Citrus Trees

Irrigation: Frequency depends on soil type, temperature and humidity. For a sandy loam, irrigate about once every week to ten days in summer and every two to three weeks in winter. In hot dry areas, twice a week or more may be necessary in summer. The important thing to remember is to never let new trees dry out. Fill the basin slowly. Do not spray leaves because they will absorb salts in the water and may burn. Slightly wilted leaves indicate immediate need for irrigation. Heavy clay soils need less frequent irrigation; sandy soils need more. In very hot weather (110F, 43C), newly planted trees may need water every day. Taper off frequency of irrigation in fall to harden tree for winter. (See page 37 for suggestions on emitter placement.)

Sun protection: Protect bare trunks from the sun by white-washing with a water-based paint or by wrapping with burlap for the first year or more until branches shade the trunk.

Pruning: Young citrus require little pruning, but you should remove suckers growing below the bud union. Pinch the rapidly growing leader to encourage bushiness and uniform growth. Wide arching branches sometimes need cutting if they grow too long.

Frost protection: In colder areas, wrap trunk with burlap to keep from freezing. Put temporary framework over tree for the first three or four winters while tree is at its most tender. Cover with a sheet or light blanket during the night and remove covering during the day. Avoid using plastic, and don't allow covering to touch tree. Trees not uncovered during the day may prematurely start new growth that will be extra tender. For mildly cold areas, hang flood lights, trouble lights or Christmas tree lights in the tree for added warmth. If you can find them at a nursery, petroleum coke blocks will burn all night like giant candles, providing heat.

Feeding: Except in very poor soils, do not feed the first year. To be safe, it's much better to underfeed than overfeed, which can burn or kill the plant. The second year sprinkle a good citrus fertilizer on the soil to the drip line and irrigate immediately. Follow the package directions for amounts and application methods. Do this four times during the growing season starting in late winter or early spring. Thereafter feed the tree three times a year with a balanced citrus fertilizer available at nurseries. Feed the end of February or the first of March, in May and around the first of September.

Minneola tangelo *(Citrus paradisi* x *Citrus reticulata)*

Valencia orange *(Citrus sinensis* 'Valencia')

Barriers (for trees in areas where wildlife may damage them): A strong high barrier will protect young citrus from becoming browse for wildlife or nest-building material for pack rats. If trees are planted in an area open to animals, you can protect the tree with a 1-inch (2.5-cm) mesh chicken wire hoop at least 4 feet (1.2m) high and at least a foot (0.3m) larger than the foliage. Stake the hoop with four or five rebars (reinforced bars) woven through the fencing from the top to the base and set a foot (0.3m) or so into the ground.

Care of Mature Citrus Trees

A citrus tree is considered mature at twelve years of age. If you move into a house with trees in the landscape and they are not small or dwarf varieties, consider them mature and treat them as such.

Irrigation: Soak the root zone heavily

Calamondin *(Citrofortunella mitis)*

in mid February to wash away salts and to prepare for feeding after which it should be soaked again. Then irrigate as needed between feedings. It is best to supply a constant supply of moisture, especially during fruit production. Establish a schedule short of allowing leaf wilt, as this creates stress. For sandy loam soils, every three to four weeks may be enough in winter, every ten days in summer. High temperatures and low humidity may call for more. Fill the basin slowly, but don't allow water to stand or the trunk to stay wet. Continue to protect trunk from moisture with an inner soil dike near its base.

Feeding: Use a balanced commercial fertilizer made especially for citrus and follow the directions on the package label. Feed after the first heavy irrigation described above. Feed again around Memorial Day, when the fruit should be golfball size, then the Fourth of July. In the warmer zones, the last feeding will be on Labor Day. Always soak the root zone again after feeding.

Pruning: Prune only as needed to remove dead wood, inside shoots or suckers below graft or bud union, or very long arching branches. Skirt of lower branches may be removed if you prefer, but they shade trunk and produce much of the fruit. If trunk is exposed to the sun, cover with water-based paint or wrap with burlap to keep it from being burned. Pinch the leader to encourage bushiness and uniform growth.

General Care

Enlarge tree basins as the tree grows. The berm of earth should be just beyond the drip line—the outer reach of branches—and should be 2 to 4 inches (5.1 to 10.2cm) high. Maintain an inner dike a short distance from the trunk to prevent wood from becoming damp, which can cause gummosis fungus. Keep grass and weeds pulled and prevent competition for water by not planting in the basin around the tree. Mulch the basin in

summer with ground bark, straw or other material to preserve moisture, cool soil and discourage weeds.

Remove mulch in winter to allow sun to warm soil. In areas with highly alkaline-saline soils or water, it is necessary to leach soil at least once a year to remove damaging salts. In February, just before feeding, give a long, slow soak of 8 to 12 inches (20.3 to 30.5cm) of water. This will wet soil to 6 feet (1.8m) or more and carry salt accumulations away from roots.

Feed after soaking so the soil is thoroughly damp and the roots are completely hydrated. Then water again to wash some of the dissolved fertilizer down, but avoid high concentrations, which burn the roots. Some growers recommend a second deep watering in March. Afterward you should begin a summer watering schedule as the weather warms up.

Citrus in Containers

Growing citrus in containers greatly extends the range of conditions in which they can be grown. And, where soil problems are severe, containers provide a near-perfect growing medium. Citrus in containers are also attractive additions to patios, decks or entryways—anywhere you would normally locate a container plant. Due to the restricted area for root growth, container plants are smaller than those grown in the ground, but they still produce tasty fruit.

By far the most valuable aspect of containers is their mobility. In the high zone where winter cold prevents citrus from being grown outdoors, plants in containers can be moved indoors when temperatures drop. Many gardeners in all parts of the United States are discovering that citrus can be an attractive indoor plant. Choose a bright location for your indoor citrus and keep an eye out for pests that may like the tender foliage. If you follow this indoors-outdoors routine, make the transition from one place to another gradually. For example, don't move a tree that has been indoors all winter directly into bright spring sun. Sudden changes in temperatures and sunlight can defoliate a tree.

Container culture: Growing citrus in containers calls for special cultural requirements. Plants generally require more frequent watering and fertilization. Although most native soils contain ample amounts of the necessary micronutrients, container or potting soil mixes sometimes do not. If regular applications of nitrogen fertilizers do not improve a chlorotic condition (yellowing

of plant leaves), it is probably due to a lack of iron, manganese or zinc. Each of these elements can be purchased in chelated or sulfated forms at nurseries. Some citrus fertilizers already contain them.

Choosing a Tree

Grafted trees are named varieties of predictable fruit type and quality. While disagreement exists on the best root stock for home garden plants, some experts feel plants for home use should be on sour orange root stock for grapefruit, orange, tangerine (mandarin) or tangelo. This root stock is best for heavier soils, most resistant to cold and the sturdiest. It also keeps the tree at a manageable size. Commercial orchards often use macrophylla stock. Trees on this stock grow rapidly and become very large. They are also not as cold-resistant. Lemons should be grafted to rough lemon stock.

To avoid disappointment years later, take care in the selection of a citrus tree, especially one for fruit production. There are certain precautions you can take to be sure your tree is free of disease and is on a suitable root stock. You also want to be sure to choose the correct kind or variety of citrus. Make your purchase from a reliable nursery. Also, ask your nursery about tagged trees. Tagging is a program initiated by the Crop Improvement Association in some states. Trees certified by the association have a blue tag, which includes a plant registration number. It also warrants the tree to be free from disease. The tag is put on at the time of the grafting and is nonremovable. Sometimes, a tree's identity is unknown if its paper label falls off. Be certain the tree you select has the original label or your orange may taste like a lemon.

A Selection of Citrus

Because of the confusion resulting from citrus hybridizing, we have listed common names first, botanical names second. Plants mentioned are by no means the entire citrus selection but are reliable performers in the climates covered in this book. They are generally listed in order of hardiness from the toughest to the most tender.

Citrus as fruit trees are considered standard for the low zone. In the high zone citrus should be grown only when it can be brought indoors or given ample shelter in winter. If fruit is your goal in the middle zone, place citrus in a warm spot away from the winter frosts, such as on south or southwest sides of buildings where trees will receive winter sun and shelter from winds.

Calamondin, Calamondin lime, Sour acid mandarin
Citrofortunella mitis

Usually seen as a dwarf with a columnar or rounded form. Grows at a moderate rate 8 to 10 feet (2.4 to 3.1m) tall and 6 to 8 feet (1.8 to 2.4m) wide. Produces decorative 1-inch (2.5-cm) orange fruit by the hundreds. Fruit is usually sour; sweeter ones are merely tart. Fruit sets over a period from March through December and remains for a long period on the tree.

Outstanding ornamental value as a standard tree, street tree or near patios. Excellent as large container plant or as clean plant around swimming pools. Clip or use unclipped as a hedge or screen spaced 4 or 5 feet (1.2 to 1.5m) apart. Good in limited spaces and for close-up viewing.

Kumquat
Fortunella margarita

A close relative of citrus with oval or round orange-colored fruit to 1-1/2 inches (3.8cm) long ripening November through March. Fruits have sweet skin and tart flesh, which makes a flavorful marmalade. Individuals grow at a moderate to slow rate from 6 to 25 feet (1.8 to 7.6m). 'Nagami' is probably the most common; 'Meiwa' is best for eating.

Grafted dwarfs make excellent colorful container plants. Seedling-grown types may be used as clipped standards, espaliers, shrubs or small trees where there is limited space. Excellent around pools. Attractive for close-up viewing. Accepts pruning and shaping.

Sour orange, Seville orange, Bitter orange, Bigarade
Citrus aurantium

Grown in Spain for the rough and bitter fruit shipped to England for marmalade, sour orange was brought by the Spaniards to the New World. A seedling tree in the original botanical form, it is a durable, decorative, vigorous grower to 15 to 20 feet (4.6 to 6.1m) tall, rarely 30 feet (9.2m), spreading 10 to 15 feet (3.1 to 4.6m). White, waxy spring flowers produce an unsurpassed fragrance for several weeks in spring. Spiny crowns are densely foliated with dark green leaves 4 inches (10.2cm) in length, which are fragrant when crushed. Colorful orange fruits ripen in fall, remaining on the plant as a cheery accent in winter, dropping in spring.

Outstanding ornamental tree for the garden, poolside, patio or street. Clips well into formal shapes. Well mannered for smaller spaces. The fruit is very acidic but can be used for pies, drinks, garnishes and especially marmalade.

'Bouquet' orange, 'Bouquet des Fleurs,' Bergamot orange
Citrus aurantium bergamia

This moderate grower reaches 8 to 10 feet (2.4 to 3.1m) tall and spreads about 8 feet (2.4m) wide. Distinctive curling leaves cover the tree to the ground. Showy fragrant flowers in clusters are followed by yellowish fruit suitable for marmalade, but flowers are not outstandingly attractive. This plant is very hardy and tolerates much heat.

Distinctive ornamental shrub. Space 5 to 6 feet (1.5 to 1.8m) apart as a large hedge or windbreak. Good plant for containers. Flowers are especially fragrant and large; reputed to be the orange blossoms used by florists for bridal bouquets.

Grapefruit
Citrus paradisi

Grapefruit has become very popular in the home garden; it is one of the easiest citrus trees to grow. Grapefruit trees grown in the hot arid climates probably produce the finest fruit found anywhere in the world. Fruit are basically of two kinds—pink or white (yellow)—and ripens November to June. Pink selections are sweeter. 'Marsh,' the main white selection, is highly acidic and nearly seedless. Best in May or June when it contains more sugar. Both pink and white keep well on the tree and reach full flavor with a long period of high summer heat. Trees reach about 12 to 20 feet (3.7 to 6.1m) with a spread of 20 to 24 feet (6.1 to 7.3m). All are vigorous growers that bear consistently.

Tangerine, Mandarin orange
Citrus reticulata

There are many varieties of this plant. Most popular and widely planted is 'Clementine,' the Algerian tangerine. Other fine varieties include 'Fairchild,' said to be a good pollinator for 'Clementine,' 'Kara' and 'Kinnow.' Trees reach 12 to 15 feet (3.7 to 4.6m) high, spreading 16 to 20 feet (4.9 to 6.1m). Fruit ripens November through January and is deep orange, seedy and easy to peel. Yields are irregular, usually with a heavy set about every

Calamondin *(Citrofortunella mitis)*

Kumquat *(Fortunella margarita)*

Kumquat *(Fortunella margarita)*

Grapefruit *(Citrus paradisi)*

Minneola tangelo *(Citrus paradisi x Citrus reticulata)*

Washington navel orange *(Citrus sinensis 'Washington')*

Lemon *(Citrus lemon)*

other year. Tangerines benefit from cross-pollination with other tangerines or tangeloes. They are generally best eaten as soon as they are ripe.

Tangelo
Citrus paradisi x *Citrus reticulata*

The tangelo is a cross between a tangerine and a grapefruit. Most popular is 'Minneola,' which produces large, flavorful red-orange fruit that is easy to peel. Fruit ripen in February and March, and store well on the tree for two months. Fruit are more sensitive

to cold than the tree and may be lost in cold winter areas. 'Orlando' is less vigorous but is slightly more cold tolerant. Yellow-orange fruit ripen from November to January. Trees often grow rapidly with distinctive cupped leaves and are regular heavy producers of fruit. If you have room, plant one of each of the above for cross pollination. Trees are about the same size and have the same growth rate as the tangerine.

Sweet oranges
Citrus sinensis

Oranges found in grocery stores and grown in groves for juice and eating originated in China and South Vietnam. They are classified in four groups based on fruit characteristics (naval or blood) and on geographical ancestry (Spanish or Mediterranean). They are widely cultivated in subtropical and tropical areas of the world and are considered to be among the most prized of the world's fruits.

"Arizona Sweets" is the name given to a group of Valencia-type oranges that does well in the hot inland valleys. They are probably easiest to grow and most dependable for the home gardener. 'Diller' is said to be hardiest of all, producing small seedy fruit excellent for juice. Fruit ripens in November and December before heavy frost can damage it. Tree size is 15 to 20 feet (4.6 to 6.1m) high and 20 to 24 feet (6.1 to 7.3m) wide. 'Trovita,' a California variety, is vigorous, tolerant of cold and heat and a dependable producer of thin-skinned fruit that ripens in early spring. In warm areas, grow 'Valencia.' It ripens March through May and produces medium-size fruit good for juice and eating. Trees grow to 20 to 25 feet (6.1 to 7.6m) high and 20 to 24 feet (6.1 to 7.3m) wide.

'Washington' navel does well as a crop tree in the warm interior valleys of California but is often a disappointing producer in the home garden in hot arid climates. It may flower abundantly, but it sheds most of the flowers and produces a few small fruit that split readily. It does best in medium to heavy soils, very poorly in sandy soil. Fruit ripen November through February. Allow 16 to 20 feet (4.9 to 6.1m) for spread.

'Robertson' navel is similar to 'Washington' but smaller, thus it takes up less space. It has similar needs as 'Washington' and tends to fruit in clusters. Ample fruit ripen two to three weeks earlier than 'Washington.'

One dwarf citrus variety that deserves

mention is the 'Shamouti,' grown on dwarf root stock for home garden use. It was developed in Palestine and is reported to produce large crops of big seedless oranges. It grows wider than high, with large leaves.

The blood orange is also worth planting. The best varieties for the hot arid climate are 'Sanguinella' and 'Moro.' These are vigorous open trees with fruit that ripen in late spring. The pulp of ripe blood oranges is suffused with red or pink. To have fruit of tasty quality, pick early while still slightly tart.

Lemon
Citrus lemon

Lemon is the fastest growing of the citrus and quite tender to frost. Grafted trees are best on rough lemon rootstock. Improved 'Meyer' is the hardiest lemon, with round, thick-skinned orange-tinted (and less tart) fruit, but it is currently banned in some states—Arizona for one—because it hosts citrus quick decline, a serious virus. 'Lisbon' is a dense, thorny tree of vigorous growth that likes the high heat of summer. It grows 20 to 25 feet (6.1 to 7.6m) high and 22 to 26 feet (6.7 to 7.9m) wide. Fruit ripen in fall but may be picked early, when they become juicy, to avoid frost damage. 'Eureka' is the standard fruit of the market. It is similar to 'Lisbon' but smaller, more open and less vigorous. Fruit are borne throughout the year. 'Ponderosa' is actually a lemon-citron hybrid that produces giant bumpy fruit with thick skin and a mild flavor. It grows fast, bears early and is angular and open with large leaves. Trees grow rapidly to 10 feet (3.1m).

Lime
Citrus aurantifolia

Lime is the most tender of the citrus and is usually seen as a thorny bush 12 to 15 feet (3.7 to 4.6m) high. There are basically two kinds of limes: the 'Key' lime, also known as 'Mexican' and 'West Indian,' and the Persian lime. 'Bearss,' a seedling of the Persian lime, is said to be hardier. It grows well in the low zone and in protected areas in the middle zone. The yellow fruits are seedless, very acidic and aromatic. It can grow in the same climate as lemons. Form is open in youth, dense at maturity.

Cocculus laurifolius

Family: Menispermaceae
Cocculus
Laurel-Leaf Cocculus
Laurel-Leaf Snailseed

Cocculus is an exuberant dark green shrub to small tree from southern Japan and the Himalayas. Bold laurel-like leaves densely cover the plant. It can be kept at 6 feet (1.8m) or will grow at a slow to moderate rate to become a small tree 15 feet (4.6m) high, occasionally to 25 feet (7.6m). The crown makes a dense canopy of leaves 20 feet (6.1m) or wider. Trunks bend and weave and usually lean to one side. Inconspicuous greenish flowers in spring produce a scattering of 1/4-inch (0.6cm) black berries in summer. Plants drop leaves in spring just as new leaves appear.

Special design features: Luxuriant deep green creates a cool oasis or woodsy effect.

Uses: General purpose shrub or background plant. Wide unclipped screen or clipped hedge to 6 feet (1.8m) or higher. Espalier on cool walls. Trained as a patio tree, it creates a wide umbrella of dense shade, producing an effective screen.

Disadvantages: Iron chlorosis and leaf-tip burn in alkaline soils. Slow to develop good form.

Planting and care: Plant from containers any time. Space 4 to 6 feet (1.2 to 1.8m) for a screen or hedge. To form a tree, stake and tie up young plants, gradually remove lower branches until the crown is as high as desired, then allow to spread. Once or twice a year, soak deeply to leach soil salts. Feed with iron sulfate if leaves turn yellow.

Cocculus laurifolius

Cocculus laurifolius

Low zone and warmer areas of middle zone
Evergreen
Soil: Prepared garden soil on the acidic side. Needs good drainage. Avoid alkaline situations.
Sun: Open or filtered shade. Part to full sun.
Water: Moderate to ample, especially in summer.
Temperature: Hardy to 20F (-7C), lower if sheltered. May lose leaves below 20F (-7C) and can be badly injured at 15F (-9C). Recovers quickly in spring.
Maintenance: Periodic.

Cordia boissieri

Family: Boraginaceae
Texas Olive • Anacahuita

A moderate- to fast-growing tree 10 to 25 feet (3.1 to 7.6m) high or, with pruning, a shrub 3 to 5 feet high (0.9 to 1.5m) with a single or multiple trunk. It forms a dense crown of large slightly grayed green leaves 5 inches (12.7cm) long that are soft and coarse. A profusion of soft, large white flowers with yellow throats in terminal clusters decorate the tree if moisture is present. Flowers bloom March through October, stopping when the weather becomes too cold. Fruit is rounded and yellow-green, resembling green olives.

Special design features: Dense foliage and long period of bloom.

Uses: Patio tree; small tree for small spaces; background plant or screen at property edges; foundation plant for large buildings, medians; tropical effect.

Disadvantages: Fallen leaves and flowers create litter. Leaves turn brown and stay on the tree for a long time after a hard frost.

Planting and care: Plant from seed or a nursery container in spring after frosts. Seeds take a long time to germinate. Garden care.

Cordia boissieri

Low and middle zones; warm areas of high zone
Evergreen unless leaves are frozen
Soil: Accepts most soils if they drain well.
Sun: Full to reflected sun or part shade.
Water: Drought tolerant once established. Give a good soak once a week to keep it blooming and looking good, especially during the warm growing and flowering season.
Temperature: Leaves will freeze at 28F (-2C), so it may look poor in the middle and high zone part of the year. Recovers in spring.
Maintenance: Periodic garden care.

Cordia boissieri

Cordia parvifolia

Family: Boraginaceae
Little-Leaf Cordia

A large rangy plant from the Sonoran and Chihuahuan Deserts that grows fast to 4 to 8 feet (1.2 to 2.4m) high and 4 to 10 feet (1.2 to 3.1m) wide. This large shrub with arching gray-barked branches and small-toothed oval grayish to olive-green leaves is rough to the touch. Showy white flowers to 1 inch (2.5cm) or more in diameter appear in small clusters beginning in spring and with a scattering at intervals over the warm season or after a rain when the soil is damp.

Special design features: A mass of rangy twiggy branches. Flowers over the warm season can be a snowy mass with ample moisture.

Uses: Boundary plant for a large property; medians; foundation plant for large buildings set in a Xeriscape or areas given low maintenance as a specimen, hedge or screen. A contrast to Mexican fan palms and bold succulents.

Disadvantages: Leaf and flower litter. Twiggy look not considered attractive by some. Foliage may drop completely during extended drought or a hard frost. Usually looks sparse in winter.

Planting and care: Plant from container any time. Pruning and shaping or little to no maintenance as desired. Tolerates very little irrigation.

Cordia parvifolia

Low and middle zones; protected locations in the high zone
Deciduous to evergreen
Sun: Reflected to full sun or part shade.
Water: Weekly irrigation until established, then soak once a month to maintain growth and flowering.
Temperature: Leaves freeze at 28F (-2C) but don't seem to hang on afterward. Plants propagated from the Chihuahuan Desert natives will be hardier to cold.
Maintenance: Periodic care once established. Selectively head back longest branches to encourage denser growth.

Cordia parvifolia

Cotoneaster species

Family: Rosaceae

Currently out of fashion, but still good plants, this group of shrubs from Europe and Asia includes plants that reach up to 20 feet (6.1m) in height as well as low-growing ground-covering plants. We cover only three of the many species. While these are large, you will find others that are smaller, deciduous or more appropriate for particular climate zones. They tolerate minimum care and fairly dry conditions. Most have angled to arching thornless branches, gray-green leaves, white flowers and red fall berries. *Cotoneasters* are members of the rose family, closely related to the *Pyracantha* species. They even suffer from the same diseases and are most susceptible to Texas root rot. A few kinds perform well in the warmer zones; most do best in cooler areas.

Special design features: Angular, arching gray-green form. Informal. Winter color.

Uses: Borders; foundation plant; clipped hedge; space definer.

Disadvantages: Subject to fireblight, Texas root rot, iron chlorosis and red spider mite.

Planting and care: Plant from containers in any season, but spring is best. Space 4 to 6 feet (1.2 to 1.8m) apart as an informal screen, mounding planting or clipped hedge. Add iron occasionally to prevent iron chlorosis. Prune as desired in late winter.

Cotoneaster glaucophyllus

Cotoneaster species

All zones
Evergreen to partly deciduous
Soil: Prefers loose, well-drained, improved soil with some humus added.
Sun: Part shade to full or reflected sun.
Water: Occasional deep irrigation to moderate watering.
Temperature: Hardy to cold, but may become all or partly deciduous in cold winters. Tolerant of heat.
Maintenance: Little to none.

Cotoneaster glaucophyllus
Bright-Bead Cotoneaster

Bright-bead cotoneaster is a shrub reaching 6 feet (1.8m) high and as wide but easily kept at any height. It is often seen at heights of 2 to 3 feet (0.6 to 0.9m). Stiff angled to arching branches covered with gray-green leaves up to 2 inches (5.1cm) in length are closely set on the branches. Small pinkish white flowers in dense clusters appear in spring and 1/4-inch (0.6-cm) orange-red berries follow in fall for a long period. The best *Cotoneaster* for the hot arid climates.

Cotoneaster lacteus
(*C. lactea, C. parneyi*)
Red Clusterberry

The red clusterberry is an informal arching evergreen shrub with the appearance of a large-leafed but softer and thornless *Pyracantha*. If unclipped, it grows rapidly 6 to 7 feet (1.8 to 2.1m) high and about as wide, sometimes wider. May be clipped and kept at any size. Loose open form bears leathery 3-inch (7.6cm) round-tipped leaves, deeply veined and dull gray-green above, whitish and hairy beneath. Foliage reaches to the ground. In spring, pink-tinged buds open in clusters of small white flowers. Dull red berries follow in fall and hang on a long time. Native to western China. In addition to uses listed above: espalier on cool walls; transitional plant; containers. Does well in areas somewhat neglected, or in hot sun, wind, poor soil and some drought.

Cotoneaster lacteus

Cotoneaster pannosus
Silverleaf Cotoneaster

A large, rangy, informal shrub, silverleaf cotoneaster grows at a fast to moderate rate, forming a fountain of arching branches 6 to 10 feet (1.8 to 3.1m) high and as wide. Dense clusters of small pinkish-white blossoms in spring produce soft red berries in fall. Leaves to 1-1/4 inches (3.1cm) in length are dull gray-green above, silvery and felty beneath. This native of China is widely tolerant of poor soil, heat, wind and cold. Use as a filler plant for large semi-neglected areas; wide screen, windbreak or foundation plant for large buildings; transitional gardens. Can be clipped as a hedge, but it loses its distinctive shape and character.

Cotoneaster pannosus

Dalbergia sissoo

Family: Fabaceae (Leguminosae)
Sissoo Tree
Indian Teakwood
Rosewood

Large evergreen to semideciduous tree of moderate to fast growth with a mature height of 30 to 50 feet (9.2 to 15.2m) in most arid regions; trees are said to reach 80 feet (24.4m) in their native India. Lush, medium to light green, compound leaves densely cover the spreading, usually round-headed crown, creating heavy shade. Abundant but inconspicuous pale-yellow pea-shaped flowers (April to May) produce small green pods that blend into the foliage-supplying little visual interest or litter problem. As a legume tree, the spreading root system has the potential to fix nitrogen in the soil in the wide area of its root zone.

Special design features: Luxuriant splash of bright green in arid landscapes. Medium to large shade tree. Erosion control. Roots will prevent erosion when planted along an intermittent drainage way or ditch.

Uses: Parks, roadsides, large residential gardens. Stabilizes banks and ditches with thick network of roots that prevent erosion.

Disadvantages: Can be damaged by cold, which browns foliage and causes thin and wan appearance in late winter. Recovers quickly in spring.

Planting and care: Plant from containers in spring or early summer. Space 30 to 40 feet (9.2 to 12.2m) apart for street planting, closer for groves or banks. When grown as residential tree, control size by pruning in January. Thin interior to allow wind to blow through.

Dalbergia sissoo

Low zone and warmer areas of middle zone
Evergreen to partly deciduous
Soil: Tolerant of a wide variety of soils.
Sun: Full sun.
Water: Weekly until established. Mature trees need monthly deep irrigation.
Temperature: Leaf damage in mid 20s F (-3 to -5C), wood damage in low 20s F (-5 to -7C). Young trees may be damaged in high 20s F (-1 to -3C).
Maintenance: Periodic. Prune carefully to develop strong branch structure in late winter. Remove any cold-damaged wood in spring that may occur in borderline hardiness areas.

Dalbergia sissoo

Dalea species

Family: Fabaceae (Leguminosae)

This genera did not attract much interest and was not used for landscaping until the water shortages emerged in the West. It is now one of the more promising groups of native plants, providing a number of species for drought tolerance and landscape performance. Plants have interesting and varied forms, color and blooms, which have brought them into favor. Some are winter bloomers when nothing much else is blooming. They blend well with other Xeriscape plantings. Protect newly planted daleas from animals until they develop woodiness. Several attract bees or butterflies. Plant propagators continue to look at new species for landscape possibilities.

Special design features: Varied forms and color. Some are winter bloomers.

Uses: Foundation plants. Excellent ground covers. Buffer, screen, median plant. Border or space definer. See also individual species descriptions.

Disadvantages: Young *Daleas* require protection from small animals, especially rabbits, until established.

Planting and care: See individual species for planting requirements. Cut back severely in late winter for fast regrowth in spring. Prevent spread beyond designated area. Weed until plants spread to cover or use a pre-emergent. Protect all young newly planted *Daleas* from rabbits until they develop some woodiness.

Dalea species

Low and middle zones; warmer areas of high zone
Evergreen to deciduous
Soil: Tolerant, but needs good drainage.
Sun: Light shade to full or reflected sun.
Water: Young plants need daily, then weekly irrigation to start. Drought resistant when established, but irrigation at wide intervals will encourage growth, spreading and an attractive appearance. Restrict water in mid-fall to harden young plants.
Temperature: Mature plantings tolerate temperatures into the teens F (-8 to 11C), or even lower, but young plants with tender growth may be damaged in the mid- to low 20s F (-3 to -7C).

Dalea capitata

Dalea frutescens

Dalea bicolor argyrea
Silver Dalea

A compact moderate-growing deciduous shrub to three feet (0.9m) high and wide. Lush silvery foliage. Purple and yellow pealike flowers bloom in late summer. Hardy to 5 to 10F (-15 to -12C). There are cultivars that have special features or a larger size. Its cousin, *D. bicolor bicolor*, is a larger plant with blue flowers from fall into early spring.

Dalea capitata
Golden Dalea

Low-growing, densely foliaged, flowering evergreen ground cover for small areas, borders, edging, and small banks. One plant grows at a moderate to fast rate to 12 inches (30.5cm) high and spreads to 3 feet (0.9m) or so. Fine-textured foliage is medium green. Yellow blooms come in late spring and again in fall when it is the showiest. It attracts whiteflies. Hardy to 0F (-18C). Cultivar 'Sierra Gold™' is more regular in form.

Dalea frutescens
Black Dalea

Evergreen to deciduous in colder areas, this shrub grows to 4 feet (1.2m) high and 5 to 6 feet (1.5 to 1.8m) wide, with delicate, lacy deep green foliage. Bright rose-purple flower clusters adorn tips of branches in September through November. Use in the subtropical, desert or natural garden. 'Sierra Negra™' is an improved selection. Cut back in early spring to enjoy fresh new spring growth. This Xeriscape plant is tolerant of tough conditions but performs better and looks its best if given some irrigation. Attracts bees and butterflies. Hardy to 0F (-18C).

Dalea greggii
Trailing Indigo Bush

Native to the Chihuahuan desert, this dense, trailing, mounding evergreen ground cover grows about 6 inches (15.2cm) high and spreads to 4 or 6 feet (1.2 to 1.8m), rooting itself as it spreads where conditions are favorable. Plant is densely covered with tiny pearly gray leaves. Numerous unspectacular small purple flowers appear in spring. Trailing indigo bush comes the closest of any plant now available to developing into a complete ground cover solely on limited rainfall. Younger and more lush plantings are a light gray green. Mature or drought-stressed plantings are a darker gray. To cover an area fully without sparse, open spaces, and for a more lush appearance, it needs some supplemental water. A bonus is that while young plants need protection from rabbits, older ones appear to be rabbit-proof. Use as a berm or bank cover, container or planter spiller, median plant, or in Xeriscapes as a low foreground planting with larger plants. Does not tolerate foot traffic. Looks nicely groomed when lightly sheared. Best planted fall to spring and spaced 3 to 6 feet (0.9 to 1.8m) apart. Single plant can spread 8 feet (2.4m).

Dalea pulchra
Pea Bush • Indigo Bush

An evergreen upright shrub that grows at a moderate rate to 5 to 6 feet (1.5 to 1.8m) high with a 6-foot (1.8-m) spread. Leaves are small, hairy and silvery gray. Rose-purple flowers on spikes at branch tips bloom from October to February. A rugged informal plant with considerable drought tolerance as well as ornamental value in a Xeriscape with other plants. Tolerates drought when established but looks drab. Best planted fall to spring and set 4 to 5 feet (1.2 to 1.5m) apart. Attracts bees. Shear in early summer. Hardy to 0 to 5F (-18 to -15C)

Dalea versicolor sessilis
Dalea

A tough and hardy evergreen shrub to 4 feet (1.2m) high and as wide or wider with a prolonged bloom of purple flowers from fall through spring. Hardy to 10F (-12C), making it suitable for high zone as well as low and middle zones. Needs full or filtered sun and severe pruning in January to encourage dense growth. Cultivar 'Mountain delight™' is one of the favorite *Daleas* because of its long bloom season over the cool of the year.

Dalea greggii

Dalea pulchra

Dasylirion wheeleri

Family: Agavaceae
Desert Spoon • Sotol
Wheeler's Sotol • Spoon Flower

A favorite dependable plant of the Southwest and northern Mexico. Used by the Indians for food, fiber and to make an alcoholic beverage. White settlers dismembered this plant to obtain the trunk ends of the leaves, displaying them as "desert spoons," popular in dried arrangements. In recent years, the desert spoon has become a favorite of plant rustlers who sell it without the required legal tag from the United States Commission of Agriculture. Young plants are available in nurseries.

Slender, toothed gray-green leaf blades radiate from the center in all directions. Growth is moderate to 5 to 8 feet (1.5 to 2.4m) or higher, with equal spread. Older plants occasionally develop several heads on a short trunk, especially in the home garden. From late spring through late summer some plants send up a bloom stalk 5 or 6 feet (1.5 to 1.8m) above the foliage, topped by a long plume of straw-colored flowers like a sheath of grain. Fortunately, bloom does not spell the end of the plant as it does with *Agaves*.

Cultivars and other notable species: *Dasylirion acrotriche* (green desert spoon, green sotol) is a slightly larger and greener plant than *D. wheeleri*, so it looks at home in tropical effects as well as subtropical, naturalistic, desert or wild gardens.

Special design features: Explosion of long slender leaves from center of plant creates a rounded form.

Uses: Subtropical, naturalistic, desert or wild gardens.

Disadvantages: None if planted in the proper place.

Planting and care: Plants may be obtained from some nurseries or grown from collected seed, but it is not always viable. There is speculation that the moth responsible for pollination is a victim of civilization and insecticides. It is possible seed collected farther from cities would be more viable. Plant from container any season but summer. Prune in October. Remove old bloom stalk and old leaves at base to groom.

Dasylirion wheeleri

Dasylirion wheeleri

All zones
Evergreen
Soil: Any soil with good drainage.
Sun: Full sun to open shade.
Water: Drought tolerant, but needs occasional water during the hot season to look its best.
Temperature: Hardy to 0 to 10F (-18 to -12C).
Maintenance: Periodic, to remove old bloom stalks.

Dodonaea viscosa

Family: Sapindaceae
Hopbush • Hopseed Bush • Switch Sorrel

A tough, drought-resistant shrub grows fast to 15 feet (4.6.1m) and spreads almost as wide in an irrigated situation. In less favorable situations, it is often much smaller. Foliage is variable in color and density. Lush growth is dense, with slender medium green leaves. In difficult situations, shrubs look angular and sparse. Plants are usually irregular in shape but are sometimes symmetrical. Insignificant flowers at the end of winter produce clusters of decorative, flat, round seeds in late spring that resemble hops. Plants may bloom and produce fruit at other times of year, such as after summer rains.

Cultivars and other notable species: 'Purpurea' is more symmetrical and erect in form and less hardy to cold. Its foliage has a bronze to purple cast and is less dense. 'Saratoga' is dependably purple. This is the form that is most often trained into a small tree in mild winter areas.

Special design features: Untrimmed plants give a willowy effect. Evokes the mood of the mountain canyon, upper grassland or chaparral belt. Purple-foliaged plants give color contrast but will turn greener in summer.

Uses: Waterside or water effect gardens, subtropical or desert gardens, and transitional areas. Large informal screen. Clipped hedge anywhere, especially the shrubbier forms such as 'Purpurea.' Foundation plant or espalier. Small trees or standards.

Disadvantages: Young plants, especially the purple-leafed forms, can be set back by a long, hard freeze. Strong odor at close proximity during certain times of year, especially when plant is producing pollen. Greedy roots take water from less aggressive plants nearby. Attracts whiteflies.

Planting and care: Plant from containers any time in warm areas when danger of frost has passed in cooler areas. Space 6 to 8 feet (1.8 to 2.4m) for a wide screen or mass planting, 3 to 4 feet (0.9 to 1.2m) for a clipped hedge. Trim leaders to promote bushiness and control height.

Dodonaea viscosa

Dodonaea viscosa

Low and middle zones; warmer parts of high zone
Evergreen
Soil: Tolerant of alkaline, rocky or heavy soils. Does best in improved garden soil.
Sun: Part, full or reflected sun.
Water: Best with occasional irrigation for large plants. Plants grow well with extra runoff in areas of 12 inches (305mm) of rainfall.
Temperature: Tolerant of heat. Young plants are damaged at 20F (-7C) and frozen to the ground around 15F (-9C).
Maintenance: None to constant, depending on use.

Elaeagnus ebbingei

(*E. macrophylla* 'Ebbingei')
Family: Elaeagnaceae
Ebbing Silverberry

This versatile hybrid shrub grows at a moderate to slow rate to 9 feet (2.7m) high and nearly as wide, but the thornless character makes it easy to keep as a smaller plant 3 feet by 3 feet (0.9m by 0.9m) with selective pruning or shearing. Its most fascinating feature is the foliage. Crinkly edged leaves to 4-1/2 inches (11.4cm) long are green above, nearly white beneath. The whole leaf is covered with scalelike silver flecks that shimmer. A few brown flecks on the leaf undersides concentrate on the shrubby stems, giving the plant a metallic bronze cast. Foliage densely covers the thornless branches to the ground. Plants are attractive at close range as well as from a distance. They are well-behaved, easy to train and adaptable to many growing situations. Tiny flowers occasionally appear within foliage, not noticeable except for scent.

Cultivars and other notable species: *E. pungens*, the thorny *Elaeagnus*, is a sprawling, irregular, densely foliated shrub, brown or olive green when viewed at a distance. The sometimes spiny branches support oval wavy-edged leaves 2 to 4 inches (5.1 to 10.2cm) in length. It grows at a moderate rate 6 to 12 feet (1.8 to 3.7m) high and as wide if left untrimmed. With favorable conditions, it can reach up to 15 feet (4.6.m). Unimportant flowers sometimes produce edible fall fruit in red, silver or brown.

Special design features: Shimmering leaf form.

Uses: General purpose large shrub for use as a specimen or massed as a background or wide, freely growing screen. Can also be used as an informal hedge if carefully shaped. Adapted to irrigated gardens or transitional gardens. Outstanding as an espalier for a large wall or against fences. Clips well as hedge, but loses the decorative quality of the leaves.

Disadvantages: Occasional scale problem.

Planting and care: May be planted any time, but best in spring. Some shaping or pruning can be done as required. Plants in transitional areas require no care other than some irrigation.

Elaeagnus ebbingei

Elaeagnus ebbingei

All zones
Evergreen in mild climates
Soil: Tolerant. Prefers improved garden soil.
Sun: Open or filtered shade, part or full sun. Accepts reflected sun in cooler areas and in middle and low zones if given more water.
Water: Moderate. Needs ample in hottest weather. Accepts occasional in cool season.
Temperature: Accepts heat and cold. May lose leaves in cold winters.
Maintenance: Periodic, or as desired for special uses, such as hedges or espaliers.

Eriobotrya japonica

Family: Rosaceae
Loquat • Japanese Plum
Japanese Medlar

A small- to medium-size tree, the loquat is one of the most decorative and versatile plants around. Reaches 15 to 30 feet (4.6 to 9.2m) high and as wide. The attraction is primarily the bold, dense foliage that grows in a decorative rosette pattern at the branch tips. Young plants have wide, low, irregular crowns. Mature plants develop picturesque single or multiple trunks with rounded umbrellalike crowns. Fuzzy, leathery, deeply veined leaves are dark gray-green above, whitish beneath. Fragrant, fuzzy, often incomplete flowers in fleshy, woolly, cream-colored clusters form in the leaf rosettes in fall and winter. They produce small, delicious pearlike fruit in clusters in late spring in warm-winter areas, but fruit are lost to frosts in cooler areas because it's a winter bloomer. Most plants are sold as seedlings, but to have fruit of a predictable quality, seek a grafted named variety. In some areas, commercial trees are available that produce fruit for the market. Native to China and Japan.

Cultivars and other notable species: *E. deflexa* (bronze loquat) is a smaller and more refined version of the above. It is usually grown as a shrub or small tree. This tree requires a sheltered location because it is more sensitive to heat and wind. White flowers appear in late winter and spring, but no edible fruit is produced. Requires same basic culture as *E. japonica*.

Special design features: Tropical or oriental effect. Bold foliage. Bronze new growth.

Uses: Small patios and tight spaces. Espaliers on cool walls. Lawn, patio or street tree. Hedge on stilts to extend upward the screening effect of a wall. A good understory tree that enjoys the dappled shade of taller trees.

Disadvantages: Very susceptible to fireblight. Sometimes attacked by red spider mites. Leaf drop is a nuisance, especially in spring, but occurs whenever tree is growing. Fruit is blighted by hard frosts.

Planting and care: May be grown from seed. Plant from containers any time, but best before summer heat. Shade young newly set plants from the sun during hot periods. Prune sparingly to train.

Eriobotrya japonica

Eriobotrya japonica

All zones
Evergreen
Soil: Tolerant, but needs good drainage.
Sun: Open to filtered or part shade. Full sun in middle and high zones. Afternoon shadow in low zone.
Water: Moderate, but accepts ample, especially as fruit ripens and as new growth appears. Tolerates periods of drought when established.
Temperature: Hardy to 15F (-9C) or below. Flowers and fruit damaged at about 28F (-2C).
Maintenance: Little to constant, depending on the neatness desired.

Erythrina bidwillii

(*E. crista-galli* x *E. herbacea*)
Bidwill's coral tree

This hybrid becomes a large shrub or small tree, growing vigorously to as high and wide as 20 feet (6.1m). In frost-free areas, produces an abundance of spectacular 3-foot (0.9-m) spikes of deep red pea-shaped blooms over the warm season, a dramatic contrast to its crisp bright green foliage. Large plants develop a thick trunk and branch structure, eventually becoming gnarled trees. In frosty areas, *Erythrina bidwillii* remains a shrub.

Special design features: Fantastic flowering display for color in the landscape throughout the warm season. Gnarly structure adds interest.

Uses: Tropical effects. Flowers attractive to birds. Containers.

Disadvantages: This is a thorny plant, so prune with care and plant away from walkways and other high-traffic areas.

Planting and care: Propagate with cuttings, or even branch sections. Prune to remove old bloom stalks or to keep as a shrub. Prune annually to enhance trunk and branch structure, particularly if you want to encourage a gnarly growth habit.

Erythrina bidwillii

Erythrina bidwillii

Low and middle zones
Partly deciduous
Soil: Improved.
Sun: Part shade to full sun.
Water: Moderate in warm bloom season to little in winter.
Temperature: mid- to low 20s F (-3 to -7C).
Maintenance: Seasonal. Remove old bloom stalks to harden wood before new spring growth.

Eucalyptus species

Family: Myrtaceae

Eucalyptus is the most commonly planted skyline tree in warmer parts of the Southwest and in similar climates throughout the world. There are also varieties of residential size that are less well known. More than 500, possibly as many as 750, kinds are found in Australia and Tasmania, with some ranging to the Philippines, Java and New Guinea. More than eighty species were introduced into southern California before 1900; about twenty species are now commonly planted. There are many shrubs called mallees and trees of various sizes that deserve attention. Only a few are covered here. Many are commonly found in nurseries. If you know of a kind you would like to have and can't find it, or if you want a lot of a certain kind, contract with a grower to start them for you. Good trees come from freshly grown stock not rootbound for indefinite periods in a nursery. They are mostly fast growers, so don't worry about the wait.

A similarity in appearance and scent makes almost all *Eucalyptus* easily recognizable. The differences are interesting and essential when choosing plants for the landscape. Some are extra fast growers and get too large for an average residence. Others have round or very narrow leaves or especially fragrant foliage. Color, form, rate of growth, eventual size, even the bark varies from species to species. Some are hardier to cold than others, or have especially beautiful flowers. The tallest reach over 100 feet (30.5m) high. There are also round headed types that may reach only 20 feet (6.1m) or so. Most *Eucalyptus* are drought and heat tolerant, grow fast and provide welcome shade or wind screen in hot dry areas. Not to be forgotten are the mallees, the shrubby *Eucalyptus*, which are multiple-branched and lower growing. Prune to open up and train into an interesting multitrunk tree.

In the colder parts of the West the number of successful species is more limited. Two more recent problems for the *Eucalyptus* are the borer and the unfortunate introduction of a pest, called the *redgum lerp psyllid*, from Australia that has been decimating trees in California. (See page 42 for more information on this pest.) The redgum lerp psyllid infests red gums and certain other *Eucalyptus*, but none that we know of other than *E. camaldulensis* and *E. sideroxylon* are covered in this book. If you are in a fairly isolated area you may be safer from infestation, but you also might consider other types of *Eucalyptus* trees or other species entirely.

Special design features: Handsome informal silhouette. Fast shade. Mostly vertical form.

Uses: Specimen, row or grove. Excellent for shade, windbreaks or open areas.

Disadvantages: Some species shed bark annually producing a litter of bark, leaves, flower parts and seed capsules. Most have greedy invasive roots that enable them to survive adverse situations but make them unsuitable for planting near structures, terraces, walks, garden beds or lawn areas. Larger trees sometimes break in the wind and drop branches. Iron chlorosis is a problem in some places, especially after freezes or if planted in a well-watered area. A symptom is new foliage that is bunchy and pale and sometimes tinged reddish or reddish brown. If not corrected, trees may languish and die. You can call a professional to spray iron chelates on the foliage or try the following method: To give a tree immediate treatment, place iron chelates in common gelatin pill capsules. Follow package directions for dosage amounts. Insert them into holes of equal diameter drilled into the trunk in an ascending spiral. Plug holes with chewing gum or caulking. Once the tree is treated with a spray or the pills, administer iron sulfate at the base of the tree to the drip line in little "banks" of iron poured into holes made with a pole, and irrigate deeply. Foliar sprays are also effective but are temporary and difficult to administer to large trees.

Planting and care: Plant frost-tender species in spring or summer, other species any time in an area large enough for eventual size of the tree, unless you plan to remove it when it gets too big. Select vigorous plants with roots that fill its container but are not rootbound. Young established trees in five-gallon containers are good buys. Be sure the species you select is suited to temperatures in your area or to a special microclimate or situation. Also be aware that many *Eucalyptus* species grow quite tall. Avoid planting the giants under power lines, or you will be plagued with pruning troubles for the life of the tree. Most young trees need staking until a strong vertical trunk develops. Some experts recommend planting only small one-gallon trees and never staking. The taller older trees in the nursery are grown too close to each other, becoming spindly, thus requiring staking. One-gallon trees in place will usually quickly catch up to the ones purchased in larger containers and should need no staking. Prune young trees as stated under the individual plant description. Very tall or old trees may need to be thinned or headed back to prevent wind breakage if they present a danger to structures, parked cars or passersby. This is best done by properly trained and equipped arborists. Improper heading back only increases the problem.

Eucalyptus species

Zones: See individual species descriptions. Evergreen
Soil: Widely tolerant. Deep soil and good drainage are important for best results. Trees are more likely to become chlorotic in alkaline or poorly drained soils.
Sun: Full sun.
Water: Give occasional deep irrigation, more often for young plants until they are established. Established trees grown where they receive extra runoff or in areas receiving 10 to 12 inches (254 to 305mm) annual rainfall will need little or no supplemental irrigation. Most trees benefit from monthly soakings through summer, especially in hot areas receiving no summer rains. Taper off irrigation to prepare trees for winter.
Temperature: See individual species descriptions.
Maintenance: None to constant, depending on the tree and its location.

Eucalyptus citriodora

Eucalyptus camaldulensis
(E. rostrata)
Red Gum • River Red Gum
Murray Red Gum

Red gum is a tall, majestic tree with weeping branches and long, slender medium green leaves. Its bark is mottled tan to light gray (sometimes white) and sheds in patches except on the lower trunks of older trees, where it becomes a consistent dark gray. Individuals vary widely in form and tolerance to cold, perhaps because of hybridization or the seeds point of origin. Too large for the average residence except at distant property edges. Very fast growing: It may grow 10 to 15 feet (3.1 to 4.6m) a year, eventually reaching around 120 feet (36.6m) in height. Best used in open areas, parks, large public spaces or for roadsides or shelter belts. Space 15 feet (4.6m) apart for windbreak, 20 to 30 feet (6.1 to 9.2m) or more for row planting. Damaged by cold at 15F (-9C) for a brief period. Best in low and middle zones.

Eucalyptus campaspe
Silver-Topped Gimlet

Decorative tree to 25 to 30 feet (7.6 to 9.2m) high, with a spreading crown 20 to 25 feet (6.1 to 7.6m) wide. Leaves are light silver and narrow. A cinnamon brown trunk is so smooth it looks polished. Inconspicuous late winter to spring bloom. A tough and undemanding tree that can exist on 7 inches (17.8cm) of rain a year but does better with a weekly summer watering or monthly soak in the root zone. Also accepts garden conditions. Good drainage is essential. Moderate to rapid growth depending on temperature and moisture availability. Not for formal landscapes, but looks good in all others. Grows in low and middle zones. In high zone, it sustains serious damage from freezes, resulting in major branch removal the next spring. Trees usually have an irregular branch structure.

Eucalyptus cinerea
Spiral Eucalyptus • Mealy Stringbark
Argyle Apple • Ash Gum

This irregular tree has a leaning trunk and gray juvenile leaves of great interest that spiral around the twigs. Moderate to fast grower to 20 to 50 feet (6.1 to 15.2m) high and 20 to 30 feet (6.1 to 9.2m) wide. Long, slender mature leaves eventually take over unless tree is pruned back. A pruned tree may

Eucalyptus campaspe

Eucalyptus camaldulensis

Eucalyptus cinerea (mature)

Eucalyptus erythrocorys

Eucalyptus microtheca

exhibit both juvenile and mature leaves. The foliage is valued in flower arrangements and bunches are sold in cities to freshen the air in apartments. Usually planted as an accent, character or silhouette plant, but not for use where a symmetrical tree is wanted in formal landscapes. It is perhaps most attractive when grown with multiple trunks. Handsome even in maturity, it maintains the gray foliage color. Tolerates more shade and more water than some *Eucalyptus* and generally does well in lawns. Space 10 to 15 feet (3.1 to 4.6m) apart for a mass effect. If grown for form and foliage, keep it pruned to 15 feet (4.6m). Adapted to high zone; hardy to 17F (-8C).

Eucalyptus citriodora
(E. corynocalyx)
Lemon-Scented Gum

Best where there are no heavy frosts, this tall, elegant and graceful tree has a smooth,

slender, pinkish white trunk, a strong vertical form that eventually produces an open, spreading crown, and narrow medium green leaves. Trees grow rapidly to 70 or even 100 feet (21.3 to 30.5m) high, gradually shedding branches to about 20 to 30 feet (6.1 to 9.2m) from the ground. Spreads 20 feet (6.1m), rarely to 30 (9.2m). Do not use where it will need to be topped because topping ruins the form. It is best used on hills or along roadsides where it can grow freely to its full magnificence. Its silhouette is especially attractive against structures or the sky. Safe to grow near walls and walks because roots don't heave. Accepts large or small amounts of water. Sturdily stake young trees. Thin and cut back until trunk becomes strong. When leaves are crushed, they give off a delightful fragrance resembling lemons. Bark peels and drops annually all at once, revealing first a smooth greenish white color, soon changing to a tan or pinkish white color.

Tenderness to cold is the only drawback besides annual bark litter. Frost damage may permanently distort its form. Hardy to about 23F (-5C) in the low zone and warm pockets of the middle zone. Becomes chlorotic in overwatered situations or in poorly drained or calcareous soils. Space 6 to 12 feet (1.8 to 3.7m) apart for grouping of tall slender trunks, 20 to 30 feet (6.1 to 9.2m) for a grove. Usually low branches will shed when young but can be trimmed off to enhance the high trunk and silhouette effect. Roots are not greedy, so other plantings nearby do well. In marginal climates, place trees in sheltered locations such as against south sides of tall buildings.

Eucalyptus erythrocorys
Red-Cap Gum • Illyarrie

Striking as a large shrub or small tree, red-cap gum is a moderate grower reaching 10 to 20 feet (3.1 to 6.1m) or higher, spreading 15 feet (4.6m). Attractive at close range with smooth light tan to whitish bark, irregular, somewhat open crown and very green 7-inch (17.8-cm) lance-shaped leaves.

This tree has one of the largest and most striking bud caps of the *Eucalyptus* group— bright scarlet, square, with a raised cross. They shed as showy yellow brushlike flowers in clusters appear (usually from fall to spring, but can appear any time). Seed capsules are large with wavy margins—decorative in arrangements. Grow as a single or multitrunk tree or as a large shrub. Roots are less greedy than other *Eucalyptus* and it remains in scale

with the average residence. Massed, it makes a handsome irregular grove. Low zone and protected microclimates of middle zone.

Plant any time of year from containers, but best set out in spring. Space trees 10 to 12 feet (3.1 to 3.7m) for a wide, loose screen or at random intervals for a grove. Cut back main shoots several times to form dense bushy growth or a multitrunk tree. Needs controlled staking and pruning to look good. Grows in lawns, but may need extra iron to prevent chlorosis. In its native Australia it grows in sandy or calcareous soils, so it should tolerate them in the arid Southwest. This plant is hardy to 23F (-5C) and tolerates high heat in arid climates when given moderate amounts of water.

Eucalyptus leucoxylon
White, Pink or Purple Ironbark

This is a tree of variable form that grows to a height of 20 to 50 feet (6.1 to 15.2m) or more. Usually has a light, open and slender appearance with pendulous branches. Eventual size and spread depends on soil and moisture conditions. Juvenile leaves are round and dark gray-green; mature leaves are the same color but long, slender and slightly curved to one side. Smooth whitish bark sheds in irregular flakes, revealing pinkish white inner bark. White blossoms appear among the foliage all year, with the heaviest show in winter. Widely tolerant of adverse conditions, including heat, wind, drought and heavy or rocky soils. Excellent as roadside or open-area tree. Often grown for timber or as an aid in honey production.

'Rosea' is the most popular white ironbark for landscape use because of its stunning hot pink flowers, which appear throughout the year with heaviest bloom in winter. 'Purpurea' has purple flowers. Both are variable in shape and size but usually are smaller than is typical of the species, reaching heights of 15 to 20 feet (4.5 to 6.1m), spreading 12, sometimes 20 feet (3.7 to 6.1m). All are very ornamental.

Select plants carefully, in bloom if possible, because they vary widely in form and color. Space the species 20 to 30 feet (6.1 to 9.2m) apart for roadsides, smaller forms at random distances 8 to 12 or 15 feet (2.4 to 3.7 or 4.6m) for small grove or informal screen. Depending on local conditions, soak root zone weekly or monthly. Hardy to 15F (-9C), so it can be used in low and middle zones and warmer microclimates in the high zone.

Eucalyptus microtheca
Flooded Box • Coolibah Tree

One of the most temperature tolerant and drought tolerant of the *Eucalyptus*, this single or multitrunk tree survives heat, drought and poor soil as well as cold. It is a picturesque, often leaning tree that grows at a moderate rate, eventually reaching 35 to 40 feet (10.7 to 12.2m) high with a slender, then spreading crown to about 25 feet (7.6m) wide. In caliche (or hardpan), reaches only 20 to 30 feet (6.1 to 9.2m) high. Selections have long, slender, ribbony silver-gray or green leaves that hang from pendulous branches. These trees can tolerate lawn conditions without becoming chlorotic. While very drought tolerant, they need intermittent irrigation in order to grow and develop. They are cleaner and less likely to break in the wind than many of the other *Eucalyptus*. Trunks of young trees are smooth and mottled white to gray. Older trees have wrinkled, cracked, fibrous gray bark on the lower trunk. Its smaller size makes it appropriate as a street tree or for use in smaller spaces than many other Eucalyptus trees. Young single-trunk trees need staking to develop vertical trunks, but they resist training and must be stoutly tied. Space 10 to 15 feet (3.1 to 4.6m) apart for windscreen, 20 to 30 feet (6.1 to 9.2m) or more for a street tree. Also makes a handsome, multitrunk tree.

Foliage may burn in a hard freeze, but winter-hardened trees usually survive to 5F (-15C). It is adapted to low, middle and high zones as well as to very arid conditions in the Middle East. Give young trees deep periodic irrigation until they are established. Trees once established can live on runoff water in areas of 10 to 12 inches (254 to 305mm) of rain a year if placed at the bases of banks or along streets where water collects at the edges. In hot areas with no summer rain, give monthly irrigation.

Eucalyptus nicholii
Nichol's Willowleaf Peppermint • Narrow-Leaved Black Peppermint

This graceful, fast-growing erect tree reaches up to 40 feet (12.2m) in height, spreading 25 feet (7.6m). It has a vertical form in youth and a spreading crown when mature. Weeping branchlets support very narrow, willowlike gray-green leaves that are sometimes purplish. Leaves smell like peppermint when crushed. Bark is soft, brown and fibrous. Because the bark does not shed as much as most *Eucalyptus*, it is a desirable garden or street tree. Flowers are small and inconspicuous. Space 15 to 20 feet (4.6 to 6.1m) apart for a graceful, willowy grove or screen, 30 feet (9.2m) or more for a row or street planting. Hardy to 12F (-11C) in the low and middle zones.

Eucalyptus polyanthemos
Silver-Dollar Gum • Silver-Dollar Tree
Red Box

Silver-dollar gum is a medium-size tree of moderately fast growth to 40 to 60 feet (12.2 to 18.3m) high and 20 to 40 feet (6.1 to 12.2m) wide. Picturesque and often asymmetrical, with an angular trunk, it is appropriate in small-scale landscapes. Individuals vary in foliage color and form. Round brown-green to gray-green juvenile leaves have a silvery cast, giving the tree an unusual informal texture; they are often used dried in indoor arrangements. Older trees develop more pointed mature leaves, but that takes a number of years. Trunks are covered with fibrous to scaly reddish brown bark. Upper limbs are mottled and support pendulous branchlets. Often open and irregular in youth, trees develop a wide crown with age. Select plants carefully because individuals vary. The silver-dollar gum grows almost anywhere and under poor conditions. Marginal in lawns or other well-watered locations, where it may develop chlorosis. Good drainage is necessary. They make excellent windscreens. For a row, space trees 20 to 30 feet (6.1 to 9.2m) apart. Can be pruned and shaped when young. Beyond that, little maintenance other than some cleanup.

Hardy to 14F (-10C), but trees have survived lower temperatures without damage, making it appropriate for warmer locations in the high zone as well as the low and middle zones.

Eucalyptus pulverulenta
Silver Mountain Gum • Money Tree

A real conversation piece, this fast-growing tree is widely admired for its round, leathery gray-green juvenile leaves that appear to be skewered on the branches. Attractive with a single trunk and perhaps even more so with multiple trunks, it benefits from pruning and shaping. Looks best when kept at 6 or 7 feet (1.8 or 2.1m) or a little higher, making it a good accent piece for smaller situations. Sturdy and appealing, it has silky white bark that peels and sheds annually. If allowed to

Eucalyptus polyanthemos

Eucalyptus pulverulenta

Eucalyptus robusta (crown)

grow to 20 or 30 feet (6.1 to 9.2m), the mature leaf form develops, which is slender and pointed—similar to other *Eucalyptus*. For a shrubby sapling grove, space plants 8 to 12 feet (2.4 to 3.7m) apart; for a row, space 15 to 20 feet (4.6 to 6.1m) on center. This is not a tree for windy areas. Hardy to 15F (-9C), but has survived lower temperatures without damage. Best in low and middle zones and all but the coldest areas of the high zone.

Eucalyptus spathulata

Eucalyptus robusta
Swamp Mahogany

A large shade tree for large spaces with a broad crown to 70 feet (21.3m). With moisture it grows rapidly to 80 feet (24.4m) high, usually shorter in desert conditions. Densely foliated with dark green leathery leaves 4 to 7 inches (10.2 to 17.8cm) long that give it almost a tropical feeling. Bark is stringy, rough and a dark reddish brown. Pink-tinted whitish flowers may appear any time, mostly in winter. It withstands salinity and overwatering if in well-drained soil, but, like other *Eucalyptus*, it may become chlorotic and unattractive in poorly drained calcareous soils. Because of its height, it is subject to wind damage, but heavy pruning ruins its form, so with its heavy litter it is suitable for larger sites, away from structures, where limb breakage and litter are not of concern. Once established, give it deep soaks every month or two. Adapted to all zones. Hardy to about 15F (-9C).

Eucalyptus sideroxylon
(*E. sideroxylon* 'Rosea')
Red Ironbark • Pink Ironbark

Red ironbark is a tree of variable form, height and color, growing rapidly to 20 feet (6.1m) high as an urban tree with restricted water to sometimes 80 feet (24.4m) in larger favorable situations. Spreads 15 to 20 feet (4.6 to 6.1m) wide. A striking tree—the slender trunk has deeply fissured, rusty dark brown bark. In each fissure, the red inner bark can be seen, which is dramatic in appearance. Trees are narrow and open with gray-green foliage. Those grown in the middle zone may be structurally distorted by occasional freezes. Flowers in pendulous clusters bloom from fall to late spring and are creamy pink to deep pinkish crimson. Usually the darker the foliage, the darker the flower color. Select individual plants carefully to get the characteristics you want.

Accepts high heat and poor or shallow soil. Best in light soil with good drainage and deep periodic irrigation. Use in a residential-size garden as a windscreen. A roadside planting of tall dark trunks is impressive. Space 15 to 20 feet (4.6 to 6.1m) apart for a grove, 30 feet (9.1m) or more along roadsides. Hardy to 25F (-4C). Use only in low zone and warmer areas of middle zone.

Eucalyptus spathulata
Narrow-Leaved Gimlet • Swamp Mallee

This small erect plant suitable for residential situations reaches 15 to 20 feet (4.6 to 6.1m) in height, with a single trunk or, usually, multiple trunks. Spreads about 15 feet (4.6m). Form is slender and bushy. Narrow ribbonlike bright green leaves are 2 to 3 inches (5.1 to 7.6cm) long. Bark is smooth and reddish brown. Tolerant of drought, poor drainage, lawn situations and heat. Actually a shrub, or mallee, it can be used in smaller spaces than can the full-size *Eucalyptus*. Excellent as a tall garden hedge, wind or privacy screen. Place plants in southern exposures or warmer microclimates if frosts are common. Space 6 to 8 feet (1.8 to 2.4m) apart for hedge or screen or randomly for small grove or filler planting. Hardy to 15F (-9C) in the low zone and warmer areas of the middle zone.

Eucalyptus torquata
Coral Gum

A tree for small or narrow spaces, this handsome, somewhat delicate-appearing tree makes a good grove, street, median or residential tree, with handsome flowers usable in arrangements. May need staking to achieve tree form. It is slender and upright and grows at a moderate rate to 15 or 20 feet (4.6 to 6.1m) high with equal spread. Unlike most *Eucalyptus*, it tolerates part shade. Light green leaves may be long and narrow or blunt an roundish. It has dark brown flaky bark. Numerous flower buds make a show on and off all year. They resemble Japanese lanterns and open to reveal coral and yellow flowers followed by 1/2 inch (1.3cm) seed capsules. The weight of the blooms and capsules may weigh down or even break the branches off. While it is reasonably drought resistant, this plant is most attractive if it gets a good soaking every week or two during the warm season and is in well-drained soil. It is best used in the low and middle zones, where it tolerates temperatues down to 17 to 22F (-8 to -6C).

Eucalyptus torquata

Euonymus fortunei

(E. radicans)
Family: Celastraceae
Common Winter Creeper

This evergreen vinelike shrub deserves wider use. It sprawls over the ground or will climb a wall to 20 feet (6.1m) or more, clinging by rootlets. Thick leaves are rich dark green above, whitish beneath, 1 to 2-1/2 inches (2.5 to 6.4cm) in length with scalloped edges. Branches are densely covered with tiny bumps and numerous leaves; some turn red in cold weather. Mature plants are shrubby and bear fruit. Plants on the ground sometimes root as they go. Native to Japan and South Korea.

Cultivars and other notable species: *E. fortunei vegeta* (big-leaf winter creeper) is woody enough to support itself as a mound or to train as a vine. It will cover an area of 15 to 20 square feet (4.5 to 6 square meters). Orange-seeded fruits come in fall. Spring growth is yellow-green. Grows in an irregular manner at first, sending out large branches. *E. fortunei radicans* has 1-inch long (2.5-cm) leathery leaves of dark green. It can trail or be used as a densly covering wall plant.

'Colorata' (purple-leaf winter creeper) is similar to *E. f. radicans* but its leaves turn dark purple in the cool of the year. 'Kewensis' climbs or trails with 1/4-inch (0.6cm) leaves that form a delicate tracery or dense ground cover.

Special design features: Leafy. Deep green color.

Uses: A plant for partially shaded to sunny walls. Spills over containers. Ground cover. Porch posts or trellises.

Disadvantages: Foot traffic destroys it. Subject to Texas root rot, powdery mildew and sometimes root knot nematodes. Rabbits sometimes eat it.

Planting and care: Plant any time. Space 3 to 4 feet (0.9 to 1.2m) apart for a ground cover. Apply a systemic or spray if mildew occurs. Responds to the same bug and pest prevention program as roses.

Euonymus fortunei

Euonymus fortunei

All zones
Evergreen
Soil: Tolerant. Prefers improved garden soil.
Sun: Part shade to full sun. Afternoon shade in middle and low zones. Reflected sun burns plants.
Water: Moderate.
Temperature: Tolerant of heat and cold to 0F (-18C).
Maintenance: Periodic.

Feijoa sellowiana

(Acca sellowiana)
Family: Myrtaceae
Pineapple Guava • Feijoa

An attractive, versatile and underused plant, pineapple guava does well in heat, cold and poor soil with little water. Growth rate is slow to moderate to 15 feet (4.6m) high with equal spread, but this South American native is easily kept at any size with clipping. Slightly fuzzy leaves are 3 inches (7.6cm) long, gray-green above and woolly white beneath, and are spaced at intervals along the twigs, giving the plant a distinctive character. A natural, somewhat open small tree with bending, weaving trunk or trunks, it accepts training to any form. Unusual fleshy, pinkish white flowers with long dark red stamens appear in May through June. Petals are edible and may be used to liven up fruit salads. Green fruit 3 inches (7.6cm) long ripen in fall—delicious eaten fresh or in jellies. Fruit that is still on the plant is not yet ripe. Wait until they fall to the ground. They will keep for about a week and can be gathered any time.

Special design features: Gray-green durable plant with strongly patterned foliage and beautiful flowers suitable for close-up viewing.

Uses: A wonderfully adaptable plant for all zones. Use as a small patio tree. Train as a dense, erect, clipped round-headed standard. Wide loose screen, clipped hedge or wall espalier. Adapted to large containers. While this plant can be sheared, this treatment removes the plant's distinctive character and produces minimum bloom.

Disadvantages: Problems are minimal. In well-watered locations such as lawns, plants can become chlorotic.

Planting and care: Plant from containers any time. Space 4 feet (1.2m) apart for clipped hedge, 5 to 6 feet (1.5 to 1.8m) apart for loose screen. Prune selectively in late winter to maintain shape and size, but prune only as needed. Clipped plants lose their natural character and produce fewer flowers and set less fruit.

Feijoa sellowiana

Feijoa sellowiana

All zones
Evergreen
Soil: Tolerant. Prefers good drainage.
Sun: Part shade to full or reflected sun.
Water: Best with occasional deep irrigation. Accepts moderate to ample. Established plants tolerate much drought and neglect.
Temperature: Hardy to about 15F (-9C), possibly lower. Tolerant of heat.
Maintenance: Trim and train to desired shape in winter. Otherwise none to periodic.

Ferocactus species and similar barrel cactus types

Family: Cactaceae
Barrel Cactus • Compass Cactus • Fishhook Cactus

The dramatic cylindrical form of the barrel cactus is a stand-by in the cactus garden. There are about twenty-five species of this plant group, native to the Southwest and Mexico. Those most commonly seen are about 16 inches (40.6cm) in diameter. They have a fluted form and green waxy skin. Clusters of spines grow on the outer ridges of the fluting, with several straight thorns and one heavy spine curved like a fishhook. Mature plants vary in size, depending on the species, with some kinds growing up to 8 to 11 feet (2.4 to 3.4m) high. Most in nature are seen at 2 to 4 feet (0.6 to 1.2m). Although the shape is similar to the unbranched young saguaro, this cactus is heavier in form and has hooked thorns, which the saguaro lacks. Most plants found in nature lean toward the south. This is caused by faster plant growth on the north side. Yellow to orange to red waxy flowers appear at the top of the plant. Bloom may come in May to September, depending on the species. Fruit like small greenish to yellow pineapples follow, filled with tiny round black seeds. There is no truth to the story that a decapitated cactus will produce a barrel of water for the desert wanderer dying of thirst. That is only a myth that has unfortunately contributed to the destruction of many cacti.

Special design features: Bold desert form. Desert and subtropical effect.

Uses: Emphasis plant for corners or entrances, but not too near walkways. Often used as a key plant in compositions with other succulents.

Disadvantages: Protected by law and illegal to obtain without tag. Slow to grow.

Planting and care: Plant any time. Buy tagged plants to ensure the cactus was acquired legally. Try to plant with same orientation to the south as the plant had originally. Irrigate occasionally during the first summer after planting, and anytime where the rainfall is less than 10 to 12 inches (254 to 305mm) a year.

Ferocactus species

Ferocactus species

All zones to 5,000 feet (1,524m) elevation, depending on species
Evergreen
Soil: Prefers sandy or gravelly soil with good drainage.
Sun: Full or reflected sun to part shade, except for plants collected in subtropical Mexico: They require more shelter from sun in middle and low desert climates.
Water: Occasional to none, depending on local rainfall.
Temperature: Species are hardy to where they are found naturally. Plants collected in warm subtropical regions need winter protection in cooler high zones, but there are numerous cold-hardy species, enabling you to avoid the tender ones.
Maintenance: None.

Ficus species

Family: Moraceae

Ficus species may not seem significant when you consider there are only one or two species that grow outdoors in the middle and high zones. But you might be familiar with these plants even if you live in a very cold area—many are grown as houseplants, such as *Ficus benjamina*. In areas that are nearly frost free, *Ficus* are important outdoor trees. The majority of the following plants are used as hedges and street trees in mild climates. They are truly tropical trees and are not dependable even in cooler parts of the low zone, but they are extremely versatile and attractive landscape plants to use where climate permits.

Special design features: Handsome silhouette. Bold, lush foliage.

Uses: Tropical effect. *F. benjamina* and *F. microcarpa* make excellent street or patio trees. All but *F. carica* can be trained as container plants.

Disadvantages: Fruit and leaf litter. Subject to Texas root rot and fig mosaic virus. Some species are tender to frost. The sap of *F. carica* green fruit is toxic.

Planting and care: Plant *F. carica* from cuttings or containers any time or bare root in winter. Plant other species from containers in spring, after danger of frost has passed. Provide sufficient room for root development or some species can buckle nearby pavement. Prune only to shape, create a formal tree, control size or remove dead branches. Trees damaged by root knot nematodes may need severe pruning. Varieties have different pruning requirements. Do any final pruning in late summer so tree can harden off before winter.

Fertilize outdoor trees in spring and early summer; indoor trees should be fed lightly with irrigation any time they seem to need a boost.

Ficus species

Zones: See individual species descriptions.
Evergreen (except F. carica, **which is deciduous)**
Soil: F. carica prefers gravelly soil with good drainage. Other species covered here prefer improved garden soil.
Sun: See individual species descriptions.
Water: Moderate to ample. F. carica can thrive on deep irrigation at wide intervals, but more during the growing season for better fruit.
Temperature: See individual species descriptions.
Maintenance: Periodic to constant, depending on species and use.

Ficus benjamina
(F. nitida)
Weeping Fig • Benjamin Tree • Weeping Chinese Banyan Tree

This is a handsome dark green tree with shiny, wavy-edged 3-inch (7.6-cm) leaves and an open irregular crown that broadens with age. Native to the Malay Archipelago, southeast Asia and north tropical Australia. A moderate grower, its ultimate size in arid lands is not yet known, but probably 20 to 30 feet (6.1 to 9.2m) high is maximum in frost-protected spots. This cold-tender plant is best grown in the warmest areas of the low zone or anywhere if kept indoors as a container plant. It is hardy to about 30F (-1C), but it seems to enjoy desert heat and sun with little evidence of leaf burn or low humidity stress. Grow in open shade to full sun, even reflected sun if new plant is gradually exposed to it before planting. Once adapted to reflected heat, weeping figs seem to enjoy it. Trunk is slender, erect and covered with light-gray bark; side branches are weeping. Mature plants are lush and tropical, producing many tiny, hard, inedible but decorative orange figs.

Excellent for confined spaces because it can be pruned or clipped and kept small. Clip into a hedge or formal tree shape. Oriental effect. Large or small containers on terraces or indoors if light is adequate. Tolerates full shade. Container plants develop into miniatures of trees growing in the ground. Sometimes scale or mealy bugs infest plants grown indoors. Laurel mite deforms leaves on plants grown outdoors (control with systemic). General garden care will help it look its best.

Ficus carica
Common Fig • Edible Fig

This deciduous tree has been grown in the Mediterranean region for thousands of years for its pear-shape fruit. Usually a sculptural

Ficus carica

Ficus pumila

gray-bark form in winter and a bold-leaf rounded form in summer. Its hairy, deeply lobed leaves to 8 inches (20.3cm) across and 10 inches (25.4cm) in length are lush but itchy and irritating to skin. A naturally low-branching tree, it must be pruned up continually if you wish to walk under it. Grows at a moderate rate 10 to 15, sometimes 20, feet (3.1 to 4.6, sometimes 6.1m) in height, spreading 8 to 10 feet (2.4 to 3.1m) wide, sometimes 20 to 30 feet (6.1 to 9.2m) if large tree. First crop of figs sets with the new leaves in spring and ripens in June, sometimes later, depending on variety. A second crop may ripen later in summer or appear continuously into fall only to be interrupted by autumn chill when leaves turn yellow and drop. Grow in full to reflected sun (tolerates some shade). Mature wood is fairly hardy, but succulent new growth may be killed by heavy winter freezes unless irrigation is tapered off from late summer onward to harden wood. Recovers from freeze rapidly. Prune in January. Best in the low zone, middle zone to about 2,500 feet (762m) and warm microclimates in the high zone. Hardy to 20 to 25F (-7 to -4C).

Although grown mainly for fruit, which attracts birds, or for sentimental reasons rather than as landscape subjects, there are many handsome mature fig trees in arid regions. Best planted alone, in the farther reaches of the garden, with room to spread. They are most attractive when viewed from a distance. If not planted alone, space trees 20 to 30 feet (6.1 to 9.2m) apart, depending on

the variety. There are many Cultivars and other notable species: 'Black Mission' (or 'Mission') with dark purple figs is best for low and middle zones, and is the best landscape tree. 'Brown Turkey' is better for the higher zone, smaller, with brownish purple fruit. A nice garden tree but needs to be cut back severely to fruit well and to make harvesting easier. 'Black Mission' has attractive sculptural branches when bare in winter. Both cultivars have bold foliage in summer.

Ficus microcarpa
Indian Laurel Fig • Glossy-Leaved Fig

Originally from India to the Malay Peninsula, this spreading tree has a dense round crown to 25 to 30 feet (7.6 to 9.2m) or more with pendulous side branches and smooth gray bark. Tolerant of high heat, this is a plant for the low zone or the warmest microclimates of the middle zone (or any zone as an indoor plant). It grows best in full sun to some shade, especially afternoon shadow. Damaged at about 25F (-4C), tender to frost and subject to foliage distortion when attacked by the laurel mite.

This dense *Ficus* is excellent for shearing or shaping. Effective as a spreading overstory tree or for formal topiary gardens. It provides welcome shade for large areas, although the surface rooting and trunks form buttresses—a problem near paving or lawns. This species will develop aerial roots from the branches in coastal arid regions, but the roots seldom reach the ground or form secondary trunks.

Shallow soil over impenetrable soil layers increases surface rooting problems. Prepare a deepened plant pit where caliche (hard pan) or other soil problems exist. Trees tend to be low branching and will need training and staking for a canopy shape.

F. microcarpa nitida, Laurel de India, is the tree most often seen in Mexican parks and plazas. It is smaller than the species (to 20 feet; 6.1m), at least in youth, and is more upright and stiffer in form. The crown is more conical at top and the foliage is stiffer and more pointed. Symmetrical growth habit makes it easy to shear and train for formal effects. Also a good plant in tubs. Can get thrips that curl leaves. Use systemics to control. 'Green Gem' is darker in color and seems less subject to thrip damage.

Ficus pumila
(F. repens, F. stipulata)
Creeping Fig • Climbing Fig

Creeping fig, a native of eastern Asia, is prized for the delicate tracery formed by its charming juvenile leaves on masonry walls. A self-climbing vine, it attaches itself tightly to walls with aerial rootlets. A few inedible figs form among foliage of mature plants. Once established, and when most of available wall space is covered, 2- to 4-inch (5.1- to 10.2-cm) mature leaves appear. They cover the plant densely, giving it a completely different appearance. Eventually the vine develops woody branches 2 feet (0.6m) or longer, which stand out perpendicularly from the wall. Sometimes slow to begin climbing, vines will cover a large building and are very aggressive once they catch on. The roots are invasive and vigorous vines may disrupt roof tiles or cover windows if not controlled. Filaments cling to masonry after the vine is removed. Never allow it to grow on wooden structures, because it will cause damage.

This vine for all zones creates a deep green woodsy feeling with a minimum of spatial depth. Damaged at about 15F (-10C), but usually survives freezes well if protected by warmth radiated from supporting wall. Prefers open or filtered shade to part sun. Best used on north or east masonry walls, against partly shaded pillars, in the recesses of buildings. Space 10 feet (3.1m) or more apart. Tying up growth at the time of planting sometimes helps, but it will climb when it is ready. To keep juvenile leaf and to control size, cut back all or partway every few years. The cultivar 'Minima' is smaller, with leaves that appear to stay juvenile longer.

Fouquieria splendens

Family: Fouquieriaceae
Ocotillo • Coach Whip • Vine Cactus

This dramatic plant is native to the U.S. Southwest and northern Mexico. It grows slowly to 12, sometimes 18 feet (3.7 to 5.5m) high. A few to several woody, thorny, mostly unbranched canes rise upward and outward from its base. After several years, plants may reach a diameter of 10 feet (3.1m) under favorable circumstances. Each spring and after summer rains, canes suddenly sprout green leaves their whole length. Leaves remain for several weeks (depending on soil moisture) before turning yellow and dropping. Spiky flamelike clusters of red tubular flowers from new growth develop at cane tips from April to July. They remain for several weeks before plant goes dormant. Ocotillo quickly responds to moisture, putting out leaves in four or five days. Conversely, plants go dormant equally fast when moisture dries up. Ocotillos are protected by the native plant laws of some states and cannot be sold or moved without a tag from the United States Commission of Agriculture.

Fouquieria splendens bloom

Warning: Most of the plants for domestic use are transplanted from the wild rather than grown in nurseries. There is a high mortality rate because many plants are not gathered or planted well. Some are infested with a borer that hollows out the whips and eventually kills the plant.

Special design features: Stark and dramatic silhouette against masonry or sky. Bold emphasis. Groupings, especially "living fences," are more striking than single plants. To create a living fence, wire canes together with the bottoms buried in the soil. These canes often take root, turn green and grow branches.

Uses: Dry areas, desert or natural gardens. Minimum landscaping with rocks or a few low plants with a decomposed granite or gravel mulch.

Disadvantages: Subject to rust or powdery mildew in cultivation.

Planting and care: Plant bare root from the nursery any time. Plants are most effective set with random spacing when used as a grouping. Plants root easily from cuttings, either long whips or short pieces, especially in spring and early summer. To be dug properly, a plant should have a few inches of root, which has been cleanly cut and sulphured, sticking out on all sides. Plant in the ground or a bank of sand the same day so the roots don't dry out. Its short trunk should not be buried in the ground. A few rocks around the roots will help it grab hold. Support with stakes and ties until it has had time to reroot. Besides having the roots well dug and the plant well set, check the canes (or whips). They should be firm with tough-looking greenish lines or cuticles down them, which indicates a healthy plant. The fresher a "living fence" is, the more likely the harvested canes will root and grow. Besides irrigation, spraying the fence twice weekly after installation and periodically for two or three months will encourage it to root and live. Also spray for rust or powdery mildew.

Fouquieria splendens

All zones
Deciduous
Soil: Rocky soil with good drainage.
Sun: Full to reflected sun.
Water: Irrigate newly set-out bare root plants weekly until established. Later, allow soil to dry out in between. Supplemental water is needed only in dry years or where rainfall is under 6 or 7 inches (152 to 178mm) annually. Constant or regular irrigation may kill plants. They also absorb water through the whips. Lightly spray them with the hose to encourage green leaves.
Temperature: Hardy to about 5F (-15C).

Living fence *(Fouquieria splendens)*

Fouquieria splendens

Fraxinus greggii

Family: Oleaceae
Little-Leaf Ash
Greg Ash
Gooding Ash

Small tree or large shrub with multiple trunks that grows at a slow to moderate rate to 9 to 12 feet (2.7 to 3.7m) high and spreads to about 9 feet (2.7m) wide, with smooth gray bark and small compound gray-green leaves. A five-gallon size tree can get to 10 feet (3.1m) high in five or six years and can eventually reach 18 feet (5.5m) in height and spread to 15 feet (4.6m) wide. Blooms in July and August. It is widely tolerant of conditions from the oasis to transitional or desert landscapes, where it will be smaller.

Special design features: A good tree for small spaces or in the open country

Fraxinus greggii

because it does not seem to be eaten by rabbits or javelinas.

Uses: Patio, courtyard or entry tree. Transitional areas to Xeriscapes.

Disadvantages: Slow to develop.

Planting and care: Wind pollinated. No particular care unless pruning and shaping to make a tree. Remove lower branches.

Fraxinus greggii

All zones
Evergreen to partly deciduous
Soil: Widely tolerant, but good drainage a must.
Sun: Reflected to full sun or part shade.
Water: Once established, can withstand erratic watering, but will grow faster with weekly irrigation.
Temperature: Hardy to at least 10F (-12C) or lower, probably to 0F (-18C).
Maintenance: None to periodic.

Fraxinus uhdei

Family: Oleaceae
Evergreen Ash
Shamel Ash
Mexican Ash

This upright tree grows 25 to 30 feet (7.6 to 9.2m) high in only ten years. A native of Mexico, it is a favorite in the lower zone due to its fast growth. In twenty years, trees in favorable situations may reach 40 to 60 feet (12.2 to 18.3m) in height. Young trees are narrow but in time develop billowing crowns as wide as the tree is high. Trees are nearly evergreen, except for old foliage that thins or falls just before new dark green 4-inch (10.2-cm) leaflets appear in February. Some seasons, new foliage appears before the last date of killing frost, damaging the tree. A young tree may lose branches as well as leaves from the cold, but it recovers quickly. Unimportant blooms come out as leaves appear. Winged fruit follows.

Cultivars and other notable species: 'Majestic Beauty' is more dependably evergreen and has a better form and larger leaves.

Special design features: Vigorous, upright, billowing form. Fast shade.

Uses: Shade tree for large areas, such as parks or large lawns or near tall buildings. Not for narrow spaces or areas near pavement; its buttressed trunk and surface roots will heave structures.

Disadvantages: Cold damage. Leaf burn from hot dry winds. Seed and flower litter. Limb breakage from high winds.

Planting and care: Plant from containers in spring when danger from frost has passed. Space young trees 30 feet (9.2m) or more apart. Correct pruning helps form a strong tree. Cut back long side branches of young trees. Prune weak branches at deep V-shaped crotches, which may split off in the wind. Leave only well placed, strong side branches to develop as the tree's scaffold— its basic framework. Correct buttress roots on old trees by cutting below the ground surface and forcing development of deeper brace roots. Irrigate deeply to encourage deeper rooting. If tree shows signs of iron chlorosis (yellowing of leaves), apply an iron foliar spray for immediate treatment. Annual applications of iron sulfate will usually prevent chlorosis from occurring.

Fraxinus uhdei

Fraxinus uhdei

Low zone; marginal in middle zone
Evergreen to briefly deciduous
Soil: Deep soil.
Sun: Part shade to full sun.
Water: Give ample deep irrigation, especially in summer.
Temperature: Branch and foliage damage occurs at approximately 22F (-6C). Serious damage occurs at 15F (-9C).
Maintenance: Periodic garden care.

Fraxinus velutina

(*F. toumeyl*)
Family: Oleaceae
Ash • Velvet Ash

This tree and its cultivars are some of the best and fastest-growing shade trees for the home garden to be found in the zones covered in this book. Native to the Southwest, trees grow naturally in canyons and along water courses. Trees are erect and grow to 30 to 50 feet (9.2 to 15.2m) high, with a spread of 20 to 30 feet (6.1 to 9.2m). Somewhat open, irregular crown of strong scaffold branches supports medium green leaflets, duller and more velvety than some of the cultivars. Inconspicuous flowers appear in spring, before foliage comes out, and in late spring, they bear winged fruit among the leaves of female trees. Trunk is covered with a gray bark of even roughness.

Cultivars and other notable species: 'Modesto' is vigorous and more refined and symmetrical than the species, usually smaller and more compact. 'Rio Grande,' also known as 'Fantex Ash,' has large, darker green leathery leaves, resistant to burn from the hottest sun or wind. It is vigorous, fast growing, highly resistant to drought and less subject to chlorosis caused by soil alkalinity than *F. velutina* or 'Modesto.' It also stays green, holding its leaves later in the fall.

Special design features: Handsome, upright shade tree. Yellow fall color.

Uses: Fast shade for lawn, patio, street or park. Excellent for summer-shade/winter-sun combination. In combination with evergreens. Specimen, row or grove.

Disadvantages: Iron chlorosis in poorly drained or heavily alkaline soils. Occasional mistletoe infestations. "V" crotch on 'Modesto' is subject to breakage by wind. Heart rot may infest pruned or damaged trees that have not been properly treated.

Planting and care: Plant from containers any time of year or bare root in winter. Space trees 25 feet (7.6m) or more apart for rows or groves. Carefully prune and shape young trees to remove weaker branches at each crotch to avoid wind damage. Treat cuts or wounds. If tree yellows, treat with iron foliar sprays and then feed iron sulfate once or twice a year.

Fraxinus velutina 'Fantex'

Fraxinus velutina

All zones
Deciduous
Soil: Tolerant. Prefers loose soil with good drainage and some humus added.
Sun: Part to full or reflected sun.
Water: Occasional deep irrigation.
Temperature: Hardy to 10F (-12C). Tolerant of heat.
Maintenance: Periodic.

Gazania rigens

Family: Asteraceae (Compositae)
Gazania • Treasure Flower

Gazanias hug the ground in leafy clumps and produce daisylike flowers on stems rising above the foliage. Narrow gray-green, sometimes lobed leaves radiate from the center of the clump. They bloom mostly in late winter and spring in low and middle zones before the heat of summer. In cooler summer areas, they may continue to bloom throughout the growing season. Yellow and white clumping types tend to be everblooming.

Cultivars and other notable species: 'Copper King' is generally considered to be the hardiest and blooms only in winter and spring. It has large orange flowers with wine-red markings toward the center—very dramatic as a mass planting. 'Gold Rush' is bright orange-yellow with brown spots at the base. Blooms are abundant and long-lasting. 'Royal Gold' has bright double yellow blooms. The 'Colorama' strain comes in white, cream, yellow, gold, yellow-orange or pink with purple undersides. Crosses between various *Gazanias* have produced clumping hybrids with bright colors and decorative markings. They grow moderately fast to form a dense, low mound of foliage to 6 or even 12 inches (15.2 to 30.5cm) high and as wide with daisylike flowers on stems above plant. Most have flowers that need sun to open and are closed on cloudy days or at night. Get seeds of named plants or purchase small plants at a nursery.

Special design features: Brilliant color at ground level.

Uses: Borders, ground cover, under trees producing only filtered shade. Bedding plant or filler between young plants of a more permanent nature, which are slow to mature.

Disadvantages: In heavy soils, an unidentified root rot or damping off fungus may wipe out parts of plantings in summer. Plants fail to cover, become stunted or die out, leaving bare areas. They often decline during hot weather.

Planting and care: Plant from flats, root divisions, seed or containers in fall or spring. Space plants or thin seedlings to one plant 9 to 12 inches (22.9 to 30.5cm) on center to cover. Refurbish bare spaces in spring and fall. Divide every three to four years.

Gazania rigens 'Copper King'

Gazania rigens

All zones
Evergreen perennial
Soil: Prefers enriched soil with good aeration and good drainage.
Sun: Part to full sun but accepts filtered shade. Flowers open best in full sun.
Water: Moderate. Allow the ground to dry out slightly between waterings, especially in summer. This helps avoid damping off. Avoid wetting foliage if possible. Watering early in the day will let foliage dry out before night when damp foliage is more likely to become diseased.
Temperature: Hardy to 15F (-9C). Languishes in intense heat.
Maintenance: Periodic grooming or winter replacement of dead plants to refurbish.

Geijera parviflora

Family: Rutaceae
Australian Willow
Wilga

A graceful weeping tree with medium green, fine-textured foliage, this distant relative of citrus looks like a refined, willow-leafed *Eucalyptus* and is just as hardy. Branches grow upward with the branchlets holding narrow 3- to 6-inch (7.6- to 15.2-cm) leaves that hang down like a willow. A moderate grower to 15 to 25 feet (4.6 to 7.6m) high with a spread of under 20 feet (6.1m). Bloom is insignificant. Although drought resistant, it will grow in well-watered places such as lawns. This well-behaved Australian native deserves wider use in warm climate areas. It has the grace of a willow, the toughness of a *Eucalyptus*, without the latter's invasive roots. Long-lived and pest-free.

Special design features: Willowlike weeping form. Light shade. Rustle of leaves.

Uses: Patio or street tree. Effective in grove or row plantings as a visual, wind or sun screen. Does well in neglected areas, on south sides or in lawns.

Disadvantages: Damaged by severe freezes.

Planting and care: Plant any time in low zone, in spring after frost is past in middle zone. Space 15 feet (4.6m) apart for a grouping or screen, more for a street tree. Only light pruning is necessary.

Geijera parviflora

Geijera parviflora

Low zone; protected areas in middle zone
Evergreen
Soil: Tolerant. Needs good drainage.
Sun: Full to reflected sun. Tolerates part shade, but looks thin and spindly.
Water: Tolerates drought when established. To promote growth, supply moderate to ample water. Once it reaches the size you want, taper off and give only occasional deep irrigation.
Temperature: Tree may defoliate at around 18F (-8C) and lose branches below that, but it recovers quickly.
Maintenance: Little.

Gelsemium sempervirens

Family: Loganiaceae
Carolina Jasmine
Confederate Jasmine
Yellow Jessamine

This is not a true jasmine, but its flowers resemble the Italian jasmine. It grows at a moderate rate to 20 feet (6.1m), providing an uneven and tangled cover. Shiny pointed leaves are yellowish green and densely cover the billowing, twining growth. Clear yellow trumpet-shaped flowers to 1-1/2 inches (3.6cm) long bloom in profusion along slender stems during late winter and early spring. Bloom is sometimes fragrant. Native to the southeastern United States.

Special design features: Vivid color when little else is in flower. Woodsy effect.

Uses: A vine for porch posts, fences, walls and trellises. It can also be used as a ground or a bank cover, but may tangle and mound, covering unevenly. It is also effective spilling from containers or draped over walls.

Disadvantages: All parts of plant are poisonous. In time it becomes overgrown and top heavy with dead underbranches. Flowers can be a litter problem.

Planting and care: Plant from containers any time. Space 3 feet (0.9m) apart for a ground or bank cover, 4 to 10 feet (1.2 to 3.1m) apart to make an attractive and interesting fence or wall plant. Tie to supports to train. For a ground cover, use U-shape wires like giant hairpins to spread out and stake stems to the ground in the pattern desired. Prune overgrown plant severely after the bloom is over; plants make a fast recovery.

Gelsemium sempervirens

Gelsemium sempervirens

All zones
Evergreen
Soil: Tolerant. Prefers improved garden soil.
Sun: Open to part shade, even full shade but blooms later in spring. Full or reflected sun for early bloom.
Water: Moderate. Established plants are reasonably drought resistant.
Temperature: Loves heat. Hardy to 15F (-9C) or below. Recovers from cold damage quickly.
Maintenance: Periodic.

Gleditsia triacanthos inermis

Family: Fabaceae (Leguminosae)
Thornless Honey Locust • Sweet Locust
Honeyshuck

Thornless honey locust is erect, growing at a moderate rate to 30 or even 75 feet (9.2 to 22.9m) high in the warm arid zones, spreading as much as 50 feet (15.2m). Train trees to have a tall trunk before scaffold branches spread out in a vase shape to form an eventual oblong crown. Also attractive as a multitrunk tree. Small leaflets range in color from bright spring green to deep green in summer, then turn yellow in fall. Unimportant greenish flowers produce large, flat black pods that hang on the tree through winter. A long dormant period prevents new leaves from being damaged by late spring frosts.

Cultivars and other notable species: 'Sunburst' has golden green foliage and an irregular form. 'Moraine locust,' a better known cultivar, is faster growing, more spreading in form. 'Imperial' is a symmetrical cultivar that, at maturity, reaches only 35 feet (10.7m). Its dense foliage produces great shade. 'Shademaster' is less spreading and a rapid grower to 24 feet (7.3m) high and 16 feet (4.9m) wide in about 6 years, eventually reaching 40 to 50 feet (12.2 to 15.2m). Other cultivars are also available.

Special design features: Erect vertical form. Handsome silhouette. Delicate summer foliage. Fall color.

Uses: Lawns, parks, boulevards, large patios. Deep roots do not heave paving. Foliage allows enough light to pass through to sustain lawns. Withstands city air pollution.

Disadvantages: Occasional infestations of mistletoe. Sometimes slower growing in low deserts. Pods can be unsightly. A pod gall may deform leaves in some locations. No known control.

Planting and care: Plant from container any time or bare root in winter. Easy to transplant large specimens during dormant period. Space 20 to 40 feet (6.1 to 12.2m) apart for boulevard plantings, 15 to 20 feet (4.6 to 6.1m) for groves.

Gleditsia triacanthos inermis

Gleditsia triacanthos inermis

All zones
Deciduous
Soil: Tolerant except for very heavy soils.
Sun: Full sun.
Water: Occasional deep irrigation. Young trees need frequent watering during growing season.
Temperature: Endures heat and cold, Prefers sharply defined winters and summers, but performs well in the milder low zone.
Maintenance: Cleanup and periodic pruning to encourage a balanced branch structure and to remove lower limbs.

Grevillea robusta

Family: Protcaceae
Silk Oak

Erect and columnar to pyramidal in form, silk oak grows rapidly 40 to 60 feet (12.2 to 18.3m) high with a spread of 20 to 30 feet (6.1 to 9.2m) when grown in deep soil. In desert areas, it rarely reaches its maximum height of 150 feet (45.7m). In shallow soils it may reach only 30 feet (9.2m) with a 15-foot (4.6-m) spread. Medium to dark green fernlike foliage densely covers the tree. Mature trees become broad-crowned and picturesque. Dense flat clusters of colorful yellow-orange flowers appear in May on short leafless branches of old wood; they attract birds and bees. Small woody pods with black seed follow. Silk oak is considered evergreen but can lose leaves from cold or become briefly deciduous in spring at bloom time just before new leaves come out. Native to Queensland and New South Wales, Australia.

Special design features: Strong vertical for a skyline silhouette.

Uses: Specimen or row in parks, by roadsides or in large public areas in warmer low zone. In the middle zone it is best on south exposures, protected from the full force of a cold winter, but older trees are quite hardy and reliable.

Disadvantages: Very susceptible to Texas root rot. Neglected or older trees develop dead unsightly branches that require pruning. Susceptible to iron chlorosis, especially in lawns.

Planting and care: Can be grown from seed. When planted from containers set out in spring after frosts. Space 15 to 20 feet (4.6 to 6.1m) apart for massing or a grove, 25 to 30 feet (7.6 to 9.2m) or more for a row. Stake willowy young trees against the wind. Shorten side branches to balance framework. Give iron if trees become chlorotic.

Grevillea robusta

Grevillea robusta

Low and middle zones
Evergreen
Soil: Tolerant. Prefers deep soil. Good drainage is essential.
Sun: Part, full or reflected sun.
Water: Best with occasional deep irrigation. Accepts more water with good drainage. Tolerates drought when established but grows slowly and looks poor.
Temperature: Young trees are more sensitive, damaged at about 24F (-4C). Older trees tolerate temperatures to approximately 15F (-9C), with minor foliage damage but they recover quickly.
Maintenance: None to periodic.

Hedera canariensis

Family: Araliaceae
Algerian Ivy
Canary Ivy
Madeira Ivy

Algerian ivy is an appealing plant with large, deep green, lobed leaves that vary from 3 inches (7.6cm) wide when young to 6 or 8 inches (15.2 or 20.3cm) wide when mature. Foliage is supported on wine-red stems that add color to the dark green form. Mature growth is stiff and woody, producing elliptical leaves and greenish flowers, but these are rarely seen. Once established, Algerian ivy grows aggressively to cover a large wall area. Bolder and more casual in appearance than English ivy, but not as good a clinger. Weight of mature leaves is likely to pull the vine away from its attachment. Vines are best tied to supports or grown on the ground.

Cultivars and other notable species: 'Variegata' (variegated Algerian ivy, Hagenburger's ivy, gloirede marengo ivy) is an often preferred form of Algerian ivy. Leaf edges are a creamy color and the center appears to be a grayer green. It is a bright contrast to dark wood or deep shade and dark green plants.

Special design features: Bold foliage. Tropical feeling.

Uses: Shaded places as a ground cover, especially beneath deciduous trees. Tie to porch posts, cool walls, fences or trellises where it will get afternoon shade.

Disadvantages: Subject to sudden death by a damping off fungus in summer. Can be affected by Texas root rot and snails and slugs. May be slow to start, but then becomes very aggressive, overcoming weaker plants nearby unless restrained. Leaves burn in hot sun. May creep into house through cracks or window casements.

Planting and care: Plant any time of year. Thoroughly soak both plant and ground before planting. Space 2 to 4 feet (0.6 to 1.2m) apart for a fast ground cover. Do any severe pruning in late winter before spring growth begins. Trim lightly as needed. Feed heavily in early spring.

Hedera canariensis

Hedera canariensis

All zones
Evergreen
Soil: Tolerant. Prefers improved garden soil. Needs good drainage.
Sun: Morning sun. Full, open or filtered shade. Accepts more sun at higher elevations or in winter.
Water: Moderate to ample. Established plants withstand some drought, especially in winter. Water plants early in the day so foliage will have time to dry out to prevent fungus.
Temperature: Hardy to about 10F (-12C). New growth may be damaged below 20F (-7C).
Maintenance: Periodic control of aggressive vines that spread in or over adjacent plantings.

Hedera helix

Family: Araliaceae
English Ivy

An old favorite, English ivy is a widely adaptable, self-climbing vine originally from Europe, Western Asia and North Africa. It covers densely, climbing walls, posts and tree trunks with tightly clinging aerial rootlets. Leaves are a dark dull green, 2 to 3 inches (5.1 to 7.6cm) long with three to five lobes and whitish veins.

Cultivars and other notable species: 'Baltica' has small juvenile leaves that turn purplish in winter. It trains well as a pattern plant on walls. 'Pittsburgh' ('Hahn's Self-Branching') has lighter green leaves with dense branches. Juvenile leaves become larger on mature plants. Both take at least as much sun as *H. helix*, perhaps more. Many other cultivars, some with miniature leaves, make excellent houseplants. There are also variegated forms.

Special design features: Dense cover of cool dark green. Woodsy.

Uses: North and east masonry walls, porch posts, ground covers, under stairwells or trees.

Disadvantages: Rootlets remain on masonry walls after vine removal. Aggressive and invasive once established. Growing tips sometimes find crannies and enter the house. Sunburn where exposed to summer sun. Harbors slugs and snails. Subject to Texas root rot and summer fungus, especially in warm moist soils.

Planting and care: Plant any time of year from containers or flats. Moisten planting hole and soil around plant in container before planting. Space 12 to 18 inches (30.5 to 45.7cm) apart from flats for a ground cover. To train on walls, one plant may be spaced 3 to 6 feet (0.9 to 1.8m) on center for cover. Do any heavy pruning in late winter before new growth starts. Trim lightly any time. At times ivy will overgrow and requires severe pruning to clear out old growth and to rejuvenate. Feed heavily in early spring.

Hedera helix

Hedera helix

All zones
Evergreen
Soil: Tolerant. Best with some organic material added to top 6 inches (15.2cm) of soil.
Sun: Full, open or filtered shade to morning sun. Accepts more sun in high zone.
Water: Moderate to ample.
Temperature: Hardy. Accepts heat with shade and ample water.
Maintenance: Periodic.

Hesperaloe parviflora

(H. yuccifolia)
Family: Agavaceae
Red Yucca
Semandoque
Red Hesperaloe

Red yucca is a clumping plant with narrow, curving straplike leaves that rise from its base to a height of 3 or 4 feet (0.9 or 1.2m), spreading as wide. Leaves are gray-green, stiff and fleshy, with numerous fibrous threads along the edges. Plants slowly enlarge by clumping outward to form an irregular cluster of foliage 3 to 4 feet (0.9 or 1.2m) wide. Tall leaning spikes with scarlet to coral bell-shaped flowers appear April through August or September. Native to Texas and Mexico.

Cultivars and other notable species: 'Yellow' has yellow flowers, is slightly smaller and has all the other attributes of *H. parviflora*. Variety *H. engelmannii* is a hardier form for the high zone.

Special design features: Tropical, subtropical or desert effect. Spring color.

Slender straplike leaves combine well with palms, yuccas and other bold-foliaged plants.

Uses: Dry areas. Natural, desert or rock gardens. Transitional gardens. Containers. Attracts hummingbirds.

Disadvantages: Slow to develop. Small plants are sometimes eaten by rodents, so protect them until they gain some size.

Planting and care: Plant any time from containers. Divide old clumps in late winter and reset to form new plants. Remove old flower spikes after bloom has passed. Prune in October.

Hesperaloe parviflora

All zones
Evergreen
Soil: Tolerant of many soils.
Sun: Full or reflected sun.
Water: Moderate to none. In areas with less than 10 inches (254mm) of rainfall, supply supplemental irrigation. Extra water as plant establishes will speed development.
Temperature: Foliage damaged around 10F (-12C). *H. engelmannii* is hardy to 0F (-18C).
Maintenance: None except for removing old flower spikes.

Hesperaloe parviflora

Ilex cornuta

Family: Aquifoliaceae
Chinese Holly

Favored for its crisp, spiny evergreen leaves and occasional red berries, Chinese holly is marginal, except in the high zone, and grows slowly to make a large shrub or a small tree, reaching an eventual height of 6 to 10 feet (1.8 to 3.1m). Its open form bears leaves to 2 inches (5.1cm) long with sharp spines at each of the four corners and at the tip. Chinese holly is not as dependable or as widely used in arid zones as the cultivar 'Burfordii.'

Cultivars and other notable species: Although most hollies seem to languish in the warmer zones, 'Burfordii' does very well, especially if it gets afternoon shadow in hot summer areas. It grows at a slow to moderate rate up to 6 feet (1.8m) high and 4 feet (1.2m) wide but is easily maintained at a smaller size. Leaves are usually thornless. Berries are large, bright red, long lasting and need no pollinator. Berry production in the desert is usually sparse, especially on clipped plants. 'Dwarf Burfordii' is smaller, slower growing and more compact.

Special design features: Crisp, bright to deep green. Woodsy effect.

Uses: A plant for under trees, north sides and other shaded places as a shrub, foundation plant, espalier or standard tree. Clipped hedges or screens. Pool areas or anywhere litter would be a problem. North and east exposures. May use larger plants as a loose screen but they have an uneven growth pattern and shape that doesn't match the neatness of the foliage. Usually more attractive when clipped. The dwarf looks good close-up and can be used in small intimate gardens, such as entryways and atriums.

Disadvantages: Leaves may sunburn in hot sun. Subject to iron chlorosis in alkaline or calcareous soils. Usually a problem-free plant, however.

Planting and care: Plant from containers any time. If pruning is necessary, do it in late winter before new growth starts. Mulch roots against summer heat. Do not cultivate around roots, because it disturbs them. Flowers appear on old wood. Pruning and clipping lessens their number and the number of berries. Feed iron if plants become chlorotic.

Ilex cornuta

Ilex cornuta

Middle and high zones; shaded areas of low zone
Evergreen
Soil: Tolerant. Best with improved garden soil.
Sun: Open or filtered shade. Morning sun.
Water: Moderate is best. Accepts occasional soakings once established. Tolerates little to ample water.
Temperature: Hardy to cold. Accepts heat with shade.
Maintenance: Periodic to almost none depending on taste and use.

Jacaranda mimosifolia

(J. ovalifolia, J. acutifolia)
Family: Bignoniaceae
Jacaranda • Green Ebony

This Brazilian native produces a breathtaking sight in mid- to late spring when it produces large sprays of lavender-blue flowers. It grows at a fast to moderate rate reaching 25 to 50 feet (7.6 to 15.2m) high, spreading 25 to 40 feet (7.6 to 12.2m) wide. This tree revels in heat and requires it in order to flower. Flower clusters appear any time from April to September, but the majority are usually seen in May or June. Tree normally drops its leaves in February or March (some will retain a little foliage) and stays bare until flowering time or sprouts new leaves soon after dropping old ones in warmer areas. Individual flowers are 2 inches (5.1cm) in length and look like clusters of trumpets. Some cultivars have blooms of white or orchid pink. White selections may blossom over a longer period, but with less profusion and lusher foliage. All forms have dark, rounded 2-inch (5.1-cm) seed capsules shaped like castanets.

Special design features: Tropical effect. Color during the warm season. Shower of petals on ground or pavement is pleasant to some, a nuisance to others. Handsome ferny foliage texture.

Uses: Specimen or grouping on south or west sides of tall buildings or at north end of courtyard where it receives southern sun and reflected heat. Plants can be located in the open in warm areas of the low zone and microclimates of the middle zone.

Disadvantages: Cold sensitivity may preclude bloom. Unattractive for a period in spring. Litter of leaves, blossoms and seed capsules.

Planting and care: Plant in spring from containers after weather warms up. Space 15 to 25 feet (4.6 to 7.6m) apart for a grouping. Stake young trees to form a single erect trunk or grow as a multistemmed or multitrunk shrubby plant, especially where plants are frozen back periodically. Prune in August to develop basic branch structure.

Jacaranda mimosifolia

Low zone; middle zone if sheltered
Winter deciduous; briefly deciduous in early spring
Soil: Tolerant. Prefers loose, sandy soil.
Sun: Full to reflected sun.
Water: Once established, occasional deep irrigation, such as a good weekly soak in summer, and about twice during winter dormancy. Too much water in late summer and early fall produces succulent growth tender to frost. Taper off watering as fall approaches.
Temperature: Young trees damaged at about 25F (-4C). Older ones can tolerate temperatures a few degrees lower. Recovers vigorously after freezing, but will have a distorted structure and won't bloom. When last season's new wood is damaged in hard freezes, the next spring's flowers are destroyed.
Maintenance: Periodic garden care.

Jacaranda mimosifolia

Jasminum species

Family: Oleaceae

Jasmine is usually thought of as a fragrant vine. Many are. Some are not. All the plants below prefer garden soil and garden care, require support to climb, and need frequent pinching and shaping to direct their growth. Some, if not trained to climb, can make good hedges. Several are mentioned briefly here along with the zones in which they are known to grow and any unique characteristics. They join the needed parade of vines for the oasis garden.

Special design features: A bold plant. Spring color. Informal.

Uses: Large-scale ground cover, foundation plant or background plant. A wide screen or space divider. Excellent as a clipped hedge. Trains well over walls or high planters or banks.

Disadvantages: Rank growth unless cut back every few years or clipped regularly. Becomes woody with age. Develops iron chlorosis in overwatered situations, yet shows drought stress quickly.

Planting and care: Plant from containers any time. Space 6 feet (1.8m) apart for a mounding effect; 18 to 24 inches (45.7 to 61cm) on centers for a low clipped hedge; 3 feet (0.9m) apart for a higher one. Shear any time for a hedge. To rejuvenate, cut back overgrown plants nearly to the ground in spring after bloom has passed. Plants tolerate neglect but become woody and unattractive. If plants yellow, give extra iron.

Jasminum species

Zones: See individual species descriptions.
Evergreen to deciduous: See individual species descriptions.
Soil: Tolerant. Appreciates improved garden soil with good drainage.
Sun: Part to full or reflected sun. Prefers moist but not soggy soil.
Water: Tolerates moderate to ample. Does well with occasional deep irrigation, but wilts quickly when the soil dries. It recovers rapidly when water becomes available.
Temperature: Accepts heat of south and west sides. Cold hardiness varies among species.
Maintenance: Constant garden care for the most attractive plants.

Jasminum grandiflorum
(*J. officinale grandiflorum*)
Spanish Jasmine

A deciduous vine that grows in the low and middle zones. It grows fast to 10 or even 15 feet (3.1 to 4.6m) and bears fragrant 1-1/2 inch (3.6cm) white flowers in clusters all summer that remain on the plant. Leaves are glossy and green, with five to seven leaflets, 2 inches (5.1cm) long. Open and airy in aspect. Train on a support. Handsome leafy silhouette on walls. Low zone and warm microclimates of middle zone.

Jasminum humile
Italian Jasmine

A yellow-flowering jasmine, similar to *J. mesnyi*, but with smaller single flowers that are very fragrant. Foliage is light green. This sprawling evergreen shrub or shrubby vine grows to 6 feet (1.8m) high or higher. Train and support vine, which tends to be erect and willowy, with long arching branches. Will make a large mound if not restrained. Can also be clipped as a hedge or planted in a row. Best in low and middle zones. 'Revolution' has larger leaves and flowers that are twice the size of *J. humile*.

Jasminum mesnyi
(*J. primulinum*)
Primrose Jasmine • Yellow Jasmine
Japanese or Chinese Jasmine

Primrose jasmine is a bold, sprawling shrub with branches trailing 6 to 10 feet (3.1m) in length. Untrained and untied, its natural form is a spilling fountain of rapid growth. It trains well into a wall plant and is one of the few plants for clipped hedges that will bloom profusely even when sheared. Medium green leaflets of three along the square stems are rather coarse in texture. Clear yellow single or double nonfragrant flowers bloom for a long period in late winter or early spring. Flowers are wide open and evenly spaced in pairs along the slender stems and look like popcorn after they dry out. No seeds are produced and there is no fragrance. This native of western China is hardy in all zones.

Jasminum nitidum
(*J. magnificum*)
Angelwing Jasmine

Evergreen in the low zone to semideciduous in the middle zone, this jasmine likes a long warm growing season and grows at a moderate rate to 10 or 20 feet (3.1 or 6.1m) high. Leaves are leathery, glossy and medium green to 2 inches long (5.1cm). Flower buds are purplish. Flowers to 1 inch (2.5cm) wide are very fragrant and look like little white pinwheels with purple bases. It needs drastic pruning, can make a shrubby ground cover or an attractive container plant where it can stay evergreen in the middle zone if it is protected from cold.

Jasminum grandiflorum

Jasminum nudiflorum
Winter Jasmine

A deciduous vine with slender willowy branches that can grow to 10 to 15 feet (3.1 to 4.6m) with support. Foliage is a glossy green and somewhat tender to cold. Nonfragrant 1-inch (2.5-cm) flowers are yellow and appear in spring before the leaves are out. It is adapted to the high zone, but can also grow in the middle and low zones. Train it as you would *J. mesnyi*.

Jasminum mesnyi

Jasminum polyanthum
Evergreen Vine

This evergreen from the low and middle zones climbs fast to 20 feet (3.1m). Its leaves are dainty, divided into leaflets. It has dense clusters of little pink buds that open into fragrant white flowers in midspring and may last to July in higher and cooler locations. It needs heavy pruning to keep it from becoming a tangle and, besides being trained as a vine, can be used as a ground cover as well as a container plant. Prefers regular irrigation.

Jasminum sambac
Arabian Jasmine • Pikake

An evergreen shrub that prefers the warmer low zone because of its sensitivity to cold (tolerant to 28F; -2C). Famous for its fragrance, its spring white flowers with pink exteriors are 3/4 to 1 inch (1.9 to 2.5cm) in diameter. In Hawaii, where it is called pikake, it is a favorite for leis. It is the jasmine of perfume and, in Asia, is added to tea to make jasmine tea. As a shrub it grows to 5 feet tall (1.5m) with glossy 5-inch (12.7-cm) leaves. Can be used in a container in the middle zone where it can be moved to a warm spot in winter or trained on a trellis as a vine in warm winter areas. A double flowered variety is called 'Grand Duke' jasmine.

Jasminum mesnyi

Juniperus species

Family: Cupressaceae

Junipers are a numerous group of coniferous plants originating from parts of the Northern Hemisphere. They seem somewhat out of place in arid regions, but because they are easy to grow, dependable and tolerant of a range of conditions, they are frequently planted in western gardens. Colors range: silvery, blue, bright green, deep green, yellow-green and gray-green, as well as variegated. Juniper forms are also many: prostrate or creeping, low spreaders to knee high and shrubs 6 to 8 feet (1.8 to 2.4m) high. Some kinds become small to medium trees after many years—others grow into tall trees seldom seen in home landscapes.

Form varies from horizontal or spreading to those with fountainlike, upward-pointing branches. There are upright columnar types and weeping forms. All are recognizable as junipers because of their dense, scaly, sometimes needlelike foliage, similar to that of cypress.

Over the years junipers have been the subject of much manipulation and selection by horticulturalists. There are many, many varieties available, and a complete list would require many pages. Juniper admirers in every region have different opinions of which junipers are the best. The following includes a few selections in each general landscaping category.

Special design features: Dense evergreens with medium to fine-textured foliage. Woodsy feeling. Some produce an oriental effect. Transitional when used with dry, desert-type plants, but also fits into the well-watered landscape.

Uses: Varied landscape uses according to plant.

Disadvantages: Large mature plants usually lose their form and charm when branches are cut back beyond the foliage. Foliage does not regrow quickly and may not come back at all if pruned severely. Foliage is somewhat prickly when handled. In hot areas the inner foliage on some types burns from the sun and becomes straw-colored and unattractive. Some very low types burn out completely because the foliage does not shade the soil over their roots to keep them cool. Junipers are subject to infestations of spider mites. Aphids cause falling needles, sticky deposits and sooty mildew. Twig borers cause branch tips to brown and die back. Control by spraying from mid May to mid June with Sevin or Diazinon or with copper sprays in mid and late summer. As with all ground covers, plantings of low-growing junipers suffer from invasions of Bermudagrass or weeds. Plant only where Bermuda has been removed or destroyed to prevent this. Infestations of unwanted plants may be controlled by pulling or by careful application of an herbicide. Preemergents can be effective in controlling weeds. Because of the prickly, mounding, dense character of the genus, trees trap airborne trash and leaves, which looks bad and is difficult to remove.

Planting and care: Plant any time of year from containers. Avoid crowding. Because most junipers are slow to moderate growers, space between plants can be filled with annuals, perennials, small shrubs or a mulch until junipers grow to fill the space. Do not plan to remove plants later in a closely set planting, which is sometimes suggested. Roots of individual plants usually intertwine, so removal of any plant may injure others. Be sure to place plants at least 3 to 4 feet (0.9 to 1.2m) away from curbs or paved edges to prevent them from growing into an area where they will be in the way. In hot regions, mulch roots of young plants to keep them cool until foliage spreads out to shade itself. Transplant junipers in fall or winter so they can regrow roots in cool weather. Never give heavy feedings of nitrogen fertilizers. As with all conifers, junipers are sensitive to all but the lightest touch of nitrogen and can be injured by heavy applications. The best fertilizer is a manure mulch. As plants reach the desired size, trim them by removing the main leaders inside the foliage where the cut will not be visible. This leaves the secondary or side branches and helps maintain the plant's appearance while still containing it. Shearing and shaping destroys the natural form of junipers, but they can be successfully clipped and trained into dense hedges or bonsai. Clipping and shearing are answers to overgrown plants if removal is the only alternative. Note that junipers placed closer together than their natural width will grow taller than normal. As they begin to crowd together, the only direction they can grow is up.

Ground Covers

Juniperus horizontalis
(J. prostrata, J. chinensis prostrata, J. virginiana prostrata)
Prostrate Creeping Juniper

Flat heavy branches of this dark green juniper support dense short twigs. Space a minimum of 3 to 5 feet (0.9 to 1.5m) apart and 4 to 5 feet (1.2 to 1.5m) from any edge. Slow growing to 18 inches (45.7cm) high, spreading 8 feet (2.4m) or more.

Juniperus horizontalis 'Wiltonii'
(J. h. 'Blue Mat')
Blue Carpet Juniper

This plant makes a dense, undulating cover of silver-blue, sometimes taking on a purple cast in cold weather. It is the flattest-growing juniper, with long trailing branches and short side branchlets. Sometimes burns from reflected heat, especially new plantings in the low and middle deserts. Organic mulches, such as wood chips, keep the soil surface cool until plants fill in. Space a minimum of 3 to 4 feet (0.9 to 1.2m) apart and from any edge. Growth is slow to moderate to 4 inches (10.2cm) high, spreading 8 to 10 feet (2.4 to 3.1m).

Juniperus sabina 'Buffalo'
Buffalo Juniper

This juniper is bright green, with soft feathery branches and foliage that spreads out laterally. Massed, it gives a crosshatched effect, which makes a pleasing pattern. It is very hardy and prefers some humidity or a little shade in the low and middle zones.

Juniperus species

All zones
Evergreen
Soil: Good drainage is important. Species are tolerant but prefer enriched porous soils.
Sun: Full sun to part or even full shade.
Water: Best with occasional deep irrigation—allow soil to dry between waterings. Do not allow young plants to dry out completely until they have become established. Good-looking plantings are often seen adjoining lawns, but as a rule, avoid soggy soil because plants will often collapse from poor drainage.
Temperature: Hardy to 0F (-18C). Those listed are tolerant of heat and low humidity.
Maintenance: Plants tolerate neglect but look best with periodic shaping and cleanup. Weed and grass invasions of immature plantings are the chief maintenance problem.

Juniperus sabina 'Buffalo'

Juniperus sabina 'Tamariscifolia'

Juniperus chinensis 'Pfitzerana Compacta'

Space 4 to 6 feet (1.2 to 1.8m) apart and 3 to 4 feet (0.9 to 1.2m) from any edge. Growth is slow to moderate to 12 inches (30.5cm) high, spreading to 8 feet (2.4m).

Juniperus sabina 'Tamariscifolia'
(J. tamariscifolia)
Tam • Tamarix Juniper

This juniper is dark blue-green and spreads to make a dense, symmetrical form. Varies from a low, spreading habit to one with more ascending branches, which makes a higher plant. Pick plants with the habit you want. One disadvantage is that occasional plants in a mass planting fail for no known reason. Space 5 to 6 feet (1.5 to 1.8m) apart and 4 to 5 feet (1.2 to 1.5m) from use areas. Growth is slow to 1-1/2 to 3 feet (0.5 to 0.9m) high, spreading 8 to 20 feet (2.4 to 6.1m).

Shrubs

Juniperus chinensis 'Blue Vase'
Texas Star Juniper

The square, blocky form of this plant is covered with prickly blue foliage. Attractive as a shrub or barrier, space 10 feet (3.1m) apart for specimen plantings in hot areas, closer in cooler regions for a continuous planting. Keep 6 feet (1.83m) away from edges or use areas. Growth is slow to moderate to 3 to 4 feet (0.9 to 1.2m) high and as wide, but it gets much larger in hot areas.

Juniperus chinensis 'Mint Julep'
Mint Julep Juniper

Upward-jutting branches covered with bright green foliage give this juniper the effect of "taking off." Dependable green color for sunny places, hot or cold. Space 5 feet (1.5m) apart and from any edge. Grows 2 to 4 feet (0.6 to 1.2m) high or higher, spreading to 6 feet (1.8m).

Juniperus chinensis 'Pfitzerana'
Pfitzer Juniper

This is one of the all-time durable plants for hot sunny spaces. Pfitzer has dense, deep, gray-green feathery foliage on upward-sweeping branches that jut out at a 45-degree angle. Space 10 feet (3.1m) or more apart and 10 feet (3.1m) from any edge. Growth is slow to moderate to 5 to 8 feet (1.5 to 2.4m) high, spreading to 15 feet (4.6m).

Juniperus chinensis 'Pfitzerana Compacta'
(J. pfitzerana nicksi, J. nicksi compacta)
Compact Pfitzer Juniper

Compact, densely branched and gray-green, this juniper has proved to be popular in the desert. It is low growing but does not spread quite as much as a ground cover plant. Space 4 feet (1.2m) apart and 5 feet (1.5m) or more from any edge. Growth is slow to moderate to 2 feet (0.6m) high, spreading 4 to 6 feet (1.2 to 1.8m).

Juniperus chinensis 'Pfitzerana Glauca'
Blue Pfitzer

Similar to pfitzer juniper in every way except its color is silvery blue. Space 10 feet (3.1m) or more apart and 10 feet (3.1m) from any edge. Growth is slow to moderate to 5 to 8 feet (1.5 to 2.4m) high, spreading to 15 feet (4.6m). There is also a variegated form with yellow-tinged foliage, but most landscape plants variegated with yellow or gold look chlorotic in arid lands because chlorosis is a problem with so may landscape plants.

Juniperus sabina 'Arcadia'
Arcadia Juniper

'Arcadia' is low growing, with rich, green, lacy foliage that juts outward, forming an attractive tiered pattern. Plants open up in the center, making them less dense than other junipers, but they are very dependable growers. Space 3 to 4 feet (0.9 to 1.2m) apart and place about 5 feet (1.5m) from any edge. Growth is slow to moderate, 2 to 4 feet (0.6 to 1.2m) high, spreading 4 to 5 feet (1.2 to 1.5m).

Small Trees

Juniperus chinensis 'Kaizuka'
(J. c. 'Torulosa')
Hollywood Juniper • Twisted Juniper

This interesting, twisted, irregular and upright form makes a dramatic silhouette. It looks frozen in the wind. Deep rich green in humid climates, dusty olive-green in hot arid regions. Aside from the color difference, it grows well in these zones. Space 8 to 12 feet (2.4 to 3.7m) apart. Growth is slow to moderate to 15 feet (4.6m) or higher, spreading 6 to 8 feet (1.8 to 2.4m).

Justicia spicigera

(*J. ghiesbreghtiana, Jacobinia ghiesbreghtiana, Cyrtanthera ghiesbreghtiana*)
Family: Acanthaceae
Mexican Honeysuckle • Desert Honeysuckle • Firecracker Plant

A wonderfully dependable nonwoody shrublike plant, Mexican honeysuckle is one of the most welcome introductions in recent years. It provides color more or less all year in mild-winter climates. Soft, fuzzy-surfaced medium green leaves are slender elongated ovals that taper to a point. Erect stems grow fast to 5 feet (1.5m) unless trimmed back; plants are easily kept at 2 or 3 feet (0.6 to 0.9m) with occasional trimming. A gallon-size plant will spread to 2 feet (0.6m) or more at the base; with foliage it may be 3 feet (0.9m) or wider. Clusters of red-orange tubular flowers loved by hummingbirds are heaviest in spring, appearing after a growth spurt.

Cultivars and other notable species: *J. californica* (chuparosa) is a similar plant with a sparser appearance than Mexican honeysuckle. Responds well to rain or irrigation. It is native to the low zone so is not particularly hardy, damaged at about 28F (-2C). It can be grown in the middle zone where it recovers quickly from winter cold setbacks.

Special design features: Lush, almost tropical effect. Some color nearly all year.

Uses: Containers. Small planting areas such as entryways, large planters, atriums and patios. Bedding or foundation plant. Does well in hot places or under trees with filtered shade, as a filler plant or an underplant. For clumps, masses or rows in irrigated, natural, desert or tropical gardens. East, south or west walls. Also on the north, but less bloom.

Disadvantages: May become rank or look bad in cold weather. Occasionally yellows from chlorosis.

Planting and care: Plant when frost is past in the middle zone, any time in the low zone. Pinch tips to encourage bushiness. Feed to encourage fast growth; feed iron if it yellows. Trim back occasionally to keep neat and to rejuvenate.

Justicia spicigera

Justicia spicigera

Low and middle zones
Evergreen perennial
Soil: Average garden soil with good drainage.
Sun: Filtered shade to part shade to full or reflected sun.
Water: Moderate to ample. Tolerates less in cool weather.
Temperature: Freezes back at about 25F (-4C). Recovers rapidly in warm weather.
Maintenance: Periodic. Some trimming.

Lagerstroemia indica

(*L. elegans*)
Family: Lythraceae
Crape Myrtle

Crape myrtle grows at a slow to moderate rate to 15 feet (4.6m) high, sometimes to 20 feet (6.1m), spreading 8 to 12 feet (2.4 to 3.7m) or more. Plants usually take on a vase shape, but are sometimes trained as small trees with a single or multiple trunk. Shiny long leaves are bright green, often tinged with bronze, especially when new. Depending on the weather, they are golden, orange or red in fall before dropping to reveal a handsome outline. When bare, crape myrtle lends interest to the landscape with clusters of rounded seed capsules that remain at the branch tips. Smooth dappled gray to light brown bark may shed to reveal a pinkish inner bark. Large clusters of delicate flowers in shades of red, white, purple and pink may bloom when hot weather arrives, from May to September. It loves heat and grows best when protected from wind and in deep soil.

Cultivars and other notable species: Many outstanding hybrids and cultivars are available.

Special design features: A change-of-season plant—spring green and summer flower color, fall color, winter silhouette. Informal but luxuriant.

Uses: Color feature plant for summer. Combines well with plants in any type of garden. Transitional plant. Group, row or specimen.

Disadvantages: Chlorosis in alkaline soils. Hot winds can also cause leafburn. In cool, humid coastal locations, powdery mildew may be a problem; seek resistant plants.

Planting and care: Plant any time from containers. Space 6 feet (1.8m) apart for an eventual loose screen with continuous summer color. Prune old wood 12 to 18 inches (30.5 to 45.7cm) back on large forms. Prune twiggy growth and spent flowers on dwarf forms in the dormant season to increase next year's bloom. Give moderate feeding and leach the soil periodically (deep soaking) where water or soil are high in alkalinity. Spray for mildew just before bloom.

Lagerstroemia indica

Lagerstroemia indica

All zones
Deciduous
Soil: Prefers enriched deep soil with good drainage.
Sun: Tolerates part shade. Prefers full sun, even reflected sun.
Water: Best with occasional deep irrigation. Tolerates moderate watering or ample water when planted in lawns. Avoid overhead irrigation.
Temperature: Hardy to cold. Revels in heat.
Maintenance: Seasonal to periodic.

Lantana camara

Family: Verbenaceae
Bush Lantana • Shrub Verbena
Yellow Sage

This native of tropical and semitropical regions provides color off and on all year as it cycles into bloom in frost-free areas. It grows to 4 feet (1.2m) high and as wide with sometimes prickly foliage and stems. Leaves are rounded at the tips, with toothed edges and deeply veined fuzzy surfaces. They usually appear in pairs along stems. Flowers are multicolored, blooming from March into November, all year in warm areas. Many hybrids and cultivars of this plant are widely available and often preferred.

Cultivars and other notable species: Dwarf forms reach 2 to 4 feet (0.6 to 1.2m) high, spreading 3 to 4 feet (0.9 to 1.2m). They are densely branched and more tender. They prefer garden conditions as well as heat. They include 'Dwarf Pink,' bright-pink flowers; 'Dwarf White,' a white-flowered form; 'Dwarf Yellow,' corn yellow flowers; and 'Radiation,' orange-red flowers. There are many other cultivars.

Special design features: Vibrant warm weather color. Informal.

Uses: Color accents for masses, containers, foundation planting, espalier, hedges or feature areas. Desert, transitional or natural gardens. Butterfly gardens.

Disadvantages: Foliage is pungent. Tiny berries in clusters resembling blackberries are poisonous. Foliage and stems are prickly and abrasive. Poor winter appearance, but less objectionable if combined with hardy evergreens.

Planting and care: Plant from containers in spring when danger from frost has passed and nights are warm. Place 3 feet (0.9m) apart for massing shrub forms, 3 to 4 feet (0.9 to 1.2m) for spreaders. Overfeeding and too much water may diminish bloom and encourage foliage. Pinch tips to encourage fullness. Mulch plants in cold winter areas. Cut plants back in late winter or early spring after frost to remove unsightly or dead leaves and branches or to shape and encourage compact dense growth. Do this even in mild climate areas. In summer, most plants are encouraged to bloom again more quickly after a bloom cycle if clipped or pinched lightly at the tips.

Lantana camara

Lantana camara

Low and middle zones; protected microclimates or annual in high zone
Evergreen perennial in frost-free areas to dormant with frost
Soil: Tolerant.
Sun: Part, full or reflected sun. Revels in heat of south sides.
Water: Moderate. Avoid giving plants too much water in winter.
Temperature: Foliage damaged at 28F (-2C). Most established plants recover quickly in spring. Roots are hardy to below 20F (-7C).
Maintenance: Little. Minimum amounts of pruning and grooming.

Lantana montevidensis

(L. delicata, L. delicatissima, L. sellowiana)
Family: Verbenaceae
Trailing Lantana • Weeping Lantana •
Lavender Lantana

Trailing lantana, a native of South America, has naturalized in warmer parts of the United States. It is a constant bloomer in warm weather with a profusion of 1-inch (2.5-cm) verbenalike lavender flowers. Leaves are small, prickly, gray-green and crinkly. Slender stems root along the ground so plants spread to an indefinite width and mound less than a foot high. Single branches may trail to 6 feet (1.8m) and find their way up fences, walls or other supports. When the soil dries out, plant becomes dormant. As soon as water is available, it sprouts green leaves, begins to grow and blooms again. This heat-loving plant will tolerate periods of neglect. It is a joy to the casual gardener who wants fantastic results with very little care.

Cultivars and other notable species: 'Lavender Swirl' has both lavender and white flowers.

Special design features: Trailing plant with constant bloom when given water in warm weather. Informal.

Uses: Ground cover or wall climber for warm weather or warm microclimates. Desert, wild, natural or rock gardens. Transitional areas. Spiller for banks or containers. Grows over hot pavement. Does well on south or west sides.

Disadvantages: Pungent smell. Prickly foliage. Very aggressive in flower beds and may take over. Unattractive winter appearance in cool areas.

Planting and care: Plant from containers or transplant rooted runners in warm weather. Space 3 feet (0.9m) apart for massing. Cut back any time to control or if plant looks poor. Best planted in a well-defined area to prevent unwanted spreading. Prune back once a year to control its invasiveness. Mulch plants in colder areas in winter.

Lantana montevidensis

Lantana montevidensis

All zones
Evergreen perennial
Soil: Tolerant.
Sun: Part, full or reflected sun. The more sun, the better.
Water: Accepts occasional irrigation, but best with moderate water.
Temperature: Foliage is damaged at 25F (-4C), frozen to the ground at about 20F (-7C). Fast recovery in warm weather. Dormant perennial in coldest winter areas.
Maintenance: Periodic pruning to no maintenance.

Leucophyllum species

Family: Scrophulariaceae

Sturdy, rounded shrubs that have always been standby workhorse plants for water-efficient landscapes. There is a wide range of newer selections in size, foliage and flower color, some of which are covered here. This has come about through horticultural breeding and cultivar selection within the original species of *L. frutescens,* but also through additional plant exploration. The result is the introduction of several outstanding species, allowing nurseries to offer an ever-increasing range of choices. Most *Leucophyllum* species bloom all summer with moisture. They grow from 3 to 8 feet (0.9 to 2.4m), depending on the species.

Special design features: Informal pearl gray to gray-green foliage on some species, silver on others. Desert effect. Sporadic warm season flowering can be spectacular. Small to large rounded shrubs that serve a wide range of situations.

Uses: Informal shrub with room to spread as a specimen, screen, clipped hedge or random informal planting. Foundation plant. Border plant. Natural or desert gardens. One of the most important plants in the transitional or Xeriscape garden. Blends well with a green garden on one side and the desert on the other. Foliage contrast. Some work well as accents or specimens. Use to revegetate disturbed areas.

Disadvantages: Will die out if overwatered. Can look sparse and scraggly in late winter or in long periods of drought. Some are susceptible to Texas root rot.

Planting and care: Plant from containers any season. Give regular irrigation at first to establish and warm-season irrigation as a supplement in hot dry weather and if there is no summer rainfall to encourage growth and bloom. Can be cut back to a few inches from the ground to renew growth.

Important note: Do not subject these plants to hedge trimmers unless you desire a formal clipped hedge. Select the correct plant for the area it is to occupy so it will not overgrow the space. If a plant needs size reduction, prune it selectively. Using hedge trimmers ruins the natural shape. Leaves will form thickly on the exterior and sometimes leave large bare spots. Shearing also reduces flower production.

Leucophyllum species

Zones: See individual species descriptions.
Evergreen to partly deciduous
Soil: Tolerant, but good drainage is a plus.
Sun: Part to full or reflected sun. Can tolerate part shade, but may show spindly growth.
Water: Best with occasional deep soakings. Tolerates none to moderate, the latter only with good drainage.
Temperature: See individual species descriptions. Most are hardy to about 10F (-12C).
Maintenance: None to periodic.

Leucophyllum candidum
Cenizo • Violet Silverleaf

One of the dependably small evergreen Texas rangers that grows at a moderate rate to 3 feet (0.9m) high and as wide. Small rounded leaves are covered with silvery hairs that form a dense mat over the surface. There are two cultivars. 'Thunder Cloud' has very light silvery foliage, nearly black buds that open as intense purple flowers contrasting dramatically with the foliage. It blooms more frequently and profusely than 'Silver Cloud.' 'Silver Cloud' has whitish foliage, grows a little larger and blooms less. Both plants can come into bloom several times over the warm season with the heaviest bloom in late summer. Adapted to all zones, this plant is cold hardy to about 10F (-12C). Roots are sensitive to too much moisture, so good drainage is a must. Use as a small silver accent that will not become a monster, in addition to the uses listed in the genus introduction.

Leucophyllum frutescens
(*L. texanum*)
Texas Ranger • Ceniza
Barometer Bush

Texas ranger is a striking large evergreen plant, covered with rosy lavender bell-shaped flowers in the high humidity of a summer rainy season, but can bloom any time over the warm season. This native of Texas and Mexico grows slowly to moderately up to 8 feet (2.4m) high and as wide unless trimmed. Planted for its gray feltlike foliage and open to dense rounded form, it blends with the desert or contrasts nicely with dense green plants or desert succulents. Foliage is thicker in warm weather. Where moisture is available, it becomes luxuriant, almost succulent. Flowers need hot weather to bloom, and often appear briefly after summer showers, which is why it is sometimes called "barometer bush." Endures great heat. This is the hardiest of the Texas rangers so far: It endures great heat and cold to about 5F (-15C). Although adapted to all zones and tolerant of cold, dry or adverse conditions, Texas ranger may lose much of its foliage except at branch tips and look struggling and unattractive. Use this form of Texas ranger in areas needing large shrubs. Shearing with a hedge trimmer ruins the shape and is contrary to its natural form, though it performs well as a formal clipped hedge. The cultivar 'Compacta' is smaller, to only 4 feet (1.2m) high by as wide. A good low foundation plant. 'Green Cloud' has green leaves and is otherwise similar to the species. 'White Cloud' has white flowers and is otherwise similar to the species.

Leucophyllum laevigatum
Chihuahuan Rain Sage

This broad-spreading evergreen shrub grows 3 to 4 feet (0.9 to 1.2m) high and about 5 feet (1.5m) wide. Character is more open and loose than most other *Leucophyllum*. The upturned branch tips create a flat-top effect. The small leaves are fine textured and deep gray green. Fragrant little lavender flowers with a bluish cast bloom along the branches

Leucophyllum candidum

Leucophyllum laevigatum

Leucophyllum langmaniae

in spring and also appear frequently during the warm season. Use in a shrubbery border, on banks, in a foundation planting, as a space definer or transitional plant between the green landscapes and in desert gardens. Hardy in all zones to about 18 F (-8C), including warmer parts of the high zone.

Leucophyllum langmaniae
Cinnamon Sage
Langmanie's Sage
'Rio Bravo™' Sage
Canyon Rain Sage

One of the outstanding new Texas ranger introductions, this plant somewhat resembles the plant above but has a lusher, greener, fuller foliage mass and grows at a moderate rate into a rounded form reaching about 5 feet (1.5m) in height and width. Summer moisture brings out lavender flowers. The trademarked 'Rio Bravo™' is a more uniform and compact plant. Grow in low and middle zones and probably warmer areas of high zone. Sensitive to soggy soil. Good drainage is a must.

Leucophyllum zygophyllum
Blue Rain Sage
Blue Ranger

Blue rain sage is a slow-growing, dense, evergreen shrub with a round form to about 5 feet (1.5m) high. Small dusty gray-green leaves cup upward and contrast nicely with little blue-violet to purple flowers that bloom several times a year, but heaviest in summer. A selection sold as *L. z.* 'Blue Ranger' has especially good form and color. The naturally dense and rounded form, plus interesting dusty green foliage and colorful flowers, add a special design dimension in combination with other plants. Use as medium shrub for banks, foundations, space definition, shrub combinations and gardens. Shear as hedge or clipped shrub in formal situations. Good for smaller areas where its slow growth is an advantage. Hardy to low and middle zones, to 5F (-15C). Although not yet tested, it is probably hardy in the warmer locations of the high zone. *L. z.* 'Cimmaron' to three feet (0.9m) high and wide is good for tight spaces.

Ligustrum japonicum

(L. texanum, L. kellermannii)
Family: Oleaceae
Waxleaf Privet
Japanese Privet

An elegant subject in the right location, waxleaf privet is a handsome garden plant of many uses. It grows at a moderate rate to 10 to 12 feet (3.1 or 3.7m) high with an equal spread if unclipped. Keep at almost any size by shearing and shaping. Habit is dense, compact and erect. Leathery, almost spongy leaves are shiny and crisp, dark green above, whitish beneath, forming wide-pointed ovals to 4 inches (10.2cm) long. Foliage reaches to the ground if left untrimmed. Whitish, somewhat fragrant flowers appear in clusters at branch tips of unclipped plants in April and May. Small dark, almost black, berries follow. Native to Japan and Korea.

Cultivars and other notable species:
L. japonicum 'Silver Star' is a new introduction—a variegated medium-size shrub with creamy silver leaf edges. A slow, compact grower, good brightener for shady gardens and as a contrast to deep green plants.

Special design features: Formal architectural form. Rich foliage is pleasant close up. Outstanding for clipping and topiary in formal or small gardens.

Uses: Clipped as a high or low hedge. Topiary plant, small standard tree, column or globe. Feature plant for containers. Adaptable to narrow spaces because it clips so well. North or east sides. Swimming pool areas and patios.

Disadvantages: Berries are poisonous. Pollen can be quite bothersome to those allergic to it. Foliage may sunburn in low or middle zones when exposed to reflected sun in summer. Subject to root knot nematodes and brittle leaf, although the latter is easily cured with an application of ammonium sulphate. Very susceptible to Texas root rot.

Planting and care: Do not plant in soil known to have Texas root rot. Prepare planting hole to prevent it. Plant from containers any time of year. Space 1 foot (0.3m) apart for a low hedge, 3 feet (0.9m) apart for a 6-foot (1.8-m) hedge or screen. Shear any time, but do any heavy pruning in October.

Ligustrum japonicum

Ligustrum japonicum

All zones
Evergreen
Soil: Improved garden soil with good drainage and a high percentage of humus.
Sun: Open to filtered shade and part sun. Avoid planting in hot pockets under midday sun in warmer climates. Accepts full sun at elevations or in cooler places. Avoid intense, reflected heat.
Water: Moderate, but accepts a range from occasional to ample if soil is well drained.
Temperature: Hardy to 20F (-7C) or below. Tolerates heat with shade and water.
Maintenance: As desired, from periodic to constant in the case of a hedge or topiary.

Ligustrum lucidum

Family: Oleaceae
Glossy Privet • Chinese Privet
Nepal Privet

Glossy privet is one of the basic hardy evergreen trees and shrubs in the desert landscape. This native from China and Korea is usually seen as a clipped hedge, but is often planted as a slow-to-develop round-headed tree. It reaches up to 30 feet (9.2m) high with a spread of 20 feet (6.1m) at maturity. As a hedge it grows at a moderate to fast rate to 6 feet (1.8m) high and may be coaxed to 10 feet (3.1m) or more. Plant is as wide as it is high unless clipped or trained. Crisp, dark green, pointed, elongated oval leaves curve backwards. Privet may produce an abundant to sporadic bloom of whitish flowers in pyramidal clusters in late spring. Bloom is mildly fragrant, appearing at the branch tips, and lasts for several weeks. Small black berries follow bloom.

Special design features: Formal feeling. A strong and richly foliated tree. One of the surest broadleaf trees for midwinter green. Neat and adaptable to many uses.

Uses: Erect round-headed tree with one or more trunks for patios, rows, street plantings or formal settings. Clipped hedge at any height from 3 to 12 feet (0.9 to 3.7m). Wide unclipped screens. Pool areas.

Disadvantages: Blue-black berries are poisonous and create litter, but a quick shearing corrects the litter problem. Bloom is rather coarse, not too attractive at close range, and may cause allergies. It eventually fades to brown. Subject to root knot nematodes and privet weevil. Occasionally gets Texas root rot.

Planting and care: Plant any time from containers. Space 12 to 18 inches (30.5 to 45.7cm) apart for a quick low hedge, 3 feet (0.9m) for a 6-foot (1.8-m) hedge, 3 to 4 feet (0.9 to 1.2m) for a 12-foot (3.7-m) hedge. Space up to 10 feet (3.1m) for a wide unclipped screen. Clip so bottom of hedge is wider than the top. This enables the sun to reach all parts of the plant to produce denser foliage. Do any heavy pruning in October. Shear as needed to shape or keep neat. Trim blossoms when they fade or to prevent berries.

Ligustrum lucidum

Ligustrum lucidum

All zones
Evergreen
Soil: Tolerant. Prefers improved garden soil with good drainage.
Sun: Filtered to open shade or part to full sun.
Water: Prefers occasional deep irrigation. Accepts moderate or ample. Tolerates limited periods of drought when fully established.
Temperature: Hardy to 15F (-9C) or below. Tolerant of heat.
Maintenance: Periodic to constant, depending on use and preference.

Lonicera japonica 'Halliana'

Family: Caprifoliaceae
Hall's Honeysuckle

An old-fashioned garden vine, Hall's honeysuckle is probably the most commonly grown cultivar of *Lonicera japonica*. Although this eastern Asian native has become a pest in the Middle Atlantic states, it is welcome in arid regions for its adaptability and vigor where little else will grow easily. Soft medium green leaves are oval, to 3 inches (7.6cm) long. Flowers in pairs along the stems are white, then turn golden as they age. Bloom is heavy and very fragrant in early spring and may continue in summer with less profusion. Plants are aggressive growers once established and can cover up to 1,200 square feet (366 square meters) or more. Not a plant for close range, but very pleasant on the back fence or trellis or at the end of the patio where its shade and fragrance can be enjoyed. Tolerates some drought, hot winds, poor soil and hot sun. Check with a nursery in your area for other honeysuckles that grow in your zone.

Special design features: Fragrance in spring and summer. Quick shade on a support or trellis. Old-fashioned garden effect.

Uses: Erosion control on banks, although it may not spread evenly and may need some training. Fast shade or screening on trellises, fences, arbors or porches.

Disadvantages: Mature plants become woody underneath and need to be cut back. Runners spread, reroot and can be invasive. Avoid planting too near shrubs or trees, where it can climb and take over. Difficult to eradicate once established.

Planting and care: Plant in spring when the weather warms up. Set plants 2 to 3 feet (0.6 to 0.9m) apart for a ground cover. Plants are easy to propagate from divisions or cuttings. Space 8 to 10 feet (2.4 to 3.1m) apart for a wall, fence or trellis cover. Prune severely in late winter to give it a fresh start and to keep the plant from becoming woody. Train as desired.

Lonicera japonica 'Halliana'

Lonicera japonica 'Halliana'

All zones
Evergreen to all or partly deciduous
Soil: Tolerant.
Sun: Open shade to part, full or reflected sun. Revels in heat.
Water: Accepts a wide range from occasional to moderate to ample. Best with occasional root-zone soaking. Tolerates long periods of drought and neglect but looks mangy and sections will die out. Comes back quickly when water becomes available.
Temperature: All to partly deciduous in frosty winter areas, but hardy and quick to leaf out in warm weather.
Maintenance: Periodic to thin, groom and control.

Lysiloma watsonii thornberi

(L. thornberi)
Family: Fabaceae (Leguminosae)
Feather Bush • Feather Tree

The feather bush from southern Arizona and northern Mexico lends a tropical mood to the garden or patio. It is a shrub or tree with large, finely cut, medium to dark green feathery foliage. A moderate to fast grower, it reaches 15 to 20 feet (4.6 to 6.1m) high in frost-free areas and spreads its canopy of ferny leaves as wide as high. In cooler locations or in unprotected areas of the middle zone, it is a summer foliage plant. When frosted back, it grows to only 4 or 5 feet (1.2 or 1.5m) by late spring or midsummer. Recovers from cold damage in spring with lush feathery new growth. Numerous creamy white flowers like clusters of puffballs appear from May to June as new leaves come out. Flat brown pods 4 to 8 inches (10.2 to 20.3cm) long follow bloom and hang from branches for a long period.

Tolerant of drought and great heat.

Special design features: Luxuriant feathery to ferny foliage. Tropical to subtropical feeling. Filtered shade.

Uses: Summer feature plant with rocks or structural features. Silhouette plant. Textural foliage contrast. Natural, desert, tropical or transitional gardens. Patio or garden tree in frost-free areas. Summer effect in colder areas. Planting with evergreens will mask its winter dormancy.

Disadvantages: Sensitive to cold. Occasional chlorosis from too much water. Beans can be unsightly and produce litter.

Planting and care: Plant from seed or from containers in spring when weather warms up. Plant in a sheltered spot in areas of frost. Prune selectively; only shape or remove dead branches. If frozen, cut plant to the ground.

Lysiloma watsonii thornberi

Lysiloma watsonii thornberi

Low and middle zones
Evergreen to deciduous in cold winters
Soil: Tolerant. Prefers good drainage.
Sun: Part, full or reflected sun.
Water: Best with occasional deep irrigation. Accepts moderate irrigation or none at all in areas of 10 to 12 inches (254 to 305mm) of annual rainfall and in somewhat porous soil. It remains a shrub with meager irrigation, but becomes a tree in mild zones when given moderate water.
Temperature: Hardy to 25F (-4C). Recovers quickly in spring.
Maintenance: Periodic.

Melia azedarach

(M. australis, M. japonica,
M. sempervirens)
Family: Meliaceae
Chinaberry • Bead Tree
Pride-of-India • Texas Umbrella Tree

The chinaberry grows so easily from seed that nurseries seldom carry it. A rapid grower in youth to 20 to 30 feet (6.1 to 9.2m) high, rarely reaching 50 feet (15.2m), with an equal spread if not trimmed back. Crown form varies depending on selection. Branches of the species are more loosely arranged than those of cultivars. Foliage is made up of compound leaves with numerous tooth-edged leaflets. Looks velvety in the wind. Bouquets of fragrant small lavender flowers appear in spring. Foliage is deep green in summer and golden in fall. Winter silhouette is decorated with clusters of hard yellow berries that hang until spring. Usually erect with a single trunk, young trees are slender and tall, attractive when massed.

Cultivars and other notable species: 'Umbraculiformis,' Texas umbrella tree, has a very erect trunk with branches radiating in a regular pattern like ribs of an umbrella. Some gardeners prefer its more regular symmetrical form.

Special design features: Interest all year. Dense shade. Desert oasis.

Uses: Shade tree for hot places—patios, lawns and streets. Sapling groves along walls for silhouette and screening above walls. A good plant for alkaline soils.

Disadvantages: Susceptible to Texas root rot and heart rot. Branches break in strong winds, especially on older trees or trees infected with heart rot. Berries are said to be poisonous and have an unpleasant odor between ripening and the time they are dried out. Trees may sucker at base. May naturalize and become a pest.

Planting and care: Plant seed after berries have ripened. Young trees may be planted from containers any time, or bare root in winter. Select nursery stock that has a predictable form. Space 5 to 6 feet (1.5 to 1.8m) apart for a temporary sapling grove. Space 15 to 20 feet (4.6 to 6.1m) for a grouping or row. Control berry production and branch breakage by trimming the branch tips in late winter. In January, prune inside branches of trees with dense canopies to allow wind to pass through. Do not cut branches back to nubbins near the main trunk as is so often done.

Melia azedarach

Melia azedarach

All zones
Deciduous
Soil: Tolerant.
Sun: Part, full or reflected sun.
Water: Moderate to occasional irrigation. Tolerates lawn watering.
Temperature: Hardy. Accepts heat of low deserts.
Maintenance: Seasonal.

Muhlenbergia species

Family: Poaceae (Graminaea)

These recently introduced grasses create a whole new effect in the landscape. They give an informal feeling and created rounded mounds that play well against other plant structures. One, *M. capillaris* 'Regal Mist', gives a colorful fall seed display. From August to December, a filmy wine bloom rises above the plant. *M. rigens* also blooms from August to December. *M. dumosa* gives a bamboo effect and blooms from March to May. *M. emersleyi* blooms from August to December. Any of these handsome clumping grasses will add a unique informal effect to your landscape.

Special design features: Each grass has a special character for informal, open country or waterside effects.

Uses: Suitable for landscape use as clumps, specimens, drifts, foundations or in combinations with other plants for specific needs.

Disadvantages: There is always a danger that the grasses covered will become pests in your area. Check around with horticulturists and your county cooperative extension service to see if it is safe to use the grasses mentioned here. Rabbits can finish off young plants. Protect the plant until it develops substantial foliage.

Planting and care: Best planted in spring or summer. Can be cut back if too large, unkempt, or to rejuvenate after winter browning. Shear in late winter each year. Can be trimmed or cut back any time if they appear brown and unattractive.

Muhlenbergia species

Low and middle zones; protected microclimates of the high zone
Sometimes evergreen
Soil: Most soils with good drainage. *M. capillaris* performs better with garden treatment.
Sun: Full sun to part shade.
Water: Drought tolerant when established. Moderate water best for attractive foliage over the warm season. *M. capillaris* will perform best with weekly summer soaking. *M. dumosa* can be neglected once established but will turn brown during dry spells. Best with weekly or biweekly water, or at least every month or two for a decent appearance. *M. emersleyi* does best with weekly to biweekly summer water. *M. rigens* can tolerate monthly irrigation once established, but more frequent irrigation makes a larger, lusher, greener plant. All need occasional irrigation in winter.
Temperature: Most are root hardy to 0F (-18C).
Maintenance: Periodic or seasonal.

Muhlenbergia capillaris 'Regal Mist'
Pink Mulhy

Grows rapidly into a clump 3 to 4 feet (0.6 to 1.2m) high and wide. In late summer through fall, it is stunning with wine pink seed plumes that look like a mist above the plant. Most dramatic if backlit by the sun.

Muhlenbergia dumosa
Bamboo Mulhy

A densly clumping grass that grows fast to 3 or even 6 feet (0.9 to 1.8m) high with equal spread. The many stems are strong and woody with leaf blades that resemble bamboo. Usually green if it gets water, it looks tan in spring as the flower clusters on woody stems produce seeds. It is dramatic in an informal rock garden, giving an oriental effect to a dry wash or massed as a background. Contrast with other foliage types or succulents. Cut back in June.

Muhlenbergia emersleyi
Bull Grass

A more traditional grass form that grows at a moderate rate to as high and wide as 5 feet (1.5m). Becomes a dense mound of evergreen foliage that bears loose, delicate reddish flower spikes to 16 inches (40.6cm) above the foliage in fall. Because of its size, it is mainly used for textural interest in transition gardens and Xeriscapes as well as

for erosion control and revegetation of a disturbed area. Cut back in January.

Muhlenbergia rigens
Deer Grass

A semi-evergreen perennial grass that grows fast into a large rounded clump 2 to 3 feet (0.6 to 0.9m) high by 3 to 5 feet (0.9 to 1.5m) wide, with a refined texture. Inconspicuous brown 5-inch (12.7-cm) flowers appear on thin white stalks as 3 feet (0.9m) or higher. A dramatic touch in transitional gardens, rock gardens, naturalistic landscapes and even oasis gardens. Leaves may brown in cold winter areas, but plant revives quickly in the spring. Space 6 to 8 feet (1.8 to 2.4m) apart when planting.

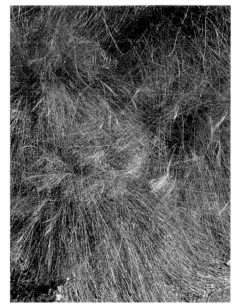

Muhlenbergia emersleyi

Muhlenbergia capillaris 'Regal Mist'

Muhlenbergia rigens

Myoporum parvifolium

(*Myoporum parvifolium* 'Prostratum')
Family: Myoporaceae
Prostrate Myoporum

This ground cover features bright green narrow leaves to 3/4 inch (1.9cm) long evenly spaced in spirals around the horizontally spreading stems. A profusion of small white flowers appear from March to May; some blooms also appear during the summer. Small purple berries may follow bloom. Where space allows, one plant may spread as a 3-inch (7.6-cm) high mat to as much as 9 feet (2.7m) in diameter. Where space is restricted, a plant will mound to several inches high. Its good looks belie its toughness.

Special design features: Bright green ground cover with pleasing texture and attractive white flowers.

Uses: Ground cover for sunny spaces in residential or public situations. Cascades over pots or planters. Combines well with rocks and mulches as a limited-area ground cover.

Disadvantages: Looks unattractive for a period after spring bloom. Areas may die out from a fungus. Nematodes can be a problem.

Planting and care: Plant from containers any time. Space 5 feet (1.5m) or more apart to give room to spread; closer for faster cover and denser look. Mass plantings require some refurbishing in early spring: Fill in with new plants where old ones have died or look unattractive.

Myoporum parvifolium

Myoporum parvifolium

Low and middle zones
Evergreen
Soil: Tolerant. Prefers prepared garden soil with good drainage.
Sun: Full sun to light shade.
Water: Moderate to occasional deep irrigation once established; more in hottest regions.
Temperature: Hardy to the low 20s F (-5 to -7C).
Maintenance: Periodic replanting when plants die out. Some trimming to maintain appearance.

Myrtus communis

(*M. boetica, M. italica, M. latifolia,*
M. romana)
Family: Myrtaceae
Classic Myrtle • True Myrtle
Greek Myrtle • Roman Myrtle

Dependable, neat and easy to grow, myrtle always looks attractive whether clipped or left natural. It gives long service and requires little care. A moderate grower becoming a shrub 5 to 6 feet (1.5 to 1.8m) high in a few years, with a spread of 4 to 5 feet (1.2 to 1.5m), mature plants reach 12 to 15 feet (3.7 to 4.6m) high and spread as wide unless clipped. Foliage is dark green, shiny and compact, densely covering the plant to the ground. Numerous delicate white to pinkish flowers 3/4-inch (1.9cm) across appear in April and May. Small blue-black berries may follow.

Cultivars and other notable species: 'Variegata' has white-edged leaves. 'Compacta' (compact myrtle) grows slowly 2 to 3 feet (0.6 to 0.9m) high and as wide. It has small, pointed, closely set leaves, used for low hedges or edges. Susceptible to root rot in summer if soil is too damp. If soil is well drained, there is usually no problem. 'Microphylla' (dwarf myrtle) grows 1 to 2 feet (0.3 to 0.6m) high, densely covered with tiny overlapping leaves. Excellent as a low, dense clipped hedge, edge or space definer. It is susceptible to summer root fungus in wet

soils. 'Boetica' (twisted myrtle) is quite different in appearance from the others. It is an angular, rugged, upward-pointing and informal deep green shrub, growing slowly up to 12 feet (3.7m). It can be trained into a little gnarled tree when it reaches this size.

Special design features: Formal to informal appearance depending on use. Dense deep green statement in the landscape. Oriental quality. All myrtles have aromatic foliage.

Uses: Wide informal specimen or screen. Clipped hedge or background plant. Excellent for clipping and shaping as topiary plants or standard trees. Older specimens may be clipped into small trees. Highly resistant to Texas root rot.

Disadvantages: Chlorosis in poorly drained soil or from shallow watering.

Planting and care: Plant any time from containers. Space 1-1/2 to 3 feet (0.5 to 0.9m) apart for a clipped hedge, 4 feet (1.2m) or more for a wide unclipped screen or background planting. Prune in February. Shear at any time.

Myrtus communis

Myrtus communis 'Boetica'

Myrtus communis

All zones
Evergreen
Soil: Adaptable. Should have good drainage.
Sun: Part, full or reflected sun.
Water: Prefers occasional deep irrigation. Established plants tolerate some drought.
Temperature: Hardy. Tolerates heat and cold, to 20F (-7C).
Maintenance: None to constant, depending on use.

Nandina domestica

Family: Berberidaceae
Heavenly Bamboo • Nandina
Sacred Bamboo

The grace and class of this plant belies its toughness and drought resistance. Heavenly bamboo is not a bamboo at all, but it looks a little like one. Delicate foliage grows outward from one or more vertical canelike stems. Individuals vary in size unless grown from cuttings of the same plant. Plants grow at a slow to moderate rate to as much as 8 feet (2.4m) high, but usually 4 to 6 feet (1.2 to 1.8m). Some plants spread by underground roots. Most keep their slender form and seldom get more than 4 feet (1.2m) wide. Easy to grow and very neat, heavenly bamboo adds interest to the landscape in each of the seasons. Sprays of tiny white flowers appear in April and are occasionally followed in fall by long-lasting sprays of red berries. Foliage turns reddish or bronze in the winter sun; fresh green growth reappears in spring. Plants are highly resistant to pests, diseases and most soil problems, requiring little maintenance, even tolerating periods of neglect.

Cultivars and other notable species: 'Compacta' dependably reaches 4 to 5 feet (1.2 to 1.5m) high and about 3 feet (0.9m) wide. 'Nana Compacta' is a small mound, 12 to 18 inches (30.5 to 45.7cm) high by 15 inches (38.1cm) wide. 'Purpurea Dwarf,' the same size, is often preferred for its deep red color. Both have wide, drooping, cupped leaves and are best used under south-facing overhangs in low and middle zones so they get summer shade and winter sun. 'Harbor Dwarf' is a recent introduction that grows to about 2 feet (0.6m) high and spreads by underground runners to fill as a ground cover. There are other cultivars not covered here.

Special design features: Oriental effect. Refined and attractive at close range.

Uses: Specimen or accent plant. Foundation plant. Narrow spaces. Entryways, atriums or intimate patios. Container plant. Taller forms can be used as informal hedges or space definers and are effective as background plants, especially in a flower garden.

Disadvantages: May yellow from iron chlorosis in alkaline soils. Sometimes stunted in hottest locations. Dwarf types may not survive intense sun of desert summer afternoons.

Planting and care: Plant from containers any time of year. Space larger forms 18 to 30 inches (76.2cm) apart for a solid hedge or screen, farther for a more casual effect. Do not clip or shear as a hedge because it ruins the form. Exposed canes look unattractive and awkward. Space dwarfs 12 to 18 inches (30.5 to 45.7cm) apart; 'Harbor Dwarf,' 18 to 24 inches (45.7 to 61cm).

Nandina domestica

All zones
Evergreen
Soil: Average garden soil. Avoid highly alkaline conditions.
Sun: Open, filtered or part shade to full sun. Dwarf forms need afternoon shade in the middle or low zones; all forms require shade in low deserts.
Water: Tolerates a wide range of irrigation practices from ample to periods of neglect, from which it recovers quickly when water is again available.
Temperature: Hardy, but can lose leaves at 10F (-12C). Recovers quickly.
Maintenance: Periodic to none.

Nandina domestica

Nandina domestica

Nerium oleander

(N. indicum, N. odurum)
Family: Apocynaceae
Oleander • Rosebay

One of the more dependable plants for hot climates, oleander is a bright bouquet in the warm season. Growth rate varies from moderate to fast depending on conditions and plant type. Vigorous growers produce a dense hedge to 6 feet (1.8m) high in three years with favorable conditions. Mature hedges have been seen 20 feet (6.1m) high and higher. Plants are about half as wide as they are high unless pruned. Erect in form, stems are almost canelike in youth, supporting narrow, dark, dull green leaves to 10 inches (25.4cm) long that densely cover to the ground. Older plants may be trimmed up as trees, revealing gnarled single or multiple trunks.

Except as patio trees (and possibly the dwarf varieties), oleanders are best used in farther reaches of the landscape. They are not for a refined intimate space. Flowers may be single or double and appear in profusion on the branch tips, with the heaviest bloom in mid- to late spring; some flowers bloom through summer until nights cool in fall. There are numerous varieties with varied blossom color: red, pink, salmon, soft yellow and white—some are scented. Seedpods may follow, releasing airborne seeds. Native from the Mediterranean across Asia to Japan.

Cultivars and other notable species: Largest and most vigorous grower is white single-flowering 'Sister Agnes.' Many other color selections grow nearly as large. 'Hawaii' will grow to a 6-foot (1.8-m) shrub with double salmon pink flowers. Two medium growers from North Africa are 'Casablanca,' with single white flowers, and 'Algiers,' with single red flowers. The more refined 'Petite' series is a fairly recent introduction. Most common are 'Petite Pink,' with profusions of delicate pink flowers throughout the growing season, and 'Petite Salmon,' with salmon pink flowers. There are also red, light yellow and deep pink selections. These tightly branched dwarf plants grow 3 to 5 feet (0.9 to 1.5m) high, occasionally larger in hot summer areas. They are effective in containers or for low unclipped borders, hedges or background plantings.

Special design features: In general, the species provides wonderful spring to summer color. Dense deep green foliage.

Uses: Best as unclipped hedges, screens and borders. Effective along roads or drives, at property edges or as background plantings. Oleanders may be clipped to any size, but yield fewer flowers when clipped. Larger forms make handsome single- or multitrunk trees when trained. Trees are adapted to grow in patios, median strips or as street trees for color, character and shade.

Disadvantages: All parts of the plant are poisonous. Sap may irritate skin or eyes. Smoke from burning leaves is irritating. Airborne seeds may cause hay fever at close range and reseed where they aren't wanted, in springs and other natural wet spots. Plants are sometimes subject to yellow oleander aphids and scale. Warty growths and splitting branches as well as blackened deformed flowers may indicate bacterial gall. Very severe infections of this disease may follow a hard freeze, which will split the bark on mature twigs, allowing bacteria to enter. Plants must be cut back beyond any galls that show on stems or trunks. Disinfect pruning cuts with a 50/50 bleach and water solution and treat pruners or saw between each cut to avoid spreading the disease. Yellowing and dropping of old leaves, especially in spring, may indicate drought stress. A new disease, *Sylella fastidiosa*, that causes Pierce's disease (killing older plants) is appearing in some areas of California, spread by the insect the glassy-winged sharpshooter. Contact your local county cooperative extension service or a qualified landscape professional to find out if this is a problem in your area. Yellowing of new leaves sometimes occurs if plants are overwatered. Flowers litter pavements. Plants trained as trees eternally sprout suckers from the base, which must be pulled out rather than trimmed off.

Planting and care: Plant or transplant in any season, but best in spring. Space 2 to 2-1/2 feet (0.8m) apart for a fast hedge, 3 to 6 feet (0.9 to 1.8m) for an eventual tall hedge, up to 9 feet (2.7m) for a wide, loose screen. Prune in June to control size and form or to remove seedpods. To maintain desired height or shape, trim branch tips lightly or shear any time. Train tree forms carefully, supporting trunks with sturdy stakes. To rejuvenate older plants, cut a few old stems to the ground each year. Spray as needed for aphids and scale.

Nerium oleander

Nerium oleander 'Petite Pink'

Nerium oleander 'Double Pink'

Nerium oleander

All zones
Evergreen
Soil: Tolerant of a wide range of soils, including heavy, poor and alkaline.
Sun: Full to reflected sun. Tolerates part shade, but may be poor or leggy and have few flowers.
Water: Best with ample. Not really a drought-tolerant plant, but survives while waiting for regular water.
Temperature: Plants revel in heat. Damaged by cold below 20F (-7C), severely at 10F (-12C). They recover rapidly in spring.
Maintenance: Usually periodic. Depends on location and use. Otherwise, maintenance depends on use.

Olea europaea

Family: Oleaceae
Olive • European Olive

Gracious yet picturesque, the billowing crown and gnarled trunk of the olive tree make it one of the most desirable plants for the arid landscape. The olive is believed to be native to Asia Minor, where it has been grown since prehistoric times. Greeks and Romans carried it to other parts of the Mediterranean where olive groves are a familiar sight. Some of the earliest trees in cultivation in the United States were seedlings planted in the 18th century by Franciscan padres at the San Diego Mission. These trees are now widely known as the mission olives. Olives live for hundreds of years, enduring drought, heat and poor soil.

Although older single-trunk specimens grown in deep soil reach 40 to 50 feet (12.2 to 15.2m) tall, the olive is usually a multitrunk, round-headed tree that grows slowly to 15 to 30 feet (4.6 to 9.2m), with a spread almost as wide. Young trees may gain height quickly, but take time to develop substance. Leaves are stiff and leathery to 2 inches (5.1cm) long, medium gray-green above, white to nearly silvery beneath. Gray-barked trunks become rough, gnarled and buttressed with age. Clusters of tiny yellow-white flowers in March and April produce fruit that ripens in fall. Fruit may be pickled or pressed for oil. Recipes are available from county agents or university extensions. Banned in some areas because wind-blown pollen from flowers of fruiting trees causes allergies in some. There is a fruitless grafted variety ('Swan Hill™') that avoids both the pollen and the litter caused by blossoms and fruit.

Cultivars and other notable species: 'Swan Hill' is a totally fruitless grafted tree that has been tested and accepted for planting even in communities where flowering and fruiting trees are banned. 'Fruitless' does produce some fruit, though not as much as fruiting trees. Two varieties are commonly grown for landscape or commercial use where allowed: 'Manzanillo,' which has a round-headed, open and spreading form with excellent olives, and 'Mission,' a taller, more compact tree that is hardier but with smaller fruit. Three kinds commonly grown in commercial groves are also used as landscape trees: 'Ascolano,' which has large fruit; 'Barouni,' which

thrives in heat; and 'Sevillano,' which has very large fruit.

Special design features: Informal and picturesque. High quality tree. Filtered shade from silvery evergreen foliage. Tolerant of arid climate conditions. Mediterranean.

Uses: Patio, street or lawn tree. Specimen, row or grove. Large containers. Roof gardens. Espalier on large walls. Silhouette against structures. Looks at home in wild or natural gardens where it blends with other plants, especially gray-colored ones. Can be used as a canopy tree in a raked earth or paved patio, with plants in pots or as a specimen. Not for lawn areas unless soil has good drainage.

Disadvantages: Basal suckering, flower and fruit litter, and hay fever are objections to fruiting trees. Verticillium wilt, a fungus present in some root stock often appears after a cool spring followed by rapidly rising temperatures. Occasionally a whole tree will die, but more often it affects a single branch on an otherwise healthy-looking tree. Seek treatment advice from a qualified landscape professional. Also subject to black scale and olive knot. Buttressing and spreading roots can heave walks and terraces.

Planting and care: Plant or transplant container plants at any time. Stake and train as desired. Do any heavy pruning in January or February. Periodically remove basal suckers. If you don't want the flowers to fruit on fruit-bearing trees, have a tree professional spray the blossoms in spring to discourage fruit set. Although fertilization is not necessary, trees respond to an annual feeding of nitrogen and added potassium, boron and phosphorus in some soils. Do not cultivate beneath olive trees, because they develop a dense mat of feeder roots near the ground surface. This is why olives are easy to transplant. The dense mat of near-surface roots support the tree after transplanting while it regrows the deeper root system that had to be cut when the specimen was moved.

Olea europaea

Olea europaea

Olea europaea

All zones
Evergreen
Soil: Prefers deep rich soil, but tolerates poor, stony, shallow and alkaline soils.
Sun: Full sun. Tolerant of part shade to reflected sun.
Water: Moderate to no supplementary irrigation in areas with ample rainfall. Best with occasional deep irrigation, especially in summer. May be neglected in winter.
Temperature: Damaged at 15F (-9C). Prefers temperatures above 20F (-7C). For good fruit production, olives prefer hot summers and a certain amount of winter chilling—about 12 to 15 weeks of temperatures fluctuating from 35F (2C) to 65F (18C) between day and night.
Maintenance: Periodic to constant. Trees over paved areas require more cleanup. Remove suckers from base of trunk several times a year.

Olneya tesota

Family: Fabaceae (Leguminosae)
Ironwood • Palo Fierro • Tesota

Ironwood is a dry-climate native found in warm-winter desert areas of California, Arizona and northern Mexico. It grows slowly 12 to 20 feet (3.6 to 6.1m) high, sometimes higher with a nearly equal spread. Gray trunk and lower branches are very thorny in youth, gradually absorbing the thorns as they enlarge to become rough and fissured at maturity. Trees naturally branch low, often have multiple trunks and must be trained to become effective patio subjects. Fine-textured gray-green foliage may shed just before bloom or as a result of drought or a hard frost. Masses of small dusty lavender-pink flowers appear in clusters in late May to June. Dark, hairy 2-inch (5.1-cm) pods follow. At a distance, ironwood is similar in appearance to an olive tree. Where it grows naturally indicates a climate belt warm enough for citrus culture. Wood is hard, heavy and dense, valued for carving and as firewood. A tree to value and train if you have it on your property, but not the best choice if you are starting it from scratch, unless you are in no hurry to achieve a tree. It is very heat and drought resistant.

Special design features: Picturesque character. Informal. Spring color.

Uses: Hot areas. Natural, wild, transitional and arid-climate gardens or patios.

Disadvantages: Spiny branches. Slow to develop. Blossom, pod and leaf litter.

Planting and care: Mature plants salvaged from a desert site are sometimes available. Plant from containers in spring. Prune only to shape and to remove objectionable branches in October. Withstands neglect but grows fastest with some irrigation.

Olneya tesota

Olneya tesota

Low zone; warmer areas of the middle zone
Evergreen to deciduous in cold winters
Soil: Tolerant. Best with loose sandy or gravelly soil with good drainage.
Sun: Full to reflected sun. Withstands harsh conditions.
Water: Best with occasional irrigation.
Temperature: Tolerant of heat. Foliage freezes at about 20F (-7C).
Maintenance: None to periodic, depending on location and preference. Otherwise, maintenance depends on use.

Ophiopogon japonicus

(Mondo japonicum, Liriope japonica)
Family: Liliaceae
Mondo grass • Dwarf lilyturf

This grasslike ground cover grows slowly to form a dense mound of narrow dark green leaves. Reaches 6 to 8 inches (1.8 to 2.4cm) high and up to 10 inches (3.1cm) wide. Tiny inconspicuous bluish to lavender flower spikes appear in summer among foliage. Plants may spread by underground roots. Native to Korea and Japan.

Cultivars and other notable species: 'Nana' is a dwarf form that grows to about half the size of the species. It is identical in other ways, including its cultural requirements. *O. jaburan* (giant lily turf) grows to 3 feet (0.9m) high and wide, spreading by underground stems. Leaves are also dark green. Flowers are whiter in color, produced in loose clusters. Uses and cultural requirements are the same as for *O. japonicus*.

Special design features: Oriental effect. Tufted, woodsy turf effect. Oasis gardens.

Uses: Small-area ground cover or foreground plant. Plants grow at different rates and cover unevenly, creating a bumpy, casual look. Nice effect in containers. Place around stepping stones or to fill other odd spaces. Not a plant to walk on, however. Combines well with other low woodsy plants.

Disadvantages: Dry thatch on neglected or sunburned plants is unattractive.

Planting and care: Plant from flats, containers or divisions any time of year. Space 6 inches (15.2cm) apart. When tufts become large, divide and replant. Grows fastest and looks best with regular garden care.

Ophiopogon japonicus

Ophiopogon japonicus

All zones
Evergreen
Soil: Improved. Good drainage. Avoid alkaline.
Sun: Open, filtered or part shade. Accepts full sun in higher elevations or near coast.
Water: Moderate.
Temperature: 10F (-12C).
Maintenance: Occasional.

Opuntia species

Family: Cactaceae

Opuntias are perhaps the most widely distributed cacti, with a multitude of species. Native to the Americas (as are all cacti) but planted around the world, they have become so successful at adapting that they are sometimes a pest in far off places such as Australia and the Mediterranean region. As a group, *Opuntias* are thorny succulent plants divided further into cholla and prickly pear groups. Formed of jointed segments with large spines or barely visible but sharp bristles called glochids, which appear in polka-dot clusters on their waxy surfaces. Prickly pears also have showy 2-inch (5.1-cm) wide waxy flowers, which appear in late spring or early summer in shades of yellow, orange, salmon, pink, magenta, red and, in rare instances, white. Fruit in the form of a berry or pear ripens mid- to late summer. They are green to shades of orange, red or purple, often changing color as they ripen. Many prickly pears produce large edible fruit that makes a tasty jelly.

These plants are some of the toughest and most tolerant plants in the arid climate. Entire groves can develop in a few years from segments set in the ground and more or less abandoned. They range in size from treelike plants 15 to 20 feet (4.6 to 6.1m) tall, to spreading prostrate forms less than 2 feet (0.6m) high and wide to colonies of greater width. They are bold and sculptural in form, striking against architecture or with other bold arid-climate plants such as *Agave*. Tender new leaves of certain prickly pears are prepared and eaten as a vegetable (called *nopalitos*) in Mexico and parts of the United States as well as in other places.

Note: The genus *Opuntia* also includes the many kinds of cholla with long cylindrical segments rather than rounded and flat. These cacti are usually found to have a trunk supporting "branches" of jointed spiny cylinders. Found throughout the U. S. Southwest and northern Mexico, these are true desert plants that belong in true desert-climate gardens. Since they are remarkably hard to handle, we are not including them here.

Special design features: Bold form. Desert effect.

Uses: Arid-climate gardens. Cactus fences at property edges at a distance from walks or decks. Barriers, combined with other thorny plants such as barrel cacti, *Agaves* or ocotillos. Bank cover for erosion control. Tall forms make bold silhouettes against structures. Low forms give a textural contrast against surfaces of different materials. Native plants are effective for refurbishing disturbed areas and returning them to a natural state. Plant densely and at random for this purpose.

Disadvantages: Dangerous if planted close to walkways or similar use areas. Plants require special care in handling and can invade areas where they are not wanted. Large plantings of low-growing kinds may harbor packrats, which eat and destroy them.

Rodents may eat tender new leaves. Subject to a virus that creates brown circles, as well as cochineal scale and bacterial infection.

Planting and care: Plant any time from containers. If you have plants and desire more, break off one or more continuous segments any time of year and place them partway in the ground. They will take root and grow but might not put out new pads until spring if planted in fall or winter. For rapid development of new clumps, set three to five segments in a cluster at 12- to 18-inch (30.5- to 45.7-cm) intervals. To make a fence or impenetrable barrier, set segments in a trench at 12-inch (30.5-cm) intervals. Can be cut back any time to shape or remove leaf pads too close to high-use areas. Trim off lower sections to avoid pack rat nests in desert areas.

Opuntia species

Note: These cultural needs are for arid types of prickly pears.

Zone hardiness varies: Most are hardy to cold in low and middle zones, many to all zones.

Evergreen

Soil: Usually widely tolerant. Most prefer gravelly soils with good drainage.

Sun: Part, full or reflected sun. Some kinds prefer some shade in the hottest areas.

Water: Best with occasional irrigation in spring and summer. Tolerates none in its native habitat or in regions receiving 10 to 12 inches (254 to 305mm) of annual rainfall.

Temperature: Varies according to origin of species.

Maintenance: None to periodic. Use tongs when handling plant parts.

Opuntia basilaris
Beavertail Cactus

Low and spreading, the blue-gray beavertail-shaped pads of this prickly pear are thornless but have tiny glochids in the areolas. It has a low and spreading form, with new pads starting from the base of the plant. Seldom more than 1 foot to 1-1/2 feet (0.3 to 0.5m) high, it may spread to as much as 4 feet (1.2m) wide. The brilliant magenta spring flowers give a stunning display. Gets fungus in cold wet soil.

Opuntia engelmannii acicularis
Bristly Prickly Pear
Red-Flowered Prickly Pear

A low-growing prickly pear that reaches about 3 feet (0.9 m) high at a moderate rate and spreads to an indeterminate width. It is an eye-catcher with bristly rust-colored glochids polka-dotting its light gray-green pads and fringing the pad all around the edge. The unexpected orange-red flowers in spring make a wonderful contrast not only to the pads, but to other arid-climate plants as well. Its character and flower color add unusual texture and form to the landscape. Use as an accent, barrier, foundation plant or in a combination of arid-climate plants with bold form, such as other cacti, *Agaves* and *Yucca*, as a center of interest. It is hardy in all

Opuntia with fruit

Opuntia ficus-indica

Opuntia microdasys

Opuntia phaeacantha

three zones and prefers full sun and reflected heat. Shade changes its color and character, which is not desirable because it loses its interesting color contrast and its pads elongate and distort.

Opuntia ficus-indica
(O. engelmannii, O. megacantha, O. occidentalis)
Indian Fig
Spineless Cactus
Tuna Cactus

A bold succulent treelike cactus to 12 feet (3.7m) or higher, Indian fig develops a woody trunk and several branches of smooth flat pads or segments. Segments are as long as 20 inches (50.8cm) and have no thorns but a few sharp glochids in each polka dot. Yellow spring flowers produce edible fruits of yellow to red, prized in Mexico and parts of the United States. Effective as a silhouette plant, hedge or barrier, and often used as a corral fence in Mexico. Tender to cold in high zone or heavy freezes in middle zone. Frozen pads may drop off as will pads on overwatered plants because they become heavy. However, it is not a cactus from the open desert, so it looks best with some supplemental water in midsummer heat in low rainfall areas.

Opuntia microdasys
Rabbit Ears • Goldplush • Prickly Pear

Rabbit ears prickly pear may grow to 3 feet (0.9m) high or spread along the ground. Pads or segments are deep to bright green or gray-green, 3 to 6 inches (7.6 to 15.2cm) long and set with velvety yellow polka dots of sharp glochids, which are decorative but hazardous to touch or handle. There are selections with white or rust-colored glochids. All produce unspectacular yellow flowers in spring or early summer. Effective as low fences or specimens. This native of Mexico is tender to cold in the high zone.

Opuntia phaeacantha
(O. engelmannii)
Engelmann Prickly Pear

This species covers a number of different prickly pears native to a wide area from California to Texas and south into Mexico, at 1,000 to 6,500 feet (305 to 1,982m) elevation, some to 7,500 feet (2,287m). They are well adapted to arid climates and the most effective of the *Opuntia* for refurbishing disturbed areas. Plants vary in growth habit, size of pad, number and length of thorns and to some extent the color of their flower. Fruit is green, changing to red, then purple. Excellent for jelly. Wide low-growing stands may harbor packrat nests. Cut out sections to allow coyotes to get at the rats, or remove lower segments altogether.

Opuntia violacea santa-rita
(O. santa-rita)
Blue-Blade • Dollar Cactus
Santa Rita Prickly Pear

Striking because of its color, this prickly pear has segments that are tinged with purple or totally purple, a dramatic color contrast to other arid-climate plants. Sometimes segments are a blue-green tinged with violet. Segments to 8 inches (20.3cm) long may have 2-1/2 inch (6.4cm) brownish to pink spines, or can be almost completely spineless. Yellow flowers to 3-1/2 inches (8.9cm) in diameter may turn red near the base inside and produce red to purple fruit. Excellent as color feature specimen or as a hedge of medium height. It is also spectacular as an eye-catcher in areas where its color and form contrast with other plants, even in subtropical arrangements. More vertical in growth pattern than the *O. phaeacantha*, so packrats seldom find harbor under this plant.

Opuntia violacea santa-rita

Parkinsonia aculeata

Family: Fabaceae (Leguminosae)
Mexican Palo Verde • Jerusalem Thorn •
Ratama

Mexican palo verde is native to the southernmost tip of Arizona into Mexico and other warm parts of America, but it is widely cultivated and has naturalized in many areas. It is usually an erect, single-trunk and thorny tree, completely covered with smooth yellow-green bark. As trees age, the bark becomes rough and gray. Trees grow fast to 15 feet (4.6m) high and eventually reach 20 feet (6.1m) or more with a crown spread as wide or wider. During summer and all year in warm areas, the tree bears a narrow portion of its leaf, the midrib, which is 8 to 16 inches (20.3 to 40.6cm) long. The entire leaf is made up of this midrib and tiny leaflets 1/8 inch (0.3cm) long. In late spring or early summer there is a spectacular display of yellow flowers and the whole crown becomes a giant bouquet. Slender yellowish pods to 6 inches (15.2cm) long follow. Shedding midribs creates a straw-colored thatch like pine needles.

Special design features: Glorious yellow spring and summer bloom color. The fully foliaged crown of young to newly mature trees unaffected by the mite is a glorious sight. Bright yellow-green tree color.

Uses: Easily grown where little else will grow. Street, patio or lawn tree. Arid or tropical effect gardens. Transitional areas. Fast filtered shade for short-term use.

Disadvantages: Becomes woody and less attractive with age. Palo verde beetle can be a problem. Clean up litter with a blower. Occasionally suffers mistletoe infestations and frost damage. Sharp thorns in spring. The witches' broom caused by the infestation of mites has infected most trees, making them unattractive. Mite also distorts foliage. Volunteers profusely, becoming a weed in some areas.

Planting and care: Start from seed, or set out from containers, in spring or summer. Space 20 feet (6.1m) or more apart for a street tree or row. Remove lower branches if necessary to form a high crown, although trees usually take on a handsome, high-crowned shape naturally. Prune in June.

Parkinsonia aculeata

Parkinsonia aculeata

Low and middle zones; warmer areas of high zone
Deciduous
Soil: Tolerant. Accepts alkaline. Prefers sandy soils with good drainage.
Sun: Full to reflected sun.
Water: Will grow without irrigation in low zones with 10 to 12 inches (254 to 305mm) of annual rainfall, but best with some supplemental irrigation or runoff. Tolerates ample watering, such as in a lawn.
Temperature: Thrives in heat. Young trees are badly damaged at about 18F (-8C). Older trees can tolerate slightly lower temperatures, to 15F (-9C).
Maintenance: None to periodic depending on location and taste.

Parthenocissus quinquefolia

(Ampelopsis quinquefolia,
Vitis quinquefolia)
Family: Vitaceae
Virginia Creeper • Woodbine
Five-Leaved Ivy

Virginia creeper is a self-climbing vine, clinging by tendrils or aerial rootlets to cover a large space in a short time. Native to an area that includes northeastern United States to Florida, Texas and Mexico. A vigorous grower, runners root along the ground as they travel to create a dense cover. Leaves 2-1/2 to 6 inches (6.4 to 15.2cm) across are formed of five-tooth leaflets that fan out from center. Leaves turn gold and crimson in fall.

Cultivars and other notable species: 'Engelmannii' has smaller leaves. Its flowers are unimportant features, but it produces colorful blue fruit that attracts birds.

Special design features: Intimate woodland feeling. Garlands and festoons. Autumn color.

Uses: Fences, masonry walls or trellises as a fast summer cover. May be used as a random ground cover if its bare winter form can be tolerated. Use with other plants around the foundation of a structure or as a garland up a tree or post.

Disadvantages: Sometimes invasive—it can cover windows and other openings. Sometimes attacked in summer by grape-leaf skeletonizers. Occasionally bothered by root knot nematodes, powdery mildew and Texas root rot.

Planting and care: Plant any time from containers or dig up and transplant rooted runners in winter. Give late winter clipping to control size.

Parthenocissus quinquefolia

All zones
Deciduous
Soil: Average garden soil.
Sun: Part shade to full sun. Prefers afternoon shadow in hot areas.
Water: Moderate to ample.
Temperature: Hardy. Tolerates heat and exposure.
Maintenance: Periodic.

Parthenocissus quinquefolia

Paulownia tomentosa

(P. imperialis)
Family: Bignoniaceae
Empress Tree

This is a fast-growing deciduous tree to 40 feet (12.2m) with equal width or wider with a heavy trunk and stout horizontal branches. Large light green heart-shaped leaves, which vary in length from 5 to 12 inches (12.7 to 30.5cm) by 4 to 7 inches (10.2 to 17.8cm) wide, give dense shade in summer. Brown buds form in fall, remaining until spring when fragrant purple flowers to 2 inches (5.1cm) long open in clusters before the leaves come out. Capsule fruitlike tops to 2 inches (5.1cm) long follow and stay on the tree with the lower buds.

Special design features: Bold foliage, flowers and capsules. Tropical effect in summer. If you want a large foliage mass with leaves to 2 feet (0.6m) long, cut the tree to a large shrub size every year or two. Stong trunk and branch structure add interest in the dormant season.

Uses: Fast dense shade for larger yards or open areas where litter won't matter. Useful in colder areas with a more limited palette of useful bold deciduous trees.

Disadvantages: Flowers poorly in cold winter areas. Shallow roots. Leaves may tatter in wind. Litter. Unprotected trunk can sunburn, especially in warmer zones. Dense shade and shallow roots make underplanting difficult and undesirable.

Planting and care: Protect trunks of trees that do not shade themselves with white water-based paint.

Paulownia tomentosa

Paulownia tomentosa

All zones
Deciduous
Soil: Tolerant of most soils with good drainage.
Sun: Full sun.
Water: Weekly deep irrigation in summer, about every two weeks in winter.
Temperature: Cold-hardy and heat tolerant.
Maintenance: Flower, fruit and leaf litter cleanup. Periodic pruning. Protect trunk from sunburn where appropriate.

Phoenix canariensis

Family: Arecaceae (Palmae)
Canary Island Date Palm
Pineapple Palm

A massive lush feather palm from the Canary Islands, Canary Island date palm develops slowly from an appealing pot-size plant into a majestic giant, 60 feet (18.3m) tall in about eighty years. A palm 12 feet (3.7m) high may have a crown spread of 20 to 30 feet (6.1 to 9.2m) and a trunk diameter of 3 feet (0.9m). Fronds are dark green, orange at the base, and formed of many shiny filaments that glisten in the sun. Palms bloom in spring. Males produce spathes, bracts or leaves surrounding flower clusters, and females produce broomlike structures that hold the developing edible dates, which are mostly pit and not worth the trouble except to the birds. Dates first appear orange, then turn brown in the fall before they drop.

Special design features: Bold vertical form. Eventually a skyline tree. Tropical, desert or oasis feeling. Mediterranean.

Uses: Best in large areas, such as a park or boulevard, or in large commercial, public or residential landscapes. Young trees are excellent container plants—durable and undemanding. Palms stay small a long time in containers. A clean tree for pool areas (except for female trees with ripening fruit).

Disadvantages: It takes a whole season for foliage to recover from a hard frost. Mature trees are difficult and costly to groom. Leaves have dangerous sharp-spiked leaflets at the base and split in the wind, which makes trunks and frond stubs unsightly. Subject to palm heart rot. Can suffer from mineral deficiencies, which shows up as yellow in the leaves.

Planting and care: Can be grown from seed, but very slow. Plant or transplant in late spring or summer. Large specimens can be transplanted during warm summer weather. Space 30 to 60 feet (9.2 to 18.3m) apart for a row, avenue planting or grove. Remove fruiting parts and old fronds in late spring and summer. Mulch roots. Feed and irrigate deeply in summer to encourage faster growth. If you skim leaf bases from the trunk, be sure to leave about 2 feet (0.6m) of leaf stumps below crown. This helps support leaf fronds.

Phoenix canariensis

Phoenix canariensis

Low and middle zones
Evergreen
Soil: Tolerant. Prefers rich moist soil for fastest growth, but also tolerates periods when the soil is dry.
Sun: Part to full sun.
Water: Moderate to ample, although palms of all sizes withstand considerable drought, especially in the cool season.
Temperature: Fronds can be heavily damaged at 20F (-7C).
Maintenance: Periodic grooming necessary for attractive plants, which can be costly with larger specimens.

Phoenix dactylifera

Family: Arecaceae (Palmae)
Date Palm
Arab Date

Slender and more open and lighter in appearance than the Canary Island date palm, the true date palm is characterized by a rough gray trunk to 18 inches (45.7cm) in diameter and a "feather-duster" crown of gray-green fronds. It grows slowly to 60 feet (18.3m) high with a crown to 25 feet (7.6m) wide. Both male and female trees are needed to produce edible fruit that ripens in fall. If no male trees are present, pollen may be obtained to fertilize females by hand. Date palms produce many offshoots around the base and are multitrunk by nature. If left in place, the offshoots will form a thick clump, eventually growing outward to form a many-headed, angled-trunk grouping. To keep trees neat, limit to one offshoot, three or four if you want a multitrunk specimen. Offshoots are also replicas of the parent, a means of asexual reproduction, for fruiting types. Do not waste your time on seedlings. Seek plants asexually reproduced from one of the many named varieties.

Special design features: Dramatic silhouette. Strong vertical. Symbolic of the oasis in Middle East deserts.

Uses: Specimen, accent or emphasis plant. Tropical effects. Eventual skyline tree.

Disadvantages: Sometimes gets palm heart rot or fiber rot, causing trunk and frond ends to look moth-eaten. Sometimes gets bud rot, especially during humid summer weather. Some reports of palm borer affecting recently transplanted or stressed trees. This pest bores into the trunk near the growing tip. Can get leaf spot in humid climates. Taller palms become difficult and costly to groom. Sharp spines at frond bases make leaf trimming difficult.

Planting and care: Plant and transplant in summer, preferably in June. Large specimens can be transplanted, but this should be performed by experts. Remove and plant offshoots for propagation when they reach 10 to 12 inches (25.4 to 30.5cm) in diameter and weigh 35 pounds or more. Plant palms from containers any time, but warm weather is best. Space 30 feet (9.2m) apart for grove or row. Plants tolerate long periods of neglect, but will not bloom or set fruit. Responds to fertilization and irrigation with faster growth and better fruit. Birds are a major threat to fruit: Cover clusters with a paper sack. To groom, remove old hanging fronds and fruiting blossom and remnants each year. If using for landscape effect, fruit may just cause an undesirable mess. Remove blossoms or green fruit clusters before they ripen.

Phoenix dactylifera (young)

Phoenix dactylifera

Low and middles zones; warm areas of high zone
Evergreen
Soil: Tolerant if used as an ornamental. Will grow in alkaline or saline soils, but requires garden soil for fruit production.
Sun: Full sun to part shade.
Water: Moderate to occasional deep irrigation for fruit production. Established trees used for landscape effect (no fruit) can get along on occasional irrigation, about once a month.
Temperature: Hardy to 18F (-8C). Grow in high zone only if you don't want fruit.
Maintenance: Periodic to constant, depending on use.

Photinia fraseri

Family: Rosaceae
Fraser's Photinia

This hybrid is a popular plant in the landscape, adaptable to many uses. A moderate grower 10 to 12 feet (3.1 to 3.7m) or higher and as wide but easily kept smaller. Erect in form, it is covered to the base with toothed leaves 5 inches (12.7cm) long, bright coppery red when new, becoming shiny dark green with whitish undersides at maturity. Leaves scattered throughout the plant are red-tinted in cold weather. Flat lacy clusters of white flowers appear in April and May. A scattering of blooms may appear again in fall along with a few red berries.

Special design features: Color and interest throughout year. Spring color as red new growth commences. Exceptionally dense and attractive foliage. Oasis.

Uses: Large specimen shrub or small patio tree. Massed or planted in rows as background, wide screen or clipped hedge. Does well in containers, parking strips or in other paved areas. Tolerates reflected heat. May be espaliered on large walls, except extra-hot west walls. Transitional areas.

Disadvantages: Rank growth and bare branches in spots if not pruned or clipped occasionally. May get fireblight or Texas root rot. Plants sometimes get chlorosis. If this happens, feed plants with iron, a complete mineral mix, and a balanced fertilizer. Occasionally attacked by aphids.

Planting and care: Set out from containers any time. Space 3 to 4 feet (0.9 to 1.2m) apart for a clipped hedge, 8 feet (2.4m) for wide screen or background. Do any major pruning in December or January. Trim and shear any time. Tolerates neglect, but regular garden care produces more handsome plants.

Photinia fraseri

Photinia fraseri

All zones
Evergreen
Soil: Tolerant. Prefers average garden soil. Alkaline soils may produce chlorosis.
Sun: Full sun.
Water: Moderate to occasional deep irrigation.
Temperature: Hardy to 5F (-15C). Thrives in hot sun.
Maintenance: Periodic garden care.

Photinia serrulata

Family: Rosaceae
Chinese Photinia

This plant does best in the middle and high zones where the climate is cooler and the sun less intense. It is slightly more hardy to cold than *Photinia fraseri*. A shrub or small to medium tree with bold foliage, Chinese photinia, a native of China, can grow 35 to 40 feet (10.7 to 12.2m) in favorable locations. Usually seen as shrub 8 to 10 feet (2.4 to 3.1m) high with crisp toothed leaves to 8 inches (20.3cm) long, but can be trained into a small single-trunk tree. New growth is coppery in spring and turns deep green in summer with yellowish undersides. Some leaves turn bronzy or red in fall and winter. Small white flowers in flat 6-inch (15.2-cm) clusters appear in April and May and sometimes produce a sprinkling of long-lasting red berries in fall.

Cultivars and other notable species: 'Nova' grows to about 8 feet (2.4m) high and as wide. It is generally considered a better plant than the species. 'Aculeata' is a compact variegated form often sold as 'Nova.'

Special design features: Dense bold foliage. Woodland effect. Large scale for open spaces. Interest all year.

Uses: Use as specimen in open places that have good air flow. Background or screen plant. Larger species makes a handsome tree in cooler areas. Smaller form makes a handsome small patio tree in low and middle zones when given good air circulation and some afternoon shade. Espalier on cool walls.

Disadvantages: See *P. fraseri*. This plant is also subject to mildew. Plants grown in the open are generally less susceptible.

Planting and care: Set out from containers any time. Space 3 to 4 feet (0.9 to 1.2m) apart for a clipped hedge, 8 feet (2.4m) for wide screen or background. Do any major pruning in December or January. Trim and shear any time. Close hedge clipping ruins the bold leaf texture. Tolerates neglect, but regular garden care produces more handsome plants.

Photinia serrulata

Photinia serrulata

All zones
Evergreen
Soil: Tolerant. Prefers average garden soil. Alkaline soils may produce chlorosis.
Sun: Full sun.
Water: Moderate to occasional deep irrigation.
Temperature: Hardy to 5F (-15C). Thrives in hot sun.
Maintenance: Periodic garden care.

Phyllostachys aurea

(Bambusa aurea)
Family: Poaceae (Gramineae)
Golden Bamboo • Fishpole Bamboo
Yellow Bamboo

This is a running bamboo, erect and rather stiff with hollow yellowish canes commonly used for fishing poles. It reaches up to 10 feet (3.1m), sometimes 20 feet (6.1m) high. Vigorous grower and spreader, it will form dense thickets or groves unless controlled. Leaves are light green beneath, darker above. Plants require time to become established and to gain height and width. This is the bamboo often used for staking plants or for fences.

Cultivars and other notable species: *P. nigra* (black bamboo) is a running type. Canes to 1-1/2 inches (3.6cm) in diameter are green, becoming olive or brownish, speckled with black. Mature canes are often pure black with nodes edged with white below. Leaf sheaths are greenish to reddish buff, adding still more color and interest. It appreciates shade on hot summer afternoons in low and middle zones.

Special design features: Vertical. Tropical, oriental, jungle or waterside effect. Festive, light, airy and informal.

Uses: General landscape use as a hedge, specimen or screen. Attractive near ponds, but produces too much litter for swimming-pool areas. A good container plant.

Disadvantages: May be slow to establish, but once established, it can become invasive. Occasionally gets crown rot. Litter of leaves and sheaths.

Planting and care: Plant from containers any time or from divisions in spring and fall. When purchasing a plant for containers, keep in mind that a rootbound plant will grow faster. If you plant in the ground, contain plants with an 18-inch (45.7-cm) deep metal, fiberglass or concrete edge to keep roots from running to places they are not wanted. An area surrounded by a wide dry space also prevents spreading. Control spreading by cutting 12 inches (30.5cm) deep around plants with a spade to sever lateral runner shoots. To encourage fast growth, treat as a lawn grass. Water generously and feed with a high-nitrogen fertilizer monthly. To form a screen or hedge, set new plants 12 to 18 inches (30.5 to 45.7cm) or more apart. Make an irregular row by clumping plants at varying intervals to form stands.

Phyllostachys aurea

Phyllostachys aurea

All zones
Evergreen
Soil: Prefers moist garden soil.
Sun: Open shade to part, full or reflected sun.
Water: New plantings are especially sensitive to drying out during the first year, so make sure they receive enough moisture. Established plants tolerate moderate irrigation but prefer ample.
Temperature: Hardy to 5F (-15C). Accepts heat with irrigation.
Maintenance: Periodic.

Pinus species

Family: Pinaceae

The pines are a group of single-trunk cone-bearing trees with aromatic needlelike foliage. Native to various parts of the Northern Hemisphere, they are plants of great character and are usually dominant features in the landscape. Pines can be identified by their distinctive cones. Cones are either male or female. One tree may have different sizes because it takes up to two years for cones to mature. Many young pines have similar bluish juvenile foliage that makes them difficult to identify. Foliage is often similar to that of spruce—flat and not in bundles—quite different from the needles they develop as they mature. Bundles are clusters of two or more needles wrapped by a woody base. This more mature foliage change makes trees easier to identify. A swelling of the terminal buds at branch tips in spring indicates new growth. This temporarily changes the look of some trees, such as the Canary Island pine, which looks as if it is bearing huge candelabras. Sometimes the needles behind the new growth turn brown and fall. Few pines from cooler climates have proven successful over a long period of time in warmer climate zones, but a number introduced recently from warmer semiarid areas have performed very well and should probably be used more extensively.

Special design features: Pines suggest the coolness of the forest. Some can look like the picturesque survivors of mountain crags.

Uses: Shade. Wind and dust screens. Around water bodies, such as reservoirs, it filters dust from the air. Shade where an evergreen tree is desired. Skyline silhouette.

Disadvantages: For the most part, pines require little care but are susceptible to some pests and diseases. Suspect aphids if honeydew or yellowing needles appear. Infestations of red spider mites cause the foliage to look dull and mangy. Both pests can be eliminated with systemic sprays. Pines with five needles to the bundle are subject to white pine blister rust, but this is not much of a problem in the arid climates. Pines with needles in bundles of two or three may be attacked by the European pine-shoot moth. Aleppo and some others die back at twig tips; the cause is not known. To avoid this blight, give pines regular irrigation, especially during periods of drought. Pinewood nematode is a new serious pest that plagues aleppo and may be spread by infected cutting tools. Foliage yellows and wilts, with death occurring in one to two months. No cure is yet known. Contact your county cooperative extension agent if you suspect it.

Planting and care: Plant any time from containers. The best time for planting and the only time for transplanting is late fall or early winter. This allows the tree to establish a good root system before warm weather and rapid growth begin. When transplanting small trees, do it just before or just as growth buds swell. Take a large ball of earth with the roots to help ease shock. It is difficult to move larger specimens and it's best to rely on an expert. Stake and tie young trees securely, especially in windy places. Stake and tie to ensure proper establishment of root systems, which is prevented if young trees are continuously rocked by wind. To maintain size of tree or to encourage bushiness, pinch off growing tips (terminal buds) of branches halfway or more. Do not break off terminal bud below needles or the whole branch will die back. For the most luxuriant growth and healthiest tree, place a 2-inch (5.1-cm) mulch of composted manure with a sprinkling of soil sulfur over root area basin, preferably in fall. This helps prevent blight and creates a more hospitable root environment in caliche, tight silty soil or other poor soil conditions. Keep area around tree base free of weeds and debris. If fertilizing plants or lawn nearby, do not apply more than one pound of nitrogen fertilizer for every 50 square feet (15.2 square meters) of space around tree to a little beyond the drip line.

Pinus species

All zones
Evergreen
Soil: Tolerant of poor soils, but good drainage is essential.
Sun: Part shade to full sun.
Water: Do not allow young trees to dry out during the first year or two until roots are well established. Most established trees do very well with occasional soaking of the root zone and a little irrigation after that. Many tolerate lawn watering. Overwatered trees show a yellowing of older needles and poor appearance. Pines kept too dry are slow growing, have sparse foliage and a weakness to pests, blight and diseases.
Temperature: See individual species descriptions.
Maintenance: Periodic thinning or pruning and mulching. You can leave the fallen needles to serve as a natural mulch.

Pinus pinea

Pinus halepensis

Pinus roxburghii

Pinus canariensis

Pinus eldarica

Pinus canariensis
Canary Island Pine

Native to the Canary Islands, this pine has a tiered vertical form. A rapid grower to 10 feet (3.1m) in five years, to 18 feet (5.5m) in ten years, to about 33 feet (10.1m) in twenty years. Mature trees may reach 60 to 80 feet (18.3 to 24.4m) high and develop rounded tops. Their dark bluish-green needles to 12 inches (30.5cm) long occur in bundles of three. Glossy brown cones are 4 to 9 inches (10.2 to 22.9cm) long. Young trees are leggy, with juvenile foliage resembling that of spruce, but soon take on a pyramidal form. They are quite handsome, with long shaggy foliage, but look unkempt unless old needles are shaken off. Otherwise, little care is needed. The fairly narrow form of this pine makes it appropriate for narrower spaces or as a lawn tree. Its handsome open silhouette makes an interesting pattern against the sky. Best in the low and middle zones. Needles are damaged by cold at about 20F (-7C) and are very slowly replaced. The common practice of pruning to open up the silhouette actually weakens the tree.

Pinus eldarica
(P. brutia eldarica)
Afghan Pine • Eldarcia Pine
Mondel Pine • Elder Pine

Dependable, dense, symmetrical, cone-shaped pine tree that grows rather fast to as much as 30 to 50 feet (9.2 to 15.2m) high by 15 to 25 feet (4.6 to 7.6m) wide. Medium green 4- to 6-inch (10.2- to 15.2-cm) needles appear two per bundle. Cones can be 4 to 6 inches (10.2 to 15.2cm) long. It is more drought tolerant than most other pines, accepting thorough bimonthly summer irrigation in the low and middle zones once established, but growing faster with weekly soaks. It is often sold as a living Christmas tree. Considered by some as an ecotype of *P. brutia*, it grows in all zones except for the hottest areas of the low zone and coldest areas of the high zone. Damaged by cold at about 13F (-11C), but has survived temperatures to 5F (-15C). Prune in January.

Pinus halepensis
Aleppo Pine
Mediterranean Pine
Jerusalem Pine

The Greeks traditionally cut down an aleppo pine each year and decorated it with flowers and ribbons in honor of the dead god Attis. It is believed this custom was adopted by Europeans in honor of Christ, making aleppo the first Christmas tree. Aleppo is one of the best pines for the arid climates. It takes about a year to establish and grows at a fairly rapid rate to 10 feet (3.1m) in five years, 20 feet (6.1m) in ten years, eventually reaching 30 to 50 feet (9.2 to 15.2m). Mature specimens have round to irregular billowing crowns that spread 20 to 40 feet (6.1 to 12.2m). Needles, usually in bundles of two, are 4 inches (10.2cm) long. Trees may be gray-green in dusty areas but are usually medium yellowish-green. Cones are rounded, light brown and 2 inches (5.1cm) in diameter. Most pines drop their lower branches so that the trunk is visible. Mature specimens are often seen with no branches below 10 to 15 feet (3.1 to 4.6m), making them excellent overstory trees. Aleppo pine blight can be a bothersome nuisance. It is indicated by browning of growing tips. Cause is unknown, but trees mulched with manure and irrigated regularly seem to overcome this problem. Irrigation is most important during dry periods when tree is under stress from drought. Because aleppo pines are fast growing, evergreen and adapted to tough conditions, they make excellent windbreaks and screens. In windy areas, young trees must be firmly staked to prevent trunks from bending or weaving. Best in the low and middle zones (has been killed by freezing in the high zones). Hardy to about 13F (-11C).

Pinus pinea
Italian Stone Pine
Umbrella Pine

Visitors to Spain and Italy know the form of the ubiquitous umbrella-shaped pines towering over all, with tall naked trunks and wide flat crowns. Most don't realize that this shape is not natural for this Mediterranean native. Although trees naturally develop some bare trunk, like the aleppo, it is the wood gatherers who trim trees to such heights. Stout, bushy, globe-shaped young trees grow at a moderate to slow rate 40 to 80 feet (12.2 to 24.4m) high and 30 to 50 feet (9.2 to 15.2m) wide. Thinning the tree's interior causes more rapid growth. Mature trees have wide flat crowns, but when they are unpruned, branches extend much farther down the trunk. Stiff bright green needles to 6 inches (15.2cm) long are in bundles of two. Cones are brown and oval, 4 to 6 inches (10.2 to 15.2cm) long and produce the edible pignolia nut of southern Europe. A large-scale tree that will eventually tower over the average residence, umbrella pine is best used for roadsides or in large open areas, as a background tree or one of a cluster of eventually tall overstory skyline trees. It makes an excellent silhouette and is handsome at any age. Hardy in all three zones, extending into colder temperate zones.

Pinus roxburghii
(P. longifolia)
Chir Pine • Emodi Pine
Indian Longleaf Pine

A towering tree from the Himalayan foothills, chir pine is similar in many ways to the Canary Island pine, except it is more cold hardy and has brighter green foliage and a less open silhouette. A moderate to sometimes fast grower, it reaches 60 to 80 feet (18.3 to 24.4m) in height, with some trees in favorable locations attaining heights up to 150 feet (45.7m), and spreads 30 to 40 feet (9.2 to 12.2m). Slender and pyramidal in youth, with thick foliage and slightly drooping branchlets, it becomes a spreading, symmetrical, rounded tree at maturity. Needles in bundles of three reach up to 12 inches (30.5cm) long; cones are 4 to 7 inches (10.2 to 17.8cm) long. Use this tree anywhere you want a pine, but give it room to develop. Best in the middle and high zones.

Pinus thunbergiana
Japanese Black Pine

A moderate to fast grower in the arid climates to about 20 feet (6.1m) or higher, this Japanese native can reach a towering 130 feet (39.6m) in areas where it grows naturally. Trees have spreading branches and are conical to irregular in form. Sharply pointed foliage is fresh dark green. Needles in bundles of two are 4-1/2 inches (11.4cm) long. Brown oval cones to 3 inches (7.6cm) long appear near branch ends. This pine is in scale with a small garden as a feature, mass or screen and is remarkably well adapted to training. Use as a bonsai plant or shear to form a pyramidal Christmas tree. Prune into picturesque shapes or train downward and outward to make a cascade. Outstanding as a container plant. Best in the middle and high zones. Heat is a problem in low zone.

Pinus torreyana
Torrey Pine • Soledad Pine

This romantic and craggy pine is found growing naturally along the California coast near San Diego, where it is preserved in a state park, and on Santa Rosa Island. Strangely enough, it grows very well in the hot dry climates. It will probably be difficult to locate in a nursery, but is worth considering. If your nursery doesn't have it, they can probably order it for you. As a landscape tree, this pine grows at a fast, sometimes moderate rate to 40 to 60 feet (12.2 to 18.3m) high and a sprawling 30 feet (9.2m) wide, but unless exposed to wind and weather, it is much more regular in shape and less open than the windblown trees seen on the coast, especially if grown in heavy soils. Stiff, light gray-green to dark green needles are 8 to 13 inches (20.3 to 33cm) long in bundles of five. Dark brown cones are 4 to 6 inches (10.2 to 15.2cm) long. Give trees room to develop. Best in the middle and high zones. Hardy to 12F (-11C).

Pinus halepensis

Pinus torreyana

Pistacia chinensis

Family: Anacardiaceae
Chinese Pistache

Chinese pistache, native to China and Taiwan, is similar to Mt. Atlas pistache but larger, taller and more common. It grows at a moderate, sometimes slow rate to 60 feet (18.3m) high with a rounded crown that spreads to 50 feet (15.2m) wide. Trees in shallow soils or other difficult situations may grow to only 30 feet (9.2m) high. Leaflets are 2 inches (5.1cm) long, pointed, often turning scarlet in fall. Clusters of 1/2-inch (1.3-cm) inedible fruit on females turn deep red in early fall before foliage changes, later changing to purple. Fruit remains on the tree for a while after leaf drop.

Special design features: Large, dense, quality shade tree for summer shade and winter sun. Fall color depending on temperatures (dependable in the middle and high zones). Leaves can become gold to a deep red. Fruit may also turn red.

Uses: Lawn, park or avenue tree. Good in public spaces, or in woodsy or naturalistic plantings. Should be used where it has room to spread.

Disadvantages: Sometimes gets Texas root rot and should not be planted in infected soil. Also reseesds freely and could be invasive.

Planting and care: Plant from containers any time or bare root in winter. Stake young trees if necessary. When it has grown to 8 feet (2.4m) or more, prune to form scaffold branches and a crown, high enough to walk under. Little care is needed.

Pistacia chinensis

Pistacia chinensis

All zones
Deciduous
Soil: Tolerates alkaline soils. Grows best with deep soil and good drainage.
Sun: Part to full or reflected sun.
Water: Moderate until established, then occasional deep soakings.
Temperature: Hardier to cold than the other *Pistacia* species. Tolerates heat.
Maintenance: None to periodic training or guidance to make a large quality garden tree.

Pistacia chinensis

Pithecellobium flexicaule

(Ebenopsis flexicaulis)
Family: Fabaceae (Leguminosae)
Texas Ebony

Small, highly decorative tree of slow to moderate growth to 20 feet (6.1m) high and 15 feet (4.6m) wide. With favorable conditions, this recent introduction from Texas and New Mexico can reach a height of 30 feet (9.2m). Its most striking feature is an unusual twig structure that forms a wide bushy crown supported by an erect trunk with smooth gray bark. Thorny-based leaflets are medium green. Fragrant light yellow to creamy catkinlike flowers in dense clusters appear in spring, sometimes extending into summer. Brown woody pods 4 to 6 inches (10.2 to 15.2cm) long follow and remain for a long period.

Special design features: Character tree. Silhouette. Rich dark green foliage, epecially striking in arid climate settings. Great for informal effect.

Uses: Natural, wild, or desert gardens. Specimen for patio or garden. Transitional plant. Silhouette against structures. Screen or barrier when planted in row or grouping.

Disadvantages: Thorns. Slow to develop.

Planting and care: Plant from containers in spring or fall. May be grown from seed that has been scarified (scratched) but growth will be slow. Space 6 feet (1.8m) apart for screen or barrier, 20 feet (6.1m) or more for a row. Trim as desired. Do any major pruning in late winter. Because of thorns, plant away from walks or, if used as a patio tree, trim up lowest branches above head height.

Pithecellobium flexicaule

Pithecellobium flexicaule

Low and middle zones and protected locations in high zone
Evergreen to partly deciduous
Soil: Tolerant. Grows best in deep soil.
Sun: Part, full or reflected sun.
Water: Supply occasional deep soaking of the root zone. Accepts and will grow faster with moderate to ample. Once established, it can withstand periods of drought but will not grow as well.
Temperature: Revels in heat. Hardy to cold, but becomes deciduous in the coldest winters.
Maintenance: Periodic.

Pithecellobium flexicaule

Pithecellobium mexicanum

Family: Fabaceae (Leguminosae)
Mexican Ebony

A deciduous tree of moderate growth, faster in wet summers, with a strong erect trunk. Small gray-green leaves on thorny twigs form an open to somewhat dense crown. Mature trees in favorable situations can reach as high as 45 feet (13.7m), with a spread up to 30 feet (9.2m), but they are usually smaller. Whitish catkin flowers in midspring produce small brown pods. Growth can be controlled by availability of water in the warm season and depth of soil.

Special design features: A strong tree form with a lacy branch and foliage structure and attractive spring bloom.

Uses: For smaller yards or larger patios where broken shade is important. Good background tree or for grouping in a bosque-type planting.

Disadvantages: Hooked thorns can be a problem when staking and training young trees, but no more so than with some mesquites and *Acacias*. Often available only from nurseries specializing in arid land plants.

Planting and care: Can be planted from seed or a nursery container. Needs staking and training at first to form an overhead tree.

Pithecellobium mexicanum

All zones
Deciduous
Soil: Prefers and grows larger in deep moist soil. Tolerant of many soils including gravelly types. A smaller, struggling tree in caliche or hardpan.
Sun: Full to reflected sun.
Water: Established trees are drought resistant. Give monthly soaks of the root zone in summer, more often in shallow soils or to encourage growth. Continue soaks several times over winter to encourage root growth.
Temperature: Hardy in these zones. Low temperature tolerance untested.
Maintenance: Periodic cleanup of litter.

Pithecellobium mexicanum

Pittosporum phillyraeoides

Family: Pittosporaceae
Willow Pittosporum • Narrow-Leaf Pittosporum

A slender, erect willowlike tree with long trailing branches and narrow light gray-green 4-inch (10.2cm) leaves. Native of Australia. Trained as a single or multitrunk tree, it grows at a moderate to slow rate to 15 to 20 feet (4.6 to 6.1m) high, with a spread of 10 to 15 feet (3.1 to 4.6m). It can be grown in a narrow space and trained to have a narrower crown. Tiny yellow flowers appear along drooping branches in March and April and produce attractive 3/4-inch (1.9-cm) round deep yellow seed capsules in fall. One of the more decorative small-scale trees for the arid climate patios and gardens. There is also a less willowy form that does not have pendulous branches. It sometimes turns up in nurseries but isn't listed as a cultivar. Its general bushiness and lack of pendulous branches are readily apparent even in nursery containers, and it is well worth the search if you desire a good patio tree.

Special design features: Refined arid-climate grove or evergreen waterside effect.

Uses: Decorative silhouette. Adapts remarkably well to a bosque or row as a tall hedge or screen. Parkways or median strips. Clean enough to use near swimming pools or paved patios.

Disadvantages: Seed litter in abundant years, but not always a problem. Sometimes appears sparse and twiggy. In certain situations it spreads by root sprouts and can be invasive in garden areas. Subject to Texas root rot.

Planting and care: Plant from containers any time. To form tall, erect tree, encourage vertical leaders by pruning side shoots and staking one or more central shoots. Maintain appearance by pruning dead or errant branches. Prune in May.

Pittosporum phillyraeoides

All zones
Evergreen
Soil: Tolerant. Prefers loose soil with good drainage.
Sun: Open to filtered or part shade. Full or reflected sun.
Water: Best with occasional deep soaking of the root zone. Accepts moderate water with good drainage. Established trees can withstand considerable periods of drought, but they will drop leaves and look sparse.
Temperature: Revels in heat. Probably hardy to 10F (-12C). Lower limits are not yet known. May survive colder areas of the high zone, but best to plant in warmer microclimates.
Maintenance: Periodic pruning and sweeping.

Pittosporum phillyraeoides

Pittosporum phillyraeoides

Pittosporum tobira

Family: Pittosporaceae
Tobira • Japanese Mock Orange

Tobira is a neat large-scale shrub that requires little care. Its dense dark green foliage is a welcome accent in hot arid climates. It grows at a slow to moderate rate to 6 to 8 feet (1.8 to 2.4m) high with an equal width; specimens may eventually reach 15 feet (4.6m) unless pruned. Foliage covers plant to the ground. Leathery, sometimes glossy leaves grow in rosettes and have round tips. In spring, clusters of small white waxy flowers form in the rosettes. Flowers have the heady scent of orange blossoms. They are sometimes followed by 1/2-inch (1.3-cm) blue-green berrylike capsules in fall that split open to reveal orange seeds.

Cultivars and other notable species: 'Variegata' is smaller than P. tobira, reaching only 5 feet (1.5m) high and wide. Variegated leaves are gray-green, edged in white, giving it a bright cheerful appearance. 'Wheeler's Dwarf' is very compact, somewhat more refined, with richer foliage and a mounding form. It will grow to 28 inches (71.1cm) high with a spread of 5 feet (1.5m) in four years.

Give it some shade in middle and low zones.

Special design features: Dense rounded mound. Formal. Gives a feeling of mass.

Uses: Specimen, wide screen or space definer. Background or foundation plant.

Disadvantages: Young plants may show sunburn and chlorosis in sunny locations for the first two years. Plants are brittle and break easily. Sometimes gets Texas root rot or root knot nematodes. If a plant is in poor condition, look closely to see if it has cottony cushion scale (see page 43).

Planting and care: Plant from containers any time. Space species to 6 feet (1.8m) apart for a solid row or mass. Space 'Variegata' 4 feet (1.2m) apart for a row. Plant 'Wheeler's Dwarf' 2-1/2 feet (0.8m) on centers. Plants naturally assume neat round forms, which do not need pruning unless they become too large. Never shear plants into hedges or it will ruin the shape and chop up the leaves. Any corrective pruning should be done with hand clippers in late winter before spring growth.

Pittosporum tobira 'Wheeler's Dwarf'

Pittosporum tobira

All zones
Evergreen
Soil: Garden soil enriched with humus.
Sun: Filtered shade to part or full sun. Tolerates reflected sun but may burn in early summer. 'Wheeler's Dwarf' is the most susceptible to burning from reflected heat.
Water: Moderate, but tolerates ample watering, such as in lawns. Once established, give it occasional deep soakings. Mature plants can tolerate some drought.
Temperature: Usually hardy to cold. Accepts heat.
Maintenance: None to periodic.

Platanus acerifolia

Family: Platanaceae
London Plane Tree

This is a hybrid sycamore used in Europe and many parts of North America as a street tree. It is large and erect and grows moderate to fast to 40 to 70 feet (12.2 to 21.3m) high unless pruned. It has a symmetrical pyramidal form and somewhat pendulous lower branches, with a crown spreading 30 to 40 feet (9.2 to 12.2m) wide. Short stout trunk is covered with decorative mottled bark, which is whitish and peels in patches. This gives the tree a light color that contrasts with darker grays and browns of most bare trees in fall and winter. Irregularly toothed leaves have three to five shallow lobes and are 4 to 10 inches (10.2 to 25.4cm) across. Brief bloom of unimportant flowers in spring produces decorative round, bristly 1-inch (2.5-cm) seed balls that hang in clusters through fall into winter. Foliage turns golden brown in fall.

Cultivars and other notable species: 'Pyramidalis' is more upright in form and lacks drooping lower branches common to

the hybrid.

Special design features: Large-scale. Symmetrical. Formal. Erect. Beautiful structure and cheery winter form.

Uses: Street, avenue or park tree. Good for large lawn areas. Impressive as row, grove or arbor. Tolerates city conditions of smog, soot and dust.

Disadvantages: Subject to iron chlorosis in alkaline soils, especially in lawns.

Leaves may show marginal drying during hot periods in midsummer and later on in low and middle arid climates, especially if planted in a very hot location. Sometimes attacked by red spider mites or scale.

Planting and care: Plant from containers any time or bare root in winter. Space 20 feet (6.1m) apart for an overhead arbor, to 40 feet (12.2m) or more for row. Prune during dormant season for any necessary shaping or allow to grow naturally. Feed with iron seasonally to prevent chlorosis.

Platanus acerifolia

Platanus acerifolia

All zones
Deciduous
Soil: Tolerant but best in deep rich soils. Does not do well where drainage and soil depth are limited by caliche. May become chlorotic in alkaline soils.
Sun: Part to full sun. Tolerates reflected sun but may suffer from leaf burn, especially if water is limited.
Water: Little in dormant season to moderate or ample in hottest weather. Otherwise, supply occasional deep soakings of the root zone.
Temperature: Hardy to cold. Tolerates heat.
Maintenance: Seasonal, but depends on use. Otherwise, maintenance depends on use.

Platanus racemosa

Family: Platanaceae
California Sycamore

This vigorous, usually fast-growing tree will reach up to 50 feet (15.2m) or even 90 feet (27.4m) high when grown in deep soil with ample irrigation. More irregular in appearance than the London plane tree, trunks often divide into leaning or spreading secondary trunks. Large velvety leaves are deeply lobed and turn golden brown in fall; some leaves may stay on tree all winter. Tree leafs out early in the season and new foliage is sometimes caught by late frost. Inconspicuous spring flowers produce decorative bristly seed balls that hang in clusters.

Cultivars and other notable species: *P. wrightii* (Arizona sycamore) is probably better adapted than the above to very hot dry regions; its natural habitat is the canyons bordering the Arizona arid deserts, often ranging out along streamside locations. Form is somewhat more irregular and spreading than *P. racemosa*, and it does not grow as large. Trees generally reach 40 feet (12.2m) high with an equal spread. Cultural requirements are the same as for *P. racemosa.*

Special design features: Bold tree with striking branch structure, especially in winter.

Uses: Large lawn areas, parks or roadsides. Informal or natural gardens with lots of space.

Disadvantages: May get chlorosis in lawn situations. Sometimes attacked by spider mites or leaf miners. In hot areas and without sufficient soil moisture, leaves sometimes dry around the edges in midsummer. Sometimes a host to a foliage blight called *anthracnose* that causes intermittent leaf drop through the growing season.

Planting and care: Plant from containers any time or bare root in winter. New plants may be started from branch cuttings. Space at least 40 feet (12.2m) apart for row, closer for grove. Avoid planting in dry windy areas. Prune and train young trees carefully to attain desired structure. Prune in dormant season. Apply iron if chlorosis develops.

Platanus racemosa

Platanus racemosa

All zones to 5,000 feet (1,524m)
Briefly deciduous
Soil: Tolerant. Best with deep, loose, gravelly soil.
Sun: Full to reflected sun.
Water: Accepts lawn watering. Requires occasional deep soaking of the root zone, more frequently in hot dry summers than in winter when it is dormant. This is a riparian tree that needs ample water.
Temperature: Hardy to about 10F (-12C). Early new growth is damaged at about 26F (-3C).
Maintenance: Seasonal. Considerable cleanup of leaf drop over the growing season if tree is affected by the anthracnose blight.

Platycladus orientalis

(*Thuja orientalis, Biota orientalis*)
Family: Cupressaceae
Oriental Arborvitae

A remarkably durable plant that is widely used because of its durability and low maintenance requirements. However, its most popular cultivar requires careful design use in the landscape because its bold heavy form is so dominant, and plants often outgrow the space allotted. Growth is usually moderate. The species grows to 40 feet (12.2m) high and as wide as 20 feet (6.1m) but is seldom used.

Cultivars and other notable species: Its many cultivars vary in color, shape and size, although most are globe-shaped. Ask your nursery about the mature size of the plant you intend to buy. 'Aurea' reaches 12 to 18 feet (3.7 to 5.5m) high and nearly as wide at its base. Commonly sold is the compact form 'Nana Berkman's Dwarf.' It reaches 4 feet (1.2m) high with golden foliage tints. 'Westmont' slowly reaches 6 feet (1.8m) high, with golden foliage during the warm season. 'Fruitlandii' reaches 6 feet (1.8m) high with a cone-shaped mass of deep green foliage. 'Elegantissima' grows 12 to 15 feet (3.7 to 4.6m) high and is golden green in summer with a broad base. Its upside-down-beet shape is uncompromising even in hedge plantings.

Special design features: Heavy, dense and formal.

Uses: Specimen plant for emphasis. Large formal gardens or lawns. Screen or hedge. Windbreaks or sound barriers. Planters or containers. Corners of buildings to extend line, making the structure seem larger. An inexpensive clipped hedge if clipping is started when plants are young and if a certain width can be allowed.

Disadvantages: Spider mites. Can overgrow the space allotted and become monsters that pruning can't control.

Planting and care: Plant from containers any time. Space large forms 8 feet (2.4m) or more apart for hedge or screen; smaller plants 4 to 6 feet (1.2 to 1.8m), depending on eventual size of plant. Place closer for a dense continuous line. Give ragged plants an occasional trimming to keep neat.

Platycladus orientalis

Platycladus orientalis

All zones
Evergreen
Soil: Tolerant of most soils. Best with improved garden soil.
Sun: Full sun.
Water: Moderate until established, then occasional deep soaking of the root zone. Mature plants can withstand periods of drought.
Temperature: Tolerant to about 10F (-12C) and to altitudes of at least 4,500 feet (1,372m).
Maintenance: Periodic.

Podocarpus macrophyllus

(P. longifolius)
Family: Podocarpaceae
Japanese Yew • Yew Pine • Yew Podocarpus

This versatile shrub or small tree from Japan is related to the true pine. In its native habitat, it grows to 45 feet (13.7m) high but is seldom seen over 20 feet (6.1m) high in arid-climate zones. Flat, narrow, dark green 4-inch (10.2-cm) leaves are set in a spiral on bushy horizontal branches. An excellent plant for narrow spaces, especially if trimmed. Healthy trees in favorable locations bush out and take on an irregular shape. They look nice espaliered on cool walls. Catkin flowers are 1 to 1-1/2 inches (2.5 to 3.6cm) long, but are seldom seen in arid zones.

Special design features: Oriental effect. Formal. Vertical. Rich refined foliage is attractive in small spaces and close-up.

Uses: Trained specimens make tall narrow espaliers on cool walls. Especially attractive for entryways, atriums, courtyards or small patios. Informal unclipped specimens produce an oriental effect.

Disadvantages: Occasionally gets iron chlorosis. Burned and yellowed by reflected hot sun.

Planting and care: Plant from containers any time. For a hedge or screen, space one-gallon plants 18 inches (45.7cm) apart, five-gallon plants 2 to 3 feet (0.6 to 0.9m) apart. Espalier by tying to a wall. Clip and train as desired, or allow it to grow naturally. Give yellowing plants iron or shade from sun.

Podocarpus macrophyllus

Low zone and protected areas of middle zone
Evergreen
Soil: Rich organic soil with good drainage.
Sun: Open, full or filtered shade to part sun. Accepts full sun in cooler areas, but prefers afternoon shadow in middle and low zones.
Water: Moderate.
Temperature: Hardy to 10F (-12C). Accepts heat with shade and water.
Maintenance: Little to periodic, depending on use.

Podocarpus macrophyllus

Populus nigra 'Italica'

Populus alba

Populus species

Family: Salicaceae

Populus are some of the fastest-growing trees available. Their appearance is as striking as their growth rate, with attractive bright shimmering green leaves and light-colored bark. Poplars and cottonwoods are best planted in open areas because of their large size: Many reach 100 feet (30.5m) high and 40 feet (12.2m) wide. Leaf size varies among species, from 3 to 9 inches (7.6 to 22.9cm), larger on younger, fast-growing trees, becoming smaller as trees mature. Male trees produce greenish catkins and female trees produce small seeds encased in a cottony mass that becomes airborne when ripe, efficiently distributing the seed over large areas. This usually occurs before the leaves emerge—late winter to early spring. They are often grown at higher elevations. Trees are beset by many problems in middle and low zones so they are seldom used there.

Special design features: Informal with a pleasant country feel. Interest and brightness in the landscape all year. Evokes Mexican hacienda, western ranch and field. Striking silhouette. Fall color in October (later in lower zones).

Uses: Large lawns, golf courses, parks, country roads or field boundaries. Too large for average residence and in many cases unsuitable because of disadvantages noted. Effective specimen or as a row or grove tree. They are best used as temporary trees for fast screening or shade or in open locations.

Disadvantages: Greedy invasive roots get into sewers, pipes, septic tanks and leach fields. They are invasive in small gardens and may develop buttress or surface rooting if grown in or near lawns. Roots will go under a walk or wall to adjacent areas in search of water and can eventually heave and crack them. Weakened branches may break in the wind. Susceptible to Texas root rot, cankers and heart rot from untreated wounds. Infestations of mistletoe and tent caterpillars. Floating cottony seeds in spring. Often short-lived, but aged specimens are found near an ample water supply. Litter is sometimes a problem, especially from female trees when airborne seeds are released in spring.

Planting and care: Start by planting large or small branch or twig cuttings from mature trees just before they leaf out in late winter. Plant from containers any time or bare root during the brief dormant season. Space 10 to 15 feet (3.1 to 4.6m) apart for sapling row or grove, 40 feet (12.2m) or more for roadsides. Saplings may need staking against the wind. Treat any malady immediately upon discovery to promote healthy attractive trees and prevent heart rot. This also means removal of stubs from limbs broken by wind. Treat exposed cuts with bleach to prevent disease. Prune in March.

Populus species

All zones, but best in the high zone
Deciduous
Soil: Prefers deep, damp, sandy or gravelly soils with good drainage.
Sun: Full sun.
Water: Ample. Requires deep constant soil moisture. Can be given occasional deep soakings of root zone, but soil should never dry out completely or leaves turn yellow and drop. This is a true riparian tree of the riverside.
Temperature: Hardy to 10 to 15F (-12 to -9C). Accepts heat with ample water.
Maintenance: Periodic raking of leaves. Cleanup of cottony seeds that gather in drifts. Little to none in open country.

Populus alba
White Poplar • Abele
Silver-Leaved Poplar

This is a spreading, fast-growing tree to 40 to 60 feet (12.2 to 18.3m) high, higher in favorable locations. It has especially beautiful 5-inch (12.7-cm) leaves that are medium green on top, white and woolly underneath. Leaves produce a silvery shimmer in the slightest breeze. Native to Europe and Asia, it has naturalized in North America. 'Pyramidalis' (bolleana poplar) is a narrow and columnar cultivar, quite different in form from the species. Often grown as a windbreak in the high zone where it gives a vertical effect and a formal appearance.

Populus fremontii
Fremont Cottonwood

This striking tree of the open country and wide washes is native to water courses and canyons of the Southwest and Mexico below 6,000 feet (1,829m) elevation. Although there are many poplars and cottonwoods, fremont is the one most commonly planted. Trees grow fast to 50 feet (15.2m) high, sometimes as much as 100 feet (30.5m) when supplied with ample moisture. Spread is about half as wide as high. Mature form is open branched with a flat to billowing crown and rough gray bark. Bright green foliage emerges in late winter, deepens in tone during midsummer and turns golden in late fall before it drops. Leaves shimmer in the wind. Catkins come in late winter or early spring on males. Females produce cottony seeds that drift through the air, the "cotton" for which the tree is named.

Populus fremontii wislizenii
Valley Cottonwood • Rio Grande
Cottonwood • Wislizenus Cottonwood

This tree is native to a wide area from southern Colorado and Utah to New Mexico, western Texas and northern Mexico. It is probably more widely grown in these areas than the species. A stout tree, it grows fast to 40 to 100 feet (12.2 to 30.5m) high with a flat, wide-spreading crown of large branches and triangular leaves to 4 inches (10.2cm) long and as wide.

Populus fremontii

Populus nigra 'Italica'
Lombardy Poplar

This is a columnar form often seen in rows along drives or field edges, especially in higher elevations. It is recognized by its narrow leaves and form, which is almost as vertical as the Italian cypress. Usually only male trees are planted because of their narrower form and lack of airborne seeds.

Prosopis species

Family: Fabaceae (Leguminosae)

Mesquites are very adaptable and tolerant of adverse conditions and exposure. They are outstanding choices for the warm arid and hot interior climates. These trees and shrubs are native to both North and South America and possibly other parts of the world. They have long supplied arid-climate dwellers with shade and shelter, fuel for fires, building materials, food for livestock, and shredded bark for making baskets.

Because mesquite trees hybridize and look different in varying environments, there has been great confusion in determining their botanical classification. Botanical names are important; knowing them allows you to choose the exact tree that is right for a particular landscape use. In the West, mesquites grown for the nursery trade are distributed under certain names. They are listed in the following descriptions under their current names. Synonyms are shown in parentheses.

Mesquite trees usually have dark, sometimes rough bark, with a spreading crown densely clothed in finely cut compound leaflets. It is said that new mesquite leaves do not appear until after the last killing frost. This is generally true, but not always. Still, the leafing out of mesquite is a good indication that spring has arrived. They are often thorny in youth, but thorns usually disappear with age as growth slows. Flowers are yellowish catkins and appear in spring, followed by yellowish seedpods, which may be straight, twisted or curved, depending on the species. Mesquites are not true desert or arid-climate plants in the same sense as cacti, saltbush or creosote bush; they do not store water or become dormant in drought. They will live on little water, but adverse conditions keep them small and cause them to develop twisted forms. With their long tap root and lateral roots, they are able to penetrate soil to depths of 150 feet (45.7m) to seek out water. Underlying ground water allows mesquites in low areas, washes or flood plains to grow to 30 feet (9.2m) high and wide, or even more, depending on species and water availability. Even if a mesquite is deprived of water in its youth, when given regular irrigation, it gains size but keeps its picturesque form. Ample irrigation will produce a large tree faster, but overwatered trees may blow over. Mesquites, have outstanding character and blend with a garden or natural landscape equally well. They are most attractive when trained as multitrunk trees, selectively pruned and shaped when young. Once a mesquite has obtained a desired size, reducing irrigation will slow its growth.

Special design features: Bold arid-climate tree of great character. Feeling of the West. Ferny leaves and spreading form. Tropical or subtropical mood.

Uses: One of the most effective plants for summer shade and winter sun (except for the South American evergreen species). Effective in controlling glare, cooling ground surfaces and filtering dust and breezes. Lawn, patio or street tree. Parks or roadsides. Can be used in difficult soil areas, such as sanitary landfill sites or disturbed areas. Not for narrow areas or closer to structures than 8 or 10 feet (2.4 to 3.1m) Privacy screens, bosques, windbreaks, buffer zones. Flowers attract bees that make excellent honey. Their beans are ground into food (the pinole of Mexico). Beans are also used as livestock feed and are ground into flour by Native Americans as a food staple. Beautiful wood for furniture or floors. Good firewood.

Disadvantages: Invasive roots. Do not plant near leaky pipes, sewers, septic tanks, leaching fields or swimming pools. Nonirrigated trees can send their roots to irrigated parts of a landscape, heaving terraces and walls in the way. Litter of catkins in spring, seedpods in summer and leaflets in fall. Some people are allergic to the pollen. Occasional infestations of scale and mistletoe. Texas root rot is mainly a problem in Texas and is rarely seen in arid climates farther west. Dripping dark fluid (slime flux) from pruning cuts or wounds can stain patio floors. Rabbits strip bark of young plants unless protected. Plants near houses can send roots under foundations to seek the water from plumbing leaks, causing trouble.

Planting and care: Mesquites can be grown from seed but take two or three years to equal trees you could purchase in a five-gallon container. Mature trees are available as transplants. Plant from containers any time. Space 20 feet (6.1m) or more apart for a fast canopy or closer for a sapling grove. Stake young trees for support. To make a high crown or canopy, select the most prominent leaders and trim side branches to 12-inch (30.5-cm) nubs. Tie main leaders on long poles (such as 2 x 2s) angled outward at the desired slant. Continue to cut low side branches back to 12 inches (30.5cm) until trunks are strong and permanent branches at the top are partially developed. When desired height is reached, remove stakes and cut off side branches. Prune only to train. Treat pruning cuts with a bleach solution. Remove green suckers growing from crown branches. If tree roots start to invade where they are not wanted, try to control them by making a ditch 12 inches (30.5cm) wide and at least 2 feet (0.6m) deep. Then put rigid fiberglass or spun fiberglass with a root pellant at the side most distant from the tree and fill the ditch with gravel.

Prosopis species

All zones
Evergreen to deciduous: See individual species descriptions.
Soil: Widely tolerant. Best in deep soil with a high water table. For best results, make sure planting holes in caliche or clay soils have drainage.
Sun: Full to reflected sun.
Water: Widely tolerant once established but best if root zone is soaked monthly during long hot dry periods. Occasional soaks during dry winters help maintain vigor. Tree size can be somewhat controlled by available water. When tree gets as big as you want it, reduce irrigation to maintain good foliage without stimulating growth.
Temperature: Hardiness varies with variety. Plants endure all but severest winters.
Maintenance: Periodic to none depending on location and tree type.

Prosopis alba

Prosopis alba
Argentine Mesquite

Mesquites offered by nurseries under this name come from a tree so labeled at the Desert Botanical Garden in Phoenix. Some authorities say it could be *P. nigra*, but until further identification is made, it is usually called P. alba. It is perhaps the fastest-growing mesquite and is quite vigorous. Rough dark trunks tend to grow more vertical than other trees. Crown is spreading, blue-green and dense. With irrigation, it can become a substantial tree in five or six years. Although nearly evergreen, it is not free of leaf drop. Old leaflets usually drop in spring just as new foliage emerges, but start pruning earlier, in February. This tree seldom hybridizes with other mesquites, because it flowers at a different time. Hardy to 15F (-9C) in all three zones, but sustains some twig damage in cold witners of the high zone; unusual spring frost can burn young leaves.

Prosopis chilensis
Chilean Mesquite • Algarrobo Mesquite

There is confusion about the naming of this species. For a time, trees questionably called "Chilean mesquite" have been sold by nurseries (see *Prosopis* hybrid). The true Chilean mesquite may presently be available because several growers are importing the seed directly from Chile. True Chilean mesquite resembles the species often offered as *P. chilensis* but is more upright and vigorous in appearance. It is rapid growing and needs 25 to 40 feet (7.6 to 12.2m) for proper development. Foliage is more open and ferny and the tree is nearly evergreen. Tree may be sensitive to cold at 10F (-12C) or below. In mild winter areas, it keeps its leaves all winter but will lose them with sharp cold. It bears fewer blooms and the few seedpods are curved and hang in clusters. Young trees have enormous white woody thorns, vertical trunks and a symmetrical spreading crowns.

Prosopis glandulosa glandulosa
Honey Mesquite • Texas Honey Mesquite

This tree is usually associated with Texas, but it also grows from Kansas to New Mexico and northern Mexico. It recently made its appearance in Arizona. It is believed seeds came west in manure from cattle being shipped west from Texas. Quite different from other mesquites, foliage is brighter green with large leaflets and a weeping form. It

somewhat resembles the California pepper tree, *Schinus molle*. This species tends to be completely deciduous in winter no matter what climate it is in. It develops a large picturesque structure in favorable locations. In areas hostile to its development, it may remain a knee-high shrub, forming large thickets in some places. Not as widely used or known in the West as most of the other mesquites listed here. This tree should be used more in all three zones. Hardy to 0F (-18C).

Prosopis hybrid
Thornless South American Hybrid
Chilean Mesquite

Misnamed Chilean mesquite, this is probably a thornless form of *P. alba*, collected on the west side of the Andes where it grows naturally. The one we cover here was gathered from a tree planted at a border experiment station near Yuma, Arizona. The station closed, but this outstanding tree persisted. Chilean mesquite is the best name to use for locating this tree in most nurseries, but is botanically incorrect (see *P. chilensis*). Vigorous in appearance, with a wide spreading crown and deep green leaflets, it is deciduous and has more blossoms and seeds than the true Chilean mesquite. It also looks more rugged in an arid-climate setting.

Prosopis pubescens
Screwbean Mesquite • Tornillo

This is a small, thorny deciduous shrub or tree to 20 feet (6.1m) high and wide, with an interesting twisted bean pod. It is most often used where it is growing naturally because it is not carried in nurseries. The bean pod is prized by flower arrangers for use in decorative strings of seed and pods for wall hangings. Many people tuck it into a background planting just to have the pods. It also serves as a barrrier plant and, with a little extra water in the summer, it produces blue-green foliage. Yellow catkins appear in April and May. Hardy in all three zones to 0F (-18C).

Prosopis velutina
(P. juliflora velutina)
Velvet Mesquite • Arizona Mesquite

The true name of this tree is the hardest to figure out, which is unusual because it is very common and widely distributed. The common name "velvet mesquite" is

Prosopis glandulosa glandulosa

Prosopis hybrid

Prosopis velutina

appropriate—its foliage is soft and gray-green, with a velvety appearance from a distance. Leaflets are fuzzy and small. Craggy, rough-barked and picturesque, it has nubby, usually thornless twigs. This is the mesquite surrounding populated areas of Arizona. It is the main source for firewood, woodworking and cabinet making. It blends the best with the arid climate. It is deciduous and loses its leaves with the first cold spell.

Prunus caroliniana

(*Laurocerasus caroliniana*)
Family: Rosaceae
Carolina Laurel Cherry • Laurel Cherry
Mock Orange • Wild Orange

Carolina laurel cherry is a refined small tree. Erect and elegant with shiny dark green foliage, plants grow at a moderate rate to 15 to 20 feet (4.6 to 6.1m) high. Plants can be kept lower and used as a large shrub. A large plant will spread 15 feet (4.6m) unless cut back. Well-branched, dense and pyramidal in youth, it becomes looser and more spreading with age. Foliage covers plant to the ground unless trimmed. Tiny white flowers appear in dense clusters in April and May, sometimes followed by shiny black fruit. Native to the southeast from North Carolina to Texas.

Cultivars and other notable species: 'Compacta' and 'Bright 'n Tight' are compact cultivars with denser foliage than the species.

Special design features: Formal and refined. Air of coolness and control. Oasis.

Uses: Patio or street tree. Near swimming pools. Large background shrub, clipped hedge or screen. Feature plant for small spaces and for close-up viewing. Small formal standard tree or topiary plant. Espalier on cool walls. Container plant. Use in locations protected from the full force of sun and heat in middle zone.

Disadvantages: Very prone to chlorosis in alkaline soils. Foliage yellows from reflected heat and burns from hot winds. Sometimes gets root rot or gummosis.

Planting and care: Plant from containers in cool season. Space 24 inches (61cm) apart for clipped hedge, 6 to 8 feet (1.8 to 2.4m) for unclipped mass or screen. Feed with iron regularly to prevent iron chlorosis in alkaline soils. Prune in February.

Prunus caroliniana

Prunus caroliniana

Middle and high zones
Evergreen
Soil: Deep, enriched, well-drained soil.
Sun: Part shade to full sun.
Water: Moderate. May need ample in summer, but overwatering can trigger chlorosis.
Temperature: Hardy to about 10F (-12C). Leaves will often burn in hottest locations.
Maintenance: Periodic.

Prunus cerasifera 'Atropurpurea'

Family: Rosaccae
Purple-Leaf Plum • Flowering Plum

Chief among spring-flowering trees are the purple-leaf plums with their pink blossoms followed by purple leaves that make a stunning contrast in color and texture to pines or broad-leafed evergreens. Usually a small, symmetrical, single-trunk tree that grows at a moderate rate to 10 to 15 feet (3.1 to 4.6m) high, possibly reaching 20 feet (6.1m) or more in favorable locations, spreading 15 feet (4.6m). Young trees have upward-pointing branches. Crowns become more spreading with age. Flowers may be pink, rose or white, depending on the cultivar.

Cultivars and other notable species: Other cultivars of *P. cerasifera* include the following: 'Krauter's Vesuvius' has a vertically oval crown and dark purple-black foliage. Numerous pink flowers in spring are seldom followed by fruit. 'Thundercloud' is a slightly larger variety than the above tree, growing at a moderate rate to 20 feet (6.1m) high. It has coppery purple leaves and pale pink to white flowers, sometimes followed by small red fruit.

Special design features: Spring bloom, purple foliage contrast, stunning specimen.

Uses: Color accent for patios, lawns, parks and commercial settings.

Disadvantages: Although some trees live to be old, many tend to be short-lived because of a variety of maladies. They include Texas root rot, iron chlorosis, cytosporea canker, peach tree borers that bore into trunk at or just below ground level, aphids, spicer mites, slugs, caterpillars and other problems that plague the stone fruits. Avoid planting where litter will be a problem.

Planting and care: Plant from containers any time or set out bare root in winter. Space 15 to 20 feet (4.6 to 6.1m) apart for massing, line or grove. Thin trees to increase size and spread. Prune after bloom to encourage heavy bloom on new wood the next year. From the second year on, supply an annual feeding of nitrogen at least six weeks before flowering time. If near traffic areas, prune in winter to establish above-head-height canopy and to remove inward-growing and cross branches.

Prunus cerasifera 'Atropurpurea'

Prunus cerasifera 'Atropurpurea'

All zones (prefers cooler high zone)
Deciduous
Soil: Best in deep enriched soil with good drainage.
Sun: Full sun. Young trees accept part shade.
Water: Moderate.
Temperature: Hardy to cold. Accepts heat with irrigation.
Maintenance: Constant. Keep a watchful eye and treat as a pet plant needing special care as flowers do.

Punica granatum

Family: Punicaceae
Pomegranate • Granada

The pomegranate is originally from southern Asia but has been cultivated in the Mediterranean region since ancient times. Brought by the Spanish to the New World, it is one of the legendary plants of the Southwest and Mexico. It was planted by padres in mission gardens and copied by Indian silversmiths as the misnamed "squash blossoms" on traditional Navajo necklaces. Usually seen as a large shrub, pomegranate grows at a moderate to slow rate from 12 to 20 feet (3.7 to 6.1m) high and spreads to at least half as wide unless pruned back. In most gardens, it reaches about 8 to 10 feet (2.4 to 3.1m) high. Its twiggy structure is covered with small glossy leaves that are bronze in spring, bright green in summer, golden in fall. Blossoms on most varieties are red and appear in April. Many produce round red to bronze fruit, 3 inches (7.6cm) in diameter, filled with seeds surrounded by red to pale translucent pulp. Pulpy seeds are very sweet and can be chewed or used to make juice and a delicious jelly.

Cultivars and other notable species: There are a number of cultivars. 'Nana,' a dwarf form, makes an appealing landscape or container plant. It grows to only 3 feet (0.9m) high, with tiny, single orange-red flowers and small red inedible but decorative fruit. Nearly evergreen in warm places, it blooms when it is only 12 inches (30.5cm) tall. Other fruiting varieties include 'Wonderful' and 'Sweet.' 'Chico' is a compact bush that can be kept even lower with a little cutting. It has bright red carnationlike flowers over a long season.

Special design features: Tough, durable and long-lived. Pomegranate, especially original forms, tolerates hot winds, drought, salty soils, intense sun and cold winters. Resistant to Texas root rot and other fungus diseases, it is easy to grow and withstands neglect when established. An interesting bright green form with additional attraction of bright blossoms, colorful fruit and golden autumn foliage. Unused fruit can be left on the tree into winter dormancy so that it eventually hardens and dries and is therefore not messy.

Uses: Specimen, hedge, screen or windbreak. Espalier on hot walls. Some can be trained into trees. Dwarf form is excellent as a low hedge, container or bonsai plant.

Clipped hedges do not set much fruit. All are effective plants for transitional areas, as well as arid-climate or irrigated gardens.

Disadvantages: Twiggy winter form is not especially attractive. Fruit can be infected with a variety of diseases. A leaf-footed insect makes tiny holes in outer fruit cover, allowing a fungus to enter. Internal black rot may enter through blossoms and decay fruit. Sunburn in the hottest areas or a sudden increase in moisture will cause fruit to split.

Planting and care: Plant any time from containers or bare root in winter. Start cuttings in dormant season from pencil-size twigs about 7 inches (17.8cm) long. Space larger forms 3 to 4 feet (0.9 to 1.2m) apart for hedge or screen (closer for the dwarf form, which makes an excellent low hedge. Prune as desired in late winter; clean out twiggy growth in plant interior to maintain form. Shearing eliminates the arching form and most flowers and fruit. Keep irrigation steady when fruit is developing. A sudden moisture increase can cause fruit to split.

Punica granatum

All zones
Deciduous
Soil: Tolerant. Accepts alkalinity.
Sun: Full or reflected sun. Accepts morning sun or open shade of the north side, but will be more open in form.
Water: Tolerates any amount. Prefers deep occasional soakings. Once established, it tolerates periods of drought in areas receiving 10 inches (254mm) or more annual rainfall.
Temperature: Tolerant of a wide range.
Maintenance: Periodic. Some pruning and eventual removal of unused fruit.

Punica granatum

Pyracantha species

Family: Rosaceae

Pyracantha delights gardeners and birds alike with masses of tiny white flowers in spring, bright red or orange berries in fall and dependable evergreen foliage. Slow to start, plants increase in vigor and grow rampantly once established. Plants grow from 4 to 12 feet (1.2 to 3.7m) or more high and as wide, depending on the selection and pruning practices. Form is angular with stiff branches that bear sharp thorns and dark green leaves, slightly indented at the tip, with tiny teeth along the edges. Spring flowers are about 1/4 inch (0.6cm) across and appear in large clusters along branches. They are followed by clusters of green fruit, which become very colorful as the weather turns cold in fall. Some kinds hold fruit until the following spring bloom period, but berries are usually eaten by birds before then. Once established, *Pyracantha* is a remarkably tough shrub, withstanding drought, hot winds, poor soil and beating sun.

Special design features: Dark green foliage and bright fall, winter and spring color. Oasis. Formal. Natural.

Uses: See individual species descriptions.

Disadvantages: Subject to iron chlorosis. Sharp thorns make plants difficult to handle. Fire blight and spider mites are its most common and serious afflictions. For fire blight, look for dying or dead twigs that are black or burned. Cut off twigs well below dead part and disinfect clippers with 30 percent bleach solution after each cut. Treat wounds by painting them with the bleach solution to prevent further infection. Sometimes susceptible to Texas root rot.

Planting and care: Plant from containers any time. Set larger forms 4 to 6 feet (1.2 to 1.8m) apart for hedge or screen. Set ground cover types 3 to 4 feet (0.9 to 1.2m) apart. Flowers and fruit are produced on two-year-old wood. Established plants grow vigorously and need to be pruned often during the growing season. Pinch new growth to control size and form before they set thorns. Avoid trimming flowers that will produce winter berries. Any heavy pruning should be done by shortening long branches in late winter, before new growth starts. Give iron regularly if iron chlorosis is a problem.

Pyracantha species

All zones
Evergreen
Soil: Tolerant but needs good drainage. More likely to yellow in poor drainage situations or in alkaline soils.
Sun: Part to full or reflected sun.
Water: Occasional deep irrigation is best. Tolerates moderate, but may become chlorotic. Tolerates periods of drought, but looks stressed and unattractive.
Temperature: *P. fortuneana* and varieties are hardy to 10F (-12C). *P. coccinea* is hardy to 0F (-18C) and lower.
Maintenance: Periodic. Constant in summer for clipped plants.

Pyracantha espalired as a wall plant

Pyracantha coccinea
Firethorn • Pyracantha

This the hardiest of the *Pyracanthas* described here (even into the temperate zone). 'Lalandei' produces a profusion of bright orange berries in fall. Growth habit is upright. Foliage is a very dark green and less glossy than is typical of the species. *P. coccinea* 'Lowboy' is one of many dwarf types that can be used as a ground cover or on banks. It also has orange berries.

Pyracantha fortuneana
(*P. crenatoserrata, P. yunnanensis*)
Firethorn • Pyracantha

A vigorous plant with red berries, it grows to 15 feet (4.6m) tall and spreads to 10 feet (3.1m) wide. Its cultivars (below) are widely used and better known than the species.

Pyracantha fortuneana 'Graberi'
Graberi

A fast grower to 10 to 12 feet (3 .1 to 3.7m) high, with lustrous dark green leaves, upright growth and huge clusters of red berries. Makes an excellent espalier as a wall or fence plant. Can also be used as a windbreak or barrier hedge.

Pyracantha fortuneana 'Tiny Tim'
Tiny Tim

A dwarf that grows to 3 feet (0.9m) tall with small leaves, red berries, and few if any thorns. Needs pruning once a year when fruit begins to color to expose the berries that are often hidden by the later summer growth. Cut back vertical shoots and runaway branches. Can be used in containers, for a low informal hedge or barrier.

Pyracantha fortuneana 'Walderi'
(*P. f.* 'Walderi Prostrata')
Walderi

Grows to only 18 inches (45.7cm) high, spreading to 4 or 5 feet (1.2 to 1.5m) or wider, with a few vertical shoots that should be removed. Use in containers or as a low informal hedge or barrier. A good ground or bank cover where weeds will not bother it or where you use a pre-emergence. Plant on 4- to 5-foot (1.2- to 1.5-m) centers for fast cover.

Pyrus kawakamii

Family: Rosaceae
Evergreen Pear

Pyrus kawakamii is a graceful and civilized pear that produces a breathtaking display of white blossoms in late winter before other plants begin to bloom. Usually trained as an upright, single or multitrunk tree with a dense umbrella crown, this native of Taiwan is a sprawling shrub in its natural form. Bright green glossy leaves turn golden or orange and drop just before blossoms appear. New leaves emerge as bloom ends, but branches may be bare for a brief period, especially if weather turns cold. Trees will wait for a break in the weather before putting out blossoms or leaves. Growth is moderate to 25 feet (7.6m) high with a crown spread as wide in rich deep soils, with irrigation. Plants usually reach 15 to 20 feet (4.6 to 6.1m) high in hot arid climates. If pears form at all, they are small, hard and inedible.

Special design features: Refined and elegant. Spring bloom. Oriental elegance.

Uses: Street, patio, courtyard or garden tree. Attractive as specimen or grouping. Effective espalier for narrow spaces. Untrained plants make excellent background shrubs or wide screens.

Disadvantages: Subject to iron chlorosis and occasionally zinc deficiency.

May get crown gall, root knot nematode or Texas root rot. Extremely susceptible to fire blight. Subject to other ills of the Rosaceae family.

Planting and care: Plant from containers any time in improved soil. Space 10 to 15 feet (3.1 to 4.6m) apart for massing, 20 feet (6.1m) or more for street or drive. For a tree form, obtain pruned and staked plants. Keep staked until trunks are self-supporting. Once trained, little shaping is needed. Feed with a general fertilizer and extra iron or zinc as needed. Watch for signs of fire blight and prune out immediately when discovered. Disinfect pruning implements with 10 percent bleach solution afterward.

Pyrus kawakamii

All zones
Nearly evergreen. Briefly deciduous before flowers appear
Soil: Rich garden soil with good drainage.
Sun: Filtered, open or part shade to full sun. Best with afternoon shadow in low zone. Avoid hot reflective west walls.
Water: Moderate. Drench entire root area on a weekly basis in summer.
Temperature: Hardy to cold but can become deciduous during coldest winters.
Maintenance: Periodic. Keep watch for fire blight infestation.

Pyrus kawakamii

Pyrus kawakamii

Pyrus kawakamii

Quercus species

Family: Fagaceae

In recent years oaks have become a common sight in the urban scene for their quality, durability and long life spans. Many are evergreen. Some deciduous oaks give fall color in all three zones. A few can tolerate heat and adverse conditions, while others will perform better in higher and cooler areas. Most oaks are slow growers, which makes them desirable as street trees or even for use in the yards of medium-size residences. The larger oaks serve well in large public areas such as parks, where they can be planted with other types of fast-growing trees with short life spans. When you plant an oak, you plant quality. Common oak characteristics are broad spreading crowns supported by sturdy trunks with fissured bark, strong branches, leathery leaves, and acorns. To save space we list only the outstanding differing features and needs of each oak. There are many other oaks, but this will get you started on finding the perfect oak for your landscape. Cultural needs are for established trees. Young trees always need care in planting, irrigation and possible training. Added irrigation will aid development and speed growth.

Special design features: Quality trees. Well worth the time they take to grow. Strong vertical. Formal and contained. Many have a picturesque form.

Uses: Tree for large areas such as streets, expansive lawns, parks, golf courses and patios large enough to accomodate them. Plant close together as a tall screen or clipped hedge. Takes clipping well enough to be used as a large topiary plant or standard tree.

Disadvantages: Some species are subject to oak moth larvae and a new as yet unnamed disease that is killing the coast live oak and other trees in California. (Consult a qualified landscape professional in your area or your county cooperative extension agent for more information.) Also watch for the fungal disease armillaria, or oak-root fungus. It is encouraged by excessive moisture at the plant's root zone. Native California oaks are especially susceptible. The disease can be transmitted from oaks to other plants nearby. Leaf drop in spring. Chlorosis in alkaline soils. Some species have greedy roots.

Planting and care: Plant from containers any time. Space 8 to 10 feet (2.4 to 3.1m) apart for substantial hedge or screen, 15 to 20 feet (4.6 to 6.1m) for grove or row, 20 to 30 feet (6.1 to 9.2m) or more for street tree, 30 to 40 feet (9.2 to 12.2m) apart for a spreading canopy or avenue planting. Stake tree carefully until it supports itself. Prune sparingly in late winter. If leaves turn yellow, give iron to correct chlorosis.

Quercus species

Zones: See individual species descriptions.
Evergreen to deciduous: See individual species descriptions.
Soil: Tolerant. Well-drained enriched soil is ideal.
Sun: Full sun. Some species tolerate reflected sun to part shade.
Water: Fastest growth with occasional deep soaks of the root zone. Withstand periods of drought when established. Light summer irrigation, monthly root zone soaks in winter.
Temperature: Varies. See individual species descriptions.
Maintenance: Periodic unless kept sheared as a hedge, standard or topiary.

Quercus agrifolia

Quercus buckleyi 'Red Rock'

Quercus agrifolia
Coast Live Oak • California Live Oak

This evergreen California native is slow growing in hot dry climates to 20 feet (6.1m) high, occasionally to 50 feet (15.2m) after many years. Stiff, dark leathery leaves to 3 inches (7.6cm) are hollylike with a sharply pointed tip. Dark gray bark, smooth for an oak, clothes the trunk, which becomes gnarled with age. The California live oak is appreciated for its picturesque form and for the slow growth that keeps it in scale with the average home for many years. Best in high and middle zones. Native to the arid-climate edge of interior valleys coastward in California and Mexico. Hardy to 10F (-12C).

Quercus buckleyi
(Q. texanum)
Texas Red Oak
Texas Hill Country Red Oak

A deciduous oak from the Texas hill country that grows at a moderate to rapid rate in arid regions to 30 feet (9.2m) high, usually smaller than the 50 to 60 feet (15.2 to 18.3m) it gets in its native habitat. Large lobed leaves turn red in late fall and hang on into early winter, an outstanding feature. *Q. buckleyi* 'Redrock' is an excellent choice. Grow as single or multitrunk tree in all three zones. Tolerant of many soils, including alkaline and high calcium soils. Prefers full to reflected sun to part shade.

Quercus emoryi
Blackjack Oak

Another oak with interesting bark that at maturity is thick and black and divided into plates, giving it an alligator-skin look. This evergreen southwestern tree grows slowly to 20 feet (6.1m) high, sometimes reaching 50 feet (15.2m) in optimum conditions. Its form is open to dense, with bronze-green leathery leaves to 2 inches (5.1cm) in length. Where space is restricted, it is more vertical and narrow. This tree may be difficult to find, but it is worth the search. Hardy in all three zones. Native to wetter areas of high zone.

Quercus fusiformis
Escarpment Live Oak

Similar in appearance to *Q. agrifolia* but very different in its adaptability to harsher conditions of cold and drought. Does well in Las Vegas and Albuquerque, although it may go deciduous. It has also done well in Phoenix heat. It is a slow grower to as much as 50 feet (15.2m) high and wide. Hardy to 0F (-18C).

Quercus ilex
Holly Oak • Holm Oak • Italian Live Oak

Evergreen, erect and symmetrical, this oak remains a shrub in adverse conditions but will grow at a moderate rate to as much as 60 feet (18.3m) high when planted in deep soil and supplied with adequate moisture. Pyramidal in youth, it develops a heavy crown as wide as it is high at maturity. Leaves are variable in size and form, from 1 to 3 inches (2.5 to 7.6cm) long and elliptical to lance-shaped. Although foliage appears gray-green from a distance, leaves are smooth and dark green on top, feltlike with a silvery or yellowish cast underneath. Leaf edges may be smooth or spiny. Bark is fairly smooth. Adapts well to most locations and is resistant to pests and diseases that attack other oaks. Hardy to about 10F (-12C). Tolerant of heat.

Quercus suber
Cork Oak

The bark of the evergreen cork oak produces cork from which many commercial products are made. The cork is harvested in sheets from the outer bark of trees growing in forests and commercial groves in southern Europe, Spain and North Africa, where it is native. Young trees are narrow and conical in form. They grow at a slow, sometimes moderate rate 30 to 50 feet (9.2 to 15.2m) high or higher with an equal width at maturity. Growth rate and eventual size depend on soil depth and moisture. Mature trees have a tall, erect trunk covered with deeply furrowed tan to gray resilient bark. Branches are somewhat pendulous. Foliage appears gray-green from a distance. Leaves to 3 inches (7.6cm) long with toothed edges are shiny dark green on top and grayish and feltlike underneath. Good in dry areas or near large structures, it will eventually tower over a house as a canopy. Soft cork bark invites mutilation and graffiti in public areas. Hardy to about 5F (-15C) and adapted to all zones. Tolerates heat.

Quercus virginiana
Southern Live Oak • Live Oak

Southern live oak, native to the southeastern United States, is a sentimental tree to many. It is the fastest-growing oak tree mentioned here and the most attractive for hot interior valleys. The crown is thick and twiggy in youth with pronounced lateral branches, giving it a distinctive silhouette. In its native habitat, a mature specimen is a great spreading tree with nearly horizontal branches, dense foliage and dark fissured bark on a short, massive, gnarled trunk. It is known to reach 50 to 70 feet (15.2 to 21.3m) tall in cultivation with a crown spread that is twice its height. It is not yet known how large this tree will grow in the West, because of the rigorous conditions and because there are not many old specimens. Trees grow at a moderate rate, faster in deep moist soil. Leaves to 3 inches (7.6cm) long are smooth-edged, shiny and dark green on top and fuzzy white underneath. Southern live oak is reportedly resistant to pests and diseases that attack western oaks. It is the best oak for wet or well-irrigated places, but it also withstands periods of drought after it has become established. 'Heritage Oak™,' a selection from Texas, is quite fast growing and has especially attractive lush foliage. Follow the same planting instructions for other oaks or transplant bare root plants in winter and early spring. Although hardy in all zones and evergreen, this oak loses leaves at about 15F (-9C) and is damaged by cold below 0F (-18C).

Quercus ilex

Quercus virginiana

Quercus suber

Quercus suber bark

Rhaphiolepis indica

Family: Rosaceae
Indian Hawthorn

Dependable Indian hawthorn is attractive all year, with lush foliage and pink to white spring flowers. Growth is slow to moderate. Its mature size ranges from 2 to 6 feet (0.6 to 1.8m) or higher, with a spread as wide or wider than its height. Maximum size is dependable and plants will not outgrow the space allotted. Shiny, dark green, leathery, toothed leaves are set on bronzy stems and often have a reddish or bronzy cast when new. Flowers appear in clusters in spring over a long period. Small, dark blue, berrylike fruits may follow in summer

Cultivars and other notable species: 'Enchantress™' mounds to 3 feet (0.9m) high by 5 feet (1.5m) wide and has rose-pink flowers. 'White Enchantress' has white flowers. 'Springtime™' is a medium-growing shrub to 4 to 6 feet (1.2 to 1.8m) high by as wide. 'Majestic Beauty,' to 10 to 12 feet (3.1 to 3.7m) high by 6 to 8 feet (1.8 to 2.4m) wide, has distinctive bold foliage. It can also be used as a single- or multitrunk tree that can grow to 20 to 25 feet (6.1 to 7.6m) high in favorable locations.

Special design features: Shrubby green forms for cultivated gardens. Refreshing late winter to early spring bloom.

Uses: Woodsy feeling. Oriental quality with other plants of an oriental nature. Larger types make dense background plantings, specimens or small trees. All plants are effective as foundation plantings. Informal hedges, edges or dividers. Large-scale ground covers. Foreground plants for small patios. Container plants. Formal.

Disadvantages: Iron chlorosis. Leafburn from intense or reflected sun or soil salts.

Planting and care: Plant any time from containers. Space larger forms 2 to 3 feet (0.6 to 0.9m) apart for quick massing, 4 to 5 feet (1.2 to 1.5m) apart to fill in over time. Pinch at least once after bloom to keep growth compact. Shearing and clipping ruin the character of the plant. Selective pruning, however, can shape or control its size. To encourage vertical growth, pinch side shoots. Or pinch top shoots to encourage side branching.

Rhaphiolepis indica

Rhaphiolepis indica

All zones
Evergreen
Soil: Best with enriched garden soil and good drainage.
Sun: Open or part shade. Accepts full sun in middle and high zones. Needs afternoon shade in low zone or where there are hot reflective surfaces in the middle zone, such as concrete walks or white walls.
Water: Moderate to ample.
Temperature: Hardy to about 10F (-12C).
Maintenance: Periodic garden care.

Rhus lancea

Family: Anacardiaceae
African Sumac

This tree is native to the arid lands of South Africa and is well adapted to the U.S. Southwest. Trees create a large dense screen to 15 feet (4.6m) or higher at maturity. Plants vary in growth rate from slow to fast, depending on conditions. Maximum height is usually 20 feet (6.1m) with a 30-foot (9.2-m) spread. Crowns of trees 12 to 15 feet (3.7 to 4.6m) high are flat-topped and spreading. As trees gain height, crown becomes more dome-shaped. Foliage appears dark green and fine textured at a distance. Leaves are formed of three narrow-pointed lobes 2 or 3 inches (5.1 or 7.6cm) long. Fragrant greenish flowers in late winter produce red or yellow pea-size berries in clusters on females.

Special design features: Ornamental and picturesque shade tree of bright to deep dark green. Dense shade canopy.

Uses: Shade tree for paved or unpaved areas, patios, courtyards or lawns where drainage is excellent. Set close together as a mass planting to create a continuous canopy. Street tree or in public spaces. Unpruned plants in row make a nice screen. Single plant makes a bold emphasis point.

Disadvantages: Blooms in winter and exacerbates hay fever. Reseeds in moist areas. Some trees lose much of their foliage in summer but usually recover a thick crown. Can get chlorosis in poorly drained soils or if overwatered. Flower and fruit litter. Can get Texas root rot and scale. Damaged by strong winds or extreme cold.

Planting and care: Plant from containers any time, but best in spring and summer. Space 15 to 25 feet (4.6 to 7.6m) apart for a canopy, 20 to 30 feet (6.1 to 9.2m) or more for street tree. Place 10 to 15 feet (3.1 to 4.6m) apart for a dense screen. Corrective pruning may be done any time. Never plant in an area known to be infested with Texas root rot. For best results, prepare soil before planting with the recommended mix to prevent root rot. Trim young trees as they grow and encourage high scaffold branches so that you can walk under the tree.

Rhus lancea

Rhus lancea

Low and middle zones
Evergreen
Soil: Tolerant of a wide range of soils but needs good drainage. Tolerates less than perfect drainage if given little water, but growth may be slow.
Sun: Part to full or reflected sun.
Water: Occasional to moderate. Space irrigation so soil dries out between deep root soakings. Accepts ample irrigation with good drainage, but also does well as a tree in open untended areas at property edges.
Temperature: Hardy to 15F (-9C) but foliage may burn and look unkempt below 20F (-7C).
Maintenance: Periodic: training and litter cleanup.

Rhus ovata

Family: Anacardiaceae
Sugar Bush

This broad, slow-growing shrub may reach 10 feet (3.1m), rarely 15 feet (4.6m) high after many years. It is surprisingly drought tolerant and gives the look of being well-watered, with a rounded form and crisp, leathery, bright to deep green foliage. Long leaves are often folded at midrib and curved backward. They have reddish, often wavy margins and are supported on red stems. The branches and trunk have smooth light gray bark. Deep red buds on spikes form in fall and remain for a long period. They are actually more decorative than the tiny creamy flowers that open in spring. Deep red hairy fruits occasionally follow. These plants sometimes naturalize in arid climates where they seem best adapted.

Cultivars and other notable species: A discussion of *Rhus* species would not be complete without mentioning *R. choriophylla* (Chihuahuan sumac, leather-leaf sumac) and *R. viren* (Huachuca sumac). They are very much like *R. ovata* in character but are not as troubled with damping off and may actually be the best *Rhus* species for arid climate regions. Both have compound leaves with a reddish midrib and small, shiny, crisp, leathery leaflets and clusters of tiny whitish flowers. Leaves are deep green with a rich waxy appearance. Size and cultural requirements for both plants are the same as for *R. ovata*.

Special design features: A decorative plant for dry areas, it gives a lush green look to the landscape. Dense, cheerful, leafy mound, wide shrub or small tree.

Uses: Specimen or emphasis plant. Wide screen. Arid-climate or dry natural gardens. Pool patios. Single- or multitrunk patio tree.

Disadvantages: Damping off fungus in summer is an occasional problem. Sometimes reseeds and naturalizes.

Planting and care: Plant from containers in fall, winter or early spring. Space 5 to 6 feet (1.5 to 1.8m) apart for large screen, 5 to 10 feet (1.5 to 3.1m) for informal mounds or massing. Accepts some pruning, but most attractive if allowed to grow naturally. Because of its regular form, it rarely needs training of any sort, unless you want to train a tall plant into a tree.

Rhus ovata

Rhus ovata

All zones
Evergreen
Soil: Good drainage is a must, but it is otherwise tolerant. Prefers loose rocky fill and likes to grow among boulders.
Sun: Part to full or reflected sun.
Water: Prefers moderate deep irrigation in winter and occasional irrigation in summer. Overwatering (especially in summer) and poor drainage can kill plant overnight.
Temperature: Hardy to approximately 15F (-9C) or below. Remains attractive after freezes that often destroy many plants in these zones.
Maintenance: None, except occasional leaf raking.

Rosa banksiae

Family: Rosaceae
Banksia Rose • Lady Bank's Rose

The famous rose in Tombstone, Arizona, reported to be the largest rose vine in the world, is a banksia rose. Plants grow vigorously, sending out long slender branches that arch and sprawl to make a large deep green informal mound on banks or a rooftop trellis cover. Given support, it can be trained as a tree or on a wall, fence or arbor. Shear to keep close and dense as a wall plant. Untrained and unsheared, it is best for large-scale areas. There are two kinds: yellow-flowering and white-flowering. April and May flowers consist of many crinkled petals that appear all at once in spring along the branches. From a distance they look like popcorn. Flowers have little if any fragrance (more fragrant at night).

Cultivars and other notable species: 'Albo Plena,' the white-flowering form, has thorny branches and is partly to completely evergreen. 'Lutea,' with yellow flowers, does not have thorns, is mostly deciduous, and is easier to control.

Special design features: Profuse spring bloom. Large green mound. Rampant growth. Wild informal look unless pruned and sheared. Develops a woody trunk when trained up to cover an arbor.

Uses: Use only where you are willing to give it the time and care necessary for training and control. Often used as bank plant along highways at interchanges or in median strips where it will tangle with out-of-control cars. White-flowering form makes a thorny barrier. Not a plant for close-up viewing unless given constant trimming.

Disadvantages: Rampant growth can take over. Occasional iron chlorosis. In cold winters, 'Lutea' may lose some or all of its leaves.

Planting and care: Plant from containers any time. Space 8 feet (2.4m) apart for a bank cover. Prune and shear as needed to control size and appearance in limited spaces, or train to cover an arbor or other shade structure.

Rosa banksiae

Rosa banksiae

Low and middle zones; warm spots in high zone
Evergreen to deciduous in colder areas
Soil: Tolerant. Prefers well-prepared garden soil.
Sun: Part to full sun.
Water: Moderate.
Temperature: Hardy to 10F (-12C), but may lose leaves in coldest winters.
Maintenance: Periodic as an informal bank or trellis cover. Constant where it needs control during growing season.

Rosmarinus officinalis

Family: Labiatae
Rosemary

One of the best and toughest plants for arid lands, this plant does well in poor or shallow soils. It tolerates great heat and blazing sun as well as cool spray from the ocean, and low temperatures. As a shrub, it can reach 6 feet (1.8m) high. Whatever its size, it has dark gray-green, almost needlelike foliage and a rugged, upward pointing picturesque form. Foliage densely covers the plant to the ground and may appear lighter gray in dusty areas or gain a yellowish cast during hot dry summers. Numerous small pale blue flowers appear along branches from winter into spring and sometimes bloom again in fall when the weather cools.

Cultivars and other notable species: 'Prostratus' is the most popular of the several low-growing forms, with trailing branches that mound to 2 feet (0.6m) high and spread 3 to 6 feet (0.9 to 1.8m) or wider. 'Tuscan Blue,' a shrub form, is upright to 5 feet (1.5m) tall with rigid branches, rich green foliage and blue-violet flowers.

Special design features: Informal aromatic plant for tough situations.

Transitional, arid climate or wild gardens. Birds love its tiny seeds. Fall, winter and early spring color. Rabbits will not eat it.

Uses: Upright forms as low shrubs or hedges. Prostrate forms as ground or bank covers, edgings, or cascading from planters.

Disadvantages: Older plants become woody. Sometimes attacked by a fungus if drainage is poor. Bermudagrass invasions create a tangled mess in large plantings not protected by pre-emergence treatment. Flowers attract bees.

Planting and care: Plant any time from flats or containers. Place prostrate forms from flats 18 to 24 inches (45.7 to 61cm) apart, gallon-can plants 24 to 36 inches (61 to 91.4cm) apart on centers as a ground cover or edging. Plant shrub types 3 feet (0.9m) apart. Pinch tips of young plants to encourage fullness and bushiness and to prevent long leaders from becoming woody. Trim tips lightly after bloom to groom. Shearing tops will encourage side branches to spread. Plants may be sheared into a hedge or left to grow as picturesque forms. Take care not to trim plants back beyond the last bits of foliage and into the wood. Plants cut too far back tend not to sprout new growth.

Rosmarinus officinalis

Rosmarinus officinalis

All zones
Evergreen
Soil: Widely tolerant but needs good drainage.
Sun: Part to full or reflected sun. Tolerates light shade but becomes rangy and open with too much.
Water: Moderate to little. Drought resistant when established.
Temperature: Generally hardy, but may be damaged if a hard freeze follows a springlike fall that has encouraged new growth. Tolerant of great heat, but it may yellow slightly if kept too dry.
Maintenance: Some to practically none in wild or natural areas. Sheared plants require regular trimming.

Santolina chamaecyparissus

(S. incana, S. tomentosa)
Family: Compositae
Lavender Cotton

Lavender cotton is a striking plant known for its low mounding form and gray color. It is multiple-branched with aromatic foliage densely covering the plant to the ground. Its species name is Greek and means "small cypress," referring to the dense scaly quality of the foliage. Growth is moderate to rapid to 12 to 24 inches (30.5 to 61cm) high and 2-1/2 feet (0.8m) wide. Unclipped plants produce 1/2-inch (1.3-cm) yellow buttonlike flowers on slender stems above foliage in summer. Rabbits and other rodents do not seem to like plants. Resistant to heat, drought, wind and poor soil. Native to Spain and South Africa.

Cultivars and other notable species: *S. virens* is similar to the above, except it has a rounder shape and bright green ferny foliage. It reaches 2 feet (0.6m) high and spreads 18 inches (45.7cm) or wider. It is

very attractive when combined with the gray-foliaged *S. chamaecyparissus*, and has the same cultural requirements.

Special design features: Undulating gray mound. Handsome all year if clipped. Gray or green foliage contrast with neighboring foliage.

Uses: Border or edge. Rock gardens. Formal gardens. Arid-climate or wild gardens, where it can be left to grow naturally and become a rangy shrub.

Disadvantages: Plants lose their compact form if allowed to bloom. They are likely to become woody and unattractive in a few years even if clipped and may have to be replaced.

Planting and care: Plant from flats or gallon containers any time, or start from cuttings placed in moist sand. Space 12 to 18 inches (30.5 to 45.7cm) apart for edging or low clipped border. Space 18 to 24 inches (45.7 to 61cm) apart for massing. Shear in late spring or early summer as flowers appear.

Santolina chamaecyparissus

Santolina chamaecyparissus

All zones
Evergreen
Soil: Tolerant.
Sun: Part, full or reflected sun.
Water: Moderate to occasional.
Temperature: Hardy to cold.
Maintenance: Regular clipping gives this plant a neat appearance. No maintenance is necessary for natural shrub except to remove old bloom or to discourage blooming by clipping.

Schinus molle

Family: Anacardiaceae
California Pepper Tree

Bright green weeping foliage and rough tan bark are the appealing features of this fast-growing tree. It can reach 15 feet (4.6m) high in three years and may grow to 25 or even 40 feet (7.6 or 12.2m) in favorable situations, with a crown spread of 20 to 35 feet (6.1 to 10.7m). Because it is susceptible to many problems, it seldom reaches a large size in arid climates. Numerous narrow leaflets, which are aromatic and sticky with resin, hang from pendulous branches. Trunks become large and gnarled with age. Yellowish flowers in long hanging clusters on females produce sprays of decorative dry pink berries the size of peppercorns in summer. Pink skin of berry peels off to reveal hard dark "peppers." Older trees are often misshapen from breakage and disease. To keep tree as a youthful multitrunk sapling cluster, cut it back nearly to the ground every few years—it will regrow rapidly. For a large attractive shade tree, take great care to treat all problems as they occur.

Special design features: Fresh-looking weeping foliage. Bright green color contrast with tan bark. Picturesque. Rustic. Informal.

Uses: Fast shade. Best in dry areas, but will survive lawn conditions. Plants may be set close together to form a tall screen or top-cut and clipped to form low hedge or screen.

Disadvantages: Tree drips resin and litters pavement. Subject to Texas root rot and root knot nematodes. Trees with diseased or bound roots may be blown over in wind. Heart rot enters trunk and branches through untreated cuts and wounds. It weakens structure so the brittle branches may blow off in wind. Plants can be severely damaged after an Arctic freeze. Greedy surface roots can be invasive.

Planting and care: Plant from containers any time except during cold times of year. Prepare planting pit with a soil mixture known to discourage Texas root rot. Space 30 to 40 feet (9.2 to 12.2m) apart for roadside planting, 20 feet (6.1m) apart for a grove. Space trees 15 feet (4.6m) or less apart for a low informal screen. Stake young plant firmly and head up to make a tree, allowing branches only above head height. Unstaked plants remain low, with foliage covering plant to the ground. Treat all wounds and cuts with a dressing to prevent invasion of the fungus that causes heart rot. Treat root problems immediately. Prune only as needed.

Schinus molle

Schinus molle

Low and middle zones; protected locations in high zone
Evergreen
Soil: Tolerant. Prefers deep improved soils with good drainage.
Sun: Full sun.
Water: Occasional deep irrigation. Tolerates lawn watering with good drainage.
Temperature: Hardy to 20F (-7C), but foliage is sometimes damaged above that temperature.
Maintenance: Constant. Needs careful maintenance to maintain a healthy tree, especially in residential and garden situations.

Schinus terebinthifolius

Family: Anacardiaceae
Brazilian Pepper Tree
Christmas-Berry Tree

This shade tree grows at a moderate rate to 15 to 30 feet (4.6 to 9.2m) high. It develops a wide dense crown with intertwining and twisting branches. Trees naturally branch near the ground and require pruning and training to make a wide umbrellalike crown that can be walked under. Compound leaves are 2-1/2 inches (6.4cm) long, glossy dark-green, with five to seven leaflets on rather stiff midribs. Inconspicuous flowers produce an attractive show of red berrylike fruit in clusters on female plants in late fall or winter. Select trees carefully because individuals vary widely in form and flower. Males are more rangy in form and sparse in foliage. If you want to ensure you buy a female tree, choose a plant with fruit on it. Trees are more attractive with multiple trunks.

Special design features: Spreading canopy. Winter color. Sculptural quality.

Naturalistic, informal.

Uses: Shade for street, lawn, patio or poolside in warm places. Adapted to well-watered situations such as parks, lawns or golf courses. Weave branches together overhead to create a canopy of shade.

Disadvantages: Subject to Texas root rot, verticillium wilt and winter injury. Wind sometimes breaks branches.

Planting and care: Select plants with care—avoid rootbound plants. Place plants in a well-drained planting hole prepared to prevent Texas root rot. Space 20 to 30 feet (6.1 to 9.2m) apart for grove or row, 30 feet (9.2m) or more for street or avenue planting. Stake trunks firmly and cut off lower branches so people can walk under tree. Select scaffold branches carefully so crown will have a balanced form. Thin foliage on larger trees in late summer to avoid wind damage. If branches have become too long, shorten them at that time. Apply fertilizer regularly to maintain growth.

Schinus terebinthifolius

Schinus terebinthifolius

Low zone and warmer areas of the middle zone
Evergreen
Soil: Tolerant. Prefers good drainage.
Sun: Full sun.
Water: Needs occasional deep irrigation. Tree receiving only light frequent lawn irrigation may develop nuisance surface roots over a wide area.
Temperature: Young trees may be damaged below 26F (-3C), severely at 23F (-5C). Older trees are damaged near 20F (-7C) and will brown out, with wood damage, below that temperature.
Maintenance: Careful training, then periodic pruning and clipping.

Senna species

(*Cassia* species)
Family: Fabaceae (Leguminoseae)

Sennas were grouped under the genus *Cassia* until botanists recently switched them back to *Sennas*, the genus they'd been grouped under years ago. Flowering *Sennas* fill many landscape needs and are appreciated for their spectacular bloom, especially in late winter and early spring. Species native to dry parts of Australia have gained popularity because of their water efficiency and attractive appearance. Most are evergreen; some deciduous. Of the many kinds, only a few are listed here.

Special design features: Color at various seasons, depending on the species. Lush foliage on some, gray to almost white foliage on others, enabling them to blend well with other arid and desert plants.

Uses: Desert or wild gardens as a specimen or part of grouping. Informal unclipped screen, space divider or foundation plant. Transition zone or arid-climate garden. Background plant. Large filler plant.

Disadvantages: Can be damaged by cold just as it starts to bloom. Heavy bean production may be unattractive to some and may litter. Texas root rot. Roots can be invasive. Large leaves (of coastal species) may wilt midday in the hot sun, making it look stressed. Somewhat rangy in appearance.

Planting and care: Plant from seed or containers any time, but best in spring after danger from frost has passed. Irrigate until established and occasionally afterwards, especially if annual rainfall is less than 10 inches (254mm) a year and to encourage the bloom. Most plants stop blooming if they get too dry. Trim lightly after bloom if you wish to remove the pods. This will also promote new growth and bushy form. Plants are most attractive if only selectively pruned or thinned. Hedge trimmers ruin the character and reduce the number of flowers.

Senna species

Zones: See individual species descriptions.
Evergreen (except *S. wislizenii*; which is deciduous)
Soil: Tolerant of most soils with good drainage. *S. wislizenii* prefers rocky or loose sandy soils with good drainage.
Sun: See individual species descriptions.
Water: Weekly soak in summer and bimonthly irrigation in winter. Some species can tolerate irrigation every month or two, depending on the rainfall. The more lush green group look best with regular water.
Maintenance: Periodic trimming and selective pruning to none, depending on the species and use.

Senna artemisioides

Senna artemisioides

(*Cassia artemisioides*)
Feathery Senna • Wormwood Senna
Old Man Senna

A rounded shrub of rapid growth to 4 or even 6 feet (1.2 to 1.8m) high with gray to gray-green needlelike foliage and a breathtaking display of golden yellow flowers in late winter or early spring. It is unobtrusive most of the year until it suddenly flowers. Flowers are 1/2 inch (1.3cm) across, followed by flat green pods to 3 inches (7.6cm) long that turn dark brown when mature. Space 3 feet (0.9m) or more apart in sunny protected area. Takes full to reflected sun to part shade. Adapted to the low zone and warmer microclimates of the middle zone, this *Senna* can be damaged below 28F (-2C). Avoid shearing

Senna artemisioides filifolia

(*Cassia nemophila*)
Arid-Climate Senna • Hardy Senna
Green Feathery Senna

Quite green when young and fast growing with water, this plant can get to 6 feet (1.8m) high with equal spread. At maturity, it is a grayer plant than *S. artemisioides* and a moderate to somewhat slow grower in arid conditions. The shape is rounded and dense unless selectively thinned. It is hardier to cold than the plant above and the flowers are yellower and slightly larger. It also blooms later, from late winter into spring, and resembles a fragrant golden ball. The abundant production of beans requires trimming. It provides the same design features, uses and selective cutting as the above. Attracts bees. Tolerant of great heat and full to reflected sun. Tolerant of cold to 15 to 18F (-9 to -8C) in the low and middle zones and warmer spots in the high zone.

Senna didymobotrya

(*Cassia didymobotrya, C. nairobensis*)
Nirobe Senna

A fast-growing lush evergreen shrub that reaches 8 feet (2.4m) in height and spreads 8 to 10 feet (2.4 to 3.1m). Bright green compound leaves have numerous long leaflets, giving the plant an interesting tropical look. Big yellow flowers in upright clusters bloom on and off all year or until stopped by frost. Large unattractive flat brown pods follow. Best when used in back of solid evergreen shrubs where bloom can be enjoyed without the unattractive legginess. Cut back periodically to control size, thicken growth, remove pods, and encourage bloom. Makes a bold green statement in mild winter/cool summer areas, such as coastal arid climates. Adapted to the low zone and protected areas of the middle zone, but coastal is best. Takes full sun and, if frosted back, recovers quickly.

Senna wislizenii

(*Cassia wislizenii*)
Shrubby Senna

This deciduous shrub is nondescript most of the year until it bursts into bloom. Numerous clear yellow flowers appear continuously over the warm season, usually from June to September, but sometimes from February to October in warm areas. A slow to moderate grower to 3 to 6 feet (0.9 to 1.8m) high, its performance depends on available moisture. Dark, rather rigid branches present an interesting growth pattern, especially when in leaf and flower. Leaves are gray-green, finely divided and make a lacy background for small flowers followed by slender pods. Bleak during winter period. Adapted to all zones, where it takes part shade to full or reflected sun. Hardy to 10F (-12C). Can live on occasional to no irrigation, depending on situation and local rainfall.

Simmondsia chinensis

Family: Buxaceae
Jojoba • Coffee Bush • Goat Nut • Deer Nut

Jojoba is a shrub of the boxwood family native to the Southwest, Mexico and Baja California, at elevations between 1,000 and 5,000 feet (305 and 1,524m). It grows naturally in an area of milder winter temperatures. Oil from its nuts produces a wax capable of replacing the oil of the endangered sperm whale. The plant has a long history of uses, indicated by its various common names. Indians and white settlers made a coffee substitute from the nuts. Nuts were also eaten roasted or raw, but are not very appealing because of the bitter tannic-acid content. A dense, rounded, sometimes irregular shrub, jojoba grows to 6 feet (1.8m) high or higher with an equal, sometimes wider spread. Oval gray-green leathery, almost succulent leaves to 2-1/2 inches (6.4cm) long densely cover plants to the ground, set in upward-pointing pairs along branches. Plants are male and female and produce unimportant small yellowish flowers, usually in spring. Numerous 1-inch (2.5-cm) acorn-like nuts follow on females. Plants bloom any time between December and July, depending on weather. A slow grower at first, once established, jojoba can grow at an increasingly fast rate over time, especially when water is available.

Special design features: Shrubby dense mass of gray-green. Interesting foliage pattern. Informal. Looks great with little or no care.

Uses: Wide screen, hedge (takes formal clipping) or foundation plant. Wild or transitional gardens. Median strips or low maintenance areas.

Disadvantages: Slow to get started. Young plants are particularly sensitive to cold.

Planting and care: Plant from containers in spring, any time in warm regions. Space 3 to 5 feet (0.9 to 1.5m) apart for a loose screen, which will grow together in a few years. Space about 2 feet (0.6m) apart for a clipped hedge. Protect young plants from extreme cold. Pruning is not usually necessary.

Simmondsia chinensis

Simmondsia chinensis

Low and middle zones
Evergreen
Soil: Tolerant. Prefers gravelly soil with good drainage.
Sun: Part, full or reflected sun.
Water: Moderate at first for fast growth, then occasional deep irrigation. Can be neglected completely when it reaches a desired size in areas of 10 inches (254mm) or more annual rainfall. Taper off irrigation gradually.
Temperature: Young plants are injured by frost at about 20F (-7C). Plants are badly damaged or killed at 15F (-9C), even mature established plants.
Maintenance: Periodic to none, unless used as a formal clipped hedge.

Sophora secundiflora

Family: Fabaceae (Leguminosae)
Mescal Bean • Texas Mountain Laurel
Frijolito

Mescal bean, a legume, is admired for its distinctive leaf pattern, wisterialike spring bloom, year-round good looks and lack of bothersome diseases. Tolerant of heat, cold, wind, drought and poor soil, this plant looks attractive in all but the most extreme conditions. Native to Texas, New Mexico and northern Mexico, it is usually grown as a shrub, although it can be slowly trained into a tree 20 to 30 feet (6.1 to 9.2m) high. Upright sculptural branches are covered with silvery bark. They bear 4- to 6-inch (10.1- to 15.2-cm) leaves with several pairs of oval, shiny medium green leaflets 1 to 2 inches (2.5 to 5.1cm) long. Plant is picturesque at any age. When barely more than a branch, it bears fragrant 8-inch (20.3-cm) long violet-blue (rarely white) clusters of pea-shaped flowers early in spring. Decorative silver-gray woody pods follow and split open in late summer to reveal bright red beans (*frijolitos*). They are poisonous, but their outer coat is so hard it is believed they pass through digestive systems without harm. Sometimes drilled and strung as colorful beads.

Special design features: Interesting and durable form and foliage. Spectacular spring bloom. Welcome green in poor conditions. Remains handsome in severe winters.

Uses: Specimen, mass, hedge or row. Espalier. Silhouette against structures. Shrub with spreading branches or upright, short-trunk tree for patio, lawn or median strip. Pool areas. Transitional plant. Natural or wild gardens.

Disadvantages: Poisonous seeds. Bees love flowers. Slow to develop, especially in cool summer areas. Sometimes attacked by defoliating caterpillars.

Planting and care: May be grown from seed, but slow. Plant from containers any time. Use a five-gallon plant for a good start. Space 5 to 6 feet (1.5 to 1.8m) apart for massing. More attractive as specimen. Allow it to grow naturally or stake and train for a patio tree.

Sophora secundiflora

Sophora secundiflora

All zones
Evergreen
Soil: Tolerant. Thrives in alkaline soils, but requires good drainage.
Sun: Part to full or reflected sun. Grows fastest with high heat.
Water: Drought tolerant when established. Best with moderate irrigation. Accepts occasional deep irrigation.
Temperature: Hardy to cold. Tolerates heat.
Maintenance: None to periodic pruning and training, especially to develop it into a mature tree.

Syagrus romanzoffianum

*(Arecastrum romanzoffianum, Cocos
romanzoffiana, C. plumosa)*
Family: Arecaceae (Palmae)
Queen Palm

This graceful and refined plant is very
erect in form, with a gray ringed trunk to
12 inches (30.5cm) in diameter. Feathery
fronds are shiny medium green with slender
papery filaments up to 2 feet (0.6m) or
longer. The luxuriant crown spreads 10 or
15 feet (3.1 to 4.6m) wide. In arid climates
these palms grow at a moderate to fast rate
to 20 or 25 feet (6.1 to 7.6m) high,
occasionally reaching 30 to 40 feet (9.2 to
12.2m), with crowns 20 to 30 feet (6.1 to
9.2m) wide. Palms may produce small
plumes of blossoms encased in a woody
canoelike sheath (prized by flower
arrangers), followed by miniature
coconutlike fruit that is covered with a sweet
edible skin. Old dried fronds tend to bend
down and hang on until trimmed off.

Special design features: Airy vertical
form. Tropical or subtropical effect. Light
shade. Little or no litter.

Uses: Specimen, grove or row. Silhouette
plant. Tropical groupings around swimming
pools. Small microclimates, south sides or
protected intimate gardens for close-up
viewing. Large planters. Attractive in courtyards of tall buildings or in the home garden.

Disadvantages: Leaves develop dry
straw-colored filaments from hot winds, cold
or age. Avoid planting in windy areas. Fronds
may become pale with iron chlorosis.
Fruiting streamers look messy. Old upward-
pointing frond ends look messy to some and
require professional removal, which reveals
the slim, textured trunk.

Planting and care: Plant from
containers in spring or summer. Space 8 to
15 feet (2.4 to 4.6m) apart for a grove, 15 to
20 feet (4.6 to 6.1m) or more for a row. Feed
regularly and provide extra iron to promote
fastest growth and more attractive
appearance. Protect from hot dry winds
in low elevation arid climates. Remove
old leaves to reveal attractive smooth,
ringed trunk.

Syagrus romanzoffianum

Syagrus romanzoffianum

**Low zone and protected microclimates in middle
zone**
Evergreen
Soil: Prefers well-prepared garden soil with depth,
but tolerates a range of soils, including alkaline
situations, if supplied with good drainage.
Sun: Part shade to full sun. Accepts reflected sun in
middle zone.
Water: Moderate to ample.
Temperature: Foliage damage at about 25F (-4C).
Recovers from freezes of 20F (-7C). or below, but
takes all summer to recover.
Maintenance: Seasonal. Some grooming of leaves
and fruiting parts.

Syringa persica

Family: Oleaceae
Persian Lilac

This shrub is a hybrid between a lilac from
Afghanistan and a lilac from China. It is the
best lilac known for warm, arid climates.
Growth is moderate to slow up to 5 to 6 feet
(1.5 to 1.8m) high, rarely to 10 feet (3.1m). It
spreads as wide as high if given room. Its
medium green leaves are similar to
Ligustrum species. Small lavender flowers
appear in early spring in loose plumelike
clusters. Flowers and plant are much smaller
than the common lilac often grown in the
northern and eastern United States.

Cultivars and other notable species:
S. vulgaris (eastern or European lilac) is
similar to *S. persica*, but with larger leaves
and more fragrant blooms that range in color
from deep purple or blue to violet or pink
tones—some are even snowy white. It will
only bloom in the cooler high zone, where it
seldom reaches more than 5 to 6 feet (1.5 to
1.8m) high. The cultivar 'Lavender Lady' is
an exception. It will grow to 20 feet (6.1m)
high with leaves to 5 inches (12.7cm) long. It
produces large clusters of lavender flowers in
areas that don't have a long period of winter
chill. Best in the higher elevations. Cultural
requirements are the same as *S. persica*. 'Alba'
is a white-flowering form. There are many
other selections and hybrids to choose from.

Special design features: Bloom and
fragrance are sentimental favorites. Woodsy
feeling.

Uses: Place in a cooler sheltered corner
where its spring bloom can be appreciated.

Disadvantages: Sometimes gets scale,
leaf miner and sunburned leaves in summer.
Close relative of *Ligustrum* species and
subject to the same diseases.

Planting and care: Plant from
containers any time. May be planted bare
root in winter. Space 5 feet (1.5m) apart for
massing. Pinch tips of young plants to shape.
Groom by removing spent flowers before
seed forms. When removing old flowers, cut
them just above where next year's buds are
forming, at points where the leaves join the
stems. Do not prune plants too heavily or
there will be fewer blooms the following year.
As plants become old and woody, cut a few of
the oldest stems to the ground each winter to
rejuvenate. Plants that do not get enough
winter dormancy time will not bloom. Lilacs
can be trained into small trees.

Syringa persica

Syringa persica

All zones
Deciduous
Soil: Prefers alkaline soils.
Sun: Part to full sun.
Water: Moderate to ample.
Temperature: Tolerates heat. Likes winter chill, but
this lilac, unlike most others, will perform in warm
winter areas, although it will struggle and bloom
irregularly in the low and middle zones.
Maintenance: Periodic trimming.Otherwise,
maintenance depends on use.

Tecomaria capensis

(Bignonia capensis, Tecoma capensis)
Family: Bignoniaceae
Cape Honeysuckle

A sprawling half-vine and half-shrub with luxuriant glossy deep-green foliage, this South African native bears clusters of brilliant 2-inch (5.1-cm) orange-red trumpet-shaped flowers in fall and winter (occasionally at other times). It grows fast, sending out branches up to 12 feet (3.7m) long unless controlled. Tied to a support, it can climb 15 to 25 feet (4.6 to 7.6m) high. Pruned carefully, it becomes a shrub 6 to 8 feet (1.8 to 2.4m) high and 5 feet (1.5m) wide or wider. It thrives in heat and accepts some drought and hot winds, as well as salty sea breezes near the coast. Attracts hummingbirds.

Special design features: Luxuriant tropical mood. Bright color through cool season when little else is blooming. Can bloom all year.

Uses: South or west walls under an overhang in cooler winter areas. Spills over hot banks or planters in areas of reflected heat. Mounding plant in open warm locations. Can be trained as a shrub or wall plant. Does well in planters or as a container plant anywhere. Can be brought indoors during winter to bloom in a sunny window. Plants need to gain a certain size or at least root size before they bloom.

Disadvantages: Can overgrow its allotted space and look poor if cut back. Can be nipped by frost just when it looks best and has begun to bloom. Although it grows new foliage rapidly, it may take time before it recovers to blooming size, and then it can be frozen again. Frost damage causes blackened branch tips as well as foliage damage.

Planting and care: Plant from containers when frosts are past. Space 6 feet (1.8m) apart for mass planting. Prune, pinch or tie as needed during the growing season to train. Heavy clipping reduces bloom because flowers are at tips of new growth. Most attractive as a tumbling shrub, allowed to grow naturally. Keep on dry side in fall to encourage more bloom and hardiness to winter temperatures.

Tecomaria capensis

Tecomaria capensis

Low zone and warmer places in middle zone
Evergreen
Soil: Prefers improved garden soil with good drainage.
Sun: Part to full or reflected sun, but it will remain an attractive foliage plant without much bloom in a northern exposure.
Water: Moderate to slightly less than moderate.
Temperature: New growth is damaged at 28F (-2C). Loves heat.
Maintenance: Periodic pruning and pinching.

Teucrium chamaedrys

Family: Labiatae
Germander • Chamaedrys Germander

This appealing plant is composed of numerous upright stems, densely covered with small, toothed, gray-green leaves set in a distinctive pattern. Growth is slow to moderate to 12 to 18 inches (30.5 to 45.7cm) high, spreading by underground rhizomes to 2 to 3 feet (0.6 to 0.9m), but often less. A member of the mint family, germander produces small purple (rarely white) flowers along its vertical stems in late summer. Native to Europe and southwestern Asia.

Cultivars and other notable species: 'Prostratum' is only 4 to 6 inches (10.2 to 15.2cm) high and is often preferred. It goes well with stepping stones, in rock gardens, as a lawn extender or as a small-area ground cover. Both species and cultivar are tough—tolerant of poor soil, heat, wind, drought and cold. 'Frutcsicans' grows in all zones to 4 to 8 feet (1.2 to 2.4m) high and as wide or wider with loose silvery stems and leaves. Spikes of 3/4-inch (1.9-cm) lavender flowers bloom at the branch tips most of the year. Can be used as an informal hedge, screen or specimen, especially at the bottom of the garden or in transitional areas. Needs to be cut back in late winter or early spring. A smaller form, 'Compactum' grows to only 3 feet (0.9m) high with a narrower and denser form and deep blue flowers.

Special design features: Pleasing leaf pattern. Informal character.

Uses: Smaller forms: low mass, ground cover or foreground plant. Edgings, borders, parking strips or spaces adjacent to paved areas. Larger forms: low clipped hedge or natural shrub in rock gardens or in transitional areas. Containers. Pool patios.

Disadvantages: Slow. Sometimes covers ground unevenly. Becomes woody in time if not sheared occasionally. Soggy soil causes plant to decline.

Planting and care: Plant any time. Space plants from flats 14 inches (35.6cm) on center, one-gallon plants 18 to 24 inches (45.7 to 61cm) apart for massing. Fill any bare spots with new plants the following year. Trim lightly in early summer and again after bloom to groom and renew vigor. This also forces side branching, helping create a dense cover.

Teucrium chamaedrys 'Prostratum'

Teucrium chamaedrys

All zones
Evergreen
Soil: Tolerant, but needs good drainage.
Sun: Part, full or reflected sun.
Water: Moderate with good drainage. Best with occasional irrigation, allowing ground to dry out between waterings.
Temperature: Hardy to cold. Tolerant of heat.
Maintenance: Periodic trimming.

Thevetia peruviana

(T. neriifolia)
Family: Apocynaceae
Yellow Oleander • Be Still Tree • Lucky Nut

Yellow oleander is a large, erect, fast-growing, graceful shrub, 6 to 8 feet (1.8 to 2.4m) high, or a small spreading tree (with training) to 20 feet (6.1m) high in warmer zones. Native to tropical America. Shiny dark green foliage and yellow or apricot-colored flowers 2 inches (5.1cm) across appear in clusters almost any time of year, but most often from June to November. Narrow leaves to 6 inches (15.2cm) long densely cover plant. Flowers may be followed by hard 1-inch (2.5-cm) angular fruit, first red then turning black. Plant is root-hardy in cooler areas if roots are well-mulched during winter. Recovers rapidly in spring.

Cultivars and other notable species: 'Alba' has white flowers.

Special design features: Luxuriant tropical effect. Bloom over a long period.

Uses: Against hot walls. As a tree in sheltered patios, atriums and entryways. Specimen. In warm winter areas, as a canopy tree for a gardens or as a small street tree. Combine with hardy evergreen shrubs where it freezes back in winter.

Disadvantages: All parts of this plant are poisonous. Seeds and flowers can litter.

Planting and care: Plant from containers when danger of frost has passed. Handle plants carefully when planting. Space 6 to 8 feet (1.8 to 2.4m) apart for a continuous mass. Prune to shape or to show trunks. Avoid cultivating at plant base because surface roots are easily damaged. In colder areas, apply a mulch several inches deep to protect roots and lower part of trunk from freezing.

Thevetia peruviana

Thevetia peruviana

Low zone and warm pockets in middle zone
Evergreen
Soil: Improved garden soil with good drainage.
Sun: Part, full or reflected sun.
Water: Ample is best, but avoid overwatering young plants. Tolerates moderate or occasional irrigation when established.
Temperature: Foliage damaged at 28F (-2C), but wood will survive much lower temperatures and new growth comes back quickly in spring. Revels in heat.
Maintenance: Periodic pruning and litter cleanup.

Trachelospermum asiaticum

(Rhynchospermum asiaticum)
Family: Apocynaceae
Asiatic Jasmine
Ground Jasmine
Dwarf Star Jasmine

Asiatic jasmine trails as much as 15 feet (4.6m), with branches rooting as they go. Branchlets bearing shiny 1-1/2-inch (3.6-cm) leaves rise vertically 6 to 8 inches (15.2 to 20.3cm) above the ground. Large established plantings have a dense, even-textured appearance. Fragrant small creamy yellow starlike flowers sometimes bloom in late spring, but are seldom seen in the arid climate. This twining, trailing plant needs to be tied up if used as a vine unless grown on a fence. Native to Korea and Japan.

Special design features: Very appealing at close range and looks nice all year. Cool woodland feeling. Tropical appearance when combined with tropical plants.

Uses: Best as dense ground cover in small area or as filler or underplant. Containers. Foreground plant. Attractive in small intimate patios, atriums or entryways. Swimming pool areas. Up-close viewing.

Disadvantages: May be slow to cover in hot areas and sometimes burns out in spots during summer. Sometimes gets chlorosis in wet situations.

Planting and care: Plant from containers any time. Can be planted from flats, but very slow and uncertain— one-gallon cans are better. Space 18 to 24 inches (45.7 to 61cm) apart. Mulch to keep roots and new branchlets cool in hot sunny areas, especially new plantings. Avoid planting where it will receive intense or reflected sun. Prune back occasionally in late winter after bloom.

Trachelospermum asiaticum

Trachelospermum asiaticum

All zones
Evergreen
Soil: Prefers improved porous garden soil.
Sun: Open, filtered or part shade. Full sun in high areas or in middle zone if properly mulched in summer.
Water: Moderate to ample. Established plants tolerate some drought in winter.
Temperature: Tolerant to about 16F (-9C), but may be damaged above that if frost follows springlike weather that has resulted in new growth.
Maintenance: Periodic. Some pruning and mulching.

Trachelospermum jasminoides

(Rhynchospermum jasminoides)
Family: Apocynaceae
Star Jasmine

This plant is much like its relative
T. asiaticum but on a larger scale. It is a
refined twining vine with elegant dark green
foliage, bearing a profusion of fragrant,
white, waxy starlike flowers. It grows at a
slow to moderate rate, spreading to 20 feet
(6.1m) over the ground. It is also attractive
trained up with wire or supports. With
training, it covers an area 10 by 10 feet (3.1
by 3.1m) at maturity. Shiny, leathery 2-inch
(5.1-cm) leaves are supported on rich glossy
brown branches. Because star jasmine is slow
to develop, it is best to start with five-gallon
plants.

Special design features: Sculptural
quality. Appealing at close range. Woodsy or
tropical effect. Spring fragrance. A choice
vine for garlands near entrances or
windows where its looks and fragrance
can be most enjoyed.

Uses: Walls, fences, trellises or porch
posts. A ground cover in middle zone.
Container cascade. Small intimate spaces
such as patios, atriums or entryways. Prefers
northern and eastern exposures. Pool patios.

Disadvantages: May be very slow to
cover or cover unevenly. It sometimes tangles
as a ground cover. Older plants in difficult
situations begin to look bare and unkempt.
Foliage can burn from reflected heat.
Occasionally suffers from iron chlorosis. May
be damaged by severe cold, especially on
south sides where the hot daytime sun can
dehydrate plants.

Planting and care: Plant from
containers any time. Space 4 to 5 feet
(1.2 to 1.5m) apart for fast cover on a
structure, 3 feet (0.9m) apart for ground
cover when using five-gallon plants. Plants
will climb by twining if given support. For a
ground cover, pinch branch tips to thicken
and encourage lateral growth and pin stems
down to mulched ground.

Trachelospermum jasminoides

Trachelospermum jasminoides

Low and middle zones; borderline in high zone
Evergreen
Soil: Improved garden soil.
Sun: Any exposure in middle zone, except in
locations of extreme reflected heat. Some shade in
the low zone. In high zone, use only as a garland on
a warm surface, such as a south wall.
Water: Moderate to ample.
Temperature: Damaged by cold at 20F (-7C),
especially if freeze follows springlike fall weather
that has encouraged new growth. Tolerates heat
when given water, but may show leafburn in hot spots.
Maintenance: Periodic attention.

Trachycarpus fortunei

(Chamaerops fortunei)
Family: Palmae
Windmill Palm

Windmill palm is a small fan palm reaching
only 15 feet (4.6m) high at maturity with a
crown to 7 feet (2.1m) in diameter. It grows
slowly at first, then at a moderate or even fast
rate with enough water. Trunk is erect and
slender, with upward-pointing stubs of old
fronds protruding from a dark fibrous cover,
which makes the trunk look thicker than it
actually is. Lack of fiber at the base makes
the plant look top heavy. Crown is formed of
small stiff dark green fans with toothed
bases; the whole frond is about 3 feet (0.9m)
long. Clusters of unimportant small dark
berry-like fruit occasionally follow creamy
white clusters of bloom. Fruit is strange in
appearance—almost succulent. Native to
China and northern Burma.

Special design features: Neat small-
scale palm that stays low for a long period.
Older plants make a strong vertical
statement. Appears oriental in the right plant
combination. Dramatic foliage. Somewhat

formal. Very hardy—a good tree for tropical
effects in the high zone.

Uses: Small-scale areas or narrow
spaces. Swimming pool areas, small patios or
gardens, atriums or entryways. Specimen,
pair or grouping. Overhead tree to smaller
plants or understory plant beneath taller
overhead trees, where it enjoys shade itself.
Container plant.

Disadvantages: Fronds may be tattered
by wind. Susceptible to sunburn in reflected
sun of low arid climates or in exposed
locations.

Planting and care: Plant from
containers any time. Field-grown plants or
larger specimens are best transplanted
spring to midsummer. Cut off old fronds or
seed structures to groom or leave fibrous
cover on the trunk if you prefer. Give
regular feeding for best results. Tolerates
neglect once established, but it becomes
less attractive.

Trachycarpus fortunei

Trachycarpus fortunei

All zones
Evergreen
Soil: Tolerant. Prefers improved garden soil.
Sun: Open, filtered or part shade to full sun.
Water: Moderate to ample.
Temperature: Hardiest of the palms. Tolerates
temperatures to 10F (-12C) or below and looks
good even after cold spells.
Maintenance: Periodic grooming and feeding.

Ulmus parvifolia

Family: Ulmaceae
Chinese Elm • Chinese Evergreen Elm

Chinese elm has a spreading canopy of arching branches and weeping branchlets. Fast growing, it can reach a height of 30 feet (9.2m) in five years, with an even wider spread if grown in deep moist soil. Glossy deep green leaves glisten in the sun. The slender trunk is smooth and dappled gray and tan as outer layers flake off. Unimportant flowers in late summer produce small decorative fruit. Tree is variable in form and whether it will remain evergreen, so ask about the best selection at your nursery.

Cultivars and other notable species: 'Sempervirens' is smaller and more delicate, nearly evergreen and better for residential use. 'Drake' ('Brea') is medium-size with an upright and regular form. 'True Green' is said to be nearly evergreen and more uniform in growth than the others.

Special design features: Tree of delicate charm and scale, with a refined appearance that is appealing at close range.

The somewhat uneven crown makes it blend with oasis or transitional landscapes. The vertical trunk with interesting bark makes it attractive up close even in winter, when deciduous. Weeping form. Can be grown with a straight trunk and umbrella canopy.

Uses: Street tree, commercial projects, public spaces. Fast shade for patio or garden.

Disadvantages: Subject to Texas root rot. Occasionally slow to develop canopy at first, but then rapidly develops a heavy weeping crown that can break in a strong wind if not occasionally thinned. Flakes from bark and leaves in fall can litter.

Planting and care: Never plant in soil known to be infested with Texas root rot. Prepare soil in planting pit with mix to prevent this disease and treat annually. Space 20 feet (6.1m) apart for canopy, 30 feet (9.2m) or more for row. Stake young tree firmly until trunk is strong enough to hold its crown. Remove lower branches up to the desired height for the crown to branch out, being sure to compensate for hanging branchlets. Shorten extra-long branches.

Ulmus parvifolia

Ulmus parvifolia

All zones
Partly evergreen to deciduous in sharp cold
Soil: Prefers deep soil with good drainage.
Sun: Part to full sun.
Water: Best with occasional deep irrigation once established, but tolerates ample water of lawn irrigation.
Temperature: Hardy to cold. Foliage may brown and drop at about 25F (-4C).
Maintenance: Constant at first to develop a canopy, then periodic.

Vauquelinia californica auciflora

(Vauqelinia californica)
Family: Rosaceae
Arizona Rosewood

Arizona rosewood is a large, vigorous, dense, erect shrub native to southern Arizona and northern Mexico at the 2,500- to 5,000-foot (762- to 1524-m) level. It grows slowly at first, then moderately to 8 feet (2.4m) high, sometimes up to 20 feet (6.1m). Young plants in nursery containers look gawky, but in a year or two they fill out from the base with numerous branches and become wide, sometimes globe-shaped shrubs. Can be staked or trimmed into a small tree. Foliage is dark green and leathery and covers plant to the ground. Serrated leaves are long, slender and grow in an upward-pointing pattern along stems, somewhat reminiscent of oleander (*Nerium* species). Tiny creamy white flowers in wide flat clusters appear in summer. Easy to grow and care for. Tolerant of adverse conditions of intense sun, poor soil, hot winds, cold and drought.

Cultivars and other notable species: *Vauquelinia corymbosa angustifolia* (Chihuahuan rosewood) is similar to the

above, except it has narrow serrated leaves that give the foliage an unusual threadlike effect. Its cultural requirements and landscape uses are the same as for *V. californica auciflora.*

Special design features: Handsome plant that will grow in tough conditions. Strong vertical shrub. Foliage may take on a bronzy cast in cold weather.

Uses: Specimen. Tall unclipped hedge or screen. Space divider. Wind, dust or noise screen. Trains well into patio-size tree. Can be clipped, but loses character. Transitional areas. Tough situations.

Disadvantages: Young plants are slow to get started. Sometimes infested with spider mites, aphids or powdery mildew (less of a problem with *V. corymbosa angustfolia*).

Planting and care: Plant from containers any time. Space 4 feet (1.2m) apart for clipped hedge, 6 to 8 feet (1.8 to 2.4m) for screen or row planting. Spray for pests as needed.

Vauquelinia californica auciflora

Vauquelinia californica auciflora

All zones
Evergreen
Soil: Tolerant. Prefers good drainage.
Sun: Part, full or reflected sun.
Water: Moderate until established, then occasional deep irrigation to encourage growth. Established plants in areas of 12 inches (305mm) or more annual rainfall can be left alone after their second year but will grow slowly.
Temperature: Hardy to cold. Young plants with succulent new growth can be damaged by a sudden sharp freeze.
Maintenance: None to periodic.

Viburnum suspensum

Family: Caprifoliaceae
Sandankwa Viburnum

This shrub native to Ryukyu Island near Japan grows at a moderate rate to 6 to 8 feet (1.8 to 2.4m) high with an equal spread. With its lustrous foliage, it provides a welcome splash of green in a partially sunny to shaded garden. Oval leathery leaves to 4 inches (10.2cm) long densely cover its rounded form. Tiny pinkish flowers in tightly packed 1-1/2-inch (3.6-cm) clusters appear in late winter, occasionally followed by small red fruit in summer.

Special design features: Woodsy feeling for shaded places. Attractive at close range. Rich, handsome winter foliage at a time when many plants look barren.

Uses: Specimen, hedge, screen or background plant for north or east sides of buildings. Suitable for part sun to shaded gardens and courtyards. Clipped hedge or small patio tree.

Disadvantages: Foliage may sunburn or languish in hot summer weather, but regains its vigor as cool weather approaches.

Subject to iron chlorosis.

Planting and care: Plant any time from containers, but best in fall or winter so plant has a chance to establish before the heat of summer. Space 4 to 5 feet (1.2 to 1.5m) apart for unclipped screen or background planting, 3 to 4 feet (0.9 to 1.2m) for clipped hedge. Clip as needed. Trim and prune after bloom in spring before high heat. Trimmed or sheared plants have little or no bloom. Feed regularly and give extra iron. Leach soil salts with occasional deep soakings. Avoid shearing because it cuts leaves unattractively.

Viburnum suspensum

Viburnum suspensum

Middle and high zones; marginal in low zone
Evergreen
Soil: Highly organic garden soil with good drainage. Avoid alkaline conditions.
Sun: Part sun to full or filtered shade.
Water: Moderate to ample with occasional deep soakings to leach salts
Temperature: Hardy to 10F (-12C) or below.
Maintenance: Constant feeding, clipping, pinching to shape and soaking. Otherwise, maintenance depends on use.

Viburnum tinus

Family: Caprifoliaceae
Laurustinus

A shrub from the Mediterranean region, this *Viburnum* accepts more sun than others. Growth is moderate to 6 to 10 feet (1.8 to 3.1m) high spreading 3 to 6 feet (0.9 to 1.8m). Leaves are 2 to 3 inches (5.1 to 7.6cm) long, rough and dark green on top, lighter underneath. Small pinkish flowers appear in 3-inch (7.6-cm) clusters in late winter or early spring, and are sometimes followed by clusters of tiny dark bluish black berries. There is a warm rosy glow to the plant, especially in winter, caused by a reddish coat on the stems and twigs.

Cultivars and other notable species: Cultivars are planted more often than the species, especially 'Lucidum,' which has larger leaves and is more resistant to mildew than the species, but is less hardy to cold. Best in low and middle zones. 'Dwarf' grows only 3 to 5 feet (0.9 to 1.5m) high and as wide. Good for low screens, hedges or foundation plantings. 'Robustum' has coarser, rougher leaves than the species and grows dense and erect with pinkish white flowers. It

makes a small narrow tree or medium-size shrub for a narrow space. It is more mildew resistant than the species.

Special design features: Decorative garden plant. Refined woodsy effect. Handsome form, foliage and flower.

Uses: May be used in the open in middle zone if there is air circulation around it and no reflected heat. Avoid western exposure. Specimen, screen, clipped hedge, background plant or espalier.

Disadvantages: Sometimes gets iron chlorosis. The species is subject to mildew, especially in humid areas, but the cultivars are less susceptible.

Planting and care: Plant any time from containers, but best during the cool season. If planted in a sunny location, set out in fall or winter so it can adjust to summer. Space larger forms 1-1/2 to 2 feet (0.5 to 0.6m) apart for clipped hedge, 5 feet (1.5m) for loose screen. Space 'Dwarf' 4 feet (1.2m) on center for massing, 1-1/2 to 2 feet (0.5 to 0.6m) for low clipped hedge. Prune lightly after bloom. Shear as needed.

Viburnum tinus

Viburnum tinus

All zones
Evergreen
Soil: Improved garden soil with good drainage. Avoid alkaline conditions.
Sun: Filtered, open or part sun. Tolerates full sun in middle and high zones. Shade in low zone.
Water: Moderate to ample. Give deep soakings occasionally to leach soil salts.
Temperature: The species is hardy to 5F (-15C). Cultivars may be damaged by cold at about 15F (-9C). All tolerate heat better than the other *Viburnums*.
Maintenance: Periodic feeding, pinching, trimming and soaking.

Vinca major

Family: Apocynaceae
Periwinkle
Running Myrtle
Blue Buttons

A vigorous low trailing plant, periwinkle quickly spreads on long stems that root as they go. Leaves 2 inches (5.1cm) long are dark green and grow in opposite pairs along the stems. Plantings become dense mounds in two or three years. Single blue flowers 2 inches (5.1cm) in diameter appear among the foliage in spring. Plant looks amazingly green and lush for the amount of care and water needed. Although it may look wilted if allowed to go too long without irrigation, it restores itself immediately when water becomes available. Native to Europe.

Cultivars and other notable species: *V. minor* (dwarf periwinkle) is a smaller, more delicate and refined version of *V. major*. Leaves are small, more pointed at the end and very dark green. This plant grows less rapidly but in time covers as densely, mounding 6 to 12 inches (15.2 to 30.5cm) high. It seldom flowers in arid regions but produces 3/4-inch (1.9-cm) lilac-blue blossoms in more favorable situations. It is an important ground cover in the temperate zone and is occasionally planted in the middle and high zones. Its best use is as a ground cover or container plant in a small area, where it can be enjoyed and cared for easily. 'Variegata' has leaf margins of yellowish white.

Special design features: Lush green mounding ground cover, trailing over planters and banks. Green woodland or jungle feeling.

Uses: Ground cover to extend lawns, vary texture, create patterns. Bank cover for erosion control. Filler plant for bare areas. Containers and planters. Use under trees to hide leaf litter. Naturalizes in woodsy locations of middle and high zone where it survives periods of drought and bounces back quickly when moisture returns.

Disadvantages: Invasive. Greedy roots may overcome less aggressive plants in the competition for moisture. Invasive in some natural areas. Difficult to eradicate once it has become established. Established plantings tend to take over an area. Sunburns in the hottest locations in midsummer but recovers quickly as the weather cools off.

Planting and care: Plant from containers or flats any time. Plant bare-root divisions during cool periods. Space 18 to 24 inches (45.7 to 61cm) apart for fast cover. Cut back occasionally in late winter to renew vigor and keep neat. Some gardeners cut back to the ground every three or four years to remove the mat of top growth-a big job but the fresh growth is very attractive.

Vinca major

Vinca major

All zones
Evergreen
Soil: Tolerates a wide range. Prefers improved garden soil.
Sun: Full, open, filtered or part shade. Full sun in middle and high zones, but may look poor in hottest part of summer. Looks best with afternoon shade in hot regions.
Water: Moderate to ample. Can be allowed to go completely dry, turning brown and shriveling, but recovers miraculously when irrigated.
Temperature: Hardy to cold, but may sustain some foliage damage at 15F (-9C). Recovers quickly. Tolerates heat, especially in shade and with enough water.
Maintenance: Periodic pruning to control.

Vitex agnus-castus

Family: Verbenaceae
Chaste Tree
Monk's Pepper Tree
Hemp Tree
Sage Tree

Chaste tree is a widely adaptable shrub or small tree with single or multiple trunks and a usually wide-spreading crown. It is native to southern Europe but has naturalized in warm areas of the United States. Without irrigation it normally remains a shrub, growing no more than 6 feet (1.8m) high. With moderate amounts of water it grows quickly to 15 to 25 feet (4.6 to 7.6m) high with an equal spread. It seems to need heat to develop fully and to bloom well. The trunk is often picturesque with gray stringy bark. Leaves are dark green with five to seven narrow-pointed leaflets fanning out from the center. Numerous flower spikes 7 inches (17.8cm) long appear above foliage in early summer and again occasionally through summer into fall. Flowers are usually blue; can be pink or white. Tiny, woody, round capsules ("peppers") follow bloom.

Cultivars and other notable species: 'Rosea' has pinkish flowers. 'Alba' has white flowers.

Special design features: Picturesque. Fast shade for summer. Summer bloom.

Uses: Patio or lawn tree. Garden tree as center of interest or along edge of landscape. Transitional or wild gardens as tree or shrub.

Disadvantages: Occasionally gets wood rot. Twiggy winter form is not especially attractive in gardens unless thinned and shaped a bit.

Planting and care: Plant from containers any time or bare root in winter. Prune during dormant season to remove dead wood and to groom and shape.

Vitex agnus-castus

Vitex agnus-castus

All zones
Deciduous
Soil: Tolerant of wide range of soil conditions. Grows luxuriantly in rich deep soils, but produces few flowers.
Sun: Part, full or reflected sun.
Water: Moderate to occasional.
Temperature: Hardy to 20F (-7C). Revels in heat.
Maintenance: Periodic light trimming to maintain tree form.

Vitis vinifera

Family: Vitaceae
Grape Vine • Wine Grape

The grape is a tendril-climbing woody vine, with large deeply lobed leaves and tan stringy bark. Plants produce clusters of small, round, tasty fruit in summer. But this common description doesn't quite express the history and mystique involved with this plant, originating from the Caucasus and grown widely for the wine produced from its fruit. Egyptian tomb paintings show the grape being cultivated in arbors. The Greeks held ribald festivals honoring Bacchus, god of wine. The Jews broke bread and drank wine together in the joyous sharing ceremony of the Kiddush. Christians sanctified wine as the blood of Christ. Places like Bordeaux, France, the Rhine River in Germany and the Napa Valley in California have become famous for the wines they produce. Today there is wide interest in grape growing and wine production. The grape vine is also an excellent landscape plant, growing well in arid zones. Once established, a vine can grow rapidly to cover a 20-by-20-foot (6.1-by-3.1-m) area and is easily trained to cover arbors or to drape porch posts. The fruit is a decorative and delicious. There are many kinds of grapes and the serious grape grower should investigate the varieties and special ways of pruning and caring for them.

Cultivars and other notable species: 'Thompson's Seedless' from Persia is outstanding for landscape use. It does well up to 4,500 feet (1,371m) elevation. It produces sweet, seedless pale green fruit in July. 'Golden Muscat' from Geneva, New York, is another fine eating grape. Fruit has seed, is gold tinged with bronze and very sweet. It ripens in late July and August. It does well in the high zone but is not recommended for low arid climates because it gets sunburned leaves. 'Black Monukka' is vigorous and productive. Small reddish black seedless grapes ripen in July. 'Flame,' also called 'Flame Seedless,' is an early medium-size red seedless variety for the middle and low zones.

Special design features: Informal garlands of bold leafy form for summer shade and greenery. Winter sun. Interesting classical sculptural effect, especially in winter.

Uses: Trellises, arbors, porches and fences.

Disadvantages: Vine grows rapidly and needs clipping and training often during growing season. Occasionally gets Texas root rot, bacterial crown gall or root knot nematodes. Powdery mildew sometimes causes twigs and leaves to look as if they have been dusted with flour. The most serious threat is the grape-leaf skeletonizer—armies of tiny yellow-and-black-striped caterpillars can sometimes be found on the undersides of leaves. Small numbers can be controlled by picking off infested leaves. For serious attacks, Sevin is an effective spray. Be sure to follow all label directions.

Planting and care: Plant container-grown plants any time. Plant cuttings or bare-root plants in winter. For landscape purposes, train strong leaders up the support and tie securely. Cut off any unwanted side branches or weave them in and out to form a garland. Plants may be pruned to a basic framework each winter or may be left alone until spring comes. Remember that new growth comes from previous year's wood, so leave little stubs of new wood with enough buds to bring on new spring growth. In spring you can prune again, cutting off dead wood and less vigorous canes that do not sprout. Head back new growth by pinching off or cutting tips or unwanted long branches to encourage bushiness. Or weave new growth into the trellis or grape branch structure. When grapes form, there are a number of ways to increase their size. One is to remove a number of clusters so the vine produces fewer but larger fruits. Thin the clusters themselves. Shorten long clusters of 'Thompson's Seedless' and remove one or more upper branches. Remove about one third of the cluster. Grapes as landscape plants may be small because pruning for fruit production is considered secondary to the shape of the vine. Grape clusters can be covered with paper bags as they grow, so birds and insects do not eat them. Fertilize plants lightly with composted manure in fall. Or give a light sprinkling of ammonium sulfate or complete fertilizer in February: No more than 1 pound to 100 square feet (30.5 square meters) of soil surface. You can skip fertilizing completely, because grapes can often go for many years without a feeding. Grapes can also thrive in poor soil. Seek more information if you are planning to grow grapes commercially.

Vitis vinifera

Vitis vinifera

All zones
Deciduous
Soil: Tolerant. Prefers porous or gravelly soils with good drainage and some humus added.
Sun: Part, full or reflected sun, except 'Golden Muscat'—reflected sun may burn leaves.
Water: Constant soil moisture is necessary in spring and summer for grape production. Otherwise the plant is drought resistant and tolerates periodic soakings.
Temperature: Hardy to cold, but may suffer twig damage in cold winters. Late spring frosts can injure or kill new spring growth or the grape set. Plant recovers from frost damage quickly in warm weather and loves heat.
Maintenance: Constant. Frequent clipping and training and sometimes spraying in summer. Single pruning in winter. Otherwise, maintenance depends on use.

Washingtonia filifera

(W. filamentosa, Pritchardia filifera)
Family: Arecaceae (Palmae)
California Fan Palm • Arid Climate Fan Palm • Petticoat Palm

A large-scale fan palm with a wide, heavy trunk, this native of the Southwest grows slowly as high as 80 feet (24.4m), although it is usually seen at heights of 20 to 40 feet (6.1 to 12.2m). The dense head spreads 15 feet (4.6m) or more and is composed of stiff gray-green fanlike leaves with hairy filaments. Leaves are held well away from the erect trunk on 6-foot (1.8-m) tooth-edged leaf bases. Old leaves droop to the trunk and hang, forming a dense straw-colored thatch or "petticoat." There are two strains of this palm: The California arid climate type retains its dead leaves all the way down the trunk to the ground unless they are removed. The form from Arizona stands are sometimes self-pruning and can drop old drying leaves. Long blossoms like streamers emerge from crown in summer and produce abundant small white flowers and blue-black fruit on females. Bare trunks of trimmed or self-pruned palms have a brownish fibrous look and often flair at the base. In nature, plants grow in clusters in wet spots.

Special design features: A grand-scale palm. Massive. Formal. Ponderous. Strong vertical, eventually becoming a skyline tree. Strong architectural emphasis.

Uses: Too large for the average residence. Boulevards, parks and public spaces for cadence or accent. Groves are impressive and dramatic. Rows make walls in the landscape. A single plant is like an exclamation point. Tiny young plants in containers stay small for a long period. Good transitional plant. Looks attractive rising out of the bare earth.

Disadvantages: Occasionally gets bud rot, which is almost impossible to diagnose until it is too late. Treat palms near an infected palm by saturating their crowns with a Bordeaux mixture. This helps prevent contraction of the disease and may cure early cases. Slow to develop. Trunks are occasionally infected with a rot near the base, or a borer that can damage and kill drought-stressed trees. Tall plants are expensive to groom. Dry thatch can be a fire hazard. Trees recover from fire but will always have a blackened trunk.

Planting and care: May be started from seed, but very slow. Plant from containers after frosts have passed in spring. Transplant field-grown palms with roots balled in burlap during the warm season. Their heavy weight and bulk require an expert to plant them. Space 30 feet (9.2m) or more apart for boulevard or row planting. Place at random distances for natural grove, including several close together in a clump, as they are found in nature. Feed and water generously to encourage fast growth. Established plants tolerate neglect and will grow for years with no care in areas with 10 to 12 inches (254 to 305mm) of annual rainfall, but they will gradually decline and die. To groom, trim drying fronds and remove fruit garlands.

Washingtonia filifera

All zones
Evergreen
Soil: Tolerant of saline and alkaline soils. Fastest in moist soil.
Sun: Part to full sun.
Water: Moderate to occasional, but reseeds rapidly in a constantly wet situation.
Temperature: Hardy to about 15 to 18F (-9 to -8C). Young plants are more susceptible to cold. Slow to recover from frost damage.
Maintenance: Periodic grooming.

Washingtonia filifera

Washingtonia robusta

(W. gracilis, W. sonorae,
Pritchardia robusta)
Family: Arecaceae (Palmae)
Mexican Fan Palm • Mexican
Washingtonia • Thread Palm

This fast-growing fan palm from Mexico may reach 80 to 100 feet (24.4 to 30.5m) high. The slender trunk may be only 12 to 14 inches (30.5 to 35.6cm) in diameter. Its glistening green head of fanlike leaves spreads 10 to 12 feet (3.1 to 3.7m) in diameter. Leaves are richer green than *W. filifera* and more festive and refined in appearance. Old leaves become dry and hang down the trunk as thatch. They can be left or removed, depending on your preference, but they don't hang on as well as *W. filifera*. They often fall from upper trunks, which gives them a moth-eaten appearance. Young Mexican fan palms may be differentiated from *W. filifera* by a reddish streak along the underside of the leaf stalk near the trunk, but they hybridize freely and seedlings coming up in urban areas are not dependable forms. Trunks shorn of old leaf stubs are brown to gray, fairly smooth and may taper from a stout base. It is difficult to determine how fast this palm grows, but it is reasonable to expect a 12- to 15-foot (3.7- to 4.6-m) palm at the end of ten years, perhaps less. Growth depends on the amount of moisture it receives. Long straw colored streamers in spring develop sprays of tiny white flowers followed by small dark fruit on female trees.

Special design features: Graceful. Festive tropical feeling. Luxuriant vacation mood. Strong vertical. Dramatic, especially in groups. Jungle feeling when used with such plants as bamboo. Eventually a great skyline silhouette.

Uses: Tall emphasis plant used as specimen or in pairs or clumps. Streets, parks, entrances and public places. Silhouette plant against the sky or tall structures. Two or more palms planted together develop curving trunks as they arch away from each other, or if planted at an angle.

Disadvantages: These plants get tall. Do not plant them near power lines or under structures. Out of scale in residential situations, but often planted because they are so attractive in younger years. They soon outgrow the situation. Mature palms are difficult to groom and require professional tree trimmers (an added maintenance expense). Thatch left on palms may appear ragged and uneven. Foliage on younger palms is subject to frost damage, but plant recovers by mid- to late spring after growing a new set of leaves. Volunteers in inappropriate locations of irrigated landscapes.

Planting and care: Can be started from seed, which germinates in sixty days. Container plants are much faster and not too expensive. Plant in spring when danger from frost has passed. Transplant palms April through October. Even large plants can be moved successfully at this time. Feed and give ample water for fast growth. Older plants withstand periods of neglect and more frost than young plants. This palm seems to be more resistant to disease than other palms. To groom, remove old dry leaves and flowering parts in late spring. Trunks may be skinned so no leaf bases are left. If you do leave the leaf bases, the tree will have an interesting pattern for a while but then the bases will slough off in an uneven fashion.

Washingtonia robusta

Low and middle zones; warmer areas of high zone
Evergreen
Soil: Tolerant. Prefers improved garden soil.
Sun: Part to full sun.
Water: Moderate or even ample for fast growth. Occasional deep irrigation is satisfactory, but prefers the ample irrigation of a lawn. Newly transplanted palms greatly benefit from a drip irrigation system. Tall transplants require ample water until they re-establish.
Temperature: Leaves are damaged in the low 20sF (-7 to -5C). Plants recover quickly in spring.
Maintenance: Periodic grooming and seasonal trimming of tall palms to remove old leaves and blossom stalks.

Washingtonia robusta

Wisteria floribunda

(W. multijuga)
Family: Fabaceae (Leguminosae)
Japanese Wisteria

This twining woody vine is a sentimental favorite. Flower clusters open over a period of time rather than all at once, thus prolonging the bloom period. Clusters of purple pea-shaped flowers appear long before leaves come out, creating quite a show. Velvety pods 6 inches (15.2cm) long may follow. Medium green leaves are formed of thirteen or more pointed leaflets. Trunk, twigs and branches become gray and woody as plant matures. In time, lower trunk can become up to 3 inches (7.6cm) thick or thicker and rigid. Plants accept training to almost any shape. A single plant will cover an area of 10-by-10 feet (3.1-by-3.1m) or more. Some plants are trained to become self-supporting trees. Many decorate only a small area of a trellis. Eventual size depends on care and soil conditions. Plants may grow fast at first, then slowly.

Cultivars and other notable species: 'Longissima Alba' has white flowers to 2 feet (0.6m) long. 'Rosea' has pink flowers in clusters to 1-1/2 feet (0.5m) long.

Special design features: Oriental effect. Woodsy or old-fashioned garden mood. Spring color. Refined summer shade and greenery. Sculptural structure or bare branches when dormant.

Uses: Cover for sturdy arbors, porches, trellises or other framework. Attractive on pergolas. May be trained as shrub or small tree.

Disadvantages: Watch for suckers on budded or grafted plants and remove promptly. Subject to Texas root rot—do not use in soil known to be infected. Subject to sooty canker that can be prevented by treating cuts and wounds. May get iron chlorosis, which can be cured or prevented by feeding plant chelated iron. Pods and seeds are poisonous. Some plants bloom heavily only every other year.

Planting and care: Seek cutting-grown, grafted or budded plants for faster bloom and dependably uniform characteristics. Plant any time from containers. Place in soil mix prepared to prevent Texas root rot. To train a plant on a framework, tie main stem to a strong support at frequent intervals. Trim side shoots and shorten long streamers. Train new shoots in the manner you wish. It is best to train about three shoots to separate vines on supports to prevent excessive intertwining. If a tree form is desired, it is easiest to purchase a plant already trained. Do not fertilize heavily or plants will grow rank and have few flowers.

Wisteria floribunda

Wisteria floribunda

All zones
Deciduous
Soil: Average garden soil with good drainage.
Sun: Part to full sun.
Water: Moderate to ample.
Temperature: Hardy to cold. Tolerates heat with irrigation.
Maintenance: Constant early training, then only occasional pinching and cutting.

Xylosma congestum

(X. racemosum, X. senticosum, Myroxylon senticosum)
Family: Flacourtiaceae
Xylosma

One of the choice all-purpose landscape plants, *Xylosma* always looks nice, is easy to grow and requires very little care. Growth is moderate to fast once it gets started. It may reach 8 feet (2.4m) high as a shrub in six or seven years. Trained as a small garden tree, it can reach up to 20 feet (6.1m) high in fifteen years. It is easily trained to any shape or kept to any size. Foliage is shiny and bright green with a bronzy cast when new. Leaves are pointed but wide at the base, with toothed edges. Flowers are green and inconspicuous.

Cultivars and other notable species: 'Compacta' has a tighter branching habit and can be used for low hedges, borders or screens.

Special design features: One of the most outstanding and agreeable garden plants, which looks as nice close-up as at a distance, clipped or unclipped. Versatile, refined and well behaved.

Uses: Specimen, wide screen, background planting, clipped hedge or wall plant. Topiary. Easily kept narrow for limited spaces. As a single- or multitrunk tree, it makes one of the loveliest canopies for the garden or patio. Swimming pool areas.

Disadvantages: New growth begins early and may be damaged by spring frost. Slightly susceptible to iron chlorosis and Texas root rot. Sometimes gets spider mites or scale.

Planting and care: Plant from containers any time, but best in spring. Space up to 3 feet (0.9m) apart for clipped hedge, 4 to 6 feet (1.2 to 1.8m) for screen. Do any heavy pruning in late winter or early spring. Clip any time. For a tree form, purchase a plant already trained.

Xylosma congestum

Xylosma congestum

All zones
Evergreen to deciduous in coldest areas
Soil: Tolerant. Prefers improved garden soil with good drainage.
Sun: Filtered or part shade to full sun.
Water: Moderate. Tolerant of some drought when established. Older plants may be given occasional deep irrigation.
Temperature: Hardy to 10F (-12C), but may show some damage around 25F (-4C). Early spring growth may be nipped by a late frost but plant recovers quickly. Tolerates heat.
Maintenance: Periodic to constant. After initial training, only as desired.

Yucca species

Family: Agavaceae

Yuccas are abundantly scattered over the Sonoran and especially the Chihuahuan deserts. Many are transplanted into home landscapes, even though they are not as versatile as *Yuccas* available in nurseries. Native-plant laws protect *Yuccas* and many states require a tag on plants in the home landscape or they are subject to confiscation. Desert-climate *Yuccas*, such as *Y. aloifolia*, *Y. baccata*, *Y. brevifolia*, *Y. elata* and *Y. whipplei*, are collected in the wild and are sometimes difficult to establish. Most are so large they need to be propped up until they reroot. Most need some supplemental irrigation in the low zone or to help them become established. Some varieties can be successfully grown from seed and are available in arid-land nurseries.

Special design features: Bold foliage for specimen, silhouette or dramatic accents. Effects can be desert to tropical to subtropical depending on variety and other plants neaby.

Uses: Accent plant as specimen or in grouping. They can function as large shrubs, foundation plants, large container specimens near frequented areas, such as walks, or as part of a barrier. Desert or transitional gardens. Tropical or subtropical in combination with tropical plants. Garden *Yuccas* are also useful as accent plants in a bed or garden. Dramatic emphasis at an entrance away from reflected sun. May be safely used around swimming pool patios if set away from traffic patterns. *Y. recurvifolia* may be susceptible to grubs and weevils in open areas, but very good in gardens, especially in containers.

Disadvantages: Very sharp leaf spikes require placement away from walkways or other use areas. *Y. brevifolia* and *Y. elata* may be hard to find, and large specimens are expensive. *Y. brevifolia* may be difficult to transplant. Garden *Yuccas*, such as *Y. gloriosa* and *Y. recurvifolia*, may become chlorotic in alkaline soils. *Y. gloriosa* may sunburn from reflected heat—avoid western and southern exposures. Frost-damaged leaves are unsightly and recover slowly. Occasionally weevils or grubs shorten *Yucca* lives by eating the roots. Grub-damaged plants sometimes resprout from surviving roots. Ungroomed plants become leggy or develop dry leaves at bases, which look out of place in a garden setting. Aphids may invade flowers as they begin to open.

Planting and care: Plant field-grown or container desert *Yuccas* any time. Make sure roots of dug *Yuccas* have been cleanly cut, sulfured and allowed to callus by air drying in the shade before replanting. Prop as necessary until plants take root. Trimming of dried leaves changes the desert character of these plants.

Plant garden *Yuccas* from containers any time, but best in spring. Cuttings are also best started in spring. Branches of *Y. recurvifolia* may be removed, healed in the shade for a few days and then planted. Space *Y. gloriosa* 6 to 8 feet (1.8 to 2.4m) apart to allow room for a clump to develop. Space *Y. recurvifolia* 4 to 6 feet (1.2 to 1.8m) apart for massing or rows. To groom, cut back plants or trim foliage in late winter. Remove old leaves or allow to remain as thatch according to taste. For an especially dramatic form, remove all leaves but those at the top of trunks. To reduce size and to rejuvenate clumps, cut plants back to about 1 foot (0.3m) above ground. New branches will sprout below cut. Prevent grubs by applying diazinon around the base of plant in spring. Remove old flower stalks to groom.

Yucca species

All zones (except *Y. gloriosa*, which is best in low zone)
Evergreen
Soil: Desert *Yuccas* prefer gravelly, sandy or alkaline soil with good drainage. Not suited to garden conditions. Garden *Yuccas* are more tolerant, although they also require good drainage.
Sun: Full to reflected sun and heat. All can tolerate a small amount of shade.
Water: A little water in the root area can help transplanted *Yuccas* become established. After that desert *Yuccas* tolerate drought, but do better with monthly irrigation in the middle and lower zones. Garden *Yuccas* prefer moderate to occasional. They tolerate long periods of drought, but lower foliage dries out and leaves become a light green.
Temperature: Hardy to cold. *Y. gloriosa* is more tender. Heat tolerant.
Maintenance: None to periodic.

Yucca aloifolia
Spanish Bayonet • Dagger Plant

A bold garden or desert *Yucca* from the southern United States, Mexico and the West Indies, Spanish bayonet grows slowly to 10 feet (3.1m) high. Stiff, smooth-edged, medium to deep green leaves closely set along the stalk have sharp spikes at their tips. Leaves are shorter than most *Yuccas*. Some reach only 12 inches (30.5cm) long and stay green on the stalks unless stressed by drought. Plants may be erect, leaning or sprawling, with a single head or several branching out from the central stalk. Summer blooms are clusters of white purple-tinged, lilylike flowers. They rise out of plant tips on 2-foot (0.6-m) stalks, usually one to each head. In addition to the above uses, this *Yucca* is appropriate for dunes at the seashore where it is salt tolerant. The cultivar 'Marginata' has yellow margins.

Yucca baccata
(Y. arizonica, Y. thornberi)
Banana Yucca • Datil Yucca

A desert *Yucca* easily started from seed, banana yucca grows slowly to 3 feet (0.9m) high and up to 5 feet (1.5m) wide. It establishes clumps as stemless rosettes or with sprawling trunks. Plants are stiff and erect in nature with stiff, hard, sharply pointed light yellow-green to blue-green leaves 1 inch (2.5cm) or wider and 2 feet (0.6m) long. Bloom stalks in summer with large white to creamy white bell-shaped flowers rise vertically, barely above the leaf rosette. Flowers are 2 to 6 inches (5.1 to 15.2cm) long and produce green to purple edible fruit, 4-1/2 to 6-1/2 inches (11.4 to 16.5cm) long, that fed Native Americans in the great Southwest and Mexico for centuries.

Yucca aloifolia

Yucca elata

Yucca gloriosa

Yucca recurvifolia

Yucca brevifolia
Joshua Tree Yucca

This picturesque desert plant sometimes reaches 40 feet (12.2m) tall. It is very striking, with long arms or branches that often take on irregular shapes and may even lie along the ground or close to it. Grayish or dull-green leaves are quite narrow and sharp. Clusters of greenish white lilylike blossoms appear at the end of each branch. A naturally occurring variety, *Y. b. herbertii*, reaches about 15 feet (4.6m) tall, so it's a better plant for most home landscapes. Both are native to the high desert climates but hardy in all arid climates. Dry desert effect. Stong accent.

Yucca elata
Soap Tree Yucca

A shaggy desert-climate *Yucca* often seen in home landscape plantings—perhaps the most commonly used arid-climate *Yucca* of those described here. Native to the high arid climates of northern Mexico and the southwestern United States. Form is erect to about 12 feet (3.7m) tall. Leaves are grasslike, with little threads curling along the edges. Old leaves hang down along the trunk, creating a straw-colored thatch. Top leaves are light green with a white edge, giving plants a grayish cast. Plants produce a bold effect and are especially attractive silhouetted against a plain background. Flower spikes produced in late spring are dramatic, topping the thatch of drying leaves. Blossom stalks reach up to 6 feet (1.8m) or higher and display spectacular clusters of fragrant snowy white blooms.

Yucca gloriosa
Spanish Dagger • Palm Lily
Roman Candle

Spanish dagger is a dramatic garden *Yucca* from the southeastern United States and northeastern Mexico. Bright to yellowish green leaves are 2-1/2 feet (0.8m) long, 2 inches (5.1cm) wide, fleshy and fairly stiff with pointed tips. Growth is moderate to 8 feet (2.4m) high. It may develop a number of trunks at its base, forming a clump 8 feet (2.4m) wide. When old foliage is skinned off, the resulting slender woody trunks and spiky heads look like miniature palms. Unskinned leaves stay green for several feet down the plant before dying and becoming thatch. Flower spikes are 3 feet (0.9m) tall and produce large creamy to pinkish blooms in

clusters. Unlike other *Yuccas*, bloom spikes are short, beginning down among the leaves. Secondary trunks can be removed at the base and healed for a week in shade, then planted elsewhere to make a new plant. Although leaf tips are pointed, they have no sharp spikes and are not dangerous unless at eye level. This *Yucca* is best in the low and middle zones and only warmer locations in the high zone. Damaged at 20 to 24F (-7 to -4C). Tolerant of heat and part shade. East sides.

Yucca recurvifolia
(Y. pendula)
Pendulous Yucca • Curveleaf Yucca

Pendulous yucca is native to the southeastern section of the United States and to Mexico. A fast-growing *Yucca* to 6 feet (1.8m) high, it develops one or several branches. One plant can spread up to 6 feet (1.8m) wide. Foliage is dark gray-green. Thin leaves to 3 inches (7.6cm) wide at the base are 3 feet (0.9m) long and have soft points at their tips. They bend downward from the plant about half their length. Spikes 3 to 5 feet (0.9 to 1.5m) long rise vertically above heads in early summer and bear delicate white lilylike flowers in loose clusters about 2 feet (0.6m) long. A good bloomer. More of a garden plant than an desert *Yucca*, larger plants in a garden setting need grooming to be attractive. They can be cut back every few years and will develop several branches below the cut.

Yucca brevifolia

Mix of *Zinnia* and *Salvia*

Annual Color

A question visitors often ask desert dwellers is, "When will the desert bloom?" This colorful and photogenic extravaganza has been so widely publicized that many assume it is an annual event, but the correct answer to this question is, "Sometime during February, March or April in the next five years or so." It takes properly spaced rains combined with other weather events to produce these great color shows.

When the desert does bloom, it produces more wildflowers than almost any place else. Desert plants must flower abundantly in good years to maintain the seed supply that perpetuates the species. Desert gardeners do not have to wait for just the right combination of weather to have their own wildflower show, because they control the moisture that brings the flower garden to life.

Planting Dates

Many newcomers to arid regions are surprised to learn that the seasons are more or less reversed. October is the "spring" planting time. During this period, weather conditions are ideal for setting out new plants for a traditional winter or spring garden. Plants require much less water during this cool period. Also, flower color seems to be more magnificent if it occurs during the coolness of late winter or early spring.

Cool-weather annuals should be planted when nights are cool but not cold, and days are warm but not hot. Plants are then able to reach a blooming phase before nights become too cold. If buds have formed, flowers will open throughout winter except during very cold spells. This show continues until summer heat comes in May. Many gardeners abandon flower gardening in summer, waiting until cool weather returns.

Many annuals thrive during hot weather. Year-round color is possible with a second planting season, usually beginning mid-May, for those who wish to garden through the summer. The list of summer-flowering annuals is shorter than cold-weather types and gardening problems are magnified by severe climatic conditions, but summer color can be very showy. Planting dates for summer flowers are not as critical as winter types because of the long warm season ahead. Planting summer flowers early before nights have warmed doesn't create an advantage. Most will do nothing until nights warm up.

Plants or Seed?

Most annual plants grow easily from seed, but it is better to buy plants at the nursery for fall gardens. Unless you have a cooled greenhouse or a place indoors to start seedlings in late July or August, it is practically impossible to have plants ready for transplanting in time. A delay of a few weeks in planting can cause flowers to wait until spring before blooming, thus shortening the season drastically.

Summer-flowering annuals are also usually planted as nursery-grown plants, but many species can be sown directly in the flower bed. Because the air and soil temperatures are so warm, plants develop rapidly. Plant a little more seed than you need to ensure adequate coverage, then thin seedlings if they become crowded.

Soil and Water Requirements

You can grow annuals in nearly any garden soil. Add humus and fertilizer to sandy or heavy soils. Most flower species require regular irrigation, and few are drought resistant. Locate flower beds where they will be easy to water. Containers make good flower beds and serve as focal points. Keep them full of good planting soil and then change the color plants each season as you would change flower bouquets in the house. Some drought-tolerant desert natives are occasionally grown as cut flowers but they are of limited value.

Familiar and Traditional Annuals

The winter to spring plants used in warm arid regions are the summer plants of the temperate zones. For convenience, they are often planted in containers as color spots at entrances or in patios, and may be changed seasonally. To maintain an annual bed, especially a large one, requires great dedication. Some plants considered annuals can actually be perennials, such as alyssum (*Lobularia maritima*).

The following chart and the perennial chart on pages 170 and 171 were adapted from the University of Arizona cooperative extension service as well as from our own experience. Use your zone as a guide to the planting and flowering dates.

Botanical Name Common Name	Height in inches	Low and Middle Zones Planting Dates	Blooming Dates	High Zone Planting Dates	Blooming Dates	Description
Antirrhinum species snapdragon	6-36 (15.2 to 91.4cm)	Oct. to Nov. 30	March to June	March to June	May to frost	Excellent for cutting, borders or beds. Dwarf types provide earlier and longer period of bloom.
Aster species aster	12-24 (30.5 to 61cm)	Oct. to Nov. 15	April	April to May	July to Sept.	Beautiful bedding plants for higher elevations. Well-drained soil. Pompon type most hardy.
Begonia species begonia (waxleaf)	10-12 (25.4 to 30.5cm)	Sept. to Nov. 15	All year if frost free	April to July	March to Oct.	Partial to full shade. Often used as summer bedding plant. Pots, beds and borders. Red, pink and white flower colors. Reddish bronze-foliage types take heat the best.
Calendula officinalis calendula	15-18 (38.1 to 45.7cm)	Sept. 15 to Dec.	Jan. to April	Aug. to Oct.	March to June	Hardy, early flowering, easy to grow from seed. Yellow and orange blossoms over a long season. Available in dwarf form. Not hardy in higher elevations for winter planting, but will bloom briefly into June.
Catharanthus roseus (Vinca rosea) periwinkle (Madagascar)	18-24 (45.7 to 61cm)	April 15 to May 30	June to Nov. (or to frost)	May 30 to June 30	July to frost	Hardy plant for beds or borders. One of the best summer bedding plants. Masses of white and lavender blossoms all season. Often perennial in warm pockets.
Coleus species and cultivars coleus	6-18 (15.2 to 45.7cm)	April to June	June to Nov.	June 15 to July 15	July to Oct.	Grown for its multicolored foliage. Excellent container plant, indoors and out. Tender to frost. Needs some humidity.
Consolida ambigua larkspur	24-48 (61 to 122cm)	Sept. 15 to Nov. 30	March to May	Aug. to Oct.	May to July	Tall, blue, red or pink flower spikes. Popular for cut flowers. Background plant for beds and screening. Naturalizes easily.
Cosmos sulphureus cosmos (yellow)	36-72 (91.4 to 182.9cm)	April to June	July to Nov.	May 15 to June 15	July to frost	Brilliant orange to yellow-orange daisylike flowers. Use for cutting or screening. Tolerates heat. Late summer bloom period.
Dahlia species dahlias (seed)	12-36 (30.5 to 91.4cm)	March to April	April 15 to Nov.	June to July	July to frost	Tall and dwarf varieties. Excellent for cut flowers. Well-drained soil. Part shade in lower zone. Blooms are double or single and come in a variety of colors.
Delphinium species delphinium	30-60 (76.2 to 152.4cm)	Sept. 15 to Nov.	March to June	Sept. to Oct. 15	March 15 to June	True perennial used as an annual. Tall flower spikes, use as background. 'Pacific Giant' and 'Connecticut Yankee' do well. Flowers come in a range of colors.
Dianthus barbatus dianthus	10-15 (25.4 to 38.1cm)	Sept. 15 to Nov. 30	March to June	Sept. to March	April to July	Dense clusters of double or single flowers. Mixed colors. 'China Pink,' 'Annual Carnation' and 'Sweet William' are popular. Often perennial in partial shade.
Dimorphotheca sinuata African daisy	12-18 (30.5 to 45.7cm)	Sept. 15 to Nov. 30	Feb. to May	Sept. to Oct. 15	Feb. to May	Hardy and fast growing. Brilliant yellow and orange blooms, excellent massed or in beds. Blooms freely up to six months a year. Naturalizes and reseeds easily.
Eschscholzia californica poppy (California)	10-12 (25.4 to 30.5cm)	Sept. to Nov. 30	March 15 to May 30	July to Sept.	April to August	Colorful border plant. Seeding is best. May be sown in open desert areas that get winter moisture. Naturalizes over large areas.
Gomphrena globosa globe amaranth	15-24 (38.1 to 61cm)	April to July 15	June to Nov. 15	May 15 to July 15	July to Oct.	Excellent border or low bedding plant. Cloverlike flowers are usually purple but are sometimes available in pink and white. Use in dried arrangements.
Iberis amara candytuft (hyacinth type)	12-18 (30.5 to 45.7cm)	Sept. 15 to Nov. 30	Feb. to May	Sept. 15 to Oct. April to May	March to July	White fragrant flowers, also available in pink, lavender and purple. Longer season in partial shade, sometimes perennial. Good cut flower. Beds and border.
Iberis umbellata candytuft	12 (30.5cm)	Sept. 15 to Nov. 30, Jan. to Feb.	Feb. to May	Sept. 15 to April	March to June	Flat flower clusters in assorted colors. Ground cover, rock garden and border.
Impatiens balsamina impatiens (balsam)	6-24 (15.2 to 61cm)	April to May	May to Nov. 15.	May to June	June to Oct. 30	Outstanding shade plants, especially adapted to hanging baskets. Dwarf and semidwarfs available. Bright colors.

Botanical Name / Common Name	Height in inches	Low and Middle Zones		High Zone		Description
		Planting Dates	Blooming Dates	Planting Dates	Blooming Dates	
Lathyrus odoratus / sweet pea	12-72 (30.5 to 182.9cm)	Oct. to Jan. 15	Feb. to May	March 15 to May 1	April to June	Early- and late-flowering varieties. Excellent cut flowers. Vining plant: Train on fence or trellis. Available in bush form. Plant in spring in cold areas of high zone. Blooms come in a range of colors.
Lobelia spacata / lobelia	6-10 (15.2 to 25.4cm)	Sept. 15 to Nov. 15	March 15 to May	April to May	April to May	Good for borders, edgings and rock gardens. Protect from temperatures below 28F (-2C). Summer annual in highest areas. Flowers come in small clusters of deep blue to white.
Lobularia maritima / sweet alyssum	6-9 (15.2 to 22.9cm)	Sept. to March	Jan. 15 to June	Aug. to Sept., March to April	April to frost	Excellent for borders, ground cover, edging and rockeries. Blooms profusely and reseeds. White and purple colors. Hardy; grows all year with morning sun.
Matthiola species / stock	18-30 (45.7 to 76.2cm)	Oct. to Nov. 30	Feb. 15 to June	July to Oct.	April to July	Excellent cutting, border or bedding flower. Plant early for best results. Single and double, white, pink, purple flowers are fragrant.
Papaver nudicaule / poppy (Iceland)	12-18 (30.5 to 45.7cm)	Oct. to Nov. 30	Feb. 15 to May	Aug. to Oct.	April to June	Sow or set out plants early from flats in large beds for mass effect. 'Champagne Bubbles' is one of the best varieties; it blooms early. Comes in a range of colors.
Petunia hybrids / petunia	12-24 (30.5 to 61cm)	Oct. to April	Nov. to May	April to May	May to frost	Available in a variety of forms and colors. Adapted to many uses—pots, beds, ground covers. Best to plant transplants. Long blooming season. Requires well-prepared garden soil.
Phlox drummondii / phlox (annual)	6-12 (15.2 to 30.5cm)	Oct. to Jan. 1	March to June	Aug. to Sept., April to June	April to May, June to frost	Prolific color producer, good for borders, edging or rock gardens. Also as a cut flower. Flowers are simple, with five petals.
Primula malacoides / primrose (fairy)	6-12 (15.2 to 30.5cm)	Oct. to Nov.	Feb. to May	April to May	May 15 to June	Small pink, rose, red, lavender or white flowers. Blooms in shade. Needs regular care. In cold areas, plant after major frost period has passed.
Primula polyantha / primrose (English)	6-12 (15.2 to 30.5cm)	Oct. to Nov.	Nov. to May	Oct. to March	March to May	Hybrid types in a variety of rich colors. Excellent for containers, beds and borders. Best winter color plant for shade.
Salvia patens / salvia	15-30 (38.1 to 76.2cm)	April to June 15	June 15 to Nov.	June to frost	July to frost	Bedding plant for full sun to part shade. Tall brilliant red flower spikes.
Tagetes erecta / African marigold	30-36 (76.2 to 91.4cm)	April 1 to June 30	June to frost	May 15 to June 30	July to frost	Tall flower for beds or cutting. Blossoms of many types and colors. Reseeds easily. Afternoon shade in low zone. Prone to leafhopper damage.
Tagetes patula / French marigold	12-18 (30.5 to 45.7cm)	April to June 30	May to frost	May to June 30	July to frost	Produces masses of orange and yellow blossoms. Best in fall and late spring gardens. Prone to leafhopper damage. Double or single types. Excellent color plant for higher elevations.
Tropaeolum species / nasturtium	10-18 (25.4 to 45.7cm)	Sept. to Nov.	April 15 to May 30	April 15 to May 30	June to Sept.	Protect from frost. Low beds, ground cover, borders and cut flowers. Single and double forms in a range of colors.
Verbena hybrids / verbena (common)	8-12 (20.3 to 30.5cm)	Sept. 15 to Nov. 30	All year (best in spring)	Aug. to Sept., April to May	April to Nov.	Small colorful plants for edging, ground cover and window boxes. Very hardy; often perennial. Colors range from white to lavender and purple.
Viola species / pansy (garden)	6-12 (15.2 to 30.5cm)	Oct. to Jan.	Sept. to Nov.	Sept. to Nov.	March to July	Multicolored flowers bloom over a long season. Blooms may be white, yellow, apricot, blue, purple or pink. Plant in fertile soil. Tolerates partial shade.
Zinnia elegans / zinnia	4-30 (10.2 to 76.2cm)	April 15 to July 15	June to frost	May 15 to July	July to frost	One of the best summer flowers. Loves sun, avoid shade. Tall, medium and dwarf types. Many forms and colors. Grows easily from seed.

Perennial Color

Perennials differ from annuals in that they live and flower for two or more years, depending on the species and the situation. You may note that a few perennials were listed previously as annuals, simply because that is how they are used in hot dry regions. It is marvelous to have a plant that will put on a seasonal show year after year, and many gardeners use perennials for this reason. But they are not used quite as often in these regions as in temperate zones where they are a major source of garden color. This is because desert and arid-land perennials produce color for maybe half the year or less, yet occupy garden space for the whole year. Many gardeners choose perennials that produce attractive foliage as well as flowers, so the unattractive off-season is much less noticeable.

Traditional perennials require optimum growing conditions. Some will endure drought stress, but lack of water often puts them into dormancy. It is best to plant them in a well-prepared soil and supply regular irrigation. Prune plants occasionally to initiate growth.

Many perennials regrow from the same clump year after year, so some plants should be dug up, divided and reset periodically to keep them growing and blooming well. Some plants will last only one to three years, then need to be replaced. Changing the location of a perennial species every few years is also a good idea. This will prevent build up of diseases and insects of growing area.

Botanical Name / Common Name	Height in inches	Low and Middle Zones		High Zone		Description
		Planting Dates S-Seed T-Transplant	Blooming Dates	Planting Dates S-Seed T-Transplant	Blooming Dates	
Althea rosea hollyhock	48-72 (121.9 to 182.9cm)	S-March to Oct. T-Oct. to March	April to June	S- April to Aug. T-Oct. to March	May to July	Red, pink, yellow and white flowers on giant 4- to 6-foot (1.2- to 1.8-m) spikes. Full sun. Very hardy and reseeds easily. Single and double flower forms.
Aquilegia hybrids columbine	24-36 (61 to 91.4cm)	S-March to Sept. T-Nov. to Feb.	April and May	S-April to Aug. T-Oct. to Jan.	April to July	Numerous purple, blue, pink, yellow and white flowers appear above fresh green foliage. Best in full or partial shade-good under trees. Old plants can be separated to reset, but replacements are usually grown from seed.
Aster novae-angliae aster, New England aster	24-36 (61 to 91.4cm)	S-April to Aug. T-Oct. to Dec.	Sept. to Dec.	S-June to Aug. T-Nov. to May	Sept. to Dec.	Purple, blue, pink and white daisy flowers in showy sprays. Full sun or partial shade. Very hardy; may crowd out other perennials. Clumps last indefinitely. Divide every two or three years.
Canna hybrids canna	14-36 (35.6 to 91.4cm)	T-May to June	May to frost	T-June	June to frost	Red, pink, orange, yellow and white orchid-textured flowers. Full sun. Dwarfs are best in borders. Divide and reset every other year to prevent beds from crowding.
Chrysanthemum maximum shasta daisy	18-30 (45.7 to 76.2cm)	S-April to Oct. T-Jan. to Feb.	April to June	S-May to Aug. T-Oct. to March	May to frost	Huge daisy flowers-semidouble types available. Full sun or partial shade. Divide every three or four years. Many Colors and cultvars.
Chrysanthemum morifolium chrysanthemum, mum	18-36 (45.7 to 91.4cm)	S-March to May T-Dec. to March	Oct. to Dec.	S-May to July T-Jan. to April	Aug. to Nov.	Purple, red, pink, orange, yellow and white flowers. Sun or partial shade. Cushion and hardy types best for the garden. Use early flowering varieties in upper elevations. Plants are hardy but blossoms are not. Pinch back early spring and late summer to encourage flowers and growth.
Chrysanthemum parthenium feverfew	18-24 (45.7 to 61cm)	S-April to May T-Oct. to March	April to June	S-May to Sept. T-Nov. to March	April to frost	Full sun. Very hardy. Single and double white button-shaped flowers. Bright green foliage. Old plants can be divided but it is better to replant every three to four years.
Coreopsis grandiflora coreopsis	24-36 (61 to 91.4cm)	S-April and Oct. T-Oct. to March	April to June	S-May to July T-Nov. to March	May to Oct.	Golden yellow flowers appear intermittently all summer. Medium green clumping foliage. Full sun. Very hardy. Plants last two to four years.
Dianthus caryophyllus carnation	12-24 (30.5 to 61cm)	S-April to June T-Oct. to March	Sept. to Dec. and March to June	S-May to July T-Sept. to Jan.	April to frost	Red, pink, orange, yellow and white fringed flowers. Single and multiple stems on bluish gray foliage. Full sun. Very hardy. Cutting grown types are best.
Dianthus plumarius dianthus, pinks	10-15 (25.4 to 38.1cm)	S-April to June T-Oct. to March	March to June	S-July to Sept. T-Oct. to Feb.	April to June	Dainty clusters of fragrant, carnationlike flowers in white, pink, salmon and rose. Attractive foliage all year. Very hardy. Full sun to partial shade. Needs well-drained soil high in organic matter. Clumps are long lasting. Reset new rooted cuttings when old plants become woody.

Botanical Name Common Name	Height in inches	Low and Middle Zones Planting Dates S-Seed T-Transplant	Blooming Dates	High Zone Planting Dates S-Seed T-Transplant	Blooming Dates	Description
Digitalis purpurea foxglove	24-72 (61 to 182.9cm)	S-April to May T-Oct. to Dec.	April to Sept.	S-May to July T-Oct. to Feb.	May to Sept.	Shade and partial sun. Tall spikes of bells create a bold vertical display in colors ranging from white to pink or lavender. Large grayish leaves. Replace with new plants when old ones become woody and die out.
Felicia amelloides blue marguerite	18-24 (45.7 to 61cm)	T-Oct. to April	March to Dec. All winter if frost-free	T-April to May	May to frost	Azure blue daisies form on single stems above mounds of crisp dark green foliage. Full sun. Blooms almost continuously, but tender to frost. Excellent container plant. Replace plants every three to four years.
Gaillardia grandiflora gaillardia, blanket flower	12-30 (30.5 to 76.2cm)	S-April to Sept. T-Dec. to Feb.	April to Dec.	S-May to July T-Oct. to Feb.	April to Nov.	Yellow and red daisy flowers with grayish green foliage. Best in full sun. Very hardy border plant that blooms all summer and off and on all year. Replace with new seedlings when old plants decline.
Gerbera jamesonii gerbera, transvaal daisy	12-18 (30.5 to 45.7cm)	S-April to July T-Oct. to Feb.	March to June	March to April	June to Summer	Red, pink, orange, yellow and white fringy flowers appear on long stems above pointed green foliage. Full sun or partial shade. Drainage is important.
Helianthus multiflorus sunflower	36-60 (91.4 to 152.4cm)	S-April to May T-Oct. to March	Aug. to Nov.	S-May to June T-Dec. to March	Aug. to Nov.	Spectacular clusters of orange, yellow, white and maroon flowers. Full sun. Very hardy. Tall background plant with mass of flowers-clean yellow color. Divide and reset or plant new plants every three or four years.
Hemerocallis hybrids daylily	18-36 (45.7 to 91.4cm)	T-Oct. to Jan. All year if frost-free	March to June	T-Oct. to Jan.	May to July	Yellow, orange and maroon colors. Striking lilyshaped flowers borne above clumps of straplike foliage. Sun or partial shade. Some leafburn in low elevations, where early types are best. Blooms over a long season. Very hardy. Long-lasting, multiplying clumps, but divide, thin and reset occasionally.
Iris germanica iris, bearded iris	12-48 (30.5 to 121.9cm)	T-July to Nov.	Feb. to May	T-Aug. to Dec.	April to June	Large, purple, blue, yellow, orange, pink and white flowers. Bold, gray-green, spiky, strap-shaped leaves. Full sun to partial shade. Very hardy—not too much water required after blooming. Divide in late summer or fall. Reset every four to five years.
Pelargonium hortorum geranium	12-36 (30.5 to 91.4cm)	S-April and May T-Sept to May	All year, but most stop in hot season	S-Start inside March to April T-April to June	May to frost	Variety of double and single flowers in large flat clusters. Colors come in pink, salmon, red and white. Pink is sometimes iridescent. Sun or partial shade. Very tough but frost tender in upper elevations. Long lasting if not frosted.
Penstemon gloxinioides penstemon, bearded tongue	14-30 (35.6 to 76.2cm)	S-April to Oct. T-Oct. to Jan.	April to June	S-May to Aug. T-Nov. to Feb.	May to Summer	Red, pink, white, blue and purple flowers. Vigorous upright plant, almost shrublike. Sun or partial shade. Very hardy. Good summer color.
Phlox paniculata phlox	18-36 (45.7 to 91.4cm)	T-Oct. to Jan.	July to Sept.	T-Sept. to Dec.	June to Aug.	Outstanding, purple, red, pink and white flowers. Plant in partial shade or in eastern or northeastern exposure. Divide and reset every three or four years.
Physostegia virginiana physostegia, false dragon head	24-36 (61 to 91.4cm)	S-April to June T-Oct. to March	Aug. to Oct.	S-June to July T-Nov. to March	Aug. to Oct.	Pink, lavender and white colors. Full sun to partial shade. Flowers borne in terminal spikes—good for background planting. Cut back plant in off season.
Rudbeckia hirta rudbeckia, gloriosa daisy	30-48 (76.2 to 121.9cm)	S-April to Oct. T-Oct. to Dec.	Aug. to Oct.	S-Aug. to Oct. T-Oct. to Jan.	Aug. to Oct.	Yellow and mahogany colors. Bushy plants need space. Full sun. Very hardy. Fall flowering. Divide every third year. Often better to reset with new plants when old clumps weaken.
Viola odorata sweet violet	8-10 (20.3 to 25.4cm)	T-Oct. to Feb.	Jan. to March	T-Oct. to March	Jan. to April	Purple, blue and lavender colors in winter and in early spring. Sun to shade—excellent bedding plant for shady location. Very hardy. Heart-shaped evergreen leaves. Reset every three to five years.

Seasonal Color

The plants listed here are all grown for the seasonal color they offer, but they are not traditional flowering annuals or perennials as charted above. They are divided into two categories: oasis garden plants (Gar) and more deserty plants (Des). Most of these plants look terrific while they are in season but are rather lackluster or frozen back in the off season. Dry-climate gardeners can choose to treat these plants more like annuals, replacing them with something else when they finish blooming for the year, or they can plan their gardens so various plants are always blooming, thus diverting attention from the ones that are not at their best. Some of these plants last only a few years at most and during that time will benefit from soil improved with organic materials just as with more traditional seasonal plantings.

Garden or Desert Plant	Name: *Botanical* Common	Description	Culture
Desert	*Ageratum corymbosum* Desert ageratum, blue mist flower	Herbaceous perennial to 3 feet (0.9m) high and wide with blue flowers in puffy clusters on branch ends in summer and fall.	Plant in filtered sun to shade. Any soil. Moderate to low water. Cut to ground in winter. Cut back hard in late summer if leggy.
Garden	*Aptenia cordifolia* Hearts and flowers, red apple	Succulent ground cover with bright green leaves and fringy red flowers blooming spring to summer.	Part shade to filtered sun in well-drained soil. Damaged by intense heat and cold (confine to warm pockets of high zone). Soak weekly.
Desert	*Baileya multiradiata* desert marigold	Short-lived perennial 1 foot (0.3m) high and wide with silvery green foliage and bright yellow daisy flowers on slender stems above leaves nearly year around. Reseeds.	Sun to light shade in well-drained soil. Looks best with weekly watering. Rejuvenate plant by clipping away faded foliage and flowers. Easy to start from seeds or plants in fall or spring.
Desert	*Berlandiera lyrata* chocolate flower	Flowering perennial 1 foot (0.3m) high to 2 feet (0.6m) wide, with masses of yellow and maroon daisylike blooms in summer and fall. Flowers have scent of chocolate.	Plant in full or filtered sun in any soil and water thoroughly about once a week during summer. Will reach full size within two seasons. Cut back in winter.
Desert	*Calylophus hartwegii* sundrops	Herbaceous perennial on woody base 2 feet (0.6m) high and wide, with large lemon yellow flowers covering plant in spring and summer. Perfect for use in tight planting spaces.	Plant in full sun to filtered shade in well-drained soil. Little water (overwatering will quickly cause damp-off). Reaches mature size in a season, but short-lived. Cut to ground in winter.
Garden	*Celosia argentea* *C. a.* 'Cristata' cockscomb	Showy summer bedding plants available in sizes from 3 feet (0.9m) high to dwarfs. Flower clusters have bizarre shapes in brilliant shades of pink, orange, red and gold. Use for bold color accents in borders or planting beds.	Plant in full sun in improved soil. Regular water. Sow seed in place in late spring or early summer or set out started plants.
Garden	*Centaurea cineraria* *Senecio cineraria* dusty miller	The name "dusty miller" is applied to several perennials 18 inches to 2 feet (0.5 to 0.6m) high and wide with pale white to silver leaves. Two best for dry climates are listed here. *Centaurea* produces single purple or yellow summer blooms; *Senecio*, yellowish flowers all year. Mix with green foliage plants in borders or in foreground as an accent.	Plant in full sun in soil with good drainage. Low water users, but wet thoroughly when irrigating. Trim after bloom to groom and rejuvenate. Replace with a new plant after a few years when plants loses its looks.
Desert	*Chrysactinia mexicana* damianita	Flowering shrub to 2 feet (0.6m) tall and wide. Bright daisylike flowers atop aromatic needlelike leaves in tight bunches through summer.	Plant in full sun in soil with good drainage. Low water use. Clip back early spring and late summer. Mix with *Ericameria laricifolia* (a fall bloomer) to extend bloom season.
Desert	*Dyssodia pentachaeta* golden dyssodia	Short-lived perennial to 8 inches (20.3cm) tall and wide produces tiny bright yellow daisylike flowers throughout warm season atop lacy needlelike leaves. Reseeds.	Plant in full sun in any soil. Low water use, but lasts longer with weekly waterings in summer. Can cut back to rejuvenate in winter.
Desert	*Eupatorium greggii* mist flower	Herbaceous perennial to 2 feet (0.6m) high and wide with blue flowers in puffy clusters on branch ends in summer and fall.	Plant in full to filtered sun. Any soil. Moderate to little water. Cut to ground in winter. Cut back hard in late summer if leggy.
Garden	*Euryops pectinatus* bush daisy	Evergreen rounded perennial to 4 feet (1.2m) high and wide with bright yellow daisylike flowers on slender stems most of year. Foliage green or gray depending on selection.	Plant in full sun in improved soil. Without moderate water, lower foliage dies back. Cold damage begins in mid 20s F (-3 to -5C). Recovers in spring. Replace with new plant when looks go or cut back severely to rejuvenate.
Garden	*Eustoma grandiflorum* lisianthus	Prized for vaguely tulip-shaped flowers in purplish blue, pink or white. Will bloom continuously until hottest weather if old blooms are cut off. Gray-green foliage.	Plant in full sun in improved soil. Buying started plants is best. Set out in spring, offering regular water. This short-lived perennial is usually grown as an annual in dry climates.
Desert	*Hymenoxys acaulis* angelita daisy	A 1-foot (0.3-m) high and wide clumping perennial with continuous warm weather bloom of golden yellow daisylike flowers. Fast growth. Green foliage.	Plant in full sun in well-drained soil. Regular irrigation. Remove old flower heads several times throughout the season to maintain bloom.

Garden or Desert Plant	Name: *Botanical* Common	Description	Culture
Garden	*Kalanchoe blossfeldiana* forest kalanchoe	Flowering succulent useful as a color plant in protected locations. To 18 inches (0.5m) tall and wide. Flowers range from yellow to red. Green foliage is tinged with red.	Plant in filtered to light shade, usually best in pots. Set out when cold weather has passed. Water as soil dries out. New dwarf varieties widely available, some reaching only 6 inches high and wide.
Desert	*Merremia aurea* yellow morning glory vine	Yellow flowers in classic morning glory shape on twining vine to 20 feet (6.1m) long. Good on fences, posts and trellises.	Plant in sun to filtered shade in spring and water at regular intervals when mature. Freezes back in mid 20s F (-3 to -5C), but recovers fast in spring. Remove browned foliage.
Garden	*Nierembergia hippomanica violacea* cup flower	Small rich blue to violet to white flowers on fringy foliage stand 1 foot (0.3m) high and wide. Excellent in pots, borders and perennial beds.	Plant seeds or starts in fall for summer flowering. Water regularly until established, then cut back to moderate moisture to maintain compact look.
Desert	*Penstemon* **species** (desert species) beard tongue	Spectacular spring to summer bloom of tubular flared flowers mostly in pink to red to purple on long stalks, rising from basal rosette of lance-shaped leaves. From 2 feet (0.6m) high to much larger depending on species.	Plant seeds (fall) or starts (spring) in full sun to part shade in well-drained soil. Low water. This short-lived perennial will rebloom for several years and also reseed. Plant several varieties with different bloom period to extend flower show.
Garden	*Pentas lanceolata* star clusters	Distinguished by tight cluster of small star-shaped flowers in white, pink, lilac or red on stems above multistemmed plant up to 2 feet (0.6m) plant.	Place in part sun to filtered shade in improved soil. With regular water, will last into hottest weather. Remove dead flowers to extend bloom season.
Garden	*Phlomis fruticosa* Jerusalem sage	Grown for interesting whorls of yellow tubular flowers appearing at intervals on erect stems rising 3 feet (0.9m) above woolly gray-green plant.	Sun to light shade. Best with protection from afternoon summer sun. Not picky about soil. Moderate to low water. Will rebloom if cut back after flowering.
Garden	*Portulaca grandiflora* moss rose	Widely grown for lustrous roselike flowers in many shades from reds to pastels on trailing, low-growing plants to 18 inches (0.5m) wide. Leaves are fleshy, succulent and pointed. Best in pots, improved garden soil, borders or perennial beds.	Set out these summer annuals in full sun. Watch watering in hottest weather: Keep plants from drying out, but don't overwater.
Desert	*Psilostrophe cooperi* paper flower	Clumping perennial to 2 feet (0.6m) high and wide. Showy bright yellow flowers on branch tips hold color as they dry, finally turning papery and ivory-colored, giving illusion of a very long bloom period. Mixes well with wildflowers and with other desert plants.	Plant in full sun to light shade in any soil with good drainage. Low water user. Replace straggly older plants with new plants periodically.
Garden	*Salvia farinacea* mealy-cup sage	Constant blue-violet flowers on spikes above dark green mounds to 2-1/2 feet (0.8m) in warm weather. Dwarf varieties and whites also available. Use as bedding plant, in perennial borders or in containers.	Plant spring to summer in full sun to light shade in well-drained soil. Provide regular water.
Garden	*Scabiosa caucasica* pincushion flower	Long stamens protruding beyond surface of flower cluster give the illusion of pins stuck into a cushion. Blue-lavender to white flowers on 2-1/2-foot (0.8-m) foliage mass.	Plant in part sun to light shade in improved soil. Moderate water. Set out starts in spring. Excellent plant for cut flowers. Also, the cutting encourages more blooms. Nursery plants may take time to become established in hot arid environments.
Desert	*Sphaeralcea ambigua* globe mallow	Herbaceous perennial wildflower that produces a showy profusion of cup-shaped flowers on stems rising above 2-foot (0.6-m) ball of grayish green foliage. Orange is most common flower color, but pink, lavender and red also seen.	Sow seed (fall), place starts (spring), or set out nursery plants in full sun in any soil. Very low water once established. Cut back hard after flowering and remove older dead stems anytime. Usually gets woody after several years and loses looks. Replace with new plant.
Desert	*Tagetes lucida, Tagetes palmeri* Mexican tarragon, Mt. Lemmon marigold	Both types display aromatic foliage and golden yellow flowers that offer fall bloom. *T. lucida* is smaller, at 2-1/2 feet (0.8m) high and wide. *T. palmeri* can get to 5 feet (1.5m).	Place in full sun to light shade in slightly improved soil. Moderate water. Plants freeze back readily, but return quickly in spring. Short-lived.
Garden	*Tithonia rotundifolia* Mexican sunflower	Spectacular sunflowers with orange-scarlet rays and tufted yellow centers cover plant from July to frost, but foliage is coarse in appearance, if velvety to touch. May become a perennial shrub in favored situations.	Plant at edge of the garden in full sun in any soil where it will grow to 6 feet (1.8m) in a season, lower in tough situations. Sow seed or set starts in spring. Lower-growing varieties can be used effectively closer in, but all types freeze.
Garden	*Zephyranthes candida, Zephyranthes rosea* rain lily	Grown for crocuslike flowers (white or pink depending on variety) above rushlike glossy green leaves to 1 foot (0.3m) high and wide. White-flowered form has leaves reminiscent of chives.	Plant bulbs or starts late in summer or early fall in somewhat improved soil in full sun. Keep alternately wet and dry. Wildflowers appear after rain.

Hesperaloe funifera

Pistacia lentiscus

Asclepias linaria

Encelia farinosa

Callistemon citrinus

Convolvulus mauritanicus

Cupressus arizonica

Hibiscus rosa-sinensis

Cephalophyllum 'Red Spike'

Dietes bicolor

Plants with Special Uses

In any plant compendium, the authors wish to put in more plants than there is room for. There are many plants that deserve mention for specific reasons such as toughness, color or to fill a certain niche in the landscape. One way to tell about them is to chart them in a more abbreviated form.

In the chart that follows, plants are alphabetized by botanical name, with common names beneath. If you are looking for a common name, please check the index for its corresponding scientific name. To the right of the names are zone and temperature information, whether the plant is evergreen or deciduous, a description, cultural requirements and finally columns of special design uses the plant might fill. These listings are only suggestions. Use your own sense of design to use plants you like where you want them.

Anisodontea hypomandarum

Antigonon leptopus

Arundo donax

Name: Botanical Common	Zone, Temp. EG or deciduous (EG or D)	Description
Abelia grandiflora glossy abelia	All zones. 15F (-9C). Root hardy. **EG to D**	Graceful mounding garden shrub. Glossy, fine-textured, pointed leaves are dark green with a bronze cast. Small pinkish white bell-shaped flowers appear from early summer through fall. A moderate grower to 6 feet (1.8m), sometimes higher, spreading 5 feet (1.5m) or more unless trimmed.
Acanthus mollis acanthus, architect's plant, Grecian pattern plant	All zones. 25F (-4C). **Summer D**	This herbaceous perennial is the classical plant of Greek culture. Large, lustrous, deep green, deeply lobed leaves reach 2 feet (0.6m) in length, supported by purplish green stems. Spreads by underground rhizomes. Pale purple flowers on spikes rise 2 to 3 feet (0.6 to 0.9m) above the plant in early summer, which signals summer dormancy and disappearance until fall. 3 feet (0.9m) high, spreading to 6 feet (1.8m).
Albizia julibrissin silk tree, mimosa	All zones. Hardy to cold. Accepts heat. **D**	Small tree with a flat, spreading crown of bright green ferny leaves gives broken shade. May have a constant summer bloom of fuzzy pink flowers followed by papery seedpods, which hang on through winter. To 20 feet (6.1m) high, spreading to 15 feet (4.6m).
Anisodontea hypomandarum cape mallow	Low and middle zones and protected areas of high zone. 28F (-2C) **EG**	Fast-growing, free-blooming, somewhat open and rounded perennial shrubby plant with medium green leaves and pink hollyhocklike flowers, which appear in mild weather most of the year. Plants can be seen to 6 feet (1.8m) high and 4 to 5 feet (1.2 to 1.5m) wide, but usually less in arid zones. Plants kept too wet, with poor drainage, may damp off. Can withstand some drought.
Antigonon leptopus queen's wreath, coral vine, confederate vine, rosa de montana vine	All zones. Damaged at 32F (0C). Killed at 20F (-7C). Root hardy. **D**	A festive fast-growing tendril-climbing summer vine with shocking pink flowers. Festoons over fences, trellises and walls in the hottest locations. Gets bigger each year. Size varies. Dies to the ground most winters after frost, but rapidly regrows in spring. A fine vine for hot south and west sides, or as a shade cover over sun-sensitive plants.
Arbutus unedo strawberry tree	All zones, but best in high zone. 0F (-18C). **EG**	Slow-growing small tree, large shrub or dwarf that is worth fussing over. Decorative rough brown bark and lustrous dark green leaves. Clusters of small greenish white urn-shaped flowers are followed by decorative red and yellow strawberrylike fruit in fall and winter. Edible, but tasteless and mealy. Size varies with cultivar.
Artemisia 'Powis Castle' hybrid powis castle	All zones. Widely tolerant of all temperatures. **EG**	Small herbaceous perennial with wide gray to silver mound of feathery foliage. Dense in youth, more open and woody in age. To 2-1/2 feet (0.8m) high and 3 to 6 feet (0.9 to 1.8m) wide.
Arundo donax giant reed, carrizo, cana brava	All zones. 28F (-2C). Root hardy. **EG to dormant**	Tall, coarse bamboolike grass that grows rapidly 10 to 15 feet (3.1 to 4.6m) high, spreading by underground rhizomes to form large stands. Will spread rapidly in wet areas—contain by controlling moisture. Flat light green leaf blades hug the bamboolike vertical canes. Whitish plumes 2 feet (0.6m) long.
Asclepias linaria pineleaf milkweed	All zones. Low limit unknown. **EG**	Small perennial shrub that branches from the base. Dark needlelike leaves. White to greenish flowers in flat clusters at branch tips from spring to fall. Milkweed seeds float from split pods. Attracts butterflies.
Asclepias subulata desert milkweed	Low and middle zones. Low limit unknown. **EG**	This perennial open shrub has vertical light gray-green, mostly leafless, stems with small clusters of white to creamy flowers at stem tips, which open spring to fall, attract butterflies, and themselves look like resting butterflies. Pods release flying seeds in fall. To 4 feet (1.2m) high and 2 feet (0.6m) wide or wider.

Culture	Accents	Average Tree Size	Average Shrub Size	Ground Covers	Herbaceous (No woody parts)	Vines	Requires Shade	Best Wall Plants	Succulents	Special Effects
Soil: Improved. **Sun:** Open or broken shade to full sun. **Water:** Moderate. **Maintenance:** Periodic.			medium (6 feet; 1.8m high) to large (10 feet; 3.1m high)	✔			✔	✔		Woodsy Color Oasis
Soil: Improved, good drainage. **Sun:** Full open or filtered shade, or morning sun. **Water:** Ample. **Maintenance:** Periodic grooming.				✔	✔					Tropical Color Oasis Mediterranean
Soil: Improved. garden soil, with good drainage and depth. Avoid heavy clay. **Sun:** Full to reflected sun. **Water:** Moderate. **Maintenance:** Periodic.		small (to 20 feet; 6.1m)								Tropical Color Oasis
Soil: Improved, good drainage. **Sun:** Full sun in high zone, part sun to full sun in middle zone, filtered shade to part shade in low zone. **Water:** Moderate to occasional. **Maintenance:** Little.			small (to 3 ft.; 0.9m high) to medium (to 6 feet; 1.8m high)							Tropical Natural Rustic Transitional Color Oasis Containers
Soil: Tolerant. **Sun:** Full to reflected sun. **Water:** Moderate. **Maintenance:** Very little. Remove last summer's growth after frost.						needs support				Tropical Natural Rustic Color Mexican
Soil: Improved. Good drainage. **Sun:** Shade to part sun for desert regions; full to reflected sun near coast or in high zone. **Water:** Moderate, then occasional. **Maintenance:** Little.		small (to 20 feet; 6.1m)	medium (6 feet; 1.8m high) to large (10 feet; 3.1m high)							Mediterranean Woodsy Natural Rustic
Soil: Good drainage. **Sun:** Full sun. **Water:** Occasional. **Maintenance:** Little to none.			small (to 3 ft.; 0.9m high) to med. (to 6 feet; 1.8m high)							Mediterranean Natural, Rustic Transitional Color
Soil: Tolerant. **Sun:** Part shade to full or reflected sun. **Water:** Needs some to look good. **Maintenance:** None to periodic. Cut back old clumps.										Tropical Mediterranean Natural Rustic Transitional Mexican
Soil: Tolerant. Good drainage. **Sun:** Full sun. **Water:** Occasional. **Maintenance:** Low.			small (to 3 feet; 0.9m high)							Desert Natural Rustic Transitional
Soil: Tolerant. Good drainage. **Sun:** Full sun to part shade. **Water:** Moderate, then occasional. **Maintenance:** Little to none.	✔		medium (to 6 feet; 1.8m high)		✔				✔	Desert Natural Rustic Transitional

Aucuba japonica

Bulbine frutescens 'Hallmark'

Name: *Botanical* Common	Zone, Temp. EG or deciduous (EG or D)	Description
Aspidistra elatior cast-iron plant, barroom plant	All zones. Hardy to cold. **EG**	Distinctive wide leathery leaves are shiny, dark green and pointed, with parallel veins that arch upward and outward on grooved stalks. Slow grower spreads by underground rhizomes. Flowers inconspicuous. To 2-1/2 feet (0.8m) high by varying width. Perennial.
Aucuba japonica Japanese aucuba, Japanese laurel, gold-dust plant, 'Variegata'	All zones where protected from sun and wind. 5F (-15C). Takes heat if watered. **EG**	Slow-growing erect shrub to small tree. Dense, shiny gold-dotted foliage. 3 feet (0.9m) to 10 feet (3.1m) high, 3 to 8 feet (0.9 to 2.4m) wide, depending on cultivar.
Baccharis sarothroides desert broom, rosin bush, broom baccharis (male selections only)	All zones. Cold hardy. Revels in heat. **EG**	Bright green rounded shrub that grows easily in broken or disturbed soil. Tough and tolerant. Females reseed abundantly. Usually under 6 feet (1.8m) high and wide, depending on the situation. Plant male selections.
Buddleia davidii butterfly bush, summer lilac	All zones. Cold hardy. No wind. **D**	Large rangy shrub or small tree with long tapering dark green leaves. Fragrant densely clustered purple, pink or white flower spikes appear late spring to midsummer. Groom and shape. Fast-growing to 10 feet (3.1m) high and wide. Attracts butterflies.
Buddleia marrubifolia wooly butterfly bush	Low and middle zones. Protected areas of high zone. Low teens F (-11 to -12C). **EG**	Compact, dense, rounded shrub with gray to whitish velvety rounded leaves and tiny orange flowers in round clusters on and off over warm season. 3 to 6 feet (0.9 to 1.8m) high and wide. Attracts butterflies.
Bulbine frutescens bulbine	Low and middle zones. Protected areas of high zone. Mid to low teens F (-7 to -12C). Root hardy. **EG**	Cylindrical light green succulent leaves spread by rhizomes to form mound to 12 inches (30.5cm) high and 3 feet (0.9m) wide. Small yellow flowers on slender spikes rise above plant late winter into spring.
Calliandra californica red Baja fairy duster, fairy duster	Low and middle zones. 28F (-2C). Root hardy. **EG unless drought or cold D**	Mounding shrub with feathery leaves and bright red fringy flowers in warm weather and with enough water. Inconspicuous pods scatter seeds. 3 to 4 feet (0.9 to 1.2m) high and wide. Sometimes to 6 feet (1.8m). Attracts hummingbirds.
Calliandra eriophylla fairy duster, false mesquite	Low and middle zones. Cold hardy but will become deciduous. **EG to D drought or cold**	Mounding low-growing open desert plant with finely divided feathery leaves. Fringy pink, lavender or wine flowers appear in spring and after rains. Slender pods explode and scatter seeds. To 3 feet (0.9m) high, spreading up to 5 feet (1.5m).
Callistemon citrinus lemon bottlebrush, bottlebrush, scarlet bottlebrush	Low and middle zones. 20 F (-7C). **EG**	Picturesque erect, loose, open shrub to small tree. Narrow medium green leaves. Spectacular heavy bloom of red bottlebrushlike flowers appear along branches in spring and some over summer. Fast to moderate grower. Attracts hummingbirds.
Callistemon viminalis weeping bottlebrush	Low and middle zones. 20 F (-7C). **EG**	Erect to leaning and irregular tree with weeping branches and slender bronze-tinged dark green leaves. Dark red 6-inch (15.2-cm) long bottlebrushlike flowers in spring; some over summer. Moderate growth to 15 to 20 feet (4.6 to 6.1m) to eventual 30 feet (9.2m). Narrow crown about 1/3 as wide as height. Leaves burn in winter cold of middle zone. Attracts hummingbirds.

Calliandra eriophylla

Culture	Accents	Average Tree Size	Average Shrub Size	Ground Covers	Herbaceous (No woody parts)	Vines	Requires Shade	Best Wall Plants	Succulents	Special Effects
Soil: Tolerant. Good drainage. **Sun:** Deep to open shade. Partial sun. **Water:** Moderate to ample. **Maintenance:** None to periodic grooming, reseparating clumps, resetting in ground or in pots.					✔		✔			Tropical Oriental Containers
Soil: Improved. **Sun:** Full to open shade. **Water:** Ample. **Maintenance:** Periodic.		small (to 20 feet; 6.1m)	small (3 feet; 0.9m high) to large (10 feet; 3.1m high)				✔			Tropical Oriental Containers Color
Soil: Tolerant of alkaline to shallow. **Sun:** Part shade to full or reflected sun. **Water:** Once established, occasional to none. **Maintenance:** None to some.			medium (to 6 feet; 1.8m high)							Desert Transitional
Soil: Improved, good drainage. **Sun:** Broken shade, part shade, full sun. **Water:** Moderate. **Maintenance:** Periodic. Groom spent bloom and cut back in winter.			medium (6 feet; 1.8m high) to large (10 feet; 3.1m high)							Woodsy Natural Rustic Transitional Color
Soil: Tolerant. Good drainage. **Sun:** Part to full or reflected. **Water:** Occasional to moderate. **Maintenance:** Little to none.			small (3 feet; 0.9m high) to medium (6 feet; 1.8m high)							Desert Natural Rustic Transitional Color
Soil: Tolerant. Good drainage. **Sun:** Part shade to full sun. **Water:** Occasional to moderate. **Maintenance:** None to periodic.									✔	Desert Natural Rustic Transitional Containers Color
Soil: Tolerant. Improved. Good drainage. **Sun:** Full to reflected sun to part shade. **Water:** Moderate (for blooms) to occasional. **Maintenance:** Periodic.			small (3 feet; 0.9m high) to medium (6 feet; 1.8m high)							Tropical Desert Natural Rustic Color
Soil: Tolerant. Good drainage. **Sun:** Reflected to full sun to part shade. **Water:** Occasional. **Maintenance:** Periodic.			small (to 3 feet; 0.9m high)							Desert Natural Rustic Transitional Color
Soil: Improved. Good drainage. **Sun:** Full to reflected sun to part shade. **Water:** Occasional to moderate. **Maintenance:** Little to none.		small (to 20 feet; 6.1m)	medium (6 feet; 1.8m high) to large (10 feet; 3.1m high)					✔		Tropical Woodsy Natural Rustic Color
Soil: Improved to tolerant. Good drainage. **Sun:** Part shade to full or reflected sun. **Water:** Moderate. **Maintenance:** Periodic.		small (20 feet; 6.1m) to medium (40 feet; 12.2m)	large (to 10 feet; 3.1m high)							Tropical Woodsy Natural Rustic Transitional Color

Carpobrotus chilensis

Casuarina stricta

Name: **Botanical** Common	Zone, Temp. EG or deciduous (EG or D)	Description
Campsis radicans common trumpet creeper, trumpet creeper, trumpet vine, cow itch, trumpet honeysuckle	All zones. Tolerant of heat and cold. **D**	Fast-growing rampant vine. Self-attaching and spreading or sprawling, with summer green and stunning clusters of orange to red trumpet-shaped flowers that appear midsummer until frost. Can take root if it spreads across the ground. To 20, even 40 feet (6.1 to 12.2m) high and wide.
Carpobrotus chilensis Chilean ice plant, Pacific Coast sea fig	Low and middle zones. 28F (-2C). Accepts heat. **EG**	Creeping perennial ground cover for small to medium areas. Rosy pink summer flowers to and triangle-shaped succulent leaves. Fire-retardant. Takes seashore conditions. More refined than *C. edulis* (below). One plant to 3 to 4 inches (7.6 to 10.2cm) high, spreading up to 6 feet (1.8m).
Carpobrotus edulis hottentot fig, fig marigold, common ice plant	Low and middle zones. 28F (-2C). Accepts heat. **EG**	Succulent ground cover, coarser and larger in size than above, mounding to 1 foot to 1-1/2 feet (0.3 to 0.5m) high with spreading 3-foot (0.9-m) long branches that root as they go. Yellowish pink or lavender flowers appear spring into summer. Fire hazard. Takes shore conditions.
Casuarina cunninghamiana Australian pine	Middle and high zones. 15F (-9C). **EG**	Fast-growing, erect, slender tree with dark bark and dark gray-green jointed branchlets that resemble pine needles. Good for many uses in tough situations: heat, drought, wind, poor soil.
Casuarina equisetifolia horsetail tree, south sea ironwood, mile tree	Low zone. 25F (-4C). **EG**	Fast-growing to as high as 80 feet (24.4m) in favorable conditions, and 30 to 40 feet (9.2 to 12.2m) wide. Tolerates shore conditions, brackish water, alkaline or salty soils, sand dunes, and other tough situations, but not cold.
Casuarina stricta beefwood, she oak	Low and middle zones. 15F (-9C). **EG**	Fast-growing to 20 to 30 feet (6.1 to 9.2m) high and 10 to 20 feet (3.1 to 6.1m) wide. Slender open form takes wind.
Celtis pallida desert hackberry, spiny hackberry, granjeno	All zones. 20F (-7C). Recovers fast. **EG to drought and cold D**	This densely branched, thorny, desert shrub with rough gray-green leaves grows slowly to 3 to 10 feet (0.9 to 3.1m) high and as wide. Barrier. Attracts birds.
Cephalophyllum 'Red Spike' red spike	Low and middle zones. 28F (-2C). **D**	Small clumping perennial ground-hugging cover to 15 to 18 inches wide (38.1 to 45.7cm). Upward-pointing bronze-tipped succulent leaves reach no more than 5 inches (12.7cm) high at the most. Stunning late winter display of 2-inch (5.1-cm) wide cerise red flowers.
Cercis canadensis eastern redbud, redbud	Middle and high zones. Hardy. **D**	Spectacular spring-flowering tree. Magenta blossoms profuse on bare tree before leaves come out. Pods may follow. Can grow to 20 to 30 feet (6.1 to 9.2m) high and as wide, but usually smaller because of soils. Gold in fall.
Cercis canadensis mexicana Mexican redbud	Middle and high zones. Hardy. **D**	Similar to above, this plant tolerates poor rocky soil with good drainage. Drought resistant. Grows to 10 to 15 feet (3.1 to 4.6m) high as shrub or patio tree.

Cercis canadensis

Culture	Accents	Average Tree Size	Average Shrub Size	Ground Covers	Herbaceous (No woody parts)	Vines	Requires Shade	Best Wall Plants	Succulents	Special Effects
Soil: Tolerant. **Sun:** Part shade, full or reflected sun. **Water:** Moderate in summer, occasional in winter. **Maintenance:** Periodic.						self-climbing				Tropical Woodsy Natural Rustic Transitional Color
Soil: Good drainage. **Sun:** Part shade, full or reflected sun. **Water:** Occasional. **Maintenance:** Periodic.			small (to 3 feet; 0.9m high)	✔	✔				✔	Natural Rustic Transitional Color
Soil: Good drainage. **Sun:** Part shade, full or reflected sun. **Water:** Occasional. **Maintenance:** Periodic.			small (to 3 feet; 0.9m high)	✔	✔				✔	Natural Rustic Transitional Color
Soil: Tolerant. Best with improved. **Sun:** Part shade to full or reflected sun. **Water:** Established trees can survive with 10 inches (254mm) annual rainfall. Best with occasional. **Maintenance:** Periodic to none.		medium (to 40 feet; 12.2m) to tall (to 80 feet; 24.4m) Skyline								Woodsy Natural Rustic Transitional
Soil: Tolerant. Best with improved. **Sun:** Part shade to full or reflected sun. **Water:** Established trees can survive with 10 inches (254mm) annual rainfall. Best with occasional. **Maintenance:** Periodic to none.		medium (to 40 feet; 12.2m) to tall (to 80 feet; 24.4m) Skyline								Woodsy Natural Rustic Transitional
Soil: Tolerant. Best with improved. **Sun:** Part shade to full or reflected sun. **Water:** Established trees can survive with 10 inches (254mm) annual rainfall. Best with occasional. **Maintenance:** Periodic to none.		medium (to 40 feet; 12.2m)								Woodsy Natural Rustic Transitional
Soil: Tolerant. Good drainage. **Sun:** Part shade to full or reflected sun. **Water:** Occasional to start. None once established in areas with 10 inches (254mm) or more annual rainfall. **Maintenance:** Little to none.		small (to 20 feet; 6.1m)	large (to 10 feet; 3.1m high)							Desert Woodsy Natural Rustic Transitional
Soil: Tolerant. Good drainage. **Sun:** Full sun to part shade. **Water:** Moderate for bloom to occasional. **Maintenance:** Periodic.				✔					✔	Natural Rustic Containers Color
Soil: Improved soil. Good drainage. **Sun:** Part shade to full sun. **Water:** Moderate to ample. **Maintenance:** Periodic.		small (to 20 feet; 6.1m)	large (to 10 feet; 3.1m high)							Woodsy Natural Rustic Color
Soil: Improved soil. Good drainage. **Sun:** Part shade to full sun. **Water:** Moderate to ample, good drainage. **Maintenance:** Periodic.		small (to 20 feet; 6.1m)	large (to 10 feet; 3.1m high)							Woodsy Natural Rustic Transitional Color

Cereus peruvianus

Convolvulus cneorum

Cortaderia selloana

Name: Botanical Common	Zone, Temp. EG or deciduous (EG or D)	Description
Cereus peruvianus and **C. p. 'Monstrosus'** monstrous Peruvian cereus, Peruvian cereus, Peruvian apple, totempole cactus	Low and middle zones, or inside anywhere. 28F (-2C). **EG**	Columnar spiny succulents gradually make clumps of columns to 20 feet (6.1m) high, spreading to 15 feet (4.6m), and to 4 inches (10.2cm) in diameter. Grows faster in friendly spots with warm shade and moderate water. 'Monstrosus' is slower, to 10 feet (3.1m) high, with clumps to 8 feet (2.4m) wide. Has irregular bumpy columns and no spines. Best sheltered.
Cissus trifoliata Arizona grape ivy, Sonoran grape ivy	Low and middle zones. Root hardy. **D to EG**	Sprawling tendril-climbing vine with shiny grape-shaped leaves and drought-tolerant tuberous roots. Protect skin from irritating sap when cutting. Can be invasive as runners root and spread over moist soil. Reaches 10 to 20 feet (3.1 to 6.1m) high and wide.
Clytostoma callistegioides violet trumpet vine, love charm	Low and middle zones. Damaged at 28F (-2C), killed at 20F (-7C). Root hardy. **EG to D**	Woody tendril-climbing vine with shiny medium green leaves and a profuse bloom of large lavender trumpets in spring. With support, can cover area 12 by 20 feet (3.7 to 6.1m). Good on posts. Somewhat temperamental.
Convolvulus cneorum silver bush morning glory	All zones. 15F (-9C). Recovers fast. **EG**	This perennial forms mounds to as high as 2 feet (0.6m) and as wide as 3 feet (0.9m). Silky silver leaves. Small white morning glories in spring, a scattering over the entire warm season.
Convolvulus mauritanicus ground morning glory, Morocco glorybind	All zones. 15F (-9C). Recovers fast. **EG**	Low perennial plant, continuously blooming in warm weather, with gray-green foliage and little blue-lavender flowers. Reaches 6 to 11 feet (1.8 to 3.4m) high and spreads 2 feet (0.6m). Heaviest bloom in spring.
Cortaderia selloana pampas grass, selloa pampas grass	All zones. 28F (-2C) Root hardy. Recovers fast. Revels in heat. **EG**	Giant perennial grass of the South American pampas quickly forms a fountain of cascading leaves up to 10 feet (3.1m) high and 7 feet (2.1m) wide or wider. Ribbonlike slender bright green leaves with sharp edges and erect plumy straw-colored flowers on 3- to 4-foot (0.9- to 1.2-m) stalks above foliage last for months. Pink to lavender plume forms available. Check to see if plant escapes as pest in your area.
Cotinus coggygria smoke tree	All zones. Best in high. Hardy. **D**	Shrub or tree with distinctively spaced roundish leaves, bluish green turning to orange-red and yellow in fall. Some cultivars have purple foliage. Wide urn shape may eventually become tree 25 feet (7.6m) high and wide. Fading sterile flowers elongate into fuzzy purple hairs that look like smoke.
Cupressus arizonica Arizona cypress, rough-barked Arizona cypress	All zones. Tolerant of heat and cold. **EG**	Trees range from tall and pyramidal to flat and broad or globe-shaped. Colors may be silvery to dark or gray-green. Scaly foliage to the ground can be trimmed up. Fissured to checkered bark. Fast growers to 20 to 50 feet (6.1 to 15.2m) high and 15 to 25 feet (4.6 to 7.6m) wide.
Cupressus sempervirens 'Stricta' Italian cypress	All zones. 10F (-12C). Revels in heat. **EG**	Tall, erect, stately skyline tree clothed nearly to ground with dense, dark, scaly foliage. The natural form is rangy with lateral branches. Cultivars of different colors, forms and sizes are available. Moderate growers to 60 or even 80 feet (18.3 to 24.4m), with a diameter at the widest part of no more than 10 feet (3.1m), often much less. Inconspicuous flowers and tiny round cones are unimportant.

Culture	Accents	Average Tree Size	Average Shrub Size	Ground Covers	Herbaceous (No woody parts)	Vines	Requires Shade	Best Wall Plants	Succulents	Special Effects
Soil: Good drainage. **Sun:** Full sun, part sun, open to filtered shade. Yellows in reflected sun. **Water:** Occasional. **Maintenance:** Little to none.	✔								✔	Tropical Desert Containers
Soil: Tolerant. Good drainage. **Sun:** Full sun to part shade. **Water:** Once established, occasional to none. **Maintenance:** Little to none.						self-climbing				Tropical Desert Woodsy Natural Rustic
Soil: Improved. Good drainage. **Sun:** Open shade, filtered or part sun. **Water:** Moderate. **Maintenance:** Periodic. Garden care.						needs support				Tropical Woodsy Natural Rustic Color
Soil: Tolerant. Good drainage. **Sun:** Part, full or reflected sun. **Water:** Moderate to occasional. **Maintenance:** Little except to prevent invasions of grass or other plants.			small (to 3 feet; 0.9m high)		✔					Mediterranean Tropical Natural, Rustic Containers Color
Soil: Tolerant. Good drainage. **Sun:** Part, full or reflected sun. **Water:** Moderate to occasional. **Maintenance:** Little except to prevent invasions of grass or other plants.				✔	✔					Mediterranean Transitional Formal/clipped Color Oasis
Soil: Tolerant. **Sun:** Part shade to full or reflected sun. **Water:** Moderate to occasional. **Maintenance:** Periodic.	✔				✔					Tropical Natural Rustic
Soil: Improved. Good drainage. **Sun:** Full sun. **Water:** Moderate. **Maintenance:** Periodic.		medium (to 40 feet; 12.2m)	medium (6 feet; 1.8m high) to large (10 feet; 3.1m high)							Oriental Natural Rustic Color Woodsy
Soil: Tolerant. Good drainage **Sun:** Full to reflected sun. **Water:** Occasional. **Maintenance:** None.		medium (to 40 feet; 12.2m) to tall (to 80 feet; 24.4m) Skyline								Woodsy Natural Rustic
Soil: Tolerant. Good drainage. **Sun:** Full to reflected sun. **Water:** Moderate to occasional. **Maintenance:** Little. Spider mites sometimes a problem.	✔	medium (to 40 feet; 12.2m) to tall (to 80 feet; 24.4m) Skyline								Mediterranean Formal/clipped

Cycas revoluta

Cyperus alternifolius

Echinocactus grusonii

Name: **Botanical** Common	Zone, Temp. EG or deciduous (EG or D)	Description
Cycas revoluta sago palm, Japanese fern, cycad	Low and middle zones. Protected areas of high zone. Damaged at 15 to 20F (-9 to -7C), but survives to 5F (-15C). Root hardy. **EG**	Small-scale palmlike to fernlike plant with shiny dark green feathery fronds closely set with sharply pointed leaflets. Old plants may form clump with two or more heads. Taller plant with frond stumps looks like miniature palm. May produce seed cone in center, then continue to grow. Adapt plants to sun in middle zone by covering with shade cloth on stakes first summer. Heads are 3 to 6 feet (0.9 to 1.8m) in diameter. Trunks to 8 feet (2.4m) high.
Cyperus alternifolius umbrella plant, umbrella palm, umbrella sedge	Low and middle zones. 28F (-2C). Recovers fast. **EG to D**	Unusual grasslike perennial sedge that grows fast to 4 to 5 feet (1.2 to 1.5m) high and gradually spreads by woody rhizomes about 6 feet (1.8m). Flat leaf blades fan out umbrellalike at top of rounded stem. May have a circlet of tiny yellowish flowers around the center of the umbrella each spring. Cut back frost-damaged plants. There is a dwarf selection, if you want a smaller plant.
Dietes (Moraea) species fortnight lily, African iris	Low zone and warmer areas of middle zone. 28F (-2C). Root hardy. Recovers fast. **EG**	Rhizominous plant forms large clumps of slender irislike leaves to 3 feet (0.9m) high. Clumps as wide. Spring to summer irislike blooms come intermittently on tall stalks just above branch tips. *D. bicolor* has yellow flowers. *D. vegeta* has whitish flowers with orange and brown blotches and some purple stippling. Do not remove branching flower stems because it will bloom again from the same stem each year. Cut off spent flowers individually. There are some named varieties and hybrids.
Drosanthemum floribundum rosea ice plant	Shore in low zone. Middle zone. 28F (-2C). **EG**	A succulent ground cover of moderate growth to no more than 6 inches high (15.2cm), each plant spreading to only 18 inches (45.7cm) or so wide. Cylindrical leaves are covered with minute glistening bumps that reflect the sun. The plant trails from the base, making a dense mat. Small pink flowers put on a show in spring.
Echinocactus grusonii golden barrel	Low and middle zones. Protected areas of high zone. Mid 20s F (-3 to -5C). **EG**	Succulent light green barrel cactus with yellow spines grows slowly to up to 4 feet (1.2m) high and 2-1/2 feet (0.8m) wide. May spawn offsets, making a clump. Dramatic when massed.
Elaeagnus angustifolia oleaster, Russian wild olive, silver berry tree	High zone. Cold hardy. **D**	This is a sturdy tree in cold and windy areas, where many plants have trouble growing. Growth is moderate to 20 feet (6.1m) high with a spread of 15 feet (4.6m) in favorable situations. In tough conditions it may remain a shrub. It can be kept to any size in the garden. The form, color and fruit are reminiscent of the true olive, although leaves are more willowlike. The angular, often spiny structure is covered with shredding bark and supports slender gray-green leaves, which are silvery beneath. Small yellowish fragrant flowers appear in spring, followed by small inedible olivelike fruit. This native of Europe and western Asia is tolerant to wind, drought, cold and poor soil.
Encelia farinosa brittlebush, incienso	Low zone and warmer parts of middle zone. Top-kill in high 20s F (-3 to -1C). Survives to 15F (-10C). **EG**	Shrubby perennial with whitish green triangular leaves on rounded form and masses of yellow daisies above the foliage in spring, sometimes also after summer rains. Survives but unsightly for a period in drought or from frost.

Culture	Accents	Average Tree Size	Average Shrub Size	Ground Covers	Herbaceous (No woody parts)	Vines	Requires Shade	Best Wall Plants	Succulents	Special Effects
Soil: Improved. Good drainage. **Sun:** Full, open or filtered sun or part shade. Can adapt to full sun in middle zone, even in the low zone with gradual hardening off. **Water:** Moderate to ample. Old plants can take periods of occasional. **Maintenance:** Little.	✔	small (to 20 feet; 6.1m)								Tropical Oriental Containers
Soil: Tolerant. Prefers moist garden soil. **Sun:** Filtered or open shade. Part, full, or reflected sun. **Water:** Ample to occasional. **Maintenance:** Periodic.					✔					Tropical Oriental Containers Mediterranean
Soil: Improved. Good drainage **Sun:** Full sun to part shade. **Water:** Moderate to ample. **Maintenance:** Little.	✔		small (to 3 feet; 0.9m high)		✔					Tropical Woodsy Oriental Natural Rustic Containers
Soil: Improved. Good drainage. **Sun:** Full sun on coast. Part shade inland. **Water:** Occasional. **Maintenance:** Periodic. Weeds can be a problem.				✔					✔	Natural Rustic Color
Soil: Good drainage. **Sun:** Full sun to part or filtered shade. **Water:** Occasional. **Maintenance:** Little to none.	✔								✔	Desert Transitional Containers Color
Soil: Tolerant. Grows best in a light, improved garden soil. Needs a heavy soil to anchor its roots if used as a windscreen. **Sun:** Reflected sun. **Water:** Moderate for fastest growth. Accepts occasional to none where rainfall is 12 inches (305mm) or more a year, but it will probably remain small. **Maintenance:** Periodic to none, depending on situation.		small (to 20 feet; 6.1m)	medium (6 feet; 1.8m high) to large (10 feet; 3.1m high)							Woodsy Natural Rustic Color
Soil: Good drainage. **Sun:** Full to reflected sun. **Water:** Occasional to moderate. **Maintenance:** None to some.			small (to 3 feet; 0.9m high)							Desert Natural Rustic Transitional Color

Eremophila 'Valentine™'

Euphorbia rigida

Fatshedera lizei

Name: *Botanical* Common	Zone, Temp. EG or deciduous (EG or D)	Description
Ensete ventricosum abyssinian banana	Low and middle zones. 28F (-2C). Recovers fast. No wind. **EG**	An exuberant colorful bananalike perennial plant with a brown to purple trunklike stem that flares from the base and wide bananalike leaves on arching stalks. In warm humidity, plants can get to 20 feet (6.1m) tall with a 15-foot (4.6-m) spread. At three to five years, unimportant blooms signal death of plant. Only for sheltered areas.
Eracameria laricifolia turpentine bush	All zones. Cold and heat tolerant. **EG**	Mounding dense shrub that grows slowly to 3 feet (0.9m) high and wide. Tolerates difficult hot situations. Needlelike dark green foliage with turpentine scent. Long fall bloom of small bright yellow daisies in clusters. White seed heads.
Eremophila 'Valentine™' emu bush	Low and middle zones. 18F (-8C). **EG**	A rounded shrub up to 4 feet (1.2m) high and wide with small dark gray-green leaves that may tinge red in winter. Dark green tubular flowers appear in January, go to at least April, and sometimes all summer. Faster in low zone. There are other emu plants available.
Euonymus japonica euonymus, spindletree	All zones. Hardy. Revels in heat. **EG**	Not popular at present, but a good tough plant covered densely with toothed, shiny thick, dark green leaves. Amazingly drought and heat resistant and durable even in poor soil and cold to below zero. Moderate grower to 8 to 10 feet (2.4 to 3.1m) high, spreading 6 feet (1.8m) or more. There are variegated forms as well as cultivars. Subject to powdery mildew where air circulation is poor. Do not water foliage.
Euphorbia pulcherrima poinsettia, Christmas star, Christmas flower, painted leaf	Low zone and protected areas of middle zone. Anywhere as houseplant. 28F (-2C). **EG to D**	Can become a large loose shrub to 10 feet (3.1m) high in frost-free areas (or in a little garden pocket) with flamboyant red bracts in December every year. Flowers are the little yellow things in the center. Leaves may drop after bloom as plant "rests." Or bracts and leaves may hang on with only some leaf drop before new growth begins. Plants saved from previous season need twelve hours of dark to start new red bracts. Best with temperatures in low 60s F (15 to 17C). There are pink and white selections. Plant outside only in warm areas, but frosted stump recovers quickly in spring.
Euphorbia rigida gopher plant, South African perennial euphorbia bush	Low and middle zones. Protected areas of high zone. 28F (-2C). **EG**	Succulent perennial with pointed chartreuse leaves, creating a striking pattern on vertical stems that splay out from the base to 2 feet (0.6m) or higher and eventually 3 feet (0.9m) wide. Showy chartreuse brachts and blooms touched with orange appear at stem ends late winter to early spring. Stems die back as seed matures and new stems arise simultaneously from base.
Fatshedera lizei botanical wonder, aralia ivy, ivy tree	All zones. 10F (-12C). **EG**	Partly erect to partly sprawling or climbing. Bold rich dark green leaves vary in size and form. Plants make an undulating and uneven ground cover or may be tied to a support to climb—or both.
Fatsia japonica Japanese aralia, formosa rice tree, paper tree	All zones. 20F (-7C). **EG**	Striking plant with extraordinarily large, rich green fanlike leaves that have a tropical appearance. Moderate to fast grower to as high as 20 feet (6.1m), but seldom seen over 5 to 6 feet (1.5 to 1.8m) in these zones. Older plants have woody stems and multiple trunks. Whitish flowers in ball-like clusters appear in fall and winter above foliage.
Gardenia jasminoides 'Veitchii' veitch gardenia	All zones. 20F (-7C). **EG**	*Gardenias* are plants to fuss over. Many cultivars exist. Most successful is the dwarf form *G. j.* 'Veitchii,' with small shiny medium to dark green leaves and very fragrant white spring flowers. Grows at a moderate rate to 3 feet (0.9m) high and wide.

Culture	Accents	Average Tree Size	Average Shrub Size	Ground Covers	Herbaceous (No woody parts)	Vines	Requires Shade	Best Wall Plants	Succulents	Special Effects
Soil: Improved. Good drainage. **Sun:** Open to filtered shade to part sun. **Water:** Ample. **Maintenance:** Periodic grooming to remove old leaves.	✔				✔					Tropical
Soil: Tolerant. **Sun:** Full sun. **Water:** Occasional. **Maintenance:** Little to none as desired.			small (to 3 feet; 0.9m high)							Desert Natural, Rustic Transitional Color
Soil: Good drainage. **Sun:** Full. **Water:** Occasional. **Maintenance:** Periodic.			small (3 feet; 0.9m high) to medium (6 feet; 1.8m high)							Natural Rustic Containers Color
Soil: Tolerant. Good drainage. **Sun:** Full or reflected sun. **Water:** Occasional to moderate. **Maintenance:** None to periodic.			large (to 10 feet; 3.1m high)					✔		Formal/clipped Containers Oasis
Soil: Improved. Good drainage. **Sun:** Full sun, part or open shade. **Water:** Moderate to occasional. **Maintenance:** Periodic to little. A lot for an attractive plant that will produce lots of blooms.			large (to 10 feet; 3.1m high)							Tropical Containers Color Mexican
Soil: Good drainage. **Sun:** Full sun to part shade. **Water:** Occasional. **Maintenance:** Periodic.	✔		small (to 3 feet; 0.9m high)		✔				✔	Desert Natural Rustic Containers Color
Soil: Improved. Good drainage. **Sun:** Part sun to filtered, open or total shade. **Water:** Moderate to ample. **Maintenance:** Periodic.				✔		needs support	✔	✔		Tropical Containers
Soil: Improved. Good drainage. **Sun:** Full, filtered or open shade. **Water:** Moderate to ample. **Maintenance:** Periodic.	✔		medium (to 6 feet; 1.8m high) to large (to 10 feet; 3.1m high)		✔		✔			Tropical Containers
Soil: Improved. Good drainage. **Sun:** Filtered to open shade to part sun. **Water:** Ample. **Maintenance:** Constant care.			small (to 3 feet; 0.9m high)							Tropical Formal/clipped Containers Color

Hardenbergia violacea

Justicia candicans

Larrea tridentata

Name: *Botanical* Common	Zone, Temp. EG or deciduous (EG or D)	Description
Hardenbergia violacea lilac vine, hardenbergia	All zones. Low limit not known. **EG**	A shrubby, twining, open and rangy vine with long, narrow medium green coarsely textured leaves and purple to pink or white flower spikes late winter into early spring. Moderate growth to 10 feet (3.1m) high and wide.
Hesperaloe funifera giant hesperaloe	Low and middle zones. 5F (-15C). **EG**	Numerous narrow, unarmed, lime green strap-like leaves with white threads radiate outward. Grows slowly to moderately, forming a bold clump to 6 feet (1.8m) high and wide. From spring into summer, dramatic stalks rise 8, sometimes 15 feet (2.4 to 4.6m) high, bearing green and white bell-shaped flowers above foliage. Old plants bloom twice.
Hibiscus rosa-sinensis Chinese hibiscus, Hawaiian hibiscus, rose-of-China, China rose	Low zone and protected areas of middle zone. 28F to 25F (2 to -4C). **EG**	Erect shrubs with almost continual bloom of large bright flowers. Single and double forms exist in many colors: red, pink, white, yellow, orange, variegated. Plants vary in size depending on selection and environment from dwarf to 4 to 6 feet (1.2 to 1.8m) to more than 8 to 10 feet (2.4 to 3.1m) high and wide.
Ilex vomitoria 'Stokes' dwarf yaupon, cassina	Middle and high zones. Cold hardy. **EG**	Rarely used sturdy small shrub that is dense, finely twigged, deep green and good for low planting or clipped box hedge. Thornless toothed elliptical leaves. Tiny whitish spring flowers in small clusters on wood from previous year may produce small scarlet berries in fall. Grows at a moderate rate to no more than 30 feet (9.2m) high and wide.
Justicia brandegeana shrimp plant, rattlesnake plant, false hop	Low and middle zones. 25F (-4C). Root hardy. **EG**	Herbaceous perennial sprawling plant with soft, fuzzy medium green oval leaves and coppery bract blooms in warm weather that look like shrimp. Can grow to 3 feet (0.9m) high and 4 feet (1.2m) wide. One form has chartreuse bract blooms.
Justicia candicans red Mexican honeysuckle, hummingbird bush, red justicia, red jacobinia	Low and middle zones. 25F (-4C). **EG**	Neat perennial shrub that grows at a moderate rate to as much as 5 feet (1.5m) high and 3 feet (0.9m) wide. Rounded, hairy bright green heart-shaped leaves. Red orange to red tubular flowers at stem tips appear in fall to spring in warm areas.
Justicia fulvicoma summer glory	Low and middle zones. **EG**	Herbaceous plant of moderate to fast growth to 2 feet (0.6m) high and 3 feet (0.9m) wide in a compact form with soft medium green leaves. Interesting blooms that look like stacks of paper and vary in color from orange to reddish brown are actually red-orange tubular flowers stacked between large, triangular, reddish brown bracts. The bloom starts any time in summer and continues until cold, when it turns brown. A good underplant to trees.
Larrea tridentata creosote bush, greasewood, guamis	All zones. Cold hardy. Revels in heat. **EG**	This shrub is the archetypical desert plant, surviving on as little as 3 inches (762mm) of annual rainfall. Bright green, olive green to dull yellow green, depending on water. 3 to 6 feet (0.9 to 1.8m) high or even higher and as wide. Small yellow flowers in spring produce fuzzy white seed balls. May bloom again after summer rains. Excellent for desert repair or screen to play an area down.
Laurus nobilis Grecian laurel, daphne, sweet bay	Low and middle zones. 20F (-7C). **EG**	Deep green tree of legend grows at a slow to moderate rate to 15 to 20 feet (4.6 to 6.1m) high with conical form and usually several trunks like a big shrub. Long, shiny, leathery leaves are the bay leaves of cookery. May have small yellowish spring flowers followed by dark inedible berries.

Culture	Accents	Average Tree Size	Average Shrub Size	Ground Covers	Herbaceous (No woody parts)	Vines	Requires Shade	Best Wall Plants	Succulents	Special Effects
Soil: Improved. Good drainage. **Sun:** Part to full sun. **Water:** Moderate to occasional. **Maintenance:** Periodic.						needs support		✔		Tropical Woodsy Natural, Rustic Color
Soil: Good drainage. **Sun:** Full sun. **Water:** Occasional to none. **Maintenance:** Periodic to little.	✔									Tropical Desert Transitional Containers Color
Soil: Improved. Good drainage **Sun:** Part shade to full sun. **Water:** Moderate. **Maintenance:** Seasonal.			small (3 feet; 0.9m high) to large (10 feet; 3.1m high)							Tropical Containers Color
Soil: Tolerant. Good drainage. **Sun:** Open to filtered shade. Part to full sun. **Water:** Moderate to ample. **Maintenance:** Little.		small (to 20 feet; 6.1m) to medium (40 feet; 12.1m)	small (3 feet; 0.9m high) to large (10 feet; 3.1m high)							Formal/clipped Containers Oasis
Soil: Improved. Good drainage **Sun:** Open or filtered shade to part sun. **Water:** Moderate. **Maintenance:** Periodic.			small (to 3 feet; 0.9m high)		✔					Tropical Woodsy Natural, Rustic Containers Color
Soil: Tolerant to improved. Good drainage. **Sun:** Filtered to part shade. **Water:** Occasional to moderate. **Maintenance:** Little.			small (3 feet; 0.9m high) to med. (6 feet; 1.8m high)							Tropical Desert, Woodsy Natural, Rustic Containers Color
Soil: Improved. Good drainage **Sun:** Filtered to part shade. **Water:** Moderate to occasional. **Maintenance:** Periodic.			small (to 3 feet; 0.9m high)							Tropical Woodsy Natural Rustic Containers Color Oasis
Soil: Tolerant. **Sun:** Part, full or reflected sun. **Water:** Occasional to none. **Maintenance:** None required.			small (3 feet; 0.9m high) to medium (6 feet; 1.8m high)							Desert Natural Rustic Color
Soil: Improved. Good drainage **Sun:** Full, filtered or part shade. **Water:** Moderate to occasional. **Maintenance:** Periodic.		small (to 20 feet; 6.1m)								Mediterranean Woodsy Formal/clipped Containers Oasis

Lavandula species

Lycianthes rantonnei

Musa paradisiaca

Name: *Botanical* Common	Zone, Temp. EG or deciduous (EG or D)	Description
Lavandula **species** lavender, French lavender, English lavender, Spanish lavender	All zones. Best in middle and high. Tolerant in these zones. **EG**	English and French are the most popular, but Spanish may be better adapted to hot arid places. All are small perennials, have grayish foliage and somewhat similar spiky and mostly purplish flowers. All are aromatic. Some plants seem to languish in summer heat, possibly from root fungus caused by damp soil. *L. dentate* to 3 feet (0.9m) high and wide. *L. angustifolia* to 4 feet (1.2m) high and wide. *L. stoechas* to 1-1/2 feet (0.5m) high and 3 feet (0.9m) wide. To harvest flowers for sachets, cut the stalks or skim off the flowers just as the flower color shows. Dry in a cool dry place. Bouquets hung upside down from rafters are a classic look.
Liriope muscari lilyturf, big blue lilyturf, variegated lilyturf	All zones. Tolerant of heat and cold. **EG**	Herbaceous perennial underplants with slender dark green grasslike leaves that grow upward and outward from the base. Slender spikes with tiny purplish flowers rise a few inches above foliage in late summer. Several cultivars vary in size. The variegated form, with white edges, is most common.
Lophocereus schottii and *L. s. forma* **'Monstrosus'** senita, totem pole cactus	Low and middle zones. Protected areas of high zone. Low 20s to high teens F (-5 to -8C). Cover tops below 28F (-2C). **EG**	Bold, vertical, medium green, somewhat spiny columns with five to seven flutes that get to 10 feet (3.1m) high, spreading as wide over time. Whiskerlike spines develop at top foot or more of old mature plants. *L. s. f.* 'Monstrosus' has bumpy medium green columns that eventually reach the same height and spread as above over many years unless restrained. Can be rooted from cuttings.
Lycianthes rantonnei Paraguayan nightshade	Low zone and warmer parts of middle zone. Damaged at 28F (-2C). **EG**	Perennial medium green shrubby vine or vinelike shrub with deep purple spring flowers. Grows fast to 6 to 8 feet (1.8 to 2.4m) high as a shrub or 12 to 15 feet (3.7 to 4.6m) high as a vine or mounding. Compact cultivars with longer bloom seasons are available.
Malephora crocea gray ice plant	Low and middle zones. 28F (-2C). Recovers fast. **EG**	Perennial succulent with colorful flowers. Makes a fast dense mound 6 to 12 inches (15.2 to 30.5cm) high, trailing to 6 feet (1.8m), with gray-green smooth leaves that angle upward. Yellow-centered red to orange spring flowers with scattered bloom appear over warm season. Hardier than other ice plants.
Melianthus major South African honey bush, honey bush	Low zone and warmer parts of middle zone. 12F (-11C). **EG**	Soft-wooded, bold-foliaged, fast-growing, sprawling gray-green plant to 12 to 14 feet (3.7 to 4.3m) high and 10 feet (3.1m) wide, but easily controlled. Striking, deeply serrated, felty leaves. Red-brown bloom stalks to 12 inches (30.5cm) high rise above foliage and nod with pyramidal flower clusters at the tips.
Musa paradisiaca edible banana, plantain	Low zone and protected areas of middle zone. Foliage damaged at 30F (-1C). Mulched roots have survived much lower temperatures. **EG**	Palmlike fast-growing banana trees are the essence of the tropics. Thin, wide, bright green leaves arch out at top of slender, succulent treelike trunks. Plants grow in clumps from fleshy base that spreads out indefinitely. Leaves can get to 8 feet (2.4m) long by 2 feet (0.6m) wide on larger plants in favorable situations. Stalks mature with blossoms and fruit if in a frost-free location (remove spent stalks). New plants spring from basal clump each year and mature rapidly. There are many cultivars of different sizes, including dwarfs, and with different fruit production. Plants that bloom in June can have ripe fruit in early to mid fall. Plants do best in junglelike environments with heat, humidity, and protection from wind. Leaves freeze in the middle zone, but stalks do not and growth quickly resumes when warm weather returns.

Culture	Accents	Average Tree Size	Average Shrub Size	Ground Covers	Herbaceous (No woody parts)	Vines	Requires Shade	Best Wall Plants	Succulent	Special Effects
Soil: Good drainage. **Sun:** Part to broken shade in hot areas. **Water:** Occasional. Irrigate twice a week in summer, weekly in winter. **Maintenance:** Prune immediately after bloom to keep plants compact. Little or no fertilizer unless plants become chlorotic from overwatering. Give nitrogen and iron chelate.			small (3 feet; 0.9m high) to medium (6 feet; 1.8m high)							Mediterranean Natural Rustic Formal/clipped Containers Color
Soil: Improved. Good drainage. **Sun:** Open, filtered or part shade. **Water:** Moderate to ample. **Maintenance:** Little to periodic.					✔		✔			Tropical Woodsy Oriental Containers
Soil: Tolerant. Good drainage. **Sun:** Part shade to full sun. **Water:** Occasional. **Maintenance:** Little to none.	✔								✔	Desert Containers
Soil: Improved. Good drainage **Sun:** Full sun. **Water:** Ample to occasional. **Maintenance:** Periodic.			medium (6 feet; 1.8m high) to large (10 feet; 3.1m high)					✔		Tropical Woodsy Natural, Rustic Containers Color
Soil: Improved. Good drainage. **Sun:** Full sun to part shade. **Water:** Occasional. **Maintenance:** Little.				✔					✔	Tropical Desert Natural Rustic Color
Soil: Improved. Good drainage **Sun:** Open, filtered to part shade. Sun by the coast. **Water:** Moderate to occasional. **Maintenance:** Constant to periodic.	✔		large (10 feet; 3.1m high)							Tropical Natural Rustic Transitional
Soil: Improved. Good drainage. **Sun:** Open to filtered shade to part sun. Full sun by the sea. **Water:** Ample to moderate. **Maintenance:** Constant to periodic.	✔				✔				✔	Tropical

Oenothera caespitosa

Osteospermum fruticosum

Pachycereus marginatus

Name: Botanical Common	Zone, Temp. EG or deciduous (EG or D)	Description
Nolina microcarpa bear grass	All zones. Tolerant in these zones. **EG**	Large, bulky grasslike plant with abundance of narrow, finely toothed, somewhat unruly cascading leaves, which form a large grassy mound to 3 feet (0.9m) high and wide, eventually doubling in size. Several slender bloom stalks above plant have greenish to white flowers in spring. Plant usually seen with combination of green and dry leaves. Bold plant for large areas.
Nolina recurvata pony tail palm, bottle palm	Low zone and protected areas of middle zone. High zone as a houseplant. 28F (-2C). **EG**	Popular Dr. Seuss-type container plant, houseplant, or sheltered garden plant. Trunk rises from a bulbous base that can fill a container. Top of tapered trunk has an unruly crop of narrow bright green leaves in the shape of a bowl haircut. Palms can eventually reach 12 to 15 feet (3.7 to 4.6m) high. Some plants develop several trunks from base and with side branches can spread 9 to 12 feet (2.7 to 3.7m) wide, but they usually stay small and neat for many years in the restricted space of a container.
Oenothera caespitosa white evening primrose, tufted evening primrose	All zones. Tops may freeze back at 28F (-2C). **EG**	A clumping perennial plant to a possible 2-foot (0.6-m) width. Rosettes have long slender leaves with reverse scallops on the edges. White primroses rise above the foliage to 12 inches (30.5cm) or so in spring and early summer, with a few blossoms appearing over the rest of the warm season. Flowers open in late afternoon or early evening, turn pink by midmorning, and then droop and shrivel. Seeds appear as slender capsules.
Oenothera stubbei Chihuahuan evening primrose (often misnamed Baja primrose)	Low and middle zones. 28F (-2C). **EG**	This vigorous herbaceous perennial ground spreader forms a dense mat to 5 inches (12.7cm) high and 3 feet (0.9m) wide or wider. Trailing stems root as they go over moist ground. Single yellow flowers appear on stems above the plant. Flowers open in the evening and last into the next morning.
Osmanthus fragrans sweet olive, fragrant olive, tea olive, sweet osmanthus	All zones. Hardy to cold. Accepts heat with ample water. **EG**	Erect, elegant dark green shrub with shiny refined foliage and clusters of fragrant, inconspicuous whitish flowers most of the year. Grows at moderate rate up to 10 feet (3.1m) high in favorable situations, usually to only 6 feet (1.8m) in arid climates. Plant may be dense or open with leaves and usually is taller than it is wide. Use as shrub, espalier or trained into a small tree. Placed by doorways, passersby can get a whiff of the flowers' delicate scent.
Osteospermum fruticosum trailing African daisy	Low and middle zones. 20F (-10C). 'White Hybrid' at 28F (-2C). **EG**	Spreading herbaceous perennial ground cover with lobed hairy leaves that mounds 6 to 12 inches (15.2 to 30.5cm). Violet-colored daisylike flowers appear November to March. Blooms fade daily to nearly white, making a multicolored bloom. One plant can spread to 2 to 3 feet (0.6 to 0.9m) in a year, with branches rooting as they go. Can form a solid cover. A white hybrid has a more profuse bloom, but is less hardy. Subject to damp-off, especially in summer.
Oxalis crassipes pink oxasis	Low and middle zones. Protected areas of high zone. 28F (-2C). **EG to D (dormant)**	Plants less than 12 inches (30.5cm) high are root-hardy perennials that form compact, rounded mounds of cloverlike bright green leaves and produce appealing pink five-petaled flowers, possibly all year. Where winters are cold, use as spring- to summer- or fall-flowering plant. In fierce summer areas, use as an underplant to summer plants such as *Lantanas*. *Oxalis* comes out as the *Lantana* fades in fall. Cultivars with different bloom colors exist.
Pachycereus marginatus Mexican fence post, organ pipe	Low and middle zones. 28F (-2C). Protect tops. **EG**	Stunning as fluted dark green vertical columns to 5 inches (12.7cm) in diameter, with white lines and spines down the ridges. This cactus makes a dramatic statement. Slow development to 10 to 12 feet (3.1 to 3.7m) high, with few side branches, eventually to 25 feet (7.6m), developing a few more columns as it grows. In Mexico, cuttings are planted tightly in rows to form a living corral.

Culture	Accents	Average Tree Size	Average Shrub Size	Ground Covers	Herbaceous (No woody parts)	Vines	Requires Shade	Best Wall Plants	Succulents	Special Effects
Soil: Tolerant. Good drainage. **Sun:** Full. **Water:** Occasional to none. **Maintenance:** Little to none.	✔		small (to 3 feet; 0.9m high)		✔					Tropical Desert Natural Rustic Transitional
Soil: Good drainage. **Sun:** Full or reflected sun to part shade. **Water:** Occasional. **Maintenance:** Little to none.	✔	small (to 20 feet; 6.1m)	large (to 10 feet; 3.1m high)							Tropical Mediterranean Containers
Soil: Good drainage. **Sun:** Part sun to full sun. **Water:** Moderate in summer, occasional in winter. **Maintenance:** Periodic grooming.					✔					Desert Woodsy Natural Rustic Transitional Color
Soil: Improved. Good drainage **Sun:** Part shade to full sun. **Water:** Moderate to occasional in winter. **Maintenance:** Periodic.				✔	✔					Woodsy Natural Rustic Color
Soil: Improved. Good drainage. **Sun:** Open to filtered or part shade. North sides. Full sun in high zone. **Water:** Moderate to ample. **Maintenance:** Periodic.			medium (6 feet; 1.8m high) to large (10 feet; 3.1m high)							Tropical Woodsy Oriental Transitional Formal/clipped Oasis
Soil: Improved. Good drainage **Sun:** Part shade to full sun. **Water:** Moderate. **Maintenance:** Periodic.				✔	✔					Tropical Natural Rustic Formal/clipped Containers Color Oasis
Soil: Improved. **Sun:** Filtered to part shade to full sun. **Water:** Moderate. **Maintenance:** Little.				✔	✔					Tropical Woodsy Oriental Natural Rustic Color Containers
Soil: Tolerant. Good drainage. **Sun:** Part shade to full to reflected sun. **Water:** Occasional. **Maintenance:** Little to none.	✔								✔	Tropical Desert Transitional Formal/clipped Containers

Passiflora alatocaerulea

Philodendron selloum

Name: **_Botanical_** Common	Zone, Temp. EG or deciduous (EG or D)	Description
Passiflora alatocaerulea passion vine	Low zone and protected areas of middle zone. Leaves damaged at 28F (-2C). Freezes to ground at 20F (-7C). Roots freeze at 10F (-12C). **EG to Partly D**	Verdant tropical vine with three-lobed leaves that climbs by tendrils and aerial roots on supports. Remarkable fragrant flowers of intricate design, in shades from white through lavender to deep purple, create scattered bloom in warm weather. Thrives in about the same climate as citrus. Several cultivars and other species, some of which can grow in the high zone.
Pedilanthus macrocarpus devil's backbone, slipper plant	Low zone and warmer parts of middle zone. 28F (-2C) if temperature doesn't remain down long. **D**	Unusual gray-green succulent with forked, upward-pointing, cylindrical stems to 3 to 4 feet (0.9 to 1.2m) high. Spring into summer bloom of red slipper-shaped structures, surrounding a tiny female flower and several male flowers. Tiny leaves appear briefly on new growth and are shed soon after they emerge if conditions are dry. Established plants in ground spread to form small thicket. Excellent in containers.
Perovskia hybrid 'Blue Spire' (_P. atriplicifolia_ x _P. abrotanoides_) Russian sage	All zones. Root hardy. **D**	Woody plant to 3 feet (0.9m) high and wide, with twiggy, lacy gray-foliaged branches radiating from a base. Spires of finely divided lavender-blue flowers are a frilly haze above the plant most of the summer.
Philodendron selloum selloum philodendron, lace leaf philodendron	Low zone and protected areas of middle zone. Anywhere indoors. Damaged at 28F (-2C). Killed at about 20F (-7C). **EG**	Exuberant, lavish, tropical-appearing, bold-foliaged plant that can develop attractive hairy leaf-scarred trunks and aerial roots that seek to anchor it in the earth. Moderate to slow grower to an eventual 10 to 12 feet (3.1 to 3.7m) over twenty years, spreading to at least 8 feet (2.4). Deeply lobed bright green leaves can reach 3 feet (0.9m) in length. They grow on herbaceous stalks the plant gradually sheds as new leaves emerge from sheaths in the plant center. Can have one or several trunks. Many hybrids, but this is probably the toughest.
Phoenix roebelenii pygmy date palm	Low zone and protected areas of middle zone. Houseplant anywhere. 28F (-2C). **EG**	Dwarf palm to eventually 6 feet (1.8m) high with a 3-foot (0.9-m) crown of feathery leaves atop its stout trunk. Multitrunk clumps fill a wider space depending on the number of heads. Trunks develop slowly, but new fronds grow at a moderate rate, forming shiny curved leaves of bright green that may make plants look top heavy.
Pistacia lentiscus mastic tree	Low and middle zones. Protected areas of high zone. Tolerant into the teens F (-7 to -11C). Revels in heat. **EG**	Large shrub or small tree with an irregular form and distinctive leathery leaves in an interesting growth pattern. Grows slowly to 12 feet (3.7m) high, eventually 15 or even 25 feet (4.6 to 7.6m). Usually spreads wider than high. Inconspicuous flowers on females pollinated by males yield small red fruits that turn black as they ripen. Aromatic resin. Dried crystals of the fallen sap are a source of amber.
Pittosporum rhombifolium Queensland pittosporum	Low and middle zones. Mid 20s F (-3 to -5C). **EG**	A seldom seen and underused large shrub or small patio tree with rich green 4-foot (1.2-m) diamond-shaped leaves and a somewhat open form. Grows slowly to 15 or even 35 feet (4.6 to 10.7m) high in favorable circumstances. Small white flowers in spring turn into decorative, round orange to yellow fruit.
Plumbago auriculata cape plumbago, leadwort	Low and middle zones. 28F (-2C). Root hardy. **EG to cold D**	Exuberant perennial shrub revels in sun and is a delight to the eye, cycling into bloom off and on during warm weather. Foliage is medium green. Clusters of pale blue phloxlike flowers bring a coolness to the garden. Plants grow at a moderate to fast rate to form a mound 3 to 4 feet (0.9 to 1.2m) high, higher when given support, and as much as 20 feet (6.1m) wide. Cultivars have varying bloom color.

Plumbago auriculata

Culture	Accents	Average Tree Size	Average Shrub Size	Ground Covers	Herbaceous (No woody parts)	Vines	Requires Shade	Best Wall Plants	Succulents	Special Effects
Soil: Improved. Good drainage. **Sun:** Part shade to full sun. **Water:** Moderate. **Maintenance:** Periodic.						needs support				Tropical Woodsy Natural Rustic Color Oasis
Soil: Good drainage. **Sun:** Part shade to full sun. **Water:** Occasional. **Maintenance:** Little to none.	✔								✔	Desert Containers
Soil: Good drainage. **Sun:** Full sun. **Water:** Occasional once established. **Maintenance:** Periodic. Cut back winter-dormant plants.			small (to 3 feet; 0.9m high)							Mediterranean Natural Rustic Transitional Color
Soil: Improved. Good drainage. **Sun:** Filtered to open or part shade. **Water:** Moderate. **Maintenance:** Little to periodic.	✔								✔	Tropical Containers Color
Soil: Improved. Good drainage. **Sun:** Full sun to part or open shade. **Water:** Moderate to occasional. **Maintenance:** Periodic grooming.	✔	small (to 20 feet; 6.1m)								Tropical Containers
Soil: Tolerant. Good drainage. **Sun:** Full to reflected sun to part shade. **Water:** Occasional. **Maintenance:** Periodic training to none.		small (20 feet; 6.1m) to medium (40 feet; 12.2m)	large (to 10 feet; 3.1m high)							Mediterranean Woodsy Natural Rustic Transitional
Soil: Improved. **Sun:** Part shade to full sun. **Water:** Moderate. **Maintenance:** Periodic.		small (20 feet; 6.1m) to medium (40 feet; 12.2m)	large (to 10 feet; 3.1m high)							Tropical Woodsy Natural Rustic
Soil: Improved. Good drainage. **Sun:** Part shade to full or reflected sun. **Water:** Moderate to ample. **Maintenance:** Little to periodic.			small (3 feet; 0.9m high) to medium (6 feet; 1.8m high)			needs support				Tropical Natural Rustic Transitional Containers Color

Plumeria rubra

Ruellia brittoniana 'Katie'

Strelitzia reginae

Name: *Botanical* Common	Zone, Temp. EG or deciduous (EG or D)	Description
Plumeria obtusa Singapore plumeria	Low zone and protected areas of middle zone. 32F (0C). **EG**	Large shrub or small tree to 24 feet (7.3m) high and about 20 feet (6.1m) wide in frost-free areas. Large shiny leaves spiral around stems and are rich green, rounded, and notched or tapered at the tip. Yellow-throated white flowers in clusters over the warm season are fragrant, especially at night. Plants rooted from tip cuttings or by air layering can begin to flower when they are only 1 to 1-1/2 feet (0.3 to 0.5m) tall. Good container plant that can be moved inside for cold protection.
Plumeria rubra frangipani, plumeria, nosegay plumeria	Low zone and protected areas of middle zone. 32F (0C). **D**	Striking bold-foliaged shrub or small tree with large pointed leaves. Large loose clusters of fragrant pink, rose, red, white or yellow flowers appear through summer into fall. Pods to 12 inches (30.5cm) long. Plants from rooted tips or cuttings can begin bloom at 1 to 1-1/2 feet (0.3 to 0.5m) high. In frost-free areas, plant gets to 25 feet (7.6m) high and wide. Move container plants inside in cold weather. Good seaside plant. Cultivars available.
Podranea ricasoliana pink trumpet vine	Low and middle zones. 26F (-3C). Root hardy. Recovers fast. **EG to cold D**	Heat-loving vine to sprawling shrub that grows fast to 20 feet (6.1) in any direction. Medium green toothed compound leaves. Large pink trumpet-shaped blooms appear most of year in warm winter areas. Beans to 12 inches (30.5cm) long. Train on support for vertical plant.
Poliomentha moderensis lavender spice	All zones. 10F (-12C). **EG**	Small, rounded, somewhat open shrub to 3 feet (0.9m) high, spreading less. Light green leaves on brittle woody twigs. Slow to fast grower, depending on conditions. Small lavender and white tubular flowers appear in clusters along the branch tips any time from spring into fall until the cold season. A comparable plant to *Salvia greggii*. Cut back to refresh, renew, make denser.
Potentilla tabernaemontanii spring cinquefoil	All zones. 28F (-2C). **EG to dormant**	Appealing bright green, somewhat tufted, creeping plant to 2 to 6 inches (5.1 to 15.2cm) high and spreading to make a fast small-scale ground cover, bulb cover, or to put between partly shaded stepping stones. Tiny yellow flowers in clusters appear among the finely divided leaflets. Can brown out temporarily in cold winter areas or in fierce summer areas. Good as underplant to such summer plants as *Lantana* in hot areas. Blooms as the *Lantana* fades in fall. Can be used as a nontraffic ground cover. Thick mats can smother weeds.
Ruellia species Mexican barrio ruellia, 'Katie' ruellia, Sonoran ruellia, Baja ruellia	Low zone and protected areas of middle zone. 28F (-2C). Root hardy. **Winter dormant**	*R. brittoniana* and *R. brittoniana* 'Katie' are flowering summer perennials and shrubs to bedding-sized plants with medium green foliage and purple flowers that bloom continuously during warm weather. *R. brittoniana* may get to 3 feet (0.9m) high and 'Katie' to 12 inches (30.5cm) high in a season. 'Katie' is a good underplant for filtered shade in summer with *Oxalis* for winter. *R. californica* is a slow to moderate grower to 2 to 4-1/2 feet (0.6 to 1.3m) high and wide. Dense summer foliage of hairy lance-shaped to oval leaves and fragrant purple flowers. Twiggy and dull when dormant.
Salvia species blue sage, chaparral sage, Cleveland sage, cherry red sage, lipstick salvia, autumn sage, Texas red sage, Mexican bush sage	All zones Root hardy. **EG to D**	The *Salvia* group is one of the best and most durable color-plant group for arid regions. Besides being perennials of various sizes, they are usually ignored by rodents and have a nice sage aroma. They also survive arid soils and neglect and can be cut back after they bloom or when they look rangy only to enthusiastically renew fresh growth. All are perennials, although some are used as self-seeding annuals (*S. farinacea* and *S. coccinea*). Colors range from blue to lavender to shocking pink to cultivars of scarlet or white. Hummingbirds love red varieties.

Culture	Accents	Average Tree Size	Average Shrub Size	Ground Covers	Herbaceous (No woody parts)	Vines	Requires Shade	Best Wall Plants	Succulents	Special Effects
Soil: Improved. Good drainage. **Sun:** Part shade to full sun. **Water:** Moderate to occasional in winter. **Maintenance:** Periodic.	✔	small (20 feet; 6.1m) to medium (40 feet; 12.2m)	large (to 10 feet; 3.1m high)							Tropical Containers Color
Soil: Improved. Good drainage. **Sun:** Part shade to full sun. **Water:** Occasional. Weekly in summer. **Maintenance:** Periodic.	✔	small (20 feet; 6.1m) to medium (40 feet; 12.2m)	large (to 10 feet; 3.1m high)							Tropical Containers Color
Soil: Improved. Good drainage. **Sun:** Full to reflected sun. **Water:** Occasional. Weekly summer soak. **Maintenance:** Periodic.			large (to 10 feet; 3.1m high)			needs support		✔		Tropical Natural Rustic Transitional Color
Soil: Tolerant. **Sun:** Filtered shade, part shade, full sun. **Water:** Moderate. **Maintenance:** Periodic.			small (to 3 feet; 0.9m high)							Mediterranean Desert Natural Rustic Transitional Containers Color
Soil: Improved. **Sun:** Filtered to part shade or full sun. **Water:** Moderate. **Maintenance:** Periodic.				✔	✔					Woodsy Natural Rustic Color
Soil: Tolerant. **Sun:** Part shade to full sun. **Water:** Occasional. Weekly in summer. **Maintenance:** Periodic.			small (3 feet; 0.9m high) to medium (6 feet; 1.8m high)	✔						Tropical Woodsy Natural Rustic Color
Soil: Tolerates most soils with good drainage. **Sun:** Full sun to a little afternoon or dappled shade. **Water:** Occasional to moderate in the warm season. **Maintenance:** Seasonal.			small (3 feet; 0.9m high) to medium (6 feet; 1.8m high)							Desert Natural Rustic Transitional Color

Tecoma alata 'Orange jubilee™'

Tecoma stans

Zauschneria californica latifolia

Name: **Botanical** Common	Zone, Temp. EG or deciduous (EG or D)	Description
Setcreasea pallida setcreasea, purple heart plant	Low and middle zones. 28F (-2C). Root hardy. **EG**	A coarse-textured, succulent summer color or character plant, with bold deep purple stems and leaves. Foliage color is best in bright sun, but gives a startling ultraviolet look in the shade. Small purple flowers are not much of a color addition next to the bright green leaves. Sprawls and spreads to 1 foot (0.3m) high by an indefinite width, rooting as it goes. Freezes back in chilly winters.
Strelitzia reginae African bird of paradise, bird of paradise, crane flower	Low zone and protected areas of middle zone. Houseplant anywhere. Damaged at 28F (-2C). Killed below 20F (-7C). No wind. **EG**	Dramatic specialty plant with one of the most exotic blooms. Moderate- to slow-growing to 3 to 5 feet (0.9 to 1.5m) high and wider as it matures. Paddlelike blue-green leaf blades on slender stems rise from plant base and radiate outward toward top. Long-lasting fantastic flowers resemble multi-colored tropical birds. They bloom any time, but most likely for a long period from fall into winter. Needs frequent feeding. Plant is worth fussing over. Slow to recover from freeze damage.
Tamarix aphylla tamarisk, athel tree, athel salt cedar	All zones. 15F (-9C). Root hardy to 0F (-18C). **EG**	A tough tree of last resort that can grow from cuttings to 10 feet (3.1m) high in three years. In deep irrigated soil, grows moderate to fast to 30 feet (9.2m) high, spreading 15 to 30 feet (4.6 to 9.2m). Tree has rough brown bark, brittle branches and long grayish blue-green jointed branchlets that appear as leaves and can cover plant densely. Can live with intense heat, hot winds, drought and salty soils. Can even tolerate irrigation with brackish water. Clusters of needlelike flowers, dusty pinkish to cream, appear at branch tips in summer. Little grows under it because of salty excretions from foliage. Deep roots are invasive of water/sewer lines.
Tecoma alata **'Orange jubilee™'** orange jubilee, tecoma	Low and middle zones. 32F (0C). Root hardy into low 20s F (-5 to -7C). **EG to dormant**	Gold-tinged copper trumpets in clusters bloom all summer on this loosely growing verdant, somewhat rank shrub. Vertical to leaning branches. As high as 12 feet (3.7m). Spreads to about 8 feet (2.4m) May freeze to ground in winter; fast recovery in spring.
Tecoma stans yellow bells, trumpet bush	Low and middle zones. Protected areas of high zone. 28F (-2C). Recovers fast. Revels in heat. **EG to winter dormant**	Exuberant summer or warm area plant with medium green foliage and constant bloom of yellow bell-shaped trumpets on new growth followed by slender pods. Plant reaches 4 to 5 feet (1.2 to 1.5m) high in cold areas, to 8 feet (2.4m) or more, even 20 feet (6.1m), in warm areas, where it is sometimes trained into a small tree. Width varies. Plant has no distinctive shape. Bright green lance-shaped leaflets.
Vigna caracalla snail vine	Low and middle zones. 28F (-2C). Root hardy. **D to EG**	Fast-twining perennial vine to 10 to 20 feet (3.1 to 6.1m) long, with pointed medium green oval leaves and lavender to purple flowers that curl like a snail shell. Trailing branches can take root. Good for fast summer cover.
Zauschneria californica latifolia hummingbird flower, California fuschsia	Low and middle zones. High zone on warm south-facing banks. Root hardy to 18F (-8C) or below. **EG**	This riparian plant to 3 feet (0.9m) high or higher is medium green and lush or straggly, depending on water availability. Much of the year it is nondescript until late summer when flashes of orange-red appear along the stems in the form of trumpet flowers. Stunning against a blooming *Salvia leucantha*. Blooms persist until frost. Then cut it back.
Ziziphus jujuba Chinese date	All zones. Hardy to cold and heat. **D**	Decorative tree that grows slowly to moderately to 20 to 30 feet (6.1 to 9.2m) high and 15 to 20 feet (4.6 to 6.1m) wide. May sucker to form a thicket. Growth depends on water supply and maintenance. Erect trunk with rough gray bark and distinctive angular thorny twigs support shimmering leaves that densely cover tree in weeping cascades. Unimportant small yellow spring flowers produce edible datelike fruit, which ripen only in high temperatures. A deep-rooted plant that tolerates drought, heat, cold, and alkaline soil conditions. Thornless cultivars available.

Culture	Accents	Average Tree Size	Average Shrub Size	Ground Covers	Herbaceous (No woody parts)	Vines	Requires Shade	Best Wall Plants	Succulents	Special Effects
Soil: Good drainage. **Sun:** Part shade to full sun. **Water:** Moderate. **Maintenance:** Periodic.				✔	✔				✔	Tropical Natural Rustic Containers Color
Soil: Improved. Good drainage. **Sun:** Filtered to part to full sun when weather is cool or at shore. **Water:** Moderate to ample. **Maintenance:** Periodic grooming of old bloom stalks and dry leaves.	✔		small (3 feet; 0.9m high) to medium (6 feet; 1.8m high)		✔					Tropical Containers Color
Soil: Tolerant. **Sun:** Full to reflected sun. **Water:** Occasional to none. Accepts ample. **Maintenance:** Little to none.		medium (to 40 feet; 12.2m)								Desert
Soil: Tolerant. Best in improved. **Sun:** Full to reflected sun. **Water:** Moderate to ample. **Maintenance:** Periodic.			large (to 10 feet; 3.1m high)							Tropical Color Natrual Rustic
Soil: Tolerant. Best in improved. Good drainage. **Sun:** Part to full sun. **Water:** Moderate to ample during bloom, little when dormant. **Maintenance:** Periodic.		small (to 20 feet; 6.1m)	large (to 10 feet; 3.1m high)							Tropical Desert Natural Rustic Transitional Color
Soil: Good drainage. **Sun:** Full sun. **Water:** Moderate. **Maintenance:** Periodic.				✔		needs support				Color Oasis
Soil: Tolerant. Good drainage. **Sun:** Filtered shade to full sun. **Water:** Moderate to occasional. **Maintenance:** Periodic.			small (to 3 feet; 0.9m high)			needs support				Tropical Woodsy Natural Rustic Containers Color
Soil: Tolerant. Prefers improved. **Sun:** Part shade to full or reflected sun. **Water:** Occasional to ample. **Maintenance:** None to periodic.		small (20 feet; 6.1m) to medium (40 feet; 12.2m)	large (to 10 feet; 3.1m high)							Woodsy Oriental Natural Rustic

Easy-Reference Plant Selection Guide

Looking for a particular type of plant, such as a shrub or ground cover? Or do you need plants to fit a particular theme, such as Mediterranean? Following are lists of some of the best plants for a variety of situations. The plants are alphabetized by botanical name only, with a page number that will direct you to more information on each particular plant in this book. The abbreviation "spp." (species) means several species of the genus fit the particular category.

Ground Covers

Small Shrubs or Shrub-Size Plants
(2-1/2 to 4 feet; 0.8 to 1.2m high)

Medium Shrubs
(to 6 feet; 1.8m high)

Large Shrubs
(to 10 feet; 3.1m high)

Small Trees
(to 20 feet; 6.1m high)

Medium Trees
(to 40 feet; 12.2m high)

Chorisia speciosa 79
Cupressus arizonica 182
Cupressus sempervirens 182
Some *Eucalyptus* spp. 92
Some *Ficus* spp. 99
Fraxinus velutina 103
Geijera parviflora 104
Gleditsia triacanthos inermis 105
Parkinsonia aculeata 127
Pinus thunbergiana 133

Large Trees
(over 40 feet; 12.2m high)

Araucaria bidwillii 59
Carya illinoensis 72
Some *Casuarina* spp. 180
Some *Cedrus* spp. and selections 73
Cupressus arizonica 182
Cupressus sempervirens 182
Dalbergia sissoo 87
Some *Eucalyptus* spp. 92
Gleditsia triacanthos inermis 105
Grevillea robusta 105
Phoenix canariensis 128
Phoenix dactylifera 129
Some *Pinus* spp. 131
Pistacia chinensis 134
Platanus acerifolia 136
Platanus racemosa 137
Some *Populus* spp. 139
Some *Quercus* spp. 146
Washingtonia filifera 162
Washingtonia robusta 163

Vines and Wall Plants

Antigonon leptopus 176
Bougainvillea spp. 66
Campsis radicans 180
Clytostoma callistegioides 182
Euonymus fortunei 97
Euonymus japonica 186
Fatshedera lizei 186
Feijoa sellowiana 97
Ficus pumila .100
Gelsemium sempervirens 104
Hardenbergia violacea 188
Hedera canariensis 106
Some *Jasminum* spp. 109
Parthenocissus quinquefolia 127
Podranea ricasoliana 196
Some *Pyracantha* spp. 144
Trachelospermum jasminoides 157
Vigna caracalla 198
Wisteria floribunda 164
(Many fruit trees & climbing roses also make
great espaliers)

Rabbit- or Deer-Resistant Plants
**(most plants still need some protection
when very young)**

Agave spp. 54
Aloe spp. 58
Artemisia 'Powis Castle' 176
Baccharis spp. 62
Buddleia marrubifolia 178
Celtis pallida .180
Celtis reticulata 74
Cupressus arizonica 182
Cupressus sempervirens 182
Dalea spp. 88
Dodonaea viscosa 90
Ficus carica 99
Juniperus spp. 111
Lantana camara 114
Lantana montevidensis 114
Myrtus communis 120
Nerium oleander 122
Olea europaea 123
Opuntia spp. .125
Pinus spp. 131
Podocarpus macrophyllus 138
Rosmarinus officinalis 150
Salvia spp. 196
Tecomaria capensis 155

Really Tough Plants
**(tolerant of extremes of temperature
and drought)**

Acacia constricta 50
Acacia greggii .51
Atriplex spp. 61
Baccharis sarothroides 62
Brahea armata 68
Dodonaea viscosa 90
Ferocactus spp. 98
Opuntia spp. .125
Parkinsonia aculeata 127
Phoenix dactylifera 129
Prosopis spp. .140
Tamarix aphylla 198
Vinca major 160
Washingtonia filifera 162
Washingtonia robusta 163

Clean Poolside Plants
(plants with little or no litter)

Asparagus densiflorus selections 60
Carissa macrocarpa 71
Chamaerops humilis 77
Some *Citrus* spp. 80
Cocculus laurifolius 85
Cycas revoluta 184

Dodonaea viscosa 90
Elaeagnus ebbingei 90
Ilex vomitoria 'Stokes' 100
Some *Justicia* spp. 113
Laurus nobilis 188
Myrtus communis 120
Nandina domestica 121
Nerium oleander 122
Photinia fraseri 129
Photinia serrulata 130
Plumbago auriculata 194
Rhaphiolepis indica 148
Sophora secundiflora 153
Tecomaria capensis 155
Trachelospermum asiaticum 156
Trachelospermum jasminoides 157
Vaquelinia californica 158
Vinca spp. 160
Xylosma congestum 164

Plants that Attract Birds and Butterflies

Some *Acacia* spp. 50
Ageratum corymbosum 172
Some *Aloe* spp. 58
Asclepias linaria 176
Asclepias subulata 176
Buddleia davidii 178
Buddleia marrubifolia 178
Some *Caesalpinia* spp. 69
Calliandra californica 178
Calliandra eriophylla 178
Callistemon citrinus 178
Callistemon viminalis 178
Carnegiea gigantea 71
Celtis pallida .180
Celtis reticulata 74
Dyssodia pentachaeta 172
Eupatorium greggii 172
Hesperaloe funifera 188
Hesperaloe parviflora 107
Some *Justicia* spp. 113
Lantana camara 114
Lantana montevidensis 114
Penstemon spp. 171
Some *Pyracantha* spp. 144
Some *Salvia* spp. 196
Tecoma alata hybrid 198
Tecoma stans .198
Verbena hybrids 169
Vitex angus-castus 160
Zauschneria californica latifolia 198

Fragrant Plants
(sweet)

Acacia farnesiana 51
Buddleia davidii 178
Carissa macrocarpa 71
Citrus spp. 80
Elaeagnus ebbingei 90
Gardenia jasminoides 186
Jasminum grandiflorum 109
Jasminum sambac 110
Lonicera japonica 'Hallmark' 117
Osmanthus fragrans 192
Pittosporum phillyraeoides 135
Pittosporum tobira 136
Sophora secundiflora 153
Trachelospermum asiaticum 156
Trachelospermum jasminoides 157

Aromatic Plants
(strong)

Cupressus arizonica 182
Cupressus sempervirens 182
Eucalyptus cinerea 93
Eucalyptus citriodora 94
Some Juniperus spp. 111
Lantana camara 114
Lantana montevidensis 114
Larrea tridentata 188
Laurus nobilis 188
Lavandula spp. 190
Myrtus communis 120
Some Pinus spp. 131
Platanus acerifolia 136
Platanus racemosa 137
Rosmarinus officinalis 150
Salvia clevelandii 196
Santolina chamaecyparissus 150
Some Tagetes spp. 169

Biblical Plants

Acacia spp. 50
Acanthus mollis 176
Aloe vera 59
Arundo donax 176
Cedrus spp. and selections 73
Ceratonia siliqua 74
Cupressus sempervirens 182
Cyperus alternifolius 184
Elaeagnus angustifolia 184
Ficus carica 99
Fraxinus spp. 102
Lavandula spp. 190
Nerium oleander 122
Olea europaea 123
Phoenix dactylifera 129
Pinus halepensis 132

Pinus pinea .132
Pistacia lentiscus 194
Platanus acerifolia 136
Quercus ilex .147
Rosmarinus officinalis 150
Salvia spp. 196
Tamarix aphylla 198
Vitis vinifera .161
Ziziphus jujuba 198

Color Plants

Antigonon leptopus 176
Bougainvillea hybrids 66
Some Caesalpinia spp. 69
Cercidium spp. 75
Chilopsis linearis selections 77
Chitalpa tashkentensis 78
Euphorbia pulcherrima 186
Euphorbia rigida 186
Gazania rigens 103
Hesperaloe parviflora 107
Hibiscus rosa-sinensis 188
Some Justicia spp. 188
Lagerstroemia indica 113
Lantana camara 114
Lantana montevidensis 114
Some Leucophyllum spp. 115
Nerium oleander 122
Plumbago auriculata 194
Some Pyracantha spp. 144
Some Salvia spp. 196
Some Senna spp. 152
Tecoma alata hybrid 198
Tecoma stans 198
Tecomaria capensis 155
Vitex angus-castus 160
Zauschneria californica latifolia 198

Plants for Shady Areas
(*need shade to survive)

Agave americana 'Media Picta' 55
Agave attenuata 55
*Aspidistra elatior 178
*Aucuba japonica 178
Most Begonia spp. 168
Cycas revoluta 184
Elaeagnus ebbingei 90
Fatshedera lizei 186
*Fatsia japonica 186
Ficus pumila 100
Hedera canariensis 106
Kalanchoe blossfeldiana 173
Laurus nobilis 188
Liriope muscari 190
Ophiopogon japonicus 124
Oxalis crassipes 192
Philodendron selloum 194

Trachelospermum asiaticum 156
Trachelospermum jasminoides 157
Vinca spp., especially Vinca minor 160

The following lists include plants that can set a special mood in a landscape design. See pages 15 to 17 for definitions of these landscape themes.

Transitional Plants

Some Acacia spp. 50
Some Agave spp. 54
Some Aloe spp. 58
Some Atriplex spp. 61
Some Caesalpinia spp. 169
Celtis pallida 180
Celtis reticulata 74
Some Cercidium spp. 75
Some Dalea spp. 88
Dasylirion wheeleri 89
Dodonaea viscosa 90
Encelia farinosa 184
Eremophila 'Valentine™' 186
Justicia californica 113
Justicia candicans 188
Lantana camara 114
Lantana montevidensis 114
Some Leucophyllum spp. 115
Nolina microcarpa 192
Some Prosopis spp. 140
Rhus lancea .148
Rosmarinus officinalis and cultivars 150
Some Salvia spp. 196
Simmondsia chinensis 153
Tagetes palmeri 173

Mediterranean

Acanthus mollis 176
Some Agave spp. 54
Some Aloe spp. 58
Bougainvillea spp. 66
Chamaerops humilis 77
Citrus spp. 80
Cupressus sempervirens 182
Laurus nobilis 188
Lavandula spp. 190
Myrtus communis 120
Olea europaea 123
Phoenix spp. 128
Pinus halepensis 132
Pinus pinea .132
Punica granatum 143
Quercus ilex .147
Quercus suber 147
Rosmarinus officinalis and cultivars 150

Oriental

Formal, Tailored, Clipped or Topiary

Informal
(natural or wild landscapes)

Tropical

Subtropical

Woodsy

About the Authors

Mary Rose Duffield, a native Arizonan, is a landscape architect with an active design practice throughout the Southwest. She specializes in personalized residential design and installation of whatever size. She also does commercial design. Her work has appeared in numerous magazines, books and other publications. She has won many awards in recognition of her work. Duffield earned her master's degree in landscape architecture from the University of Arizona and is a member of the American Society of Landscape Architects. She resides in Tucson where, besides her design work, she enjoys experimenting with plants around her desert home, enjoying nature, painting, and caring for her husband, to whom this work is dedicated.

Warren Jones, FASLA, is a native Californian and graduate of Oregon State University, with two years of graduate work at the University of Oregon at Eugene. For many years he had an active landscape architecture practice based in La Habra, designing landscapes throughout California. After being invited to teach at the University of Arizona, he educated two generations of landscape architects before his promotion to professor emeritus. His excellence as a person as well as a professor brought him the honor of being named a Fellow of the American Society of Landscape Architects (FASLA). The Arizona Green Industry offers a scholarship in his name. He is coauthor with Charles Sacamano, Ph.D., of *Landscape Plants for Dry Regions* (Fisher Books, 2000). He has served as a consultant in arid regions throughout the world. He lives in Tucson where he continues to be involved in the landscape architecture program at the University of Arizona.

Bibliography

Brookbank, George.
Desert Gardening.
Tucson, Ariz.: Fisher Books, 1997.

Hansen, Michael.
Pest Control for Home and Garden.
New York: Consumer Reports Books, 1992.

Irish, Gary, and Mary Irish.
Agaves, Yuccas, and Related Plants.
Portland, Oreg.: Timber Press, 2000.

Irish, Mary.
Gardening in the Desert. Tucson:
University of Arizona Press, 2000.

Johnson, Eric A., and Scott Millard.
The Low-Water Flower Gardener.
Tucson, Ariz.: Ironwood Press, 1993.

———. *Pruning, Planting, and Care.*
Tucson, Ariz.: Ironwood Press, 1997.

Jones, Warren, and Charles Sacamano.
Landscape Plants for Dry Regions.
Tucson, Ariz.: Fisher Books, 2000.

King, Eleanor Anthony.
Bible Plants for American Gardens.
New York: Dover Publications, Inc., 1975.

Mielke, Judy.
Native Plants for Southwestern Landscapes.
Austin: University of Texas Press, 1993.

Shuler, Carol.
Low-Water-Use Plants.
Tucson, Ariz.: Fisher Books, 1993.

Sunset editors.
Sunset Western Garden Book.
Menlo Park, Calif.: Sunset Publishing
Corporation, 1995.

———. Sunset.
Western Garden Problem Solver.
Menlo Park, Calif.: Sunset Publishing
Corporation, 1998.

The authors also regularly consulted
Southwest Trees and Turf (Stone Peak
Services), a monthly publication; various
publications of Mountain States Nursery and
Starr Nursery; and issues of *Arid Zone Times,*
a publication of Arid Zone Trees.

Subject Index

Plant Name Index

Note: Scientific names are italicized. Cultivars are enclosed in single quotation marks. Unless a cultivar is a main entry in this book, it is not listed in this index. See individual plant descriptions throughout this book for cultivar information.

A